VIRGIL'S AENEID

MICHAEL C. J. PUTNAM

VIRGIL'S AENEID

INTERPRETATION AND
INFLUENCE

THE UNIVERSITY OF NORTH CAROLINA PRESS

CHAPEL HILL AND

LONDON

MICHAEL C. J. PUTNAM IS
MACMILLAN PROFESSOR OF CLASSICS
AT BROWN UNIVERSITY.
© 1995 THE UNIVERSITY OF
NORTH CAROLINA PRESS.
ALL RIGHTS RESERVED.
MANUFACTURED IN
THE UNITED STATES OF AMERICA.
THE PAPER IN THIS BOOK
MEETS THE GUIDELINES FOR PERMANENCE
AND DURABILITY OF THE
COMMITTEE ON PRODUCTION GUIDELINES
FOR BOOK LONGEVITY OF THE
COUNCIL ON LIBRARY RESOURCES.
LIBRARY OF CONGRESS
CATALOGING-IN-PUBLICATION DATA.
PUTNAM, MICHAEL C. J. VIRGIL'S AENEID:
INTERPRETATION AND INFLUENCE /
BY MICHAEL C. J. PUTNAM.
P. CM. INCLUDES BIBLIOGRAPHICAL
REFERENCES AND INDEXES.
ISBN 0-8078-2191-8
(CLOTH : ALK. PAPER). —
ISBN 0-8078-4499-3
(PBK. : ALK. PAPER)
1. VIRGIL. AENEID.
2. AENEAS (LEGENDARY CHARACTER)
IN LITERATURE.
3. EPIC POETRY, LATIN—
HISTORY AND CRITICISM.
4. LITERATURE, MODERN—
ROMAN INFLUENCES.
5. ROME—IN LITERATURE.
6. VIRGIL—INFLUENCE.
I. TITLE. PA6825.P84
1995 873'.01—DC20 94-19891
CIP
99 98 97 96 95
5 4 3 2 1

FOR THE
AMERICAN ACADEMY
IN ROME

———

1894–1994

CONTENTS

PREFACE

Individual expressions of thanks accompany several essays. I would here like to recognize more general obligations of gratitude. The first is a long-standing debt to my students and to many colleagues at Brown and in the profession. I owe special thanks to William Wyatt, for advice on Homer, to Matthew Santirocco, for his encouragement to make this gathering in the first place, to Joseph Pucci, for casting a keen eye on segments of the final manuscript, and to Kenneth Reckford, for support in this project as in much else. Anthony Hollingsworth offered both time and computer expertise at a crucial moment. Many other friends and family members have been generous in a variety of ways. My thanks go especially to Leonard Barkan, Charles and Polly Chatfield, Kenneth Gaulin, Rachel Jacoff, Daniel Javitch, Pietro Pucci, Charles Segal, and Eugene Vance. It is a pleasure also to recognize here the careful copyediting of Brian MacDonald.

Second, I must acknowledge two institutions of higher learning with which I have been privileged to be associated. Several of these essays found their genesis during a most enriching year spent at the Institute for Advanced Study. I would like to thank my fellow Members for 1987–88 and especially Professor Glen Bowersock for many kindnesses and for erudition unstintingly shared. It remains also to recognize yet again the American Academy in Rome, where splendid library and setting without peer combine to offer the scholar a remarkable haven. *Ille terrarum mihi praeter omnis angulus ridet.*

With the exception of "Wrathful Aeneas and the Tactics of *Pietas*," which was written for this volume, all the papers here collected have been published previously. Aside from chapter 11, "Virgil's Tragic Future," whose original has been condensed, any alterations from the initial publication have been essentially cosmetic. I am grateful to the editors of journals or volumes where the essays originally appeared for permission to reprint.

Except where otherwise indicated, the translations are mine. In occasional instances I have allowed minor discrepancies in rendering the Latin to stand, when the same passages recur in different essays, as offering the reader a chance to view the verses from more than one angle.

Michael C. J. Putnam, Providence, Rhode Island, May 1994

SOURCES AND
ACKNOWLEDGMENTS

I would like to thank the following journals and publishers for permission to reprint: "The Virgilian Achievement," *Arethusa* 5 (1972) 53–70. Reprinted by kind permission of *Arethusa* and the Johns Hopkins University Press. "Possessiveness, Sexuality, and Heroism in the *Aeneid*," *Vergilius* 31 (1985) 1–21. Reprinted by kind permission of *Vergilius*. "The Third Book of the *Aeneid*: From Homer to Rome," *Ramus* 9 (1980) 1–21. Reprinted by kind permission of *Ramus*. "Daedalus, Virgil, and the End of Art," *American Journal of Philology* 108 (1987) 173–98. Reprinted by kind permission of *American Journal of Philology*. "*Aeneid* VII and the *Aeneid*," *American Journal of Philology* 91 (1970) 408–30. Reprinted by kind permission of *American Journal of Philology*. "Umbro, Nireus and Love's Threnody," *Vergilius* 38 (1992) 12–23. Reprinted by kind permission of *Vergilius*. "*Pius* Aeneas and the Metamorphosis of Lausus," *Arethusa* 14 (1981) 139–56. Reprinted by kind permission of *Arethusa* and the Johns Hopkins University Press. "The Hesitation of Aeneas," in *Atti del Convegno Mondiale Scientifico di Studi su Virgilio* 2 (Milan, 1984) 233–52. Reprinted by kind permission of Professor Claudio Gallico and the Accademia Nazionale Virgiliana. "Anger, Blindness, and Insight in Virgil's *Aeneid*," *Apeiron* 23 (1990). Reprinted from Martha C. Nussbaum, ed., *The Poetics of Therapy* (Edmonton: Academic Printing and Publishing, 1990) 7–40, by permission of Academic Printing and Publishing. "Virgil's Tragic Future: Senecan Drama and the *Aeneid*," *La Storia, La Letteratura e l'Arte a Roma da Tiberio a Domiziano: Atti del Convegno* (1992) 231–91. Reprinted by kind permission of Professor Claudio Gallico and the Accademia Nazionale Virgiliana. "Virgil's *Inferno*," *Materiali e Discussioni per l'analisi dei Testi classici* 20 (1988) 165–202. Reprinted by kind permission of Professor Gian Biagio Conte and *Materiali e Discussioni*.

ABBREVIATIONS

Ernout-Meillet = *Dictionnaire étymologique de la langue latine.*
 Edited by A. Ernout and A. Meillet. Paris, 1959.

RE = A. Pauly, G. Wissowa, and W. Kroll. *Realencyclopädie
 der classischen Altertumswissenschaft.* Stuttgart, 1893– .

OLD = *Oxford Latin Dictionary.* Oxford, 1968–82.

Liddell-Scott-Jones = *A Greek Lexicon,* compiled by H. G. Liddell,
 R. Scott, and H. S. Jones. Oxford, 1968.

TLL = *Thesaurus Linguae Latinae.* Munich, 1900– .

Paulus-Festus = Sex. Pompeius Festus. *De Significatu Verborum
 and its Epitome by Paulus Diaconus.* Edited by W. M. Lindsay.
 Leipzig, 1913.

VIRGIL'S AENEID

INTRODUCTION

The essays collected here, written over the past several decades, all approach Virgil's *Aeneid* from various angles of vision. They range from detailed interpretations of individual books of the epic to more general discussions of certain themes that permeate its texture and to analyses of the poem's influence on later literature, for subsequent authors have much to tell us not only of the effect of Virgil's brilliance but also of how his genius was understood and appreciated.

The order of presentation takes us from two general discussions, of Virgil's work as a whole and then of the *Aeneid*, to six studies of individual books of the epic. There follow two essays which look with particular attention at the conclusion of the poem. I pursue theses there developed in the subsequent treatment of how the *Aeneid* influences Ovid and Lucan, and conclude by watching Virgil's effect on the tragedies of Seneca and on Dante's *Divina Commedia*. Yet, however diverse the topics studied, their primary focus rests with the end of the *Aeneid*, with the problematics it develops, as the angry hero kills his suppliant antagonist, and with the impact that this action has on any reading of the poem as a whole.

Aeneas' savagery, although it may stem, as Servius long ago observed, from piety toward the hero's protégé Pallas and his family, calls into question the most famous norm, to borrow the terminology of Gian Biagio Conte, of the poem.[1] A Roman, any Roman from Aeneas on, should, according to Aeneas' father Anchises, war down the proud but spare the humbled (*parcere subiectis et debellare superbos*, *Aen.* 6.853). To follow this ethical dictate, with its graphic play on *sub* and *super*, the winners above, the losers below, is to question the behavior patterns both of Homeric heroes on the battlefield and of Roman warriors, each bent on demonstrating private *aretē* and on pursuing vengeance for the benefit of the larger public ensemble. (For the Roman, *pietas* primarily served the needs of the state and its religion, not of the individual.)

Because Aeneas fails to meet the challenge and because the epic ends not with a paean to Roman glory but with the dead victim's life slipping resentfully away, the reader is forced back into the poem to reexamine the plausibility not so much of Anchises' prescription but of its implementation by Rome, in what would have been a major advance from Homeric ethical values. The essays contained in this volume form in large measure a series of exercises in this reinterpretation. Their purpose, as that of my earlier *The Poetry of the Aeneid*, is not so much to supplant the standard historicist approach to the poem as to offer a counterbalance to its implicit complacency, to pry as deeply as I can into the epic's connotational aspects, to heighten rather than diminish its intricacy. I mean in no way to minimize the poem's great bows to the Augustan future, in the words of Jupiter to Venus in book 1, in aspects of the extraordinary shield that Vulcan crafts for Aeneas and above all in the splendid overview of Augustus' golden time which Virgil puts into the mouth of Anchises in book 6. There is no denying the poem's iconic cogency, from this point of view, and the effectiveness of the emblems it contains, from the raging storm of book 1, calmed by a man of piety, to the defeat of Cleopatra and her monstrous, barking gods by Augustus and his Apollo in the episode of the shield that is central, spatially, and final, temporally and verbally.

The historicist view, espoused most recently by Hardie and Cairns, but stemming from a long tradition in Virgilian scholarship whose most acknowledged exponent since the Second World War is Pöschl, sees the *Aeneid* as a grandly imaginative reinforcement of Augustan ideology and power structures.[2] Its exponents view the poem as in essence superbly crafted propaganda, aiming history toward the manifest destiny of Augustus and therefore intended by Virgil to support the imperial status quo. I have little doubt that this is one way Virgil would have expected the epic to be read, whether by his contemporaries or by us. That Virgil wished his poem burned for the very reason that it confirmed rather than probed into the principles on which Augustus based his dominance is the gist of Hermann Broch's elaborate meditation on *The Death of Virgil*.

My own view complicates matters and attempts to observe how Virgil regularly creates a friction between what we might call loyalist and subversive ways of understanding its meaning. Let me look briefly at the first two examples I noted where Virgil turns to the Augustan *aurea saecula*.[3] In the first we learn from the mouth of the king of the gods that, under Augustus, Rome will enter an age where hoary *Fides* (Faith) and Vesta will join Remus and the deified Romulus in giving laws together, this in spite of the rewriting of Roman history that such twin rulership implies. We hear also that now *Furor impius* will be enchained, in the face of the revisions of nature this demands and in the context of a poem that begins with furious winds and water, initiates its second half with the goddess Juno and her Fury stimulating to madness the world around them, including mothers become *furiis accensas*, and ends with its hero, *furiis accensus*, killing his victim.

My second example, the shield of Aeneas, is more complex and deserves separate treatment. Suffice it to recall here some salient instances of ambiguity in its presentation. We find the happy forehead of Octavian-Augustus, as he prepares for the battle of Actium, "spewing forth flames" (*flammas . . . vomunt*, 8.680–81). So does the helmet that Vulcan likewise makes for Aeneas (*flammas . . . vomentem*, 8.620), but so also does the arch-villain Cacus earlier in the book (*incendia . . . vomentem*, 8.259). When the battle is over and the temple to Actian Apollo built, Octavian can be imagined sitting on its threshold, receiving the gifts of conquered peoples

and attaching them to "proud doorposts" (*superbis / postibus*, 8.721–22).
We might be inclined to accept Augustan hauteur as innocent of negative
implications were it not that the same phrase is used of Priam's palace
(*barbarico postes auro spoliisque superbi*, 2.504), with the concomitant suggestion that pride anticipates disaster, and a parallel wording appears
shortly before in book 8, applied to the doorway of Cacus, *foribus superbis*,
hung with the faces of dead men, pale with gore (8.196). Cacus precedes
Augustus as denizen of the Palatine, and the paradoxes of pride reach out
into the poem, explicitly to Hercules and Turnus, implicitly, in the end to
Aeneas, responding to the posture of his defeated opponent, now *supplex*
(8.202, 10.514).

The end of the shield is a final case in point. Vulcan-Mulciber, fiery
Soother of metal into exquisite shape, appropriately initiates the designs
on his artifact with an act of mollification (*Mulciber*, 8.724). We watch the
wolf of Mars soothing the god's twin sons as they are poised to leap
vigorously onto the pages of history (*mulcere*, 8.634). Virgil likewise initiates his poem with acts that moderate. Neptune, in the epic's first simile,
is compared to a man, revered for his *pietas*, who calms a raging mob
with his words and "soothes their hearts" (*pectora mulcet*, 1.153) and, some
forty lines later, Virgil allots the same phrase to Aeneas, soothing the sad
hearts of his tempest-tossed men with his words (1.197). Vulcan and
Virgil, or should I better say Virgil as Vulcan, round off their diverse acts
of craftsmanship on deliberately parallel notes. The shield ends not with
Augustus in glory but with conquered peoples in procession and, finally,
with "the Araxes resentful of its bridge" (*pontem indignatus Araxes*, 8.728)
and the epic concludes not with any editorial praise of Aeneas but as
Turnus'

> vita . . . cum gemitu fugit indignata sub umbras.
> (12.952)
> life with a groan flees resentful under the shades.

Once again the shield is a microcosm of the poem into which it is
embedded. The one finds nature, in the figure of the Araxes, tamed by
Roman domination and resentful, the other watches Turnus, resentful
and dead. But Aeneas, in his own way and in the poem's greatest challenge to our expectations, also takes the role of nature over culture, of
irrational violence over calming words, as he allows private passion to
supersede any larger gestures of magnanimity. Virgil's is a poem that at
once sustains the discourses of political power and questions them as
well.[4]

My work is in sympathy with the spirit of other recent examinations of
the *Aeneid*. I think particularly of the tonality of W. R. Johnson's eloquent
study of Virgil's *Darkness Visible* and the work of A. J. Boyle as well as

R. O. A. M. Lyne's scrutiny of the poet's brilliantly nuanced word usage. I rely on allusion as a major critical tool. Partly this means watching how Virgil has changed and modified his predecessors, especially Homer, and how he in turn is absorbed by his successors. He was not untouched by the anxiety of influence nor did he leave his spiritual heirs unmarked by his accomplishment. I am most interested in the force of his own internal borrowings and in how plot structures, richness of lexical play, and the reiteration of words illuminate both context and contexts. Again the ending of the poem is the major case in point. In Virgil, as in any great poet, every word matters, but the epic's conclusion offers an obvious focus to tie together what has gone before.

In his final lines Virgil encompasses the whole of the *Iliad*, from the anger of Achilles against Agamemnon and later against Hector to the pleading words of Priam to Achilles transformed into Turnus' prayer of supplication. He also brings climactic closure by having his hero's actions recall notable figurations from earlier in the poem, from Juno's initiating anger to Dido, Anchises, and Turnus himself. For just as Aeneas' final savagery brings back the full force of the epic's opening wrath and its implementation through elemental violence, so the last moments of Turnus, and of the poem, with the dying hero's limbs undone by cold (*solvuntur frigore membra*) carefully and exactly recall the situation of Aeneas during the initial Junonian storm (12.951, 1.92).

The epic is a study in the gradual empowerment of Aeneas, but with the final confirmation of that empowerment comes a metamorphosis into his former enemy (and her ruinous ways) and the killing of his earlier, suffering self. But there is a difference. Aeneas, as his limbs grow chill from fright, stretches both his palms to the stars (*duplicis tendens ad sidera palmas*, 1.93). Turnus, as he supplicates Aeneas before the final blow, is said twice over, by the narrator and in Turnus' own words, also to stretch his hands forth (*dextram . . . precantem / protendens*, 12.930–31; *tendere palmas*, 12.936). But the object of supplication is not now some anonymous stars, harboring divinities not immediately responsive, but Aeneas himself whose anger gives him the stature of Juno and whose spear, with the force of a thunderbolt, parallels him with the lord of the heavens.[5] As Aeneas' tale comes to a close he becomes godlike, containing within himself all the tensions that such a metamorphosis implies. The Virgilian watches with interest how this suggestion of allegory takes dynamic shape in Roman history and in the future of Roman epic.[6]

Memory, too, plays a role in this poetic circularity which Virgil sets up in imaginative counterpoint to the linearity we expect of epic, especially one which in appearance complements the teleology of Roman political ambitions. The ideal spiritual accompaniment to this double act of advancement, according to Anchises' ethical design, is *clementia*. To spare is to forgive and forgiveness implies forgetfulness of the past.[7] To practice clemency on a social scale is to refound Rome on a new moral basis, with brother sharing hegemony with brother, as in the grandiose vision which Jupiter holds before his daughter. Aeneas' killing of Turnus posits a different ethical scheme where the motivations of heroes, which is to say of those who hold sway in Rome, is founded on revenge stemming from memory, revenge that remains in the mind as party to the fears, desires, and resentments that, in Anchises' jarring summary of mortal existence, control our inner lives as long as we are enclosed in the body's blind prison (6.733–34). Only by forgetting our passional sides can we bear to be reborn. But life is crammed full of remembrance, whether it be the recollection of his savage resentment at Pallas' death, which impels Aeneas to kill, or the various memories that urge Juno to implement her wildness of mind as the epic starts.

The narrator and his muse are implicated in this opening outburst: *Musa, mihi causas memora*—"Muse, remind me of the reasons" for Juno's resentment and anger. The story of the poem, then, even to its conclusion, is a reminder of memories, and the poet's mouthpiece sides with the emotionality of his creatures, equating the sources of creativity with the negative energizing principles at work during the poem's framing moments, not with any triumphant Roman historical genius or newly challenging ethical standard. What Virgil adds to the *Iliad*'s opening apostrophe—"Sing, goddess, the destructive wrath of Achilles, son of Peleus"—is not the idea of anger, which motivates both poems, but merely the fact that the goddess, instead of singing directly, now recalls for the narrator the sources of anger. Memory is a crucial characteristic for both the narrator and his protagonist, memory of anger as a generating poetic impulse and, within the poem, as the container of part of its essence.

But however much in these essays I explore the epic's darker side, I mean in no way to foster the artificial polarity that has grown up in recent Virgilian scholarship between positive and negative, optimistic and pessimistic readings of the poem, between epic winners and epic losers, as if somehow only one or the other should be of ranking importance. Just as he incorporates the *Iliad* and the *Odyssey*, both concentrated and expansive forms of epic within his intellectual framework, so Virgil would have us see both visionary aspects of Roman civilization and the very humanness of those who forward its ventures. The challenge between these two aspects of the poem generates much of its forcefulness for late twentieth-century readers.

Any modifications I would make to individual essays in this collection would further complicate rather than simplify their theses. My reading of the sculptures of Daedalus is a case in point. Like the shield of Vulcan, all the ekphraseis of the *Aeneid*, even the description in book 5 of the tale of Ganymede embroidered on the prize cloak, are versions in miniature of the epic itself, forcing us to review and reponder its meanings. In the case of the opening ekphrasis of book 6 I would now stress still more how its details help clarify the problematical relationships between fathers and sons that run through the epic.

Daedalus cannot any more bring the "career" of Icarus to fruition aesthetically than Anchises can complete Aeneas morally or, on one level, Virgil make a whole of the poetry of the *Aeneid*. The fledging of the poem, whose final message is contradictory to what we might expect, is rounded off in the Daedalian realization that *dolor*, not *clementia*, rules the titular hero's last action. As the sculptor becomes more emotionally involved with his work to the point where at the last no more creation is possible, so Aeneas' emotionality, which we have been prepared for fleetingly in book 2, more intensively in book 10, takes control at the end and renders void any higher ethical purposes. All we have left is words, the extraordinary words that in each case complete by the very act of announcing incompletion, by making the hero's very emotionality a crucial part of the poem's imaginative design, as beginning and end form a round that, like Anchises' vision of life, leads constantly back again into itself.

Occasionally I would refine details. For instance, analysis of Virgil's use of the word *aurea* at *Aeneid* 8.168 would have added further point to my study, in the second essay that follows, of the role of Pallas in the epic. Evander, cataloging gifts Anchises had bestowed on him, lists quiver, arrows, a chlamys,

> frenaque bina meus quae nunc habet aurea Pallas.
> and a pair of golden bits which my Pallas now possesses.

The long separation of the adjectives *meus* and *aurea* from their two substantives, *frena* and Pallas respectively, gives the line a pointedly disjointed quality. It reads more smoothly, and shockingly, if we allow ourselves to hear the secondary resonance that arises from the juxtaposition of *aurea* and Pallas. The collocation reinforces later hints of the androgynous charm of Pallas. His name doubly feminizes him both for its etymology ("virgin," "maiden") and for its specific association with Pallas Athena. *Aurea* strengthens the suggestion. Pallas is golden because he partakes in the metal's brilliance and beauty. Aureate shimmer is, of course, the particular attribute of the goddess of love in literature from Homer's χρυσέη Ἀφροδίτη, first at *Iliad* 3.64 and ten times thereafter in Homeric epic, to *aurea Venus*, whom we meet shortly at the opening of *Aeneid* 10 (16).

In all he does Virgil is not only a crafty Daedalus but also the Sibyl, part Apollo and part Bacchus, τέχνη and μανία, *ars* and *ingenium* combined, active fashioner of words but passively molded by Apollo himself (*fingit*, 6.80). She bellows back from her cave, "wrapping the true with the

impenetrable" (*obscuris vera involvens*, 6.100). To grope toward understanding the truths and the obscurities of poetry is also the task of the
critic, a task made more daunting in the case of Virgil by the very richness
and vitality of his accomplishment. Virgil's Sibylline voice continues masterfully on. His readers hear and reproduce only an echo of this grand
utterance. But whatever our limitations as latter-day seekers after enlightenment, we must persist in the quest. These essays are part of that
unremitting enterprise.

NOTES

1. See Conte, *Rhetoric of Imitation* ch. 5 passim, for detailed discus-
    sion of the important distinction between general epic code and
    particular Roman ethical norm.
2. Cf. also most recently Feeney, *The Gods in Epic* 137: "an ideal
    synthesis of the natural order and of Rome's historical order is
    something which the poem strives to establish as attainable";
    and 152–53: "Vergil was not the first poet to be exercised by the
    problem of how the power of divine violence could be used for
    harmony. The eventual order which Jupiter's power will enforce
    is one altogether congenial to the Roman state." Though my
    views are divergent (I do not feel, for instance, that what was
    congenial to the Roman state was necessarily congenial to its
    greatest poet), I mean in no way to abridge the accomplishment
    of those who espouse this interpretative position. Hardie espe-
    cially is fully aware of Virgil's assimilative, metamorphic tech-
    niques.
3. The phrase comes from 6.792–93.
4. The last line of the poem, critics have often noted, is repeated
    exactly from 11.831, where it describes the death of Camilla. In
    killing Turnus Aeneas also kills again the figure who, more
    perhaps even than Turnus, embodies what we might call pre-
    Roman freedom of spirit. In the catalog which brings book 7 to
    an end, Camilla is given a position of greater importance than
    Turnus, bringing it at once to conclusion and climax.
5. The comparison of Aeneas' spear to a black whirlwind (*ater
    turbo*, 12.923) has a series of resonances. I have dealt in the ante-
    penultimate of these essays with its connection with Jupiter's
    Dira who descends to earth "in a swift whirlwind" (*celeri turbine*,
    12.855). Here we should note how it recalls the picture of Aeneas
    in book 10 *turbinis atri / more furens* (603–4), raging like a black
    whirlwind as he goes on the rampage after the death of Pallas.
    We are also meant to remember the "black whirlwind" (*ater
    turbo*, 1.511, and cf. 1.83 for *turbo*, 1.60 and 1.89 for blackness),
    which is a major component of the storm of book 1. Here, too,
    matters are therefore reversed between the beginning of the
    poem and the end as Aeneas becomes the inflicter rather than
    the sufferer of violence and Turnus replaces him as receptor of
    nature (now human) in all its ferocity. Cf. also 11.596 where Opis
    descends from heaven, her body "shrouded in a black whirl-
    wind" (*nigro circumdata turbine*) as she prepares to slay Arruns,
    killer of Camilla. In book 12, immediately before Aeneas is com-

pared to a destructive *nimbus*, a storm cloud closely associated
with Jupiter, he is said to sweep his "black army" (*atrum agmen*)
over the open plain (12.450).

6.   Turnus' final reaction in death, described by the narrator, replaced in part the words that Homer gives to Hector as he dies,
admonishing Achilles to beware of the θεῶν μήνιμα (*Il.* 22.358),
the wrath of the gods, that his death will bring on Achilles. At
the actual moment of death Hector's soul is only mourning
(γοόωσα, 363) as it leaves the body. This Virgil renders through
the phrase *cum gemitu*, leaving *indignata* to convey the notion of
resentment, with its implications of ongoing anger, as the epic
ends.

7.   For David Quint in his important new book (*Epic and Empire* 78)
"Clemency and revenge are both strategies for overcoming the
past, the first by forgetting, the second by undoing; the first sees
repetition of the past as regressive, the second sees in such repetition the possibility of mastery." Both messages are to be found
in the poem and both reflect "the alternative ideological messages . . . sent out by the new regime." I would take a somewhat
different approach. Augustus may have associated revenge with
undoing the past and perhaps even with mastery, but Virgil
balances forgetting with memory, and with memory comes not
the privilege to undo the past but the condemnation to relive it,
with angry Juno leading to angry Aeneas, and indignant Turnus
reechoed in the indignant Araxes. The body's destructive passions are forever restored and the mastered ever crave to gain
mastery again. For Augustus the monumentalizing of revenge in
the temple of Mars Ultor may have marked a sense of stabiliza-
tion, a victory over revenge that publicizes it while at the same
time announcing its demise. For Virgil, long dead at the time of
its dedication, it would have served as an ongoing reminder of
the perpetuity of vendetta, at least if we may trust the evidence
of his masterpiece.

THE VIRGILIAN
ACHIEVEMENT

Scanning Virgil's three major works in the search for unity, the critic is struck by an irony in the changes of genre. As the poet advances on his career, his models grow more and more distant in time, and, it could be said, more basic in theme. The *Eclogues*, modeled often on the *Idyls* of Theocritus and clearly espousing a Callimachean credo of poetic fineness, look to a Hellenistic background. In the *Georgics*, in spite of a slender debt to Aratus and other contemporaries, Virgil turns away from Alexandria first toward the more remote Greece of Hesiod, to sing in Roman towns the song of Ascra, second to Roman Lucretius whose "causes of things" will serve as an enriching influence on his own agrarian gods and their world. The *Aeneid* follows the same pattern—back further in Roman time to Ennius (who had offered direct challenge to Callimachus), in Greek past Apollonius of Rhodes (to whom book 4 is but a passing bow), past an occasional glimpse at the heroes and heroines of tragedy, back to *il miglior fabbro*, Homer himself, against whose essential insights into humanity Virgil's own achievements will always be measured. It is easy to find those who deplore such a journey from Alexandria to the shores of Troy, but Virgil's spiritual diary is worthy of some scrutiny.

Manifestly there are deeper levels to this progress than those which questions of literary influence can plumb, revelatory of taste as the latter often are. There are themes common to all three works. The challenge between idealism and realism, between life as it is often dreamed and life as it ultimately is always led, is an inexorable topic. But in a survey from the pastoral poems to the end of the epic, what is perhaps most striking is the gradual elimination of spiritual distance from the actualities and importunities of existence.

Arcadian setting specifically tends to remove the *Eclogues* from immediacies. The shepherd as poet is itself an anomalous conceit. Moreover, when so much space seems given over to scrutinizing poetry per se, verging toward an ultimately irresponsible verbalization of art's dialogue with itself, that reader is blameless who senses himself in turn the play of make-believe. Not only does Virgil at first draw us into a landscape apart, he appears to narrow his horizon still further by enforcing concentration on a poet's private vision. He orients us to those thoughts which suit or challenge his imagination. The problems of creativity are viewed from a stance of knowing uninvolvement, we could easily assume.

But there are deeper values and more primary concerns to the *Eclogues* than poetry in or of itself. Along with this apparent estrangement from life there is another whole area of intent in the *Eclogues* which is only now becoming critically clarified. Its presence is felt idealistically in the fourth poem where Virgil, at least in his thoughts, sings a symbolic marriage hymn for the union of Rome's consul and his own "woods," of history and paradise, time and timeless, power and poetry. *Carmina*, the efficacy of "charming" verse, are expected to induce the youthful symbol of an era without ambition's wars. Virgil would have us ponder a different golden age, beyond Saturn's facile primitivism and Jupiter's more realistic economics, to a Rome which could in fact embrace pastoralism within its moral bounds, a pastoralism involving a new Saturnian intellectual as well as social freedom.

But Virgil's contemporary Rome of the 40s and 30s B.C. is a more realistic entity and *Eclogues* 1 and 9 dispel any illusions. The position of *Eclogue* 1 is in itself a warning that any seeming escapism in the poems that follow must not be given undue significance. We may treat, if we choose, the differing positions of the two shepherds as a quasi-allegorical dialogue between happiness and suffering, freedom and slavery, and re-joice that the first also flourishes. But in the background lurks a Rome that might be, facing a Rome that does exist. One Rome possesses a divine youth who in turn fosters a dream shepherd. But the idealized pose of the shepherd Tityrus merely vivifies the immediate truth of a barbaric soldier possessing the power to exile another pastoral being. *Eclogue* 9 says in addition that the writing of poetry is impossible under conditions such as now prevail in the sylvan landscape. Their creator-poet exposes his shepherds to reality and then, in *Eclogue* 10, the last of the series, poises himself on the same threshold.

Eclogue 10 makes the transition to the *Georgics* easy. Verbally we are prepared by two phrases. The poet's love for Gallus grows hour by hour like a green alder in new spring, *vere novo*, the exact words with which the land's primaveral awakening is announced at the start of *Georgic* 1. Not only this, the poet himself will "spring up," renouncing the posture of the leisured bard for something more challenging and active:

> surgamus: solet esse gravis cantantibus umbra,
> iuniperi gravis umbra; nocent et frugibus umbrae.
>   (*Ecl.* 10.75–76)
> Let us rise. Shade is often oppressive to singers, the shade of the juniper is oppressive. Shade is also harmful to crops.

It comes as a surprise to learn that shade is harmful to a singer; we have so often heard differently in the *Eclogues*. On the other hand, Virgil warns the practical farmer early on in *Georgic* 1 of the hurt shade gives crops. But it is the poet's admission of affection for the soldier-elegist Gallus that is most revealing. Earlier in the *Eclogues* Virgil, speaking for himself as poet, conjured up a dream existence or pledged a Callimachean allegiance, still within what might be called pastoral convention. Now, by acknowledging a spirited connection with the literal world of the soil and with living humanity (especially with a personage boasting of martial prestige and prowess in a very intimate poetic genre), he renounces his sylvan muse.

His closer look at reality—at nature, which must be seen literally but ultimately is also symbolic—comes in the *Georgics*. The pattern of the four books is an interesting one, from the cosmological setting in which the natural world finds itself (earth and sky), to the growth of crops and trees, to the more explicit trials of animal life, and finally, to bees, partially human, partially divine, communally minded, instinctively aggressive, ignorant of love, eternal in some eyes but equally the prey of death. And then at the end we have two tales. In the first the culture-hero Aristaeus, to wrest life from death, must be initiated into the sources of existence (in a semidivine, mythical world of water) and grasp the *miracula rerum*. The second is devoted to Orpheus, poet-lover, mesmerizer of immortal death by song but unable to control his own mortal *furor*. Finally an eight-line vignette of a still more realistic life concludes the poem—Octavian thundering on the Euphrates and the slothful poet, at his leisure, penning the rhythms of life.

In the *Eclogues* the natural landscape of breeze and shade tends to blur indissolubly with ideas of poetic creation and intellectual freedom. It becomes in the *Georgics* a grander, more essential metaphor for existence. Nature is unceasingly symbolized as human and made to reveal paradigms of flowering and decay, youth and old age, spontaneity and resistance, which offer formal comment on the world of man. And, as part of this more explicit intimacy with the human situation on Virgil's part, there is the same uncordial duality between idealism and realism, between the search for perfected hopes and fallible means. Though the pastoral mode has at first an escapist effect, the actualities of suffering are far from absent in the *Eclogues*. They are a constant theme in the *Georgics*, relieved, as in the *Eclogues*, only by notions which seem deliberately tenuous if momentarily ingratiating.

The first *Georgic* tells of the signs from heaven which only warn but cannot avert disaster. There are violent harvest storms against which there is no recourse. In the middle of the book man is an oarsman propelling a tiny skiff against a heavy current, in spite of the arms at his disposal, scarcely holding his own by unremitting toil in the battle against degeneration. At the end humanity is seen only as a futile charioteer who has lost control of his horses (life's brute and brutal forces) during the exactness of a race. We are reminded at the start of the book of the *gloria divini ruris*, in the end that the plow has lost its honor, that pruning forks are forged into swords, that fields are manured with blood not dung. The initial lines of the book imply that the farmer's lot is hard (he is styled ignorant, mortal, sick); the concluding intimate that it is virtually impossible.

The second *Georgic*, on the other hand, has splendidly idealistic moments—the praises of Italy, the bursting vitality of spring's coming, the concluding eulogy of morality in former rustic days (coupled with Virgil's own commentary on his inspiration). But this last has clues which undercut any false optimism. Virgil evokes a Sabine life of pre-Jupiter days, before war came and Justice left. The realities of Rome (*res Romanae* in every sense) are different and, though this rural existence elicits the poet's approval, it is of time past (*olim*). More peculiar, it is associated with Romulus and Remus, prototypes of civil war, fit exemplars for the modern Romans who, we have just learned, rejoice in a drenching with brothers' blood (*gaudent perfusi sanguine fratrum*). In this manner Etruria grew—and so does Virgil's irony! Romulus and Remus fought each other, the Romulidae fought the Sabines, the combination overcame the Etruscans, and Rome was walled. And yet Virgil would have us believe in another moment that this was the epoch of golden Saturn, before battle trumpets sounded and swords were forged. Such is the dream he has Jupiter propose in *Aeneid* 1 as the head of the gods predicts a future moment when Romulus will cooperate with Remus (*Remo cum fratre Quirinus / iura dabunt*) and Furor is imprisoned. But such a moment never does occur, certainly never in the *Aeneid*, and Virgil's poetic impulse tells us so throughout the *Georgics*.

The third *Georgic* has no relieving optimism, in spite of an initial urge to glorify militant Octavian. Contemplated epic quickly yields to a more direct appraisal of human life. Even love is essentially bitter and destructive. The best day for pitiable mortals is fleeting; what remains is disease, old age, and hard death. The remainder of the book bears out the maxim, ending in a brutally vivid description of a plague that destroys the animal world and those humans who are unfortunate enough to come in contact with it—strange paradox for a writer of *georgica*.

The opening of the fourth *Georgic* is a welcome change. We are to be entertained by watching bees at work, by the spectacle of "light" matters—Virgil's way of telling us that the truth is far otherwise. Critics veer happily toward allegory in their view of the bees, as if they somehow embodied perfection. Yet their life, as Virgil would see it, is neither ideal nor representative, nor, for that matter, eternal. They cannot symbolize humanity (i.e., Orpheus, Aristaeus, or even us) because they experience neither love nor individuality. The principal preoccupation they share with Rome is a devotion to war and, in some instances, a blind (or, to put it more kindly, selfless) devotion to the "state," meaning fundamentally hard work and unswerving loyalty to those in power. They are prone to civil war, which makes their passion for patriotic *pietas* the more bitter. Here fortunately they differ from Rome because their conflicts can be quelled by a handful of dust and death to the leader of lesser value. Such is the power Jupiter exerts over mankind, though from another point of view "divine" force rests in the hands of thundering Octavian (or even Virgil, the leisured imaginer of these words) and who is to control him? The *Aeneid* responds to the unanswered question.

At the end we have Aristaeus who lost his hive for causing Eurydice's death (Virgil need only say that she was running away from him *praeceps*). Orpheus then sought vengeance by destroying his livelihood. The bees were helpless victims of Aristaeus' impetuosity just as Eurydice will soon be lost again through Orpheus' lack of control. Different levels of life come vividly, often unpredictably, into contact as the cycle of birth and death continues. There is always a divine side to existence. The bees have it in part (*partem divinae mentis*). Aristaeus can turn for help to Cyrene and Proteus, and apprehend the exalted lessons of source and variety in nature. Orpheus can charm death itself. But there is always the mortal world of emotion in all its forms. Virgil's suggestion is not only that life comes out of death, bees born from a slaughtered bullock, or even that death follows life. It is also too limiting to assert that, in spite of individual loss, the universe remains immortal. Rather he posits existence as made up of this strange mixture of tragic and comic, human and divine, of death and birth, on the one side, of poetry and power (once more), of Octavian and Virgil on the other, serving as complements and inextricably intertwined.

The birth of the bees is a case in point. It is twice described, with the tales of Aristaeus and Orpheus intervening. In the first instance they shriek, grab the air, and burst forth from the carcass like a summer storm or Parthian arrows. In the second they roar swirling forth from the broken ribs, great clouds of them, and settle on a treetop from whose bending branches they hang like a cluster of grapes. There are elements of violence in each parturition but the earlier dwells on the triumph of the bees' martial instincts whereas the second envisions a more fruitful, ultimately calmer rationale. In the *Aeneid* such a cluster of bees on Latinus' laurel is one harbinger of future domination by the Trojans, seeking a dwelling place, in search of an end to their "tired affairs" (*fessis rebus*, *Aen.* 3.145) just as Aristaeus turns to Proteus in like desperation (*lassis rebus*, *Geo.* 4.449). The resulting rebirth in the *Aeneid* is permeated with the same ambivalence as the *Georgics*, and the final outcome is even less reassuring.

For in the *Aeneid* Virgil finally comes to grips with the realities of contemporary Rome, and Rome, as its poetic masterpiece proves, can be viewed from two sides, each incorporated to a certain extent in its founding hero. Aeneas is the grand civilizer, the sturdy Roman whose art (and I rephrase Anchises' provocative words to his son in the underworld) rises above the mere technical prowess of science, craftsmanship, or rhetoric

to impose a custom for peace on mankind by curbing *superbia* and ex-
hibiting *clementia*—a physical effort to implement a grand spiritual design. The Roman will create and confirm a setting for life. He will mold a
society in which men can live at peace so as to have the opportunity,
within an ordered framework, of being brilliant artisans in stone and
words.[1]

But words are one thing, deeds another, and the struggle to bring into
being an actual Rome takes us out of a realm of noble platitudes into a
more realistic situation where, as in all human endeavor of a political
nature, the bad triumphs along with the good. And Virgil is no naive
dreamer. There is a delicate balance, which Virgil's commanding language conveys, between freedom and slavery inherent in any aspect of
power politics. It is a Roman's duty to rule people by *imperium*, by the
might of empire, and to impose a rationale for peace. Or, as Jupiter says of
Aeneas to Mercury in book 4, he should put the whole world under law.
But both these preachments imply a certain bondage that under some
circumstances, easily imaginable now as well as then, could make both
law and peace meaningless. In partially rejecting the nineteenth-century
attitude about the *Aeneid* as the glorification of Augustan Rome, with
Virgil merely pulling the strings at the emperor's puppet show, we are
also disposing of a basic critical fallacy, namely that distinguished poetry
emanates directly from the fabric of society. A poet is formed, no doubt,
by the culture in which he lives, but culture is conservative. It yearns for
self-preserving stability. The poet, on the other hand, comments, teaches,
argues from an intellectual and emotional distance which prods society
by applying the goad of quality.

If we believe this of the *Aeneid*, as I think we must, then several interesting questions arise. The hero himself is human as well as divine, sensing
the grand philosophical design of a perfected society but narrowed by his
own fallibility in its achievement. Must we therefore expect him to be
totally "moral"? Are we justified in offering him only sympathy and
understanding in moments of weakness? Is it correct—or even important—to visualize him as becoming a better, more virtuous man as the
epic progresses? These are views still commonly held by the most distinguished critics, but Virgil's notions about mankind are tougher, less ro-
mantic, I suggest.[2] In the first six books of the *Aeneid*, individual suffering,
the *lacrimae rerum*, is subordinate to the developing specter of Rome, a
distant image growing more distinct yet still always mental. The hero
learns the future by word of mouth, and endures. In the last six books the
hero executes the dream as fact. The vision has become a reality and, as
always in life, truth is less easy than contemplation, to lead more dangerous than to follow.

For this reason the final three books, in which Aeneas is actually
playing the role of hero-statesman with his father's moral explication of

future Rome to guide him, are of special significance. At the end of book 8, as Aeneas raises to his shoulder Vulcan's blazing shield (and becomes the model of the *fama et fata nepotum*, the reputation and "fate" of his descendants), Virgil has him rejoice in the representation of events about which he was ignorant (*rerumque ignarus imagine gaudet*). This is one of those extraordinary moments in the *Aeneid*, like the bough that "delays" before the hero's touch in book 6, where the hero and his destiny meet most intensely through the poet's symbolization. In spite of the Sibyl's assurances that the bough would come easily and willingly to those fated to pluck it, it hesitates at Aeneas' touch.[3] There is nothing simplistic about Rome's mission or its founding hero. As for book 8, what is about to happen as the epic draws to its violent close is exactly this change from *imago* to *res*, from a craftsman's dream to present reality, from the aloof absorption of destiny by the mediation of ghost or engraved shield to its actual implementation. Aeneas must orient himself away from the artistry of his father's rhetoric and his stepfather's bronze to live the actual *artes* Anchises preaches, his own molding of future Roman *mores*. The appraisal is not necessarily a positive one, for Aeneas or for Rome, but it vivifies certain unending truths.

An issue of primary importance is Aeneas' *pietas*. Does, in fact can, it develop through the epic's course? Is the Aeneas who kills Turnus so very different from the earlier Aeneas we see pondering the murder of Helen during Troy's dark night?[4] Virgil might have us think otherwise. This is the way Aeneas describes his own emotion at the sight of Helen:

> exarsere ignes animo; subit ira cadentem
> ulcisci patriam et sceleratas sumere poenas.
> (2.575–76)
> Fires blazed up in my heart. Anger overcomes me to avenge my falling fatherland and to exact punishment for her crimes.

At the end of 12, as he blazes with wrath (*furiis accensus et ira / terribilis*) upon seeing Pallas' belt on the humbled Turnus, his words sound strangely similar:

> ". . . Pallas te hoc vulnere, Pallas
> immolat et poenam scelerato ex sanguine sumit."
> (12.948–49)
> ". . . Pallas, Pallas sacrifices you with this wound and exacts punishment from your criminal blood."

I doubt that we can say of him that he grew as his responsibilities increased but rather that he stays through it all a fallible soldier given to much the same impulses even while his destiny grows more intricate.

His violent progress through book 10 after the death of Pallas is a case in point. He kills Magus, though the latter is a *supplex* and reminds him of his father and son. Over Tarquitus, whom he also does away with in an attitude of prayer (*orantis*, 10.554), he utters the following curse:

> "istic nunc, metuende, iace. non te optima mater
> condet humi patrioque onerabit membra sepulcro:
> alitibus linquere feris, aut gurgite mersum
> unda feret piscesque impasti vulnera lambent."
>   (10.557–60)
> "Lie there now, you terrible one. No loving mother will lay you in earth nor load your limbs with ancestral tomb: you will be left to birds of prey, or, sunk beneath the flood, the wave will bear you on, and hungry fish will suck your wounds."

Whatever the arrogance of Turnus as he stands over the dead Pallas, his gesture is somewhat more noble:

> ". . . qualem meruit, Pallanta remitto,
> quisquis honos tumuli, quidquid solamen humandi est
> largior . . ."
>   (10.492–94)
> "I send Pallas back even as he deserved, whatever honor in a tomb, whatever comfort there is in burial, I grant . . ."

And Pallas had not prayed for mercy![5] Finally, like a hundred-armed, hundred-handed Aegaeon, Aeneas continues his gory rampage. He meets and kills Lausus. Virgil calls him *pius* before the deed (10.783), as Lausus tries to shelter his father, and Aeneas styles himself *pius* after it is over (10.826). At the actual moment he deals the death blow Aeneas has this to say:

> "quo moriture ruis maioraque viribus audes?
> fallit te incautum pietas tua." . . .
>   (10.811–12)
> "Whither do you rush, about to die, and dare deeds greater than your strength? Your piety deceives you in your folly."

This is quite a strange accusation for our pious hero to hurl, as his weapon passes through a tunic which Lausus' mother had knitted for him out of soft gold. When the importance of Lausus' deed actually dawns on Aeneas (son of Anchises, as Virgil now carefully calls him), it is too late:

et mentem patriae subiit pietatis imago.
  (10.824)
and the picture of paternal piety entered his mind.

Lausus was an emblem of *pietas* in life, but the *imago* is also now lifeless.[6]

The death of Turnus descends from this same line of conduct. Aeneas has him at his mercy. Turnus is a *supplex* and, as he says simply, Aeneas may kill him or not. Aeneas hesitates but sees the belt of Pallas at which point he furiously utters his fateful, ultimate words and kills Turnus as the epic concludes.

We have been prepared for both Turnus' defeat and his death. To those who go against his wise judgment in book 7, Latinus warns:

> "ipsi has sacrilego pendetis sanguine poenas,
> o miseri. te, Turne, nefas, te triste manebit
> supplicium, votisque deos venerabere seris."
>   (7.595–97)
> "Poor creatures, you yourselves will pay the penalty for this with your criminal blood. For you, Turnus, guilt, for you sad punishment will remain, and you will beseech the gods with tardy offerings."

The words imply humiliation and late learning, not death. Aeneas himself predicts Turnus' punishment with no specific allusion to death:

> "heu quantae miseris caedes Laurentibus instant!
> quas poenas mihi, Turne, dabis! . . ."
>   (8.537–38)
> "Alas, how much slaughter looms for the wretched Laurentians? What a price you will pay to me, Turnus! . . ."

But throughout book 10 we know that he is fated to die.[7] Juno, in conference with her husband, can even admit this while ironically using Aeneas' own epithet:

> "nunc pereat Teucrisque pio det sanguine poenas."
>   (10.617)
> "Now let him perish and pay the price to the Trojans with his sacred blood."

It is only Evander who makes it a question of personal vendetta, reasoning that Aeneas must kill Turnus in specific revenge for the slaying of Pallas. He is talking to Aeneas who, though not present, would have heard:

"quod vitam moror invisam Pallante perempto
dextera causa tua est, Turnum gnatoque patrique
quam debere vides . . ."
   (11.177–79)
"Your right hand is the reason that I linger in this hated life now that
Pallas has been slain, (your right hand) which you see owes Turnus
to son and to father."

It is important, then, to ponder Aeneas' hesitation before killing Turnus. If vengeance for Pallas and indeed retribution for much other suffering had been uppermost in Aeneas' mind (and there would have been no
reason for him to forget, considering the emotionality of book 10), then
Virgil need not have him pause. But vengeance should not be paramount
and this, one suspects, is Virgil's way of telling us. Aeneas, without killing
Turnus, would actually perform for the first time Rome's prototypical
heroic act as defined by his father in book 6—*parcere subiectis et debellare
superbos*. Turnus has exemplified *superbia* during his career. He has now
been beaten down. (That he is fated to die means nothing. It is Aeneas'
reasoning that is important.) It is the functioning of civilizing power to
spare him. And it is false reasoning, going against the whole moral thrust
of the epic, to say that Aeneas is right finally to purge his future of
unsophisticated opposition. This is exactly the occasion to practice *clementia*, that spirit of refraining moderation which in this case reenergizes
the downtrodden and allows the defeated to become once more a part of
the state instead of exacerbating old enmities by extracting the penalty of
death for opposition.[8] Aeneas is momentarily swayed by the last words of
Turnus' brief speech: *ulterius ne tende odiis* (12.938). Cicero defines *odium*
as *ira inveterata* (*TD* 4.21).[9] It would be the most appropriate as well as
most impressive time to put away hatred, private against Turnus, public
against all Italic opposition.

But Aeneas is moved to act differently at the sight of the belt of Pallas
which Turnus wears. Virgil is specific about this symbolism. The belt is
saevi monumenta doloris, a remembrance of Aeneas' fierce grief at Pallas'
death. A tangible object draws Aeneas (and Virgil's readers) away from
any lofty sphere of abstract, universal moralizing to sudden reality. Virgil
has been at pains to stress the personal feelings Aeneas holds for Pallas.
His physical beauty is apparent to Aeneas even in death (he is called
smooth, white as snow, and compared to a soft violet or drooping hyacinth). As they travel back from Etruria to Latium, Pallas behaves in a
manner surprisingly akin to Dido:

> . . . Pallasque sinistro
> adfixus lateri iam quaerit sidera, opacae
> noctis iter, iam quae passus terraque marique.
>   (10.160–62)
> . . . and Pallas, fixed to his left side, inquires now of the stars, of the
> course of the murky night, now of what he suffered on land and on
> sea.

Later Aeneas himself symbolically accepts the analogy. At the moment
when he is preparing the body of Pallas for the funeral cortege, he brings
out twin gold and purple garments woven by Sidonian Dido (11.72–77).
In one of these he wraps the corpse. We never hear again of the other.
Finally, it is the first-person pronoun that receives double stress as Aeneas
asks his terrible concluding question:

> . . . "tune hinc spoliis indute meorum
> eripiare mihi? . . ."
>   (12.947–48)
> "Are you, clothed in the spoils of my own, to be snatched hence from
> me?"

Aeneas' "grief" is of an intensely personal sort, and it elicits a violent
outburst of rage as we have seen (*furiis accensus et ira / terribilis*). And by
using now at the end the phrase *saevus dolor* that he had of Juno at the
opening of book 1, Virgil deliberately associates Aeneas not with reason
but with the irrationality that permeates the epic. At the beginning of
book 5, as the Trojans look back on Dido's flaming pyre, Virgil makes the
comment:

> . . . duri magno sed amore dolores
> polluto, notumque furens quid femina possit,
> triste per augurium Teucrorum pectora ducunt.
>   (5.5–7)
> . . . But the hardened resentments, when a great love has been
> desecrated, and the knowledge of what an enraged woman is capa-
> ble lead the Trojan hearts in sad foreboding.

By the end of the epic, Aeneas is no longer the aloof contemplative (or
even the remote cause) of such emotion but its actual symbol. Aeneas is
finally, and after all, a human being.

Rage and anger have not been among Aeneas' trademarks up to now,
as they have been partially of Turnus. We remember Turnus' earlier
bloodlust against the Trojans:

> sed furor ardentem caedisque insana cupido
> egit in adversos . . .
>   (9.760–61)
> but frenzy and the mad desire for slaughter drove him blazing into
> the enemy.

or his reaction to Allecto's advent:

> saevit amor ferri et scelerata insania belli,
> ira super . . .
>   (7.461–62)
> Love for the sword rages in him and the criminal madness of war,
> anger above all . . .

But both *furor* and *ira* now guide the hand of Aeneas. We may defend his
action, if we are so inclined, by appealing to *pietas*, his duty to Evander
and Pallas. He himself calls Turnus' blood *scelerato*, as if the denomina-
tion of Pallas' death in battle as a *scelus* were a vindication of the slaying of
a suppliant. Aeneas is last called *pius* at line 311, moments before he
appeals to the opposing forces to contain their wrath and not break the
treaty (*o cohibete iras!*, 12.314). But the final adjective Virgil allots his hero
in the *Aeneid* is *fervidus*.

The belt of Pallas has a symbolic value, which Virgil chooses to comment upon at the moment Turnus dons it. After telling us that it has on it
a *nefas*, the slaughter of the sons of Aegyptus by the Danaids, he exclaims:

> nescia mens hominum fati sortisque futurae
> et servare modum rebus sublata secundis!
>   (10.501–2)
> Mind of men, ignorant of fate and of their future lot and of how to
> preserve the mean when lifted by success.

The wearing of the belt is a symbol not of Turnus' savagery (this in spite
of the recent death of Pallas and the scene engraved upon it) but of his
lack of *moderatio*. To borrow Horace's words to Augustus (*C.* 3.4.65),
Turnus' impetuosity, his animal force (*vis*), is not tempered by wise
counsel. It is not unwarranted to suggest (though for obvious reasons the
poet cannot do so directly) that the sight of the belt has the same effect
on Aeneas, as the epic draws to a close. If so, it is not his hero's continued
pietas to which Virgil wishes to give final emphasis but his want of
temperantia and of the very *clementia* which his father upholds in his
parting words to his son.[10]

The first detailed exposure of the future Roman ideal state comes early in the first book when Jupiter seeks to reassure Venus after the near disastrous storm. It is a vision of Rome under divinized Augustus, himself a conquering hero, with wars put aside (*positis bellis*, 1.291). Romulus and Remus together will give laws and *furor* will be enchained. In one superficial sense it would be pleasant to affirm (as major critics still do) that the end of the *Aeneid* depicts such a vision in action. Now that Aeneas has killed Turnus, the argument runs, the vista of a peaceful future opens out. The better side has won and true civilization can at last triumph over home-grown primitivism. It is a righteous violence which Aeneas displays because, though momentarily vicious, it looks toward more sophisticated ends. By a passing act of anger, Aeneas will bring an enduring peace.

The trouble is that Virgil says none of this, however much some readers may wish he did. He makes not even the slightest mention of any sense of duty or any larger, moral concerns on Aeneas' part. Granted that the deeper his connection with Pallas (call it the result of *pietas*) the harder it is to forget revenge, nevertheless the killing of Turnus does not make peace customary but war. It glorifies a tradition of irrationality, not control. Virgil presents a final vignette of his hero in a blind rage (the very emotion to which he is supposedly superior). *Furor* could now be imprisoned, but instead Aeneas is *furiis accensus*. Romulus could live with Remus, for in some ways the clash between Aeneas and Turnus is civil. Aeneas is by now *indiges*, Latinized, and he and his rival are ultimately in search of the same goal, political supremacy in Italy. But fraternal peace does not happen any more easily than the possibility of putting wars aside. Violence continues to beget violence, hatreds further hate. Larger goals are easily stated, less readily achieved.

The *Aeneid*, unlike the *Iliad* and the *Odyssey*, is neither a journey into self-knowledge nor a quest for permanence amid the unstable intensity of experience. Achilles can take life or let it alone in his search for personal value in a code of heroic action. His return to humanity leaves him still terrifyingly unique, even through the eyes of a regal old man. Odysseus can encompass the richest adventures of mortal variety while at the same time knowing and then regaining an essential stability which for him surpasses even the temptation of divinity. Virgil knew, loved, and absorbed each work deeply, but his epic and its hero are grounded on different intellectual bases. The *Aeneid* is a work very much in time. We know the history for which it forms the background. We are aware of the social constructs and political institutions which emanated from its action. Aeneas is the moral archetype of a civilization. He is heroic more at first because he suffers the loss of personal involvements in life. To fulfill a grander design, the noble individual gives his glory to the state instead of bravely opposing its usually shallow immediacies. Aeneas is no Antigone, nor would Virgil have him be. The self seems submerged in a social enterprise only partially of its own making.

But Aeneas is as anomalous as the Rome he exemplifies. We might expect that the final purgation of the past which Virgil portrays so brilliantly in the beginning of the sixth book would leave Aeneas free to act out his father's lofty statutes. Palinurus, Dido, Troy (through Deiphobus), and in one sense Anchises himself look to a time when the very vagueness of the hero's search for Rome and *Romanitas* laid special stress on the emotional occasions which seemed momentarily to impede the force of destiny. But it is not so easy as Rome progresses to shut out the irrational which the Greeks had long since taught was basic to *la condition humaine*. The end of the *Aeneid* proves its impossibility.

The past century has seen a revolution in the interpretation of Virgil and especially of the *Aeneid*. If in the *Eclogues* and *Georgics* we were expected to find only "entertainment," in the *Aeneid* we were supposed, with good Victorian sentimentality, to see Virgil the propagandist, chanting an Augustan panegyric. Then we had an Aeneas who, despite an occasional lapse, was little short of a Christian saint, St. George with his dragon, Turnus—an easy step. We are now learning to look at the darker side, to acknowledge the presence not only of suffering but of evil in Aeneas as well as in his presumably more primitive, impetuous antagonists. In other words along with the idealistic Rome we have a very real one as well, in which individual emotion, far from being repressed by a tight social fabric, bursts forth all the stronger. This is not to maintain that the accomplishments of historical Rome do not elicit Virgil's sympathetic praise. They do, and grandly, but the undercurrent of hatred and violence, especially martial violence, that courses through Roman history cannot be gainsaid. At the end of the *Aeneid* it holds center stage in the character of the hero himself. History is by and large a reflection of those who participate in its making and the molder of Roman civilization exemplifies its own inherent weaknesses.

It is important to recall that there are intimations of allegory in the *Aeneid*. Virgil himself more than once subtly suggests an equation between Aeneas and Augustus. We think of Augustus *stans celsa in puppi* during the battle of Actium and Aeneas reaching his beleaguered colleagues in book 10, likewise *celsa in puppi*, holding up the blazing shield on which this very scene is triumphantly engraved. But Virgil immediately compares Aeneas to blood-red comets and Sirius bringing thirst and disease to sick mortals. Augustus presides over an apparently peacebringing victory and Aeneas, by momentarily bringing disease, could be said to create a productive atmosphere for the future. Or does he, and if he, prime mover and founding father, does not, can Augustus?

The *Aeneid* treats complexly the turning of myth into history and at the same time its converse, history become myth. When Anchises addresses his son in the underworld as *Romanus*, he treats him as the Roman everyman, and the philosophy which Anchises propounds offers, as we have noted, a model moral basis for living as a Roman. Aeneas' actions must therefore offer a typical paradigm of how a Roman statesman would (not should) act, given his social and intellectual heritage and commitment. When Anchises says to Aeneas that he should impose a custom for peace, that he should spare the suppliant and war down the haughty, he is urging his son to put into positive operation tenets mouthed by the Greeks.[11] And Cicero can even say of Julius Caesar in the *Pro Marcello* (3.8), not without a touch of flattery: "But to conquer one's animus, to restrain anger, to moderate one's triumphs—not only to uplift an enemy brought low, an enemy outstanding for nobility, genius or courage, but also to enhance his inherited dignity—he who does these things I do not compare with the best men but I consider him most like a god."[12]

This is one side of the coin. The other is the martial instinct and the propensity for vengeance which runs throughout Roman history. And here Augustus sets an example. On the one hand we have the grand shrine to Apollo, god of reason, enlightenment, and poetry who presides over the battle of Actium, offering an instance of Horace's *vim temperatam*. On the other we find Augustus dedicating his famous temple to Mars Ultor, should he gain revenge on his enemies at the battle of Philippi. How to reconcile the two? Virgil himself had difficulties, if we can judge from his treatment of Romulus and Remus in the *Aeneid*. On the shield, the Martian wolf nourishes the twins, but it is necessarily the sons of Romulus alone who make war against the Sabines. Jupiter in book 1 can first speak of Romulus founding the walls of Mars and giving his name to his race and in the next breath announce that, with the temple of Janus closed, Romulus (Quirinus) will give laws with Remus. Anchises, however, in the catalog of book 6, singles out Romulus alone for praise.

We may apply the analogy to the end of the *Aeneid*. Sparing the suppliant is, from one point of view, sparing Remus, and sparing Remus, as *Aeneid* 1 intimates, ends civil war and renews the reign of *ius*.[13] On the other hand there is Aeneas' more immediately emotional involvement with Evander and Pallas, an unspoken *officium* based on *pietas*. The moral thrust of the epic seems to favor the former view. Witness only Anchises' anguished cry not to two brothers this time but to a future father and son-in-law: "Do not, my children, grow accustomed in your minds to such wars; do not turn the powerful strength of your fatherland against its own body."

There are two further, interconnected ironies. First, this moral stance, educative influence of the living myth of Rome, contrasts with the growing Homeric individuality of the final books and especially with the final scene, which is a reversion to more realistic living (and myth making). Second, it is often said that Turnus must die for reasons of a satisfactory epic plot conclusion. What a letdown for the reader, what a compromise to Aeneas' virility were he to display *clementia* to his enemy! But, as the ending finally stands, what an acknowledgment of his hero's failure for Virgil suddenly to revert to the ethics of Homeric Greece and spin off, in epic fashion, an individualist rather than a "civilized" molder of social peace! Does (should) the Roman mission, especially in its Augustan enterprise, as seen through brilliantly imaginative eyes, sacrifice deeper concerns for an exciting scenario? One answer outrages, the other soothes, depending in how we read Augustus. War brutalizes always. Does it ever ennoble? Does Aeneas act the part of civilizer or barbarian? In Virgil's view is there ultimately that much difference between the two sides, and is not war as corrupting of Aeneas as it apparently has been of Turnus? Is not the most enlightened politician a composite of both dreamer and realist, but when it comes to self-preservation or self-aggrandizement do not physical instincts tend to overwhelm loftier sentiments? Is the end of the *Aeneid* ambivalent or Virgil's final, bitterest moment of melancholy?

Virgil proposes for Aeneas a passionate search for Roman identity when he is in fact an outsider—Trojan instead of *indiges*, allied with Jupiter instead of Italian Saturn, an overlord fated but foreign. Aeneas has no connection with the Roman penchant for identification with ancestors, for ordering through custom and rationalizing through law. We may grant him allegiance to Latinus' rich inheritance, to Evander's primeval ways, to Hercules' vindictive heroism, but by the end the very legality of his action is more open to question than acceptance. The emotional and intellectual ties with Pallas, *pietas* toward Arcadia, are poor balance for procreating the *persona* of Roman vengeance.[14] The paradigm is Greek, not Roman, Homeric, not Stoic. Achilles rages at the death of Patroclus, but Pallas is no surrogate for Aeneas whose final deed smacks more of self-justification than humanism. The essential Roman dream, the habituation that makes peace practicable, the suppression of individual selfhood that makes clemency viable, is not allowed to enter Aeneas' mind.

Seen archetypally, Turnus' death is the (innocent) immolation whose bloodletting is vital to any foundation. Looked at against the background of Roman historical development, the killing of Turnus announces the end of the Roman Republic, of two orders balancing each other, of two consuls, of a popular tribune with veto power over aristocratic measures.[15] Tacitus speaks of the time after the battle of Actium when *omnem potentiam ad unum conferri pacis interfuit* (*Hist.* 1.1). What replaces liberty— and this is a chief significance of Turnus' loss—is peace, but a narrow peace, born of violence and founded on personal impulse and the ethics of revenge.

Frank Kermode, in his recent book *The Sense of an Ending*, speaks of the *Aeneid* (and Genesis) as an end-determined fiction. Unlike Odysseus' cyclic ritual, "the progress of Aeneas from the broken city of Troy to a Rome standing for empire without end, is closer to our traditional apocalyptic, and that is why his *imperium* has been incorporated into Western apocalyptic as a type of the City of God."[16] We may see with justice the *Odyssey* as a journey, literal and symbolic, of departure and return and the *Aeneid* as an open-ended voyage of expansive intellectual and political accomplishment. But perhaps, too, the *Aeneid* in a very different way is a type of *Odyssey*, a cyclical evocation of emotion which transcends the temporal propulsion of history. It is true that Troy leads to Rome, loss to fulfillment of a sort, tragedy to a type of comedy, and there is one whole level of intent—an idealistic level of fated prophecies, divine inspirations, and somniac revelations—where the mastery of a perfected Rome is acclaimed. But in the poetry of action, where deed challenges word and the poet's involvement runs most deeply, mortal means obscure and corrupt apocalyptic ends. And on this level the *Aeneid* is a cycle both revelatory and humane, leading from pain and wrath on the divine level ultimately to the same emotions reconstructed by the quasi-divinized hero. The *Aeneid* is a very Roman poem not so much because it presents a vision of *imperium* functioning with civilized, and civilizing, grandeur or because it predisposes us toward a higher Stoic morality than that which a Homeric hero might contemplate (and in so doing be said to anticipate Augustine's *City* and Dante's *Paradiso*). The cycle of Roman *Aeneid*, which begins in Troy and ends with Homer, is internal and metaphysical, a cycle of madness at its conclusion appraising the primal Roman myth of two brothers who do violence to each other and of the loss of liberty that any resulting triumph or defeat portends. Peace at times means suppression, as the greatest Latin historians warn. This cycle of rage reflects Rome's past and, as Virgil would have well known, mankind's future. Eternal, boundless Rome is mortal, after all.

In spite of the "mythical" setting of the *Aeneid*, there is a gradual hardening and toughening of Virgil's version of reality as his work progresses. In the *Eclogues* the outside world is only vaguely imagined by even the shepherds who most suffer its inroads. By manufacturing miraculous vistas of the future or dwelling on poetry per se, it is easy enough to escape life's more inimical pressures. In the *Georgics* Virgil faces the beauties and hardships of life with the soil, but first by metaphor and then by myth extends his ambivalent insights to the world of men. At the end we are left to ask what can reconcile the leisured poet-singer with conquering Octavian. But it is the combined tales of Aristaeus and Orpheus which both summarize and forecast the outcome of the *Aeneid*. If a bard gifted with magic sufficient to tame the Underworld and evoke the dead to life cannot restrain his mortal *furor*, what of those with lesser gifts but more power? What in fact of those like thundering Octavian whose profession by nature could all too easily lend itself to violence? In spite of the accomplishments of the *pax Augusta*, the *Aeneid* warns of the suffering and terror in the establishment and maintenance of an empire still challengingly remote in the *Eclogues*. Through the medium of myth, movement back in time ironically brings us closer to essential matters, to prospective growth and stability but also to suffering, exile, and the final exile, death. It is this realistic appraisal of Rome and of life's ultimate ambivalence—the glory but also finally the tragedy—that at the present time continues to earn for the *Aeneid* its status as a masterpiece.

NOTES

1. This will be a theme in several of the essays that follow.
2. Quinn, *Virgil's Aeneid* 123–24; Dudley, "A Plea" 52–60.
3. Segal, "The Hesitation" 74–79. On the gates of dreams that end book 6, see Clausen, "An Interpretation of the *Aeneid*" 139–47, especially 146–47.
4. This much debated passage (*Aen.* 2.567–88)—preserved by Servius but not in the main manuscript tradition—has been bracketed by Mynors in the Oxford Classical Text. On grounds of style and tradition (how did it reach Servius if Varius and Tucca had succeeded in deleting it at Virgil's wish?), its authenticity is arguable. For full bibliography (supplementing arguments for retention), see Austin, *Liber Secundus* ad loc. For a detailed study against retention, see Goold, "Servius" 101–68.
5. For an opposite view, see Otis, "Originality" 27–66, especially 62–66.
6. Virgil gives the same words to Ascanius at 9.294, as he ponders Euryalus' devotion to his mother in the face of death.
7. Note Jupiter's important words about fate and heroism at 10.467–72.
8. We may compare the posture (both real and predictive) of Aeneas as *supplex* at *Aen.* 6.91 and 6.115.
9. See also Hor. *Epi.* 1.2.59–63.
10. For Hypermnestra's saving action as an example of *clementia*, see Hor. *C.* 3.11.46.
11. See Norden, *Aeneis* 334–38; North, *Sophrosyne* 297.
12. Cf. Horace's sentiments at *Carm. Saec.* 49–52.
13. See Wagenvoort, "Crime of Fratricide" 169–83.
14. See Van Sickle, "Dialectical Methodology" 884–928, especially 926–28.
15. Mommsen, "Remuslegende" 1–23.
16. Kermode, *Sense of an Ending* 5.

POSSESSIVENESS,

SEXUALITY,

AND HEROISM

IN THE *AENEID*

As its opening lines make clear with great precision, the plot line of the *Aeneid* is a simple one. The titular hero, exiled from his homeland, Troy, after its defeat by the Greeks, brings his gods and a remnant of his people to Italy where he is to found a city, Lavinium, the precursor of Alba Longa and finally Rome itself. The epic's story takes us from the horror of Troy's last night, through seven years of wandering from shore to shore, including the hero's dalliance with Dido, until we touch land in Italy at Cumae. After being led by the Sibyl into the Underworld to visit his father, Anchises, and learn of future Roman heroes, he confronts the more immediate challenge of establishing his dominance at the Tiber's mouth. This he succeeds in doing by defeating, and killing in the epic's final lines, the Rutulian chieftain, Turnus, who took to himself leadership of the Latin coalition against the Trojans.

But the epic's opening verses forewarn us that we are to experience far more than a tale of suffering and bravery leading to heroic victory. Take the famous opening phrase, *Arma virumque cano*, whose rendering by Dryden has become standard in English: "Arms, and the man I sing." In his recent version, Robert Fitzgerald translates: "I sing of warfare and a man of war." This no doubt grasps something of Virgil's meaning, with war standing by synecdoche for the weaponry it forces soldiers to use. Yet, though he would have sacrificed the beautiful cadence of the words he actually chose, Virgil could have written *Bella virumque*, "Wars, and the man . . ." He did not. Instead, by putting a single emphasis on arms where Fitzgerald places a double stress on the larger entity, war, Virgil tells us that his poem is to be about the explicit, specific relationship of a man, or men, and the arms they use, for the two are constantly interconnected throughout the poem. His epic is concerned with force and the moral dilemmas its wielding creates.

The poem's opening propounds the thesis. Its conclusion offers the most remarkable instance of this dynamic relationship between heroes, their armory, and the ethics of power. In the poem's last thirty-four lines we have no less than four types of arms called into service. First Aeneas seriously but not fatally wounds Turnus in the thigh with his spear. Then, after Turnus has begged him for mercy and for an end to his hatred, he stands over his defeated foe *acer in armis* (12.938). He is fierce in a panoply that includes a shield engraved with major events of Roman history

culminating in the battle of Actium and the rout of Antony and Cleopatra. Turnus' words have the effect of restraining Aeneas' hand, but he
suddenly sights the sword belt of the youth Pallas which Turnus had
stripped off his body after killing him earlier in the fighting. The appearance of this baldric on Turnus enrages Aeneas and he slays him with
his sword.

Each step in this action, each weapon that is called into play, involves
emotional and ethical considerations that are crucial to our understanding of the poem as a whole. How we read the ending determines how we
read, and reread, the poem that it caps. If the final killing, after a moment
of hesitation, is motivated by Aeneas' supposedly guiding abstraction,
pietas, as some critics maintain, then the epic ends as we might expect.
His deed may seem to go contrary to the first part of his father's injunction in the Underworld to spare the suppliant and war down the proud.
Nevertheless, according to this view, sufficient provocation, and excuse,
for his action, lies in the "piety" he owes Pallas and his father, Evander, to
avenge the son's death. Evander had earlier led us to believe that Aeneas
"owed" Turnus to the bereaved parent (11.179).

It is well, in this regard, to examine the actual words Virgil uses to
describe his hero before his final brief statement and death-dealing act.
They also take us back to the epic's opening and the moral program
quietly announced there. He speaks and acts only:

> ille oculis postquam saevi monimenta doloris
> exuviasque hausit, furiis accensus et ira
> terribilis . . .
>   (12.945–47)
> after he drank in with his eyes the reminders of his ferocious anguish
> and the spoils, set ablaze by fury and frightening in his rage . . .

If the opening lines tell us of the difficulties involved in Rome's foundation and of the intertwining of arms and men as this goal is implemented,
they also establish one of the major emotional strands of the epic,
namely, the hatred of Juno for Aeneas and his goal. The terms in which
this hatred is couched by Virgil's narrator are remarkably similar to the
way we are made to see Aeneas' reactions at the end. In the first eleven
lines of the epic we hear twice of her rage, once of her ferocity, and once
of her anguish.

In contrast with this concatenation of wildness is the—still unnamed—
hero who is styled as "a man outstanding for his piety" (*insignem pietate
virum*, 1.10). This distinction in ruling abstractions is continued on in the
initial dramatic episode which, as critics have long noted, sets the tone for
much that follows. We soon learn that the "stimuli for her rage and
ferocious anguish" (*causae irarum saevique dolores*, 1.25) are her constant

companions, and that "inflamed by these" (*his accensa*, 1.29) she co-opts
Aeolus, ruler of the winds, into her design to destroy Aeneas and his fleet
through a sea storm. Virgil is fond of having external nature reflect the
inner "weather" of his characters, and it is not hard to see the tempest
which Juno's puppet devises as both literal and figurative at once—literal,
as the means to annihilate the Trojans, figurative, as a reflection of her
deep-seated hatred.

Certainly when her brother Neptune, lord of the sea, senses his realm
in turmoil, he attributes the disturbance to the deceits and "rages" of his
sister. And as the episode draws to a close, we are brought back to its
beginning, and to the start of the poem, by the extraordinary first simile
which compares Neptune's calming influence over his unruly charges to
a respected personage who stills a spirited, revolutionary mob. Once
more the same distinctions are operative. The populace "rages" (*saevit*),
and we are told that furor lends it arms. The counterposing force is a man
"respected for his piety and his achievements" (*pietate gravem ac meritis*,
1.151). Neptune and Aeneas are parallel creations. Each endures Juno's
frenzy and sets against it—directly in the first instance, presumably in the
second—a *pietas* of mind that mitigates the often physical manifestations
of its antonym's wildness. Why, then, at the end of the poem is Aeneas
made to react like Juno and not like Neptune, like a person given over to
private vendetta rather than a public-spirited soul bent on suppressing
passion?

One answer lies, I believe, in a strand of eroticism that runs carefully
through the poem, knotting its beginning and end together. But before I
discuss this I would like to remind us of how mysterious a poem the
Aeneid is and will always remain. Here are some enigmas, paradoxes,
ambiguities that will form part of my argument. I pose them as questions. Why does the golden bough, which Aeneas needs as a passport into
the Underworld and into future Roman history, hesitate as Aeneas tugs it
off, when the Sibyl has just told him that it will be broken easily by
whomever fate allows? And, allied to this, what are we to think of the
Roman mission when we learn from Anchises that time spent in the
Underworld serves merely to purge the emotionality rampant in the
doings of men while still alive? (Each hero must be made to forget his
past, as he prepares to be reborn, and even Aeneas can exclaim to his
father on the "dread desire" [*dira cupido*, 6.721] that has grasped anyone
who wishes to face life again.) My second query: Why is Erato, muse
whose name suggests that love poetry is her province, addressed as spon-
sor of the second half of the epic? And, finally, if the manufacture of arms
for the hero is a straightforward, morally praiseworthy enterprise, why,
in book 8, does Vulcan hesitate before yielding to Venus' request for them
for her son? Why must she resort to her seductive wiles to win him
over—and gloat, later, pleased with herself that they had worked—if

nothing suspicious lurked in their forging, their use, or the deeds of the Roman future which the shield will survey? Does the erotic element that enters into their origination continue in their later employment? Or, if we use this episode as a synecdoche, in what senses and ways are sexuality and armor, emotionality and warring interdependent as the *Aeneid* presses to a close?

Let me begin a search for answers to these questions by turning to an earlier episode in book 8 whose ambiguities have not always received the scrutiny they deserve, namely the fight between Hercules and Cacus. King Evander tells the tale of this half-man, half-beast, whose soil, to paraphrase the narrative, was always warm with fresh slaughter, and fixed to whose haughty portals were hanging visages of men sallow with ugly gore. To the obvious relief of the neighborhood, Hercules strangles the creature to death after he has stolen some of his cattle. It is the memory of this deed that is being celebrated as Aeneas steps ashore at the site of future Rome.

The adventure lends itself easily to a paradigmatic interpretation with clear polarities. The hero, about his task of ridding the world of monsters, kills a villain, as good triumphs over evil, civilization over primitivism, human over animal. It is an easy jump to find here an example of myth anticipating history as Hercules prefigures the last, triumphant image on the shield of Aeneas: Augustus clearing Rome of Antony, Cleopatra, and her grotesque gods. Virgil's narrative elsewhere abets the analogy. In the sixth book he has Anchises announce that the extent of the Roman empire under Augustus surpasses the territory covered by Hercules as he went about his labors (6.801–3). The implication remains that in quality of accomplishment the new emperor surpasses even his Hellenic archetype.

But just as on the shield Virgil subtly elicits sympathy for Cleopatra and Rome's enemies while questioning Augustus' pride,[1] so aspects of Evander's narrative of the Hercules-Cacus story also work against facile allegory. First of all, lexical parallels tend to equate, rather than to distinguish, the two protagonists. Cacus' doorposts are proud with the features of his victims, and Hercules is proud from the slaying and despoliation of Geryon (8.202). Each is associated with fury: the mind of Cacus is wild with fury as he goes about his thievery, while Hercules is first ablaze with fury, then furious, in response. Each takes to himself images of blackness, Cacus spewing black fires from his throat, Hercules reacting with black rage. But it is not so much parallelisms in vocabulary that demean Hercules as questions of motivation and then reaction specifically on his part.

First the reaction. Cicero, in a passage arguing that bravery and frenzy, courage and irrationality are incompatible, asks his interlocutor rhetorically: "Do you think that Hercules, who was raised to heaven by that selfsame bravery you would consider to be irascibility, was angry when he

struggled with the boar of Erymanthus . . . ?" (*TD* 4.50)[2] Not at all is
Cicero's point. Yet, if Stoic saints do not yield to hot temper as they go
about their endeavors, why is Hercules "swollen with anger" (*fervidus ira*,
8.230) as he takes on the monster Cacus? Evander, as created by Virgil,
gives us no high-minded, metaphysical reasons for the hero's behavior.
We are not told that Hercules took one look at Cacus, sized up his
brutishness, and killed him to rid the site of Rome of barbarity. Virgil has
his death-dealing action motivated purely by Cacus' robbery of the cattle,
a deed which Evander calls a *scelus*, crime. He is moved to respond not
from larger universal concerns but because of a private hurt and its
resultant vendetta. If we are generous to him, we can defend Hercules'
anguish (*dolor*) and its consequent rage (*ira*) as a result of a loss of
dignitas. The cattle of Geryon, in which he takes pride, stand for his *virtus*,
criminally assaulted by Cacus. To touch them is to affront his courage
and the dignity that results from this heroism.

But Virgil's text gives us little help in defending even such conceptual-
ization. What Evander does tell us is that the cattle were very beautiful:

> quattuor a stabulis praestanti corpore tauros
> avertit, totidem forma superante iuvencas.
> (8.207–8)
> [Cacus] stole four bulls of supreme loveliness from their steadings,
> and as many heifers of matchless form.

We sense why Cacus might like them, but we can also readily imagine
their importance to Hercules on a most basic level. They are his possessions and they are very lovely. Their loss is the loss of objects personally
attractive to him. It arouses in him anguish, anger, and fury, twice emphasized, as we have seen, in the narration.[3]

The latent sexual element in these doings is confirmed if we look back
again to the opening episode of book 1. There Juno, after commanding
Aeolus to strike force into his winds and overwhelm Aeneas' ships, forthwith offers him a bribe:

> sunt mihi bis septem praestanti corpore Nymphae,
> quarum quae forma pulcherrima Deiopea,
> conubio iungam stabili propriamque dicabo . . .
> (1.71–73)
> I have fourteen nymphs of supreme loveliness, to the most beautiful
> in form of whom, Deiopea, I will join you in steadfast matrimony
> and I will name her yours . . .

Sexual bribery is the means by which Juno stirs Aeolus suddenly to
incorporate her rage, and to storm, with his horse-winds, against the

Trojans, in spite of his having to contravene thereby Neptune's direct limitations on his sway. The beautiful possession, momentarily lost this time rather than tantalizingly offered, is also an impetus for irrational wildness on the part of Hercules. His reaction to this deprivation associates him with, rather than separates him from, his antagonist.

In this context it is well to remember the reasons behind Juno's hostility to which Virgil alludes in detail during the epic's opening lines. She "fears" for the ultimate defeat of her favorite Carthaginians at the hands of future Romans and she "remembers" the war she had waged at Troy on behalf of her beloved Greeks. Her first reasoning, in other words, is based on past and future history, on events over or to be anticipated. Next, however, Virgil takes us into her mind and the turbulence there. The motivations for her "rage and ferocious anguish" are all congruent. They are the judgment of Paris (and her beauty scorned), her hatred of the Trojans as a race, and the preferments granted Ganymede. All are based on sexual jealousy or dissatisfaction, because Paris chose Venus ahead of her and because her husband, Jupiter, granted his favors to Electra, who became mother of Dardanus and hence ancestress of the Trojans, and to the youth Ganymede. As we trace the developing inwardness of these two catalogs, we find her at the start merely anxious and mindful, but by the conclusion—as Virgil uses a metaphor he will employ at later crucial moments—she has been set aflame.

Both these paradigmatic episodes, therefore, turn on the notion of privation, with implicit or explicit sexual innuendo, and in each case loss breeds a serious reaction. With these moments in mind, continuing the search into the reasons for Aeneas' ferocity at the epic's conclusion, I would like to turn once again to the eighth book and to a close examination of Virgil's treatment of the figure of Pallas. It is received critical opinion to understand Pallas' relationship with Aeneas as an example of *contubernium* whereby the younger tiro learns from the more experienced warrior the ways of battle.[4] This notion receives confirmation in the text in the words of Evander when he hands his son over to his guest's tutelage:

> under your guidance let him grow used to military life and to the weighty work of Mars, to apprehending your deeds, and let him admire you from his earliest years.
> (8.515–17)

Also Evander earlier helps us draw an analogy between his own admiring reaction when, as a youth, he met Aeneas' father Anchises, and Pallas' response to Aeneas. Evander says of himself:

... mihi mens iuvenali ardebat amore
compellare virum et dextrae coniungere dextram.
   (8.163–64)
My mind burned with a youthful love to greet the man and to join
right hand with right hand.

And it was only moments before that Pallas had clasped the hand of
Aeneas as he stepped ashore at Pallanteum. Pallas is to look up to and
emulate Aeneas as Evander once had Anchises.

But just as the way Virgil has Evander narrate the tale of Hercules and
Cacus or Vulcan depict Augustus and Cleopatra on Aeneas' shield allows
us to read each episode in opposite ways, so also the poetry of this crucial
meeting itself speaks of a deeper emotionality, first emanating from Pallas, then from Aeneas, as events progress. Let us begin with the initial
handshake itself.[5] Virgil's remarkable line goes as follows:

excepitque manu dextramque amplexus inhaesit.
   (8.124)
[Pallas] both grasped [Aeneas'] right hand and embracing, clung
to it.

There are many realized handshakes in the *Aeneid* but no other quite like
this one. The line heaps chiasmus on chiasmus to convey, through sound
and verbal deployment, the intensity of Pallas' gesture. In fact the verse
itself represents graphically the gesture, focusing on the elision between
dextramque and *amplexus*, and from this central point the auditory "embrace" spreads out, beginning with the repetitions on either side of the
elision, first of -*am*, then -*ex*, and extending, finally, to the ends of the line
and balancing verbs which form its termini. Moreover, neither *amplector*
nor *inhaereo* appears in such a context elsewhere in the *Aeneid*. Virgil in
fact uses *inhaereo* only twice elsewhere, shortly later in book 8, as Evander
tells of Hercules squeezing Cacus to death (260), and in book 10, as
Mezentius clings to the lifeless body of his son Lausus (845). Both, I need
scarcely add, are moments of extreme emotionality, whether the feeling
expressed be hatred or love. I will examine in a moment other appearances of the simple verb *haereo* in situations that give its compound still
further power in the present setting.

   The next occasion we are made aware of the physical presence of Pallas
occurs the subsequent morning. This also involves the shaking of hands
as the two pairs, Evander and Pallas, Aeneas and Achates, converge from
their respective abodes. But later in the day we are led to experience
another example of the extreme emotionality Pallas arouses, namely the
farewell scene, which proves to be their last parting, of father and son.

Given the number of embraces in this book, their profusion here is all the more noteworthy.[6] First we have the introduction to Evander's au revoir:

> tum pater Evandrus dextram complexus euntis
> haeret inexpletus lacrimans . . .
>   (8.558–59)
> Then father Evander, embracing the hand of [Pallas] on his going,
> clings unsated, weeping . . .

The parallels with Pallas' passionate greeting of Aeneas are clear enough. Here, however, since Virgil never elsewhere connects *complector* with *dextram*, great emphasis is given the latter, with Pallas' right hand standing for his person. This is also Virgil's only use of *inexpletus*, unsated, whose erotic overtones in this setting must not be minimized.[7] And in the course of his brief speech Evander alludes first to the "sweet embrace" (*dulci amplexu*) from which he would not now be torn if his former strength were still with him (a strange, highly suggestive way of saying that father and son would go into battle together!). Then at the end he prays for a self-inflicted death before any wounding news could reach him:

> dum te, care puer, mea sola et sera voluptas,
> complexu teneo . . .
>   (8.581–82)
> while I hold you, dear boy, my only, my late pleasure, in embrace . . .

It is no accident that six lines after the end of Evander's valedictory Virgil offers a simile comparing Pallas, bright in his variegated armor, to Lucifer, the morning star,

> quem Venus ante alios astrorum diligit ignis . . .
>   (8.590)
> whom Venus loves ahead of the other starry fires.[8]

We may also be meant to think of Pallas as a *contubernalis* of Aeneas, but through metaphor and simile, not to speak of the story line itself, we see him not as an incipient warrior but as an object of beauty given to intensities of his own and capable of arousing them in others.

When next we meet Pallas, metaphor, this time supported by analogy, is again a crucial means for the poet to tell us what his surface narrative need not say. As they make the journey down the Tiber to the final conflict with Turnus, Aeneas, we are told, turns over in his mind the varying events of the war

> ... Pallasque sinistro
> adfixus lateri iam quaerit sidera, opacae
> noctis iter, iam quae passus terraque marique.
>   (10.160–62)

and Pallas, fixed to his left side, inquires now of the stars, of the course of the murky night, now of what he suffered on land and on sea.

The analogy, of course, is with Dido at the conclusion of book 1. There, now deeply in love with Aeneas through the trickery of Venus and Cupid, the Carthaginian queen first listens to a *De Rerum Natura* sung by Iopas, then to the adventures of Aeneas on land and sea, as chronicled by the hero himself.

The metaphor in *adfixus* is more complex, but its force here can be approximated by a look at Virgil's other five uses of the verb. In the *Georgics* he applies it to a vine root, to be firmly planted (2.318), and to bees leaving a sting (4.236–38). Early in *Aeneid* 8 we find the faces of the men Cacus has mutilated pierced (*adfixa*) on his haughty doorposts (196). *Adfigo* is combined with another verb of importance to us, *haereo*, in two other contexts. At the end of the fifth book we find Palinurus "affixed and clinging" (*adfixus et haerens*, 852) to the helm of Aeneas' ship, soon to tear part of the poop and rudder with him as Sleep plunges him into the water. Finally there is a moment in book 9 where Turnus attacks a defense tower of the Trojans:

> princeps ardentem coniecit lampada Turnus
> et flammam adfixit lateri, quae plurima vento
> corripuit tabulas et postibus haesit adesis.
>   (9.535–37)

First Turnus hurled a burning torch and to the [tower's] side affixed its fire, which, fanned by the wind, seized the planks and clung to the doorposts it had devoured.

Since this is Virgil's only other juxtaposition of *adfigo* and *latus*, it may be particularly with fire that Virgil means us to associate Pallas, stuck to Aeneas' side. But the destructive elements in the other appearances of *adfigo* should not be minimized. The bees leave poison and make a wound, as they put their life into their sting, and by clutching tightly to his rudder Palinurus maims his ship as he falls. We should also note that the episodes of Palinurus and of Turnus' attack on the tower both contain the verb *haereo*. Palinurus clings, the fire clings, as they mutilate the objects to which they become attached. They both thus serve to remind us of the only other moment in the epic where Pallas actually touches

Aeneas, the initial greeting where the boy clings to the hero's right hand. "Clutching" in the early episode becomes the still more violent "piercing" in the later.

Not that these moments stand alone. *Haereo, figo,* and their compounds are used frequently throughout the epic in metaphorical contexts that have a bearing on the passages under consideration. Here are two examples that extend over stretches of the epic. As Venus prepares to send Cupid to replace Ascanius at Carthage and engineer Dido's romance with Aeneas, she commands her son:

> "cum dabit amplexus atque oscula dulcia figet
> occultum inspires ignem fallasque veneno."
> (1.687–88)
> "When she will offer embraces and plant sweet kisses, you will breathe into [her] hidden fire and deceive her with poison."

And soon thereafter, as he goes about his deadly work:

> . . . haec oculis, haec pectore toto
> haeret . . .
> (1.717–18)
> she holds to him with her eyes, holds with her whole heart.

At the start of the action she is in one sense positive. She fixes kisses and clings to the love god. By the beginning of book 4, after she has prolonged the night with hearing of his adventures, the metaphors are reversed. As the wound and fire images become hers, she is the one transfixed by Aeneas:

> . . . haerent infixi pectore vultus
> verbaque . . .
> (4.4–5)
> his features and his words cling, pierced in her heart.

And, in the book's first simile which follows on reiteration of the flame and wound images, maddened Dido is compared to an incautious doe that an ignorant shepherd has pierced (*fixit*) with his arrows. Its last phrase brings the metaphor palpably before our eyes:

> . . . haeret lateri letalis harundo.
> (4.73)
> And the lethal shaft clings to her side.

And we must not forget Juno, the divine force behind much of the poem's irrationality, who begins the first half of the epic "harboring an eternal wound under her breast" (1.36) and whom we find, not far from the opening of the second half, still "pierced by sharp anguish" (*acri fixa dolore*, 7.291).[9]

We must keep the imaginative power of all these images in mind when we seek to interpret the meaning of *inhaesit* and *adfixus* as they bear on the relationship of Aeneas and his protégé. The metaphors which vivify Pallas' effect on Aeneas are drawn from an arsenal of stings, arrows, wounds, fires. The force they exert on Aeneas is not directly apparent in his behavior after Pallas' death. Virgil tells us only that, as he prepares to act, Aeneas thinks of Pallas, Evander, their reception of him in the future site of Rome and right hands clasped in compact. The depth of these feelings, however, is attested by the vehemence of the rampage on which he now embarks. He seizes eight captives to become human sacrifices and kills at least eleven people among whom are a priest and two warriors who pray abjectly for mercy and remind Aeneas of his *pietas*. As his frenzy pursues its course, Virgil compares him to the giant Aegaeon who raged against Jove's thunderbolts with a hundred arms and hands, flashing fire from fifty mouths and chests.

At this crucial juncture in book 10 Aeneas only hears news of Pallas' death which is described impersonally as a *malum tantum*, "such a misfortune" (510). Aeneas actually addresses the corpse only at the start of book 11 as preparations are made for the funeral cortege, carrying the body back to Pallanteum. What he is made by the poet to see and do before his speech will help us gauge further his feelings about Pallas. First what he views:

> ipse caput nivei fultum Pallantis et ora
> ut vidit levique patens in pectore vulnus
> cuspidis Ausoniae, lacrimis ita fatur abortis . . .
> (11.39–41)

He, when he saw the pillowed head and features of snow-white Pallas and on his smooth chest the open wound from the Ausonian spear, speaks thus as his tears well up . . .[10]

Two words are gratuitous in this description—*niveus*, snowy, and *levis*, smooth—and both are highly sensual. What Aeneas takes note of is the adolescent, androgynous beauty of the youth.[11] *Niveus* has nothing to do with the whiteness of death (Virgil would have used *pallidus*)[12] and everything with physical allure. Virgil's only other use of *niveus* in connection with the human anatomy occurs in book 8 where Venus uses her "snowy arms" (*niveis lacertis*, 387) to fondle hesitant Vulcan in her soft embrace. Catullus styles the limbs of the virgin Polyxena, slaughtered on Achilles' tomb, as *niveos* (64.364). For Horace the skin color of Briseis, Achilles' slave-mistress, is *niveo* (*C.* 2.4.3), and in an elegy of Propertius Adonis, youthful lover of Venus, is characterized as *niveum* (2.13.53). Smoothness of skin is also a mark of youthful beauty—in a late ode Horace describes smooth-cheeked Apollo as *levis* (*C.* 4.6.28)—but we must not dismiss the hint of femininity even here. For instance, it has not been long since we were told of Amata's *levia pectora* (7.349), the smooth breasts into which Allecto's snake-madness slips, or of Camilla's smooth shoulders (7.815).

Virgil confirms the impression of youthful, partially feminine beauty in a simile subsequent to Aeneas' speech, as the body is loaded on the bier. The narrator compares dead Pallas to a flower, a violet or a hyacinth, nipped by the thumb of a virgin:

> qualem virgineo demessum pollice florem
> seu mollis violae seu languentis hyacinthi,
> cui neque fulgor adhuc nec dum sua forma recessit,
> non iam mater alit tellus virisque ministrat.
> (11.68–71)
> like a flower reaped by a virgin's thumb, either of a soft violet or a drooping hyacinth, whose brightness and shape have not yet faded, but now mother earth does not nourish it and grant it strength.[13]

From Sappho on, the hyacinth is a symbol for a bride whose "plucking" connotes her deflowering in marriage (105cLP = LGS 225). The irony here is that it is a virgin who violates the flower. For Turnus, killer of Pallas, though he robs the unmarried but attractive youth of life, will himself be killed by, and lose his potential *coniunx* to, Aeneas.

Aeneas performs now one of the most symbolic gestures in the epic. He takes out two robes

> . . . quas illi laeta laborum
> ipsa suis quondam manibus Sidonia Dido
> fecerat et tenui telas discreverat auro.
> (11.73–75)
> which Sidonian Dido, delighting in her task, had with her own hand once fashioned for him and interwoven the web with strands of gold.

In one of these he swathes the corpse. We never hear of the other, but I presume that he wraps himself in it. If so, he admits the power of Dido in this, her last direct mention in the poem, by symbolically equating first Pallas, then himself, with her.

The percipient reader would have already felt her presence in Aeneas' earlier look at the young warrior's body. The tag *pectore vulnus*, which ends line 40, occurs three other times in the epic. Two of these instances concern Dido. In the first, shortly before the shepherd-doe simile in book 4, the hurt is metaphorical:

> . . . mollis flamma medullas
> interea et tacitum vivit sub pectore vulnus.
>   (4.66–67)
> A flame gnaws at her soft inwards, meanwhile, and a silent wound lives under her breast.

The second, no longer silent and very real, is the deadly wound of her suicide:

> . . . infixum stridit sub pectore vulnus.
>   (4.689)
> pierced in, the wound hisses under her breast.[14]

Wittingly or unknowingly, Aeneas is the cause of each wound, whether symbolic or actual.[15]

Virgil supports this allusiveness with even more direct attendance to the earlier telling of Dido's story. Line 75 is the same as 4.264.[16] There the narrator describes a cloak (*laena*) made for Aeneas by Dido, which he is wearing when Mercury arrives to recall him to his Roman mission and which therefore is a *monimentum* of the brief period when he and Dido were lovers. More striking still is the equivalence of book 11's initial line with:

> Oceanum interea surgens Aurora reliquit . . .
>   (4.129)
> Meanwhile Dawn, rising, left Ocean . . .

The narrator readies us for Aeneas' farewell glimpse of Pallas by reminding us of the moment in book 4 when Dido and Aeneas set out on their hunt. This departure initiates a chain of events leading to Juno's presiding over what Dido "calls a marriage, and with this label cloaked her blame" (4.172).

Such direct verbal echoes suggest again that in Aeneas' relationship to Pallas Virgil means us to observe parallels with Dido and thus to intimate that Aeneas senses for Pallas, virginal flower mowed to death by another virgin who is also soon to die, something akin to his feelings for Dido during the briefly untroubled part of their liaison. The possibility is furthered by a lexical novelty. The verb Virgil co-opts to describe Aeneas' covering of Pallas' corpse with Dido's weaving, *obnubere* (77), is unique in his usage and makes here only its second appearance in Latin letters.[17]

Since the poet elsewhere utilizes the verb *velare* to denote ceremonial veiling of the head (3.174, 3.405, 8.277), the reader rightly speculates on the particular nuances of the Virgilian *hapax* here. Servius' comment touches on what may be the poet's point:

> "obnubit" autem velavit, translatio a nubibus quibus tegitur caelum: unde et nuptiae dicuntur, quod nubentum capita *obnubantur*, id est velantur.

> "he covers" which is to say he veiled, a figuration from clouds [*nubibus*] by which heaven is covered: whence also wedding [*nuptiae*] derives its name, because the heads of brides [*nubentum*] are covered [*obnubantur*], that is, are veiled.

In pre-Virgilian usage, Varro makes the same connection between *obnubere* and *nuptiae*, and the lexicon of Paulus-Festus states that Cincius and Aelius Stilo, Varro's teacher, did likewise.[18]

Virgil, then, chose a word on the surface appropriate for Aeneas' veiling of the corpse of Pallas in death but which also suggests a deeper symbolism: that Pallas' funeral is also to Aeneas in some sense his marriage, that his funeral *torus* (66) was also a marriage bed, as it had been for Dido.[19] Using a cloth woven by Dido for her lover, Virgil has Aeneas treat Pallas as a bride in oblique allusion to a ceremony that could no more directly be Dido's than Pallas'.

Through verbal parallels, metaphorical analogy, and symbolic gesture, then, Pallas becomes again, as he had during the Tiber journey, another Dido. In a way his deadly wound, like Dido's, was caused by Aeneas' inattention, this time to the youth's activities on the battlefield. But the impact of Pallas on Aeneas is subtly different from that of Dido. We do hear in the fourth book that the hero "with an effort smothered care deep in his heart" and once that he "swayed in his mind from his great love" (332, 395). But in general for such a *histoire passionelle* there is a remarkable absence of the physical details we expect in such circumstances. All frenzy—for love, for revenge, for death—is hers, none his. We know that Dido is beautiful but we learn this from the narrator or from Rumor paraphrased, not from any response on Aeneas' part.[20] By contrast, Aeneas looks closely at Pallas just as he had at Lausus, dead from his onslaught in book 10, and himself creates an analogy between Pallas and a happy Dido, a circumstance of which we hear little or nothing in book 4. Perhaps more important still, the narrator would have us notice through metaphor, even before the palpability of his response in book 11, that Aeneas is wounded by Pallas in a pattern that begins with the intense handclasp of book 8 and continues with the youth "affixed" to the hero's side on shipboard. Pallas is not only the receiver of a physical wound, as is

Dido, but also the bestower of a spiritual one in a way which was never allowed to be hers.

The saga of Pallas ends only as the epic ends. Aeneas, contemplating restraint, sees Pallas' belt on Turnus, goes wild with grief and kills his opponent whose life flees under the shades. I quoted earlier the lines that introduced Aeneas' final words to his foe, to show that someone acting out of fierce anguish, set aflame by furies and terrible in his wrath, was not behaving under the influence of *pietas*. My analogy was the conduct of Juno at the opening of the epic, and her opposite there was the suffering hero, enduring rather than acting. But in the last moments of the poem Aeneas turns into Juno, the goddess who at the start is "harboring an eternal wound in her breast" and who, out of sexual jealousy, raises a furious storm against the Trojans that represents her fury. It is the thesis for which I have been offering evidence that the reasons for Juno's behavior are Aeneas' as well, that he, too, is acting out of deeply personal grief, caused by deprivation, and that this drives him, as it does Juno, to a delirium of revenge.

Here are Aeneas' words to Turnus before he kills him:

> ". . . tune hinc spoliis indute meorum
> eripiare mihi? Pallas te hoc vulnere, Pallas
> immolat et poenam scelerato ex sanguine sumit."
> (12.947–49)
> "Are you, clothed in the spoils of my own, to be snatched hence from me? Pallas, Pallas sacrifices you with this wound and exacts punishment from your criminal blood."

This is not the moment to examine the irrationality of these lines, though we might pause to ask who would be doing the "snatching," that is, life-saving, of Turnus except Aeneas' instinct for *pietas* or *clementia*. What I would like to stress here is the shrill note of possessiveness in Aeneas' language. Ordinarily *meorum*, which I just translated "of my own," would mean "of my people." It cannot have that sense here. What it does parallel closely is its most recent use some sixty lines earlier in the book, where Turnus' loving sister Juturna, anticipating her brother's death, asks

> ". . . quicquam mihi dulce meorum
> te sine, frater, erit?"
> (12.882–83)
> "Will anything of mine be sweet to me without you, brother?"

A comparison of Juturna's words with Aeneas' points up the private intensity in his question.[21] He is like Hercules, given to rage not to rid the world of evil but because of the loss of a possession. His loss, however, is not of cattle but of a boy who now twice over exerts Aeneas' strength to perform the poem's last, most notable act of wounding.

Nor is Dido forgotten in these lines. Aeneas, we recall, is driven to fury only "after he drank in [*hausit*] with his eyes the reminders [*monimenta*] of his ferocious anguish and the spoils [*exuvias*]." The only other context in the poem where *monimenta* and *exuviae* appear together is in the fourth book where Dido who, in the poet's dramatic image, has just conceived fury, overcome by anguish begins to plot out her suicide.[22] Her words to her sister reach out movingly into the rest of the poem, from beginning (*arma viri*) to end.[23] Build a pyre, she commands,

> ". . . et arma viri thalamo quae fixa reliquit
> impius exuviasque omnis lectumque iugalem,
> quo perii, super imponas: abolere nefandi
> cuncta viri monimenta iuvat . . ."
>   (4.495–98)
> ". . . and heap up on it the arms of the impious man, which he left fixed in my bedroom, and all his clothing and the marriage bed, on which I perished: it pleases me to destroy all the reminders of the cursed man."

In each case the literal *exuviae* are different, being garments in one instance, a sword belt in the other.[24] But their common symbolic import is confirmed from their joint role as *monimenta*—remembrances of deep psychic travail.

The two books, and the two tales, have also in common the unusual phrase *haurire oculis*, to drink in with the eyes. Dido's final, unheard words to Aeneas are a curse:

> ". . . hauriat hunc oculis ignem crudelis ab alto
> Dardanus, et nostrae secum ferat omina mortis."
>   (4.661–62)
> "Let the cruel Dardan from the deep drink in this fire with his eyes, and carry with him the omen of our death."

The Trojans, of course, do see the actual pyre aflame but have only a generalized understanding of its import.[25] But Pallas' effect on Aeneas and Aeneas' subsequent killing of Turnus is her rich revenge. To drink in with his eyes the tokens that remind him of Pallas is to fulfill her curse and to drink in spiritually her fire. The loss of Pallas makes Aeneas suffer the *dolor* she had experienced and act out her frenzy in one last deed of violence. But she is requited in a still deeper sense. Aeneas' last act is not only irrationally violent, it is impious. It goes against his father's injunction to spare the suppliant as well as war down the proud, and sets a pattern for Roman civil war and a century of fraternal bloodshed. By undermining or, better, giving the lie to Rome's ethical pretensions toward *pietas* and *clementia*, Dido gains a far more subtle repayment for her suffering than any literal defeat future Romans could inflict on her descendants. The explicit magnetism of Pallas over Aeneas, which, as the poet's verbal echoing suggests, reenacts implicitly the power once exerted by Dido, undercuts any striving on Aeneas' part toward a supposedly "higher," dispassionate heroism of restraint. Dido's strength, which is the strength of human emotion most readily experienced through the claims of sexuality, lasts until or, better, triumphs at the epic's end. Eroticism and the demands of empire, human realities and human idealism are ever, finally, at odds.[26]

We are now in a better position to propose answers to the questions we raised earlier. Why, in book 6, does the golden bough delay at Aeneas' tugging, and the hero himself consider it a "dread desire" to yearn for return to the world above? Why is the muse Erato addressed near the start of the poem's second half? And why does Vulcan hesitate to obey Venus' wishes for arms for her son, necessitating that she use her sexual wiles to assure his positive response?

Let us take the questions in reverse order. The final episode of the poem offers the epic's most vivid example of the interaction of violent feeling and the use of weaponry, but the reader is prepared for their association from the machinations of Venus in book 8. Two scenes are involved. The first, alluded to in my question, is the most explicitly erotic moment in the epic, the seduction of the god of fire by his wife, goddess of love. The metaphorical flame she touches off in her husband soon becomes the actual fire used to concoct Aeneas' *arma*. But sexuality is involved not only in the creation but in the delivery of the arms. The meeting in which mother brings armor to son is the only time in the epic where Aeneas is allowed to embrace a person he has previously loved. But it is important to observe that Venus, not Aeneas, is here the leader. When she saw Aeneas she first "offered herself of her own accord" (*se . . . obtulit ultro*, 8.611), a phrase Virgil uses elsewhere only of erotic availability.[27] Then, after a brief speech, "the goddess of Cythera sought the embraces of her son" (*amplexus nati Cythera petivit*, 8.615). She must seduce Vulcan at the creation, Aeneas at the acceptance, of the arms. As in their final use in the epic, there is something deceitful, something irrational in the initial fortunes of Aeneas' arms and in the pattern this combination of arms and man will set for Rome to come. No wonder Vulcan hesitates.

The invocation to Erato is usually explained by appeal to Turnus.[28] His failure to relinquish his claim on Lavinia, critics argue, is the reason why there must be war in Latium, and twice, once in the words of the Sibyl, once in those of the narrator, she is entitled *causa mali tanti*, reason for such misfortune (6.93, 11.480). But, though Lavinia looms large in the experience of Turnus and figures in his final words, there is never any mention of emotional involvement with her on Aeneas' part as we would expect when Erato is invoked to inspire the second half of an *Aeneid*. But, as we have already seen, Virgil uses the phrase *mali tanti* on one other occasion, to characterize the death of Pallas (10.510). It is a dreadful blow in and of itself, and because it marks a momentary military setback. But its deeper repercussions are to be felt in Aeneas' conduct—in the spate of carnage on which he now embarks, and in the final killing of Turnus, as he thinks of Pallas for the last time in the epic.

Finally, let us look at book 6 and at possible reasons for the hesitation of the golden bough, Aeneas' passport to the Underworld and, I take it, symbol of his and Rome's future mission. The final thrust of Anchises' long disquisition to his son in that book is to preach a heroism of restraint. His list of future Roman military greats ends with a general who delays, and his last injunction, to spare the beaten, is an admonition to *clementia* in the uses of power. But the most emotional moment in his catalog is a request to Caesar and Pompey not to turn their strength against their country's inwards. His special prayer is to Caesar:

"... tuque prior, tu parce, genus qui ducis Olympo,
proice tela manu, sanguis meus!—"
  (6.834–35)
"and do you first, do you spare, who draw your descent from heaven, cast the weapons from your hand, o my blood!—"

Yet, in spite of Caesar's much touted *clementia*, he used his weapons liberally in the final campaign against his son-in-law and the latter's followers.

Roman civil war finds its archetype in the *Aeneid*'s final scene, but the philosophy or, more precisely, eschatology behind it is presented earlier in book 6 by Anchises. He teaches his son that our souls are made of divine fire, but that it is our bodies which do us harm and foster in us the emotions—he lists fear, desire, anguish, joy—that prevent the soul from achieving its divine potential. Though the evil results of these emotions must be purged in the Underworld after death, nevertheless Anchises' words point only to a renewal of this pernicious cycle even for those now suffering death's refinement. Aeneas might well exclaim on the "dread desire" of those who opt, if such is the word, for rebirth. He is himself at present, even while visiting his father in the Underworld, suffering through the emotional world of the living. His epic story is, finally, a general reminder of life's negative potential as well as a particular acknowledgment that Roman history will continue to re-create the less gentle aspects of human nature.

As Aeneas fulfills his natural response, as he yields to his own living, experiencing self, he undercuts his potential as symbol of Roman idealism to become the embodiment of a very human emotionalism. Perhaps, however, this sudden burst of complex energy on Aeneas' part is a way to claim and hold at least something of the present for himself. He relives now, and psychically extends, an experience which he, or his narrator, could define as his not through the reminiscence of an irretrievable past or the hypothesis of a golden Roman future but by an act of possessive violence, immediate and self-engendered. This anger and the corresponding indignation of Turnus' soul exemplify the *Aeneid*'s final truths.

I have been following out *arma*, arms, as a clue to the *Aeneid*'s meaning, from its beginning to its conclusion. This marvelous circularity makes us also watch carefully the interrelationship between Juno and Aeneas. The characters who appear as polar opposites at the start of the poem have, by the end, become equivalents. In other words, as Aeneas changes from passive to active, from sufferer of events to their apparent ruler, his enemy proves to be the hero's double, and initial, immediate distinctions between them yield, finally, to a deep-seated affinity.

Moreover, I hope that what I have been saying rings true psychologically. Aeneas' final rage is not motivated through a reasoned application of *pietas* but results from a terrible loss for which he compensates by killing the person who had caused this deprivation. The erotic impulse behind the action we would consider repressed. It is never openly stated by either narrator or his characters and only proposed to us through poetry's indirection. In all this Dido gains a many-sided revenge. First Aeneas now relives her experience and suffers himself the suffering he had caused her by leaving a relationship unfulfilled. Her lack of reciprocity from him is transformed into his loss of Pallas, and the furies of frustration and revenge that drive her to suicide now impel him to kill the killer of his cynosure. Responsibility for death is no longer secondary but direct.

But Dido's revenge has a more Roman side. Aeneas' final act, as I observed a moment ago, gives the lie to the much-vaunted *pietas*, the loyalty to father and to Rome, which the hero had used as his excuse for leaving Carthage and abandoning her. At the last the realism, the humanity of Aeneas displaces the artificial Aeneas, emblem of duty, symbol of *clementia*, of the Romanness that, once the proud have been beaten down, spares them as suppliants. Mindless or, better, passionless, devotion to a heaven-sent ideal yields to a spontaneous emotionality not unlike Dido's response to the hero who left her out of allegiance to a supposedly more estimable goal than loving and living in Carthage. Dido's enmity, of course, will take political shape in the future conflict of Rome and Carthage. Psychologically, however, it is fulfilled within the poem. In fact the

metamorphosis of Aeneas into a Juno, or into a Dido who might venge-
fully kill her hated lover instead of herself, is one of the epic's great acts of
emotional completion.[29]

The *Aeneid* does not end the way its models, the *Iliad* and the *Odyssey*,
conclude, with a mollification or purgation of vengeance. Its cycle, from
the epic's introduction to its finale, is of anger leading to deadly action. By
breaking the artistic mold, whether it be of Roman ethical artistry or of
generic expectations, Virgil has created a novel poetic artifact with a
different, in some respects even richer unity than Homer offers. History
never completes itself. It never folds into itself neatly like a work of art.
And history's individuals, its creatures, are never finally abstract, mere
emblems of some lofty motivating virtue. At the end of the *Aeneid* Virgil
sharply and profoundly disavows the linkage between Aeneas and *pietas*.
This unmasking of Aeneas as a symbol makes his tale truly reflect history
itself. His act leaves the *Aeneid* both finished and incomplete. His tale,
therefore, is an extraordinary cycle, both emotional and imaginative, yet
it is also an open-ended admission that history, by its own continued acts
of violence, is forever fracturing the idealistic models artistry would spon-
sor for it. The last lines of the poem look not to any newfound sense of
order which might have been reached from an ethical use of arms leading
to reestablishment of order but to the life of Aeneas' final victim suffering
the ultimate indignity of death.

Interpretation of the *Aeneid* has gone through a series of metamorphoses in this century. We have had Virgil eulogizer of empire or proto-
Christian. We have seen his epic serve as definition of the classic or, in the
aftermath of World War II, exemplify the victory of light over dark, of
reason and culture over violence and barbarism. There is truth, important truth, behind all these appraisals. I have been looking at yet another
way of evaluating the epic's force.

Anchises' words about *clementia*, about a civility that spares suppliants,
may hint at a higher eros, one that Plato, or Dante, or the aging Freud
would have understood. But the tale of Aeneas, from Juno's jealousies to
the hero's own final victimization by furies, offers a different, more realistic moral, as well as a more candid, penetrating appraisal of human behavior. This honesty, perhaps even more than its role as encomiast of Roman
might, herald of a Christian sensibility, or epitome of the classical, is a
major reason why the *Aeneid* continues to speak so forcefully to our time.

NOTES
This essay is a slightly expanded version of a lecture originally
delivered in January 1985 at the University of Georgia and Agnes
Scott College, and, then, in revised form, at the University of
Tennessee, as the Russell and Kathryn Rutledge Memorial Lec-
ture, on May 14, 1985. I am particularly in the debt of Froma

Zeitlein, for the stimulation of her encouragement at the right moment, and, in recent criticism, of Daniel Gillis, for his probing discussion in *Eros and Death*.

1. The figure of the mourning Nile, spreading its garments open to receive back the conquered into its hidden streams, presents a clear contrast to Rome's public rejoicing and to Caesar accepting the gifts of subject tribes. But Apollo's doorposts, to which Caesar affixes the donations, are proud (*superbis / postibus*, 721–22) as those of Cacus had been styled not long before in the narrative (*foribus superbis*, 196). And the last figure on the shield is the river Araxes, *pontem indignatus*, resenting the enslaving bridge built over it just as, in the epic's last line, the life of dead Turnus is *indignata* as it flees under the shades.

2. I owe the reference to Dr. R. O. A. M. Lyne.

3. It is worth observing that the stag, whose chase "was the first cause of suffering" (*prima laborum / causa*, 7.481–82) "and inflamed the rustic spirits for war" (*belloque animos accendit agrestis*) was equally "of outstanding beauty" (*forma praestanti*, 7.483).

4. Cf., most recently, Williams, *Technique and Ideas* 104, 223. It is easy, and usual, to draw an analogy between Pallas and Patroclus whose armor was stripped off and worn by Hector during his final, fatal conflict with Achilles. But there is another Patroclus figure in the *Aeneid*, faithful Achates, who appears on twenty-one occasions in the poem, some of them focal for the plot, from the first book to the last. The poem's reader should ask which aspects of the Homeric figure are transmuted into Pallas and which into Achates. If Achates serves as Aeneas' alter ego, fellow voyager to Italy and Pallenteum and occasional surrogate on the battlefield (he is wounded instead of Aeneas at 10.344), what Patroclean part are we to understand Pallas as playing?

5. Gillis, *Eros and Death* 56 and n. 8, also observes the importance of this particular handshake but treats its symbolism differently, as sign of an incipient friendship that will only bring disaster as Aeneas' progress takes two more victims, a suffering father and a dead son.

6. More than one-quarter of Virgil's uses of *amplector / amplexus* occur in book 8, which also contains four out of the eighteen appearances of *complector / complexus* in the *Aeneid*.

7. Cf. also Evander's response to the dead body of his son:

    procubuit super atque haeret lacrimansque gemensque . . .
       (11.150)
    he fell over [the body] and clings, weeping and groaning . . .

8. The star is of course the planet Venus, "Lo bel pianeto che d'amar conforta" (Dante, *Divine Comedy: Purg.* 1.19).

9. As one final example of a compound of *figo* used in a context of wounding we might note 9.578–80:

    . . . ergo alis adlapsa sagitta
    et laevo infixa est alte lateri, abditaque intus
    spiramenta animae letali vulnere rupit.

    . . . so the arrow glided on its wings and was pierced deep in his left side, and, buried within, it broke with its deadly wound the breathing passages of life.

10. Cf. *Ecl.* 6.53 where the bull beloved of Pasiphaë takes on feminine
    attributes, possessed of a snowy flank and pillowed on soft hya-
    cinths.

11. The name Pallas in Greek, according to Liddell-Scott-Jones s.v.,
    meant "prob. orig. *virgin, maiden* . . ." It is cognate with Latin
    paelex, concubine (on which see Ernout-Meillet s.v.).

12. Cf. the appearances of the adjective at 1.354 and 4.644 (Dido
    pallida morte futura, anticipating Cleopatra on Vulcan's shield,
    pallentem morte futura, 8.709).

13. I will deal elsewhere with the violence implicit in the virgin-
    killer's act. Suffice it to mention that *demeto* and *pollex* are used
    by Virgil only here. Neither the action ("mow down" instead of
    "pluck") nor the instrument ("thumb" instead of "nail") is ex-
    pected. Each is unparalleled in earlier flower similes. (The sug-
    gestion of brutality in *demeto* is anticipated by Catullus at 64.354
    where the verb is applied to Achilles mowing down the Trojans
    as if they were rows of grain.) Commentators in general link the
    simile to *Aen.* 9.435–37 where Euryalus, as his strength ebbs
    finally away, is compared to a flower dying from a plow's cutting
    or a poppy, bowed down by rain. But there Virgil is carefully
    alluding, in the simile's first segment, to Cat. 11.22–24, in the
    second, to *Il.* 8.306–8. Here novelty of word usage complements
    originality of the larger statement. The "world of erotic elegy"
    into which the simile sweeps us is well described by Gransden,
    Virgil's Iliad 117–18.

14. The third example is Juno at 1.36, *aeternum servans sub pectore
    vulnus.*

15. Note the homophonic similarity between *pectore vultus* (4.4,
    quoted previously) and *pectore vulnus.*

16. The repetition is noted by Williams, *Aeneid 7–12* in his commen-
    tary ad loc.

17. The first appearance is in a quotation made by Livy (1.26.6),
    where the command *caput obnubito* is part of a potential death-
    sentence uttered by Tullus Hostilius against Publius Horatius.
    Cf. Ogilvie, *Livy Books 1–5* ad loc. as well as his comments at
    4.12.11 (on the phrase *capitibus obvolutis*) on the ancient habit of
    enveloping the head before death.

18. Varro (*LL* 5.72): "*Neptunus, quod mare terras obnubit ut nubes
    caelum, ab nuptu, id est opertione, ut antiqui, a quo nuptiae, nuptus
    dictus*"; Paulus-Festus (174.20L) s.v. *nuptiae: "nuptias dictas esse
    (aiunt) . . . Aelius et Cincius, quia flammeo caput nubentis obvolvatur,
    quod antiqui obnubere vocarint."* Cf. Paulus-Festus (201.4) s.v. *ob-
    nubit: "obnubit, caput operit: unde et nuptiae dictae a capitis oper-
    tione."*

19. Virgil is the first Latin author to use *torus* as bier (*Aen.* 6.220).
    The reader of the *Aeneid* would inevitably think of Dido's pur-
    poseful combination of marriage couch and funeral pyre (4.508,
    4.650, 4.659, 4.691).

20. Dido is styled *pulchra* once (by *Fama*, indirectly, at 4.192), *pulcher-
    rima* twice (by the narrator, at 1.496 and 4.60).

21. We may compare Aeneas' closely parallel language at 11.42–43
    and the gratuitous, nearly untranslatable *mihi* inserted by him
    into the quasi-formulaic farewell at 11.97. (Cf. also Venus' lan-
    guage at 8.386.) Some of the tone of possessiveness of *meorum* is
    also captured in the legalistic, bitingly simple phrase *haec mea*

sunt (*Ecl.* 9.4) with which the new owner of the land, backed by the spears of Mars, announces his overlordship to the former inhabitants.

22. *Concepit furias evicta dolore* (474). This and other parallels between the epic's conclusion and book 4 are discussed in telling detail by Gillis, *Eros and Death* 105–7.

23. Dido's near juxtaposition of *Arma viri* with *impius* is not without point.

24. Aeneas' *exuviae* are also mentioned at 4.507 and 4.651. (For Virgilian usage elsewhere, also in a context of lovers' "spoils," cf. *Ecl.* 8.91.).

25. Cf. *Aen.* 5.4–7.

26. In one of the most perceptive of recent essays on the *Aeneid*, Sachs, "Fury of Aeneas" 75–82, reminds us that "The story of Dido, smaller only in geographical scale, begins where the story of Rome aims" (78). That is, Dido, in the process of "reining in proud races by justice" (Ilioneus' words at 1.523) is, in part, creating a working example of Anchises' hopes for future Rome, as it imposes a custom for peace by defeating pride and sparing the downtrodden (6.852–53). Yielding to the heart's madness (*"heu furiis incensa feror!"* is her cry at 4.376) spells destruction for Dido's political orderings just as Aeneas' rage at the epic's end (he is *furiis accensus et ira / terribilis*, 12.946–47) will invalidate his potential as paradigm for Roman impersonal statesmanship. The *Aeneid* is no exception to the common ancient proposition that self-discipline is a sine qua non for the governing of others whereas a ruler's inner decadence anticipates the disintegration of his public world.

27. Cf. *Ecl.* 3.66 (*At mihi sese offert ultro, meus ignis, Amyntas*). Contrast the more matter-of-fact epiphany of Venus to her son (*cui mater . . . sese tulit obvia*, 1.314).

28. The apostrophe is modeled on the address to Erato which initiates the second half of the *Argonautica* of Apollonius Rhodius (3.2), dominated by the figure of Medea and her relationship with Jason. Cf. Hügi, *Vergils Aeneis* 57 and 75, and Zanker, "Love Theme" 52–75. Zanker (64) presumes that the muse invoked at *Arg.* 4.2 is also Erato. Both addresses are innovations of Apollonius who is imitated first by Virgil, then Ovid (Zanker, "Love Theme" 71, n. 62).

29. The constant association throughout the epic of sexuality and irrational, destructive violence, which I have only touched on here, deserves separate study. An important investigation into another figure in the epic whose sexuality foments violence, Helen, has been made by Reckford, "Helen" 85–99, but a general discussion of the interconnection still remains necessary.

THE THIRD BOOK
OF THE *AENEID*:
FROM HOMER
TO ROME

By comparison with the acclaim they have lavished on its neighbors, critics have devoted minimal attention to the *Aeneid*'s third book.[1] Though a continuation of Aeneas' narrative to Dido, dealing now with events subsequent to his retreat from Troy, it appears to lack the emotional intensity of the second book's focused account of the collapse of the hero's homeland. The initial segment of his tale is a study in concentration, centered on one time and place. The conclusion seems diffuse by comparison. The most Iliadic book of the *Aeneid*, topographically organized around the breaching and destruction of Troy, is followed by the most Odyssean.[2] We can easily dismiss such a string of episodes, bridging the considerable distance from Ilium to Carthage, as Virgil's attempt to enliven geographical inevitability with the hero's exposure to incipient history. Aeneas must reach Dido during the book's course, but he must also learn more of Italy and Rome.

Advances in knowledge alternate with setbacks throughout the hero's continuing tale. After their ill-omened settlement on Thrace, the Trojans find comfort in the command from Delos to seek their ancient mother. Subsequent plague on Crete is counterbalanced by the Penates' clearer look forward to a true settlement. Misadventure with the Harpies is followed by the potential stability proclaimed by dedication and games at Actium. After the central episode at Buthrotum, in which Helenus details the events Aeneas will endure until the Sibyl at Cumae resumes and magnifies the prophecy of Rome, the hero assumes a less active role before events, avoiding Scylla and Charybdis and watching Etna and the Cyclopes from whom he rescues Achaemenides. A brief reference to Arethusa and scant mention of Anchises' death end Aeneas' tale, at which point we are reminded that all this time we have been at Carthage, with Dido listening.

But there is more to the book than gradual revelation spread out to cover an embarrassingly large itinerary. Virgil has taken careful liberties with his literary heritage and initiated much that is novel. It is on this originality and specifically on its poetic structuring and elaboration that I would like to concentrate in this essay. The sources against which to judge Virgil's originality have often been traced.[3] The results of the poet's handling of his inherited material have not been so thoroughly studied. Sources are primarily twofold, the literary background and the previous renditions of Aeneas' adventures. The two often interact. From Homer the poet has drawn the Polyphemus episode, which, however, he places virtually at the end of Aeneas' narrative, whereas in the tale of Odysseus it comes early. The events on the Strophades combine matter in Homer and Apollonius Rhodius. From the latter come certain aspects of the Harpies' mien and action, while Odysseus' dealings with the cattle of Helios provide the model of an attack against animals that proves unfortunate. Again Virgil's placement is important. Because of their disobedience Odysseus loses all his remaining companions after they ravage the Sun's herd. Therefore it is the last of his adventures before Calypso, Phaeacia, and his return home. The parallel episode is the second major event in Aeneas' journey. It is so placed for a purpose, as we will see.

If we turn to the tradition of Aeneas' wandering, we find that although he regularly lands on the Thracian coast Virgil invents his encounter with the ghost of Polydorus. Virgil would also have known the tradition of Aeneas' crucial meeting with Helenus but he devises for the first time and elaborates at length the emotional encounter with Andromache, now Helenus' wife. Likewise, though Aeneas' sojourn on Sicily is well attested, Virgil has added his saving acceptance of Achaemenides as well as his escape from Polyphemus. To discover meaning behind these alterations and additions to the Aeneas legend we must return to the commencement of the book and watch the story unfold as Virgil would have it.

In spite of the fact that Aeneas continues as speaker, there is a sharp stylistic disjunction between the end of book 2 and the start of book 3, as if break in narrative complemented the rupture of withdrawal from Troy. Aeneas pauses to announce what we already well know—that proud Ilium has fallen into smoldering ruins. What remains is a series of exiles, *diversa exilia* (4), for the Trojan remnants and specifically for Aeneas himself (*exul*, 11). The wordplay is significant. They are "soil-less" as they make their way onto the deep and as they search out "deserted lands" (*desertas terras*), one of which might prove the fixed abode of future dispensation.[4] Active and passive compete in the way Virgil has the hero visualize his lot. To paraphrase Aeneas' words: we build a fleet and collect colleagues, Anchises gives the order and I leave the port, yet we are driven by divine augury and I am borne off into exile. It is an alternation that well accompanies the interweaving of knowledge and ignorance, revelation and uncertainty, gain and loss, in the events that loom ahead. Only when his destined land is reached and the future is fully divulged will Virgil have Aeneas adopt a pronouncedly forward stance, and in the process create a different series of more internal dilemmas.

The first major episode, which as often in books of the *Aeneid* sets the tone for much of what follows, results from Aeneas' attempt to establish a foundation on the Thracian coast. Wishing to decorate an altar to his mother with myrtle boughs, Aeneas tugs at a nearby clump.[5] When blood spurts from the broken roots, Aeneas pulls again and then again until the groaning voice of Polydorus speaks out from his tomb warning him away:

> "heu fuge crudelis terras, fuge litus avarum."
>   (3.44)
> "Ah, flee the cruel land, flee the greedy shore."

Aeneas expounds the reasons for this cruelty and greed, pronouncing in his own person against the "cursed hunger for gold" (*auri sacra fames*, 57) that drove a host to kill his guest. The land is crime-ridden (*scelerata*), hospitality has been polluted (*pollutum*), and the Trojans must leave.[6]

But the phrase *scelerata terra* returns our attention to one of Polydorus' pleas to Aeneas:

> ". . . iam parce sepulto,
> parce pias scelerare manus."
>   (3.41–42)
> "Spare me, now that I am buried; spare the tainting of your holy hands."

Aeneas also must be asked, twice, to spare. He is guilty of disturbing the dead and of a different form of *scelus* based on a different form of greed. Under his revealing touch what had seemed to be shafts of myrtle prove in fact to be murder weapons piercing a corpse. Aeneas pulls out what before had been thrown, to become the second letter of blood from the same body. But what strikes the reader is the persistence of his violence, even after the appearance of blood.[7] Greed, already associated with Polydorus, now centers not on money but on knowledge. "To make trial of causes hidden deep within" drives Aeneas three times to rend the foliage at its roots, as if the preliminary sight of blood aroused in the perpetrator a desperate need for understanding, even at the cost of further hurt.

The broader importance of the imagery of breaking and tearing that accompanies this intellectual greed and its physical manifestation will only become clear as the book progresses. Suffice it to acknowledge here that Aeneas engenders and magnifies the very *monstrum* he yearns to comprehend.[8] He is the symbolic cannibal who wrenches the body beneath the ground and as such becomes himself a form of corrupter.[9] He exemplifies the banished hero at his most unsure, the wanderer desirous of steadying knowledge acquired even through violence, the sacrificer who pollutes, the would-be re-creator of his people whose act of disturbance only reveals murder and death.

It is not the last time in the epic where the physical vehemence and impetuosity that compensate for ignorance and insecurity bring a late learning either unpleasant or dubious at best. Aeneas' spiritual hunger, as Virgil portrays it, is often understandable, especially here at a moment when extreme deprivation and loss of direction would expectedly bring heightened instability. A monstral landscape, where myrtles of love and settlement prove to be instruments for the greed-inspired death of another Trojan who left Troy, where the search for enlightenment draws blood and ends only in the sepulchral revelation of past crimes, not future permanence, is suitable accompaniment for the hero's intemperate mood. What remains prominent in the reader's thoughts is the form and irrational intensity of his action, as Aeneas yields to the landscape and becomes a continuator and parodist of the dark myth whose outrage he reveals by further outrage.

After a ceremony to the dead, the Trojans depart for the island of Delos, once wandering, now secure, where king Anius offers the book's first prophecy of fixed land and dominion.[10] Anchises' misinterpretation of the oracle leads the group to Crete where Pergamea proves as ill-omened a name as Aeneia, title given to the foundation in Thrace. Attempted renewal of the Trojan past again brings with it a type of pollution, this time elemental and celestial, not human in origin. The sky is torn open (*corrupto caeli tractu*, 138—a Virgilian play on tearing as tainting) and dripping plague (*tabida lues*) descends on bodies, trees, and crops. Compensation for withdrawal comes here in the form of a more extended prophecy given to the sleeping Aeneas by the Penates who appear in vivid light, as if to confirm the clear truth of their words. They offer chronologically the first mention of Italy in the poem, and Anchises confirms that Troy claimed ancestry in Hesperia and that Cassandra foretold that Trojans would later return there.

But, for the third and most challenging time in the first half of book 3, the movement in space, which also furthers our knowledge of a stable, future Rome, is obstructed by the presence of the monstrous and the irrational, whether provoked or endured. This in turn begets personal hurt and death. Such is Virgil's present way of viewing the distinction between history and the individual, between public advantage and private suffering, which is one of the *Aeneid*'s main themes. Here nature is the chief prognosticator. The luminosity of the Penates' epiphany is exchanged for a stormy siege of black wandering and loss of detail, obscuring even the distinction between night and day.[11] It is fitting that after such a twisting bout of darkness the Aeneadae should land on the Strophades, the Turning Islands, home of the Harpies, the Grabbers, dripping foul ooze from their bellies and pale with hunger.[12] They form the second great *monstrum* in the book that Aeneas not only confronts but activates.

The Trojans find themselves in a setting with at least one reminiscence of a golden age. Rich cattle are everywhere about with no guardian:

laeta boum passim campis armenta videmus
caprigenumque pecus nullo custode per herbas.
inruimus ferro . . .
   (3.220–22)
We see prosperous herds of cattle everywhere about in the fields and
an untended flock of goats on the grass. We rush on them with the
sword . . .

Without hesitation or hint of concern over the legality of their act, the
Trojans rush upon the animals with swords drawn, seize their booty, and
prepare for a banquet. After the Harpies twice foul the feast, Aeneas
orders his men to wage a war that not only proves unfeasible but elicits
first a question, then a curse, from Celaeno:

"bellum etiam pro caede boum stratisque iuvencis,
Laomedontiadae, bellumne inferre paratis
et patrio Harpyias insontis pellere regno?"
   (3.247–49)
"Sons of Laomedon, is it even war in return for the slaughter of
cattle and slain bullocks, is it war you are preparing to offer and to
drive the guiltless Harpies from their ancestral kingdom?"

A moral dimension is added after the fact by the sufferers, a dimension
not perceived by the perpetrator Aeneas who kills cattle and prepares
instinctively to behave like a marauding Greek against the hapless city of
Troy and its defeated. Celaeno, who is both Harpy and Fury at once,
reveals more of the future but in the form of a malediction: the Trojans
will reach Italy but will be compelled to eat their tables out of hunger, in
recompense for the slaughter they have just inflicted.

Once more, in his search for truth, self-identity, and wholeness after a
period of upheaval, Aeneas enters the territory of the monstral and yields
to its negative enticements. The Harpies externalize the monster within
us. They objectify grabbers who make us grab, living in a landscape that
turns us around or away from some more steadfast pattern of living.[13]
They literally pollute the sustenance of those invaders who have without
thought already engendered a deeper pollution and have perpetrated an
injustice (*iniuria*) that hazards unnecessary warfare and exiles the guiltless. More explicitly than in the Polydorus episode, hunger is a major
motif. At the beginning of the episode the Harpies appear with "faces
ever pale from starvation" (*pallida semper / ora fame*, 217–18). They end it
with the curse of future want (*dira fames*, 256) against the Trojans. In
between, the episode recounts the working out of physical appetite for
food and for violence that succeeds in neither of its dubious goals. If the
Polydorus adventure demonstrated physical energy misused and blood

shed in the service of a headstrong desire for knowledge, the encounter with the Harpies finds literal and figurative hunger intertwined. Late learning results, to be sure, and repentance,[14] but there is the appropriate reversal that hunger inflicted will later be endured, if only symbolically.

Dante sensed the communion between the two episodes of potential misspent that open *Aeneid* 3. In the thirteenth canto of the *Inferno* he integrates what Virgil leaves separate. Dante is expounding the vice of the suicides whom he imagines suffering punishment under the semblance of shrubs. The symbolism seems as follows. To dissociate self from body elicits the torment of permanent rooting, of the eternal weightiness of physicality alone. Suicides persist as unthinking objects, brute and largely inanimate, suffering suitable recompense for the undivine decision to take one's life, and death, into one's own hands. The conscious decision in life to separate by force what should remain together brings in death the eternal torture of survival only as vegetation. Harpies feed on the leaves of the bushes, and even a troubled Dante follows Virgil's command and breaks off the top of a shoot in order to learn what meaning the plant conveys.[15]

Dante's appalled reluctance to follow his guide's instruction and his single gesture of rending contrast with Aeneas' eager triple tugging at the whole plant sprouting from the corpse of Polydorus, roots and all, even when blood gushes out. Dante replaces Aeneas' physical prelude to learning with a token gesture leading to a dialogue of discovery. The harsh attitude of the living creature bent on suicide is adopted briefly and without enthusiasm by the pilgrim through hell, but the differentiation from Aeneas' compulsiveness is noteworthy. Already in the first episode of book 3 Aeneas is a type of harpy, seizing and, even as the process of action promotes comprehension from uncertainty, verging near pollution from the criminal shedding of blood. Dante devotes most space in his exposition to the *monstrum* itself, explaining why suicides receive their final unalterable punishment in the guise of trees. Aeneas becomes part of the *monstrum* and further hurts what had already been maimed. The quest for permanence begins ominously as myrtles are discovered to be spear shafts by the hero's fierce touch, and a landscape of apparent innocence is converted into a battleground as the Trojans adopt the attitude that by inheritance and nomenclature should be the Harpies' own.

The Trojans now sail north past Ithaca, seizing the opportunity to curse the land that nourished "fierce Ulysses" (*saevi Ulixi*, 273), and arrive at the shores of Actium. There they sacrifice to Jupiter and celebrate games. Aeneas dedicates the shield of Abas:

Aeneas haec de Danais victoribus arma.
   (3.288)
Aeneas [dedicates] these arms from the victorious Greeks.

The event is brief but significant. Instead of apprehending their settlement of Italy through prophecy, negative or positive, the Trojans now
become prototypes for modern Romans, proclaiming a more immediate
victory over a singularly divisive enemy in September of 31 B.C. This leap
into the future accounts for a reversal of stance which helps alter the
insecure tone of Trojan actions hitherto in the book. To dedicate is to
assert control. When Aeneas writes his own *carmen* attached to the offering of a Greek shield, he posits the dominance of conquered over conquerors.[16] His deed presumes a victory which the end of the book will
expound in greater detail. It also fosters a new spirit of independence
based on the security which suggestion of later history provides. The
Trojans reach out to a known event that would ultimately be crucial to
Rome's stability. In anticipation they condone its permanence by initiating the custom of festive game. Power over Greece, formalized in written
words, follows easily after a ritual performance that posits continuity of
Roman procedure, not dictated from elsewhere but begun instinctively
by the Trojans themselves.

Virgil anticipates a major strand of thought in what follows, the book's
pivotal and most lengthy episode as the Trojans meet first Andromache
and then Helenus at Buthrotum. The encounter with Andromache provides the major emotional interest in the book, of particular importance
to students of Virgil's originality because it is his most expansive addition
to the legends of Aeneas' wandering.[17] Andromache has established for
herself a fake Troy replete with memories of the past—a cenotaph for
Hector, streams modeled after the Simois and Xanthus, Scaean gates and
an imitation Pergamum. Her spirit matches the outward setting she has
manufactured. Her thoughts center primarily on her former, not her
present, spouse and are noteworthy for a pronounced disjointedness of
expression that reflects her willful withdrawal from reality. Aeneas sees
her as *furens*, yet the allure of her escapism comes at a critical moment in
the book and in Aeneas' own development.

In its idiosyncratic way, her world is as monstral to Aeneas as his
nightmare adventures with Polydorus and the Harpies. Whereas in the
latter episodes Aeneas had been the fervid inflicter of physical hurt,
Andromache's posture preaches a subtle, deadening passivity which the
reader of the first book already knows would have appeal to Aeneas.
When Aeneas asks of her present situation, she initiates her reply with an
apostrophe:

> "o felix una ante alias Priameia virgo,
> hostilem ad tumulum Troiae sub moenibus altis
> iussa mori, . . ."
>   (3.321–22)
> "O happy alone beyond the others, virgin daughter of Priam, or-
> dered to die at the enemy's tomb under the lofty walls of Troy, . . ."

It is a locution that Aeneas himself would imitate at a later moment which nevertheless we have already marked as the first words he utters in the epic:

"o terque quaterque beati,
quis ante ora patrum Troiae sub moenibus altis
contigit oppetere!"
    (1.94–96)
"O three and four times blessed whose fate it was to die before the faces of their fathers under the lofty walls of Troy!"

The last great temptation to Aeneas in book 3 is to avoid the demands of history and yield to a life of withdrawal which focuses on the illusory, if agitated, re-creation of past feelings in a temporal scheme already known and experienced, and shuns a more demanding commitment to the unknown, even if such a credo also enforces on occasion a seemingly unheroic acceptance of fate.

Almost exactly at the center of the book, however, Aeneas turns to Helenus and the prophet's reply reorients Aeneas and his listeners toward the immediate future and the tangibility of a hitherto evanescent Italy. Like the first half of the book, his speech is built on a series of alternatives and contrasts, now of a more strictly positive quality. He begins with a précis of the impending voyage as far as the settlement in Latium (374–87). Stability is assured by means of a token:

"signa tibi dicam, tu condita mente teneto: . . ."
    (3.388)
"I will tell you of signs, do you keep them fast in your mind: . . ."

The *monstrum* of a white sow with thirty white piglets by a stream under an ilex portends a settled future as the founders of Rome become intimate with a landscape of opulence, not penury. As for the voyage immediately ahead, flee (*effuge*), says Helenus, the southern areas of Italy they will first approach (396–402).

Taking our thoughts away from immediate difficulties while at the same time suggesting a further definition of stability, Helenus next explains the proper method of dress at a ceremony in which vows (*vota*) are paid:

"hunc socii morem sacrorum, hunc ipse teneto;
hac casti maneant in religione nepotes."
    (3.408–9)
"Do your allies, do you yourself keep this manner of sacrifice; let your chaste descendants persevere in this mode of worship."

Then, returning to present necessities, Helenus follows the pattern of Circe in *Odyssey* 12 and outlines the dangers the Aeneadae must confront as they near the strait separating Italy and Sicily. Once more flight is in order (*fuge*), now from a landscape rent apart by natural catastrophe and appropriately housing Charybdis and Scylla. The first creature swallows and spews forth the ships she has lured into her whirlpool. Scylla, from the hidden security of her dark cave, sticks out her mouths and draws ships against her rocks. Virgil will soon expand further upon this paradigm of intemperate energy confined and released. The detail here is essential to show a landscape of grabbing, rending, and swallowing from which Aeneas now distances himself. He will now knowledgeably avoid a course of action involving physical hurt which earlier in the book he might have maintained through ignorance or impetuosity.

In another purposefully abrupt change Helenus next urges on Aeneas the specific need to sacrifice to Juno:

> "Iunonis magnae primum prece numen adora,
> Iunoni cane vota libens . . ."
>   (3.437–38)
> "First worship the power of mighty Juno in prayer, willingly pledge vows to Juno . . ."

Then, with a final glance at matters to come, he projects Aeneas' vision toward the Sibyl at Cumae, his next and foremost prophet who writes her sayings on leaves, combining omniscience with fickleness and presenting the hero with the challenge of extracting from the world of the dead the affirmation of an ordered future.

The contrasts in Helenus' segmented rhetoric thus differ markedly from the book's earlier jolting antinomies of clarity and dimness, revelation and setback, dramatic action, repentance or wistful endurance in a context of changing topography. Advances forward in time, place, or knowledge have for the Trojans always elicited obstacles from the irrational, whether activated or suffered by them. Helenus now varies the exposition of historical and geographical change, however inexorable, with the steadyings that landscape and above all religion can bring. These will affect Aeneas for the remainder of the epic. In book 8, for instance, he will combine elements of Helenus' first and third interludes when he sacrifices the pig directly to Juno.[18] It is Helenus' role in book 3 to anchor history's relentless pace with the continuities of civilization, by establishing in his hearer's thinking those ritual customs and precedents that mark the behavior of an ordered people. Such procedures bolster society in its constant debate with the novel or the moribund as times change. They offer to Aeneas the necessary combination of firm topographical, historical, and ethical focus on an Italy soon at last to materialize. In both these last respects, and of course in geographical detail as well, Helenus distinguishes himself in profundity of ideas from Circe who, in her narrative to Odysseus in *Odyssey* 12, limits her purview to the portentous happenings soon to engage the wits of her wily guest.

The episode ends with the usual presentation of gifts, among which are the weapons of Achilles' son (*arma Neoptolemi*, 469), as if the passing on of a former enemy's relics further consolidated the transfer of power from victorious Greeks to defeated Trojans at the moment when they begin their metamorphosis from weak to strong. In the act of parting, Andromache still thinks of Hector and Astyanax, not of the present, much less the future, as she offers gifts to Iulus, and Aeneas dwells on the happiness of those whose past fortune remains their only present. Yet now he is capable of peering ahead in time to posit enduring friendship between Epirus and those who will dwell along the Tiber.[19] *Maneat nostros ea cura nepotes* (505): Aeneas has adopted a historical role which is as important as the custom of veiling one's head during the performance of ritual. Each detail must last into the future, but in mimicking Helenus' phraseology Aeneas takes to himself the union of steadfast custom and historical movement, to Italy and beyond, that the priest sees in Aeneas' and Rome's career.

As if to reinforce a newfound lucidity of mind and intent, Virgil next has Aeneas describe a landfall at Acroceraunia which has special interest because of the behavior of Palinurus. At a parallel moment earlier in the book the helmsman had lost his way, a victim of blinding waves and blackness that offered a literal prefiguration of Aeneas' impending mental darkness in yielding to the spell of the Harpies.[20] Everything now is clarity. Palinurus sees all the stars gliding in a silent heaven, all in place with sky serene. As a devoted guide Palinurus neither here nor at his mysterious demise in the fifth book peers beyond the constellations to reality. Yet to the reader his new posture as keen-eyed observer and the generous cooperation of the elements are metaphoric for a similar change on Aeneas' part toward greater penetration of thought. It is no accident that the Helenus episode intervenes.

This profundity of vision is tested when the Trojans first touch on Italian soil, spied, appropriately for a new beginning confirmed again at the Tiber mouth, when dawn first gleams.[21] An authority he had up to now lacked is granted father Anchises (a dubious leader at best earlier in the book), *stans celsa in puppi* (527). Virgil attaches the phrase elsewhere in the epic to Augustus Caesar on Vulcan's shield (8.680), driving the Itali into battle at Actium, or to Aeneas arriving, with the same shield now likened to comets red with blood or burning Sirius, for battle against the Latins (10.261). It is a posture of power and a rhetorical prognostication of wars near and far, fought on Italian soil or by Italians. Even the coming of dawn, red, with stars put to flight, intimates through metaphor an innate bellicosity which the landscape also metaphorically bears out. There is a natural *arx* on which Minerva's temple is perched. The port is "curved into a bow" (*curvatus in arcum*, 533). Turreted crags send "arms" as outworks along twin walls.[22] The temple itself "flees back" (*refugit*, 536), as if apprehensive of attack.[23]

Metaphor is soon strengthened by symbol. Anchises interprets the meaning of an omen of four white horses:

> "bellum, o terra hospita, portas:
> bello armantur equi, bellum haec armenta minantur.
> sed tamen idem olim curru succedere sueti
> quadripedes et frena iugo concordia ferre:
> spes et pacis" ait.
> (3.539–43)

"O land receiving us, you bring war: horses are armed for war, these herds threaten war. But nevertheless the same animals are wont at times to come under the chariot and to carry reins in concord with the yoke: there is even hope of peace," he cries.

Aeneas the narrator repeats *Italia* three times in two lines when land is first sighted (523–24). It is war that Anchises now thrice pronounces visible on its soil. But there is also hope of peace—though the rhetoric dwells on doubt rather than on the reality of peace itself—if the horses are tamed under harmonious reins.

R. D. Williams comments as follows on Anchises' words: "The whole concept of the Roman mission is symbolized here—first war against the proud, then civilization for the subdued peoples."[24] In other words the old man's interpretation of the omen could be said to anticipate his own famous final command to his son in the Underworld:

> "parcere subiectis et debellare superbos."
> (6.853)

"To spare the humbled and war down the proud."

There may be a still more universal validity to Anchises' precision. Any civilizing act, not just that accomplished by Roman genius, depends on the taming of the bestial by the spiritual, on the molding of energy to form, in a proper union of order and adventure. Yet Rome, especially the *Roma triumphans* which four horses suggest, can on occasion lose sight of standards which the city itself might set. The only other use of the adjective *concors* in the *Aeneid* comes earlier in Anchises' farewell speech in the sixth book. He uses it to compliment the spirits of Pompey and Caesar, harmonious in the Underworld but ready to turn their strength against the body of their fatherland in the civil wars their reincarnation will abet.[25] Italy works its negative potentiality on many of those who come in contact with it, and Anchises leaves his sentiments suitably general.

The episode again betokens a change of spirit in the titular hero from that he had displayed in the book's opening scene. Aeneas caused blood-shed in the vehemence of his zeal to know. Anchises needs only words for wise scrutiny of an imposing *monstrum*. The aura of Helenus continues to brood over the action. Immediately after the conclusion of Anchises' interpretation and after prayer to Pallas *armisona*, "sounding in arms,"[26] the Trojans veil their heads and offer sacrifice to Juno. They thus fulfill at once two of the ritual strictures that the priest had urged on his departing guests. As if to lend further credence to Helenus' words, the Trojans next safely withstand the hazard of Scylla and Charybdis, properly sighted by Anchises and skirted by Palinurus. A new passivity, with incident suffered rather than provoked, allows the Trojans to endure without mishap the most formidable absorbers and breakers of ships in the Homeric legacy.

The experience is one that Virgil will elaborate and vary in the last expansive episode of the book. Scylla and Charybdis were new to the Aeneas legend. So too is the splendid series of events that now follows, as the Trojans experience Etna and save the castaway Achaemenides, him-self a Virgilian invention, from the clutches of Polyphemus and his fellow Cyclopes. Etna and Polyphemus are kindred entities as Virgil's imagina-tion envisions them. His graphic personification of Etna finds it breaking forth a black cloud to the heavens, licking the stars, vomiting out, in belches, torn up inwards (*avulsa viscera*) of the mountain.[27] Its groaning (577) links it with Scylla (555), Polyphemus (664) and especially Poly-dorus,[28] for it too harbors an unquiet grave, this time of the giant Enceladus. The thunderbolts of Jupiter's vengeance piercing his body, whose ferocious burning the furnaces of Etna cannot contain, have their similarity with the deadly *hastilia* which sprout from the mound of Poly-dorus.

No longer imitating his action in the book's earlier segment, Aeneas only endures the sight and sound of Etna. He at first merely hears tell of Polyphemus from the mouth of Achaemenides whose imagery under-scores the similarities between Etna and the monster harbored on its slopes. After a mountain that rends itself in concert with a giant's undying restlessness, we discover a mountainous man, lofty enough, in the poet's hyperbole, to strike the high stars, with a dwelling huge like his own hugeness (*ingens*, 619, 658). This hollow within a hollow is a cannibal who feeds on human inwards and dark blood (*visceribus . . . et sanguine atro*, 622), gnawing on limbs flowing with black gore (*atro tabo*, 626). He shows his commonality with Etna by vomiting forth bloody fragments not of himself but of his victims. Yet there is a startling echo as well of the results of Aeneas' violence against Polydorus at the start of the book. Twice there we also hear the hero tell of the dark blood flowing from the wounds he was inflicting (28, 33) and of the gore that stained the earth (29).

Once again therefore we witness a pronounced change in Aeneas' attitude from that witnessed in the book's initial phase. The inflicter of torture, the render of flesh in search of knowledge, becomes not only the avoider of those who would offer similar threat but, following his father's lead, the savior of one whose life is in jeopardy. The Trojans' new protégé is a Greek abandoned by Odysseus to the mercies of a devouring landscape and its kindred creatures leagued to present a common menace. It is through him that Aeneas can now at last prove unyielding to the temptations of violence and distinguish himself from its myths.

The circumstances are special. They begin with the very name Achaemenides by which Virgil poses for his reader a series of paradoxes.[29] Though Greek he is called after one of the most opulent, wide-ruling dynasties of the ancient world, the Achaemenids of Persia.[30] He who by title should be rich is in fact reduced to wearing clothing held together by briars and to feeding on berries and stony cornels. The presumed exotic proves to be the primitive, squalid with unkempt beard, the man of power to be a helpless victim of bestial nature. This is Virgil's striking way to exemplify one of his favorite topics, the meaninglessness of *nomina*, the falsity of taking pride in nomenclature to herald immortality or even truth.

History both near and far also figures in Virgil's meaning. The recent past is suddenly reversed as a Greek becomes *supplex* before Trojans gradually gaining control over their own destiny. After only brief delay Anchises extends his hand in friendship, suppressing any wilder propensity for vengeance in order to exercise the very *clementia* toward the humbled proud that his words in book 6 would legislate for Roman practice.[31] A Roman of Virgil's time, dwelling further on the name Achaemenides, would have made a mental leap not only to Persia but to modern Parthia. He would have been reminded of the conciliatory tactics adopted by Augustus in dealing with Rome's former enemy.[32] Once again a paradigm that Virgil has initiated by Anchises remains in force in Augustan Rome, but whereas Anchises and Augustus, *stans celsa in puppi*, had before been models of achieved strength, Anchises now reverses the coin to exhibit an image of moderation and restraint.

The reconciliation of opposites in a name, the difference between seeming and being, that is operative in the case of Achaemenides bears in another way on Aeneas' present situation. Achaemenides' first words of explanation introduce himself as companion of Odysseus:

> "sum patria ex Ithaca, comes infelicis Vlixi,
> nomine Achaemenides, . . ."
>   (3.613–14)

"I am from the land of Ithaca, comrade of luckless Ulysses, by name
Achaemenides, . . ."

Aeneas, rounding out the episode in his narrational voice, reconfirms
both names and epithet in his concluding lines, as the Greek accepted
into his company elucidates the coast of Sicily which they now skirt:

talia monstrabat relegens errata retrorsus
litora Achaemenides, comes infelicis Vlixi.
    (3.690–91)
Such were the coasts that Achaemenides, comrade of luckless Ulysses, showed us as he traced again his former wanderings.

In the second book Aeneas had styled Odysseus *durus* and *dirus*, and,
earlier in the third, *saevus*. By himself accepting the latest adjective Achaemenides had chosen for his former leader, Aeneas acknowledges its truth
and further admits to a change in himself. *Saevus* segregates an enemy
through hatred. *Infelix* dwells on the communality of a suffering endured
through years of wandering that eliminates any remaining inimical distinctions between Greek and Trojan. Aeneas is practicing a verbal form of
clementia that reaches out widely. He is fostering an insight common to
contemporary Latin poetry, an insight inherent in the antinomies that the
name Achaemenides suggests: that distinctions, general between rich
and poor, ruler and subject, more specific between haughty Greek and
abject Trojan or humble Greek and powerful Trojan, are blurred by
larger leveling forces that obliterate any individual human characteristics.

The change in Aeneas' attitude to Odysseus is symptomatic of a more
general alteration in his cast of mind. The activator or abettor of deadly
monstra, who sharpens the already mortal hurt delivered to a fellow
Trojan and makes war against the innocent for the pleasure of pillage,
becomes the avoider of *monstra* who along with his men saves a Greek
from mauling by the gigantic and irrational.[33] The initial concatenation
of rending and breaking, hungers and devourings, of pollution by man,
monsters, and plague, is exchanged for unity of man with man to elude
the monstral. The Trojans offer a gesture of reconciliation; forgiveness
cleanses away past hatreds and documents a primal Roman civilizing act.

Virgil's uniqueness within his epic tradition and the alterations he
makes to that tradition all converge on this act. The poet, of course, is
dependent throughout the book on the general outlines of the tradition
of Aeneas' wanderings. But his originality within these bounds, and the
reasons behind his careful choice of allusions to the *Odyssey* and the
Argonautica, will now be clearer. These major bows to the epic past are
four in number, balanced two by two on either side of the pivotal
Helenus episode, which also has its Homeric counterpart in the revela-

tion of Teiresias and especially Circe to Odysseus. They are the episodes involving Polydorus, the Harpies, Scylla, and Polyphemus. The first, totally Virgil's invention, as we have seen sets the tone and establishes a pattern of symbolism for the book as a whole. It serves as touchstone for Aeneas' conduct. The encounter with the Harpies differs from Odysseus' adventure with the cattle of the sun because it shows Aeneas, unlike his Homeric predecessor, to be as culpably blind as his men. Virgil also transmutes a major element in the Argonauts' encounter with the Harpies as described by Apollonius Rhodius. There the Harpies grab what Phineus needs to stay alive. In the *Aeneid* it is Aeneas and his company who snatch and prepare to consume what rightfully belongs to the Harpies, who only then pollute as an act of reprisal.

After the revelations of Helenus, however, allusions to Homeric precedent take a different turn. As I noted earlier, neither Scylla and Charybdis nor Polyphemus appears to have figured in the Aeneas legend as Virgil inherited it. In each instance, and unlike Odysseus, Aeneas saves his men from a devouring landscape.[34] But it is his generous action toward Achaemenides, another Virgilian invention, that completes the intellectual cycle of the book and creates a paradigm of conduct that abstracts the reader from Homer to Rome, from literary reference to the mythic and the past into the realities of behavior patterns whose ethical aptness Virgil's contemporaries would have understood. At the beginning of the book Aeneas is the searching exile, needlessly misusing his moments of power. At the end he receives someone not dissimilar to his earlier self, an outcast suppliant, prey to a setting of natural menace, into a society newly formed, or better reformed, and secure in the knowledge that the events Helenus had predicted and the religious procedures he had stipulated could be experienced and implemented without misfortune.

Two further events briefly seal the book's close, as Aeneas completes his Sicilian itinerary. The first is his stop at the island of Ortygia and apostrophe of the water nymph Arethusa. Allusion to the tale of Alpheus who made his watery way from Greece to his beloved in Sicily may have pointed reference to the voyage of Aeneas as it presses toward its goal.[35] The naming of Ortygia has an explicit purpose. Since it is equally the name for the island of Delos, which also after wandering had become firmly anchored, it recalls for the reader the second episode of the book as Aeneas hears his future prophesied by king Anius.[36] Virgil thus further documents the change from ignorance to knowledge, from insecurity to authoritative posture that occurs gradually during the intervening time and distinguishes the first half of the book from the second.

Aeneas' last words tell of the loss of his father. The book ends as it had begun, with death. A young Trojan, resettled, murdered, and injured again in his tomb by Aeneas is counterbalanced by the death of an old Trojan, lost during his son's journey into enlightenment so that Aeneas now can become uniquely *pater*. But Anchises' presence in book 3, which is as much his book as his son's, offers crucial illustration of a positive evolution that compares with Aeneas' own. In the first half of the book Anchises' groping misinterpretation of Anius' oracle leads to plague on Crete and parallels Aeneas' wild ventures in the use of force. Nevertheless his subsequent clearheaded interpretation of possible peace on Italian soil through the domestication of brute energy and his magnanimity toward a helpless Greek set a standard of wisdom and humanity to be marked by Aeneas and later by Rome.

Still the brief remembrance Virgil has Aeneas give Anchises rings thinly to the reader after the Achaemenides episode, which is in fact the final climax of book 3. It also serves another important rhetorical purpose. We are often told that in creating the character of Sinon, who persuades her citizens to open Troy for the wooden horse, Virgil drew upon and, the implication is, refined the earlier, tentative delineation of Achaemenides which he would have improved had he been given further opportunity to polish.[37] My own sense is that, however distinct their individual characteristics, books 2 and 3 are to be read conjointly as parts of a whole, and that the clear parallels between these two focal figures, whose adventures nearly begin and end their respective books, are Virgil's further way of carefully forming Aeneas' narrative into a unity.

This unity between the two books, like that of book 3 within itself, rests paradoxically on change. The deceiving Greek, who claims to be persecuted by Odysseus but is actually his colleague in insinuation, is replaced by the Greek who has been deceived, abandoned by a now wandering Odysseus to a potentially savage doom. The fake suppliant, a figure of destructive potential whose release means the unbinding of Troy, finds a counterpart in a true *supplex* who is saved by the Trojans only to help extricate them all from a common danger. Anchises, his vision now clear and understanding, supplants Priam who yields his thinking and his city to a cozening of lies. Finally, the destructive, occasionally suicidal violence that initiates each book and endures for most of the second, yields at their respective conclusions, first, to the compliance of his father to Aeneas' will (which represents also his son's submission to Anchises), second, to an act of clemency that would seem to abhor mistreatment of a suppliant, whatever his origin.

The narrator's balance between books 2 and 3 is reinforced by the author's outer frame of introduction and conclusion. What follows easily on Dido's request—

> Conticuere omnes intentique ora tenebant;
> inde toro pater Aeneas sic orsus ab alto . . .
>   (2.1–2)

All became silent and held their faces intent [on him]; then from his
lofty couch father Aeneas began thus . . .

—when repeated at the end of the third book bears the stamp of careful
formula:

> sic pater Aeneas intentis omnibus unus
> fata renarrabat divum cursusque docebat.
> conticuit tandem factoque hic fine quievit.
>   (3.716–18)

Thus, with all intent [on him], father Aeneas alone told the destinies
decreed by the gods and taught his wanderings. At last he became
silent and here rested after he had finished.

Calculated chiasmus, as *conticuere omnes intenti . . . pater Aeneas* becomes
pater Aeneas intentis omnibus . . . conticuit, helps the reader work forward
and backward into Aeneas' unfolding story. It also serves as a reminder
that Dido has been listening all this time to his dramatic tale of the
interaction between ignorance and knowledge, impetuosity and gentleness. She would have heard of death's constancy in her future paramour's
lot.[38] Whatever her final understanding, the transition from book 1 to
book 4 seems only to continue in words the seduction of Dido initiated
before Aeneas recounts his story, by the scheming of Juno and Venus.

The metaphorical flame and wound that possess Dido as book 4 opens
and are soon to become explicit in her suicide only encapsulate what has
already been adumbrated before Aeneas' words begin, in the vocabulary
of love as fire and disease on which Virgil relies. Such reiteration reminds
the reader that the first and fourth books of the epic are also part of a
grander cycle of which Aeneas' account of his past is only the elaborate
core.[39] There are suggestive parallels neatly plotted between the two
framing books. I would like to conclude by noting one allusion which has
special bearing on the ethical problem Aeneas will face as he attempts to
practice his newly learned *clementia*. In book 1, before Aeneas reveals his
presence, Ilioneus as spokesman for the shipwrecked Trojans addresses
the Carthaginian queen:

> "o regina, novam cui condere Iuppiter urbem
> iustitiaque dedit gentis frenare superbas,
> Troes te miseri, ventis maria omnia vecti,
> oramus: prohibe infandos a navibus ignis,
> parce pio generi et propius res aspice nostras.
> non nos aut ferro Libycos populare penatis
> venimus, aut raptas ad litora vertere praedas;
> non ea vis animo nec tanta superbia victis."
>   (1.522–29)

"O queen, whom Jupiter granted to found a city and to rein in proud peoples through justice, we, pitiable Trojans, carried by the winds over all the seas, beseech you: ward off dread fire from our ships, spare a holy race and look more kindly on our situation. We have not come either to lay waste Libyan homes with the sword or to drive stolen booty to the shore. That violence is not in our mind nor does such pride remain for the conquered."

As Ilioneus sees her, Dido epitomizes an aspect of the Roman civilizing mission, reining in the proud through justice. The Trojans do not seem to offer evidence of *superbia*. Instead, conquered, pitiable, and reduced to prayer, they present Dido with the opportunity of sparing a race that is at her mercy.

As book 4 evolves matters reverse themselves. In Dido's eyes the Trojans are now preparing to depart on proud ships (*ratibus superbis*, 540), and, as her sister makes ready to serve as her surrogate in dealing with her departing lover, she urges on her the posture of suppliant against his pride:

"I, soror, atque hostem supplex adfare superbum . . ."
(4.424)
"Go, sister, and as a suppliant address the proud foe . . ."[40]

But reaction to Aeneas' conduct is not left solely to statement by the one most injured and hence imputed to a character alone by her spoken words. A few lines before Dido's command to her sister, Virgil calls Aeneas *pius*. He then takes the reader directly into his confidence, addressing him, as he does only rarely, in the second person:

migrantis cernas totaque ex urbe ruentis:
ac velut ingentem formicae farris acervum
cum populant hiemis memores tectoque reponunt,
it nigrum campis agmen praedamque per herbas
convectant calle angusto; . . .
(4.401–5)
You could see them streaming and in a rush from the whole city: even as when ants, mindful of winter, lay waste a huge heap of grain and store it in their home, a black column makes its way over the fields and on a narrow path they carry their booty through the grass; . . .

The simile suggests that, as Virgil would now have us see it, Ilioneus' disclaimer in book 1 was in fact unintentionally fraudulent. The Trojans have become symbolic despoilers of the land, absconding darkly with its booty, and Dido, literal builder of a grand domain, alters in image to a besieged city, falling in ruins after the enemy has been allowed to enter.[41] Such is the extraordinary subtlety of Virgil's art that whatever blame Aeneas retains throughout the episode is largely attached by the innuendo of metaphor, not by any direct authorial statement.

Virgil leaves questions of responsibility unanswered and readers will continue to debate the problem of guilt and blame in the actions of the two lovers. Aeneas remains the passive hero, driven to leave Carthage by the dictates of Jupiter who is merely implementing fate. Yet, willingly or not, he brings misfortune with him. He is not allowed to practice the *clementia* he had espoused at the climax of his narrative, even if he would. It is the reader who is left to ponder the tension, which Catullus had already presented brilliantly in his sixty-fourth poem, between history, its heroic makers, and the suffering they experience or cause. There is a later moment at the end of the epic when Aeneas, in a not dissimilar situation, is at last in a position of responsibility and made by the poet to ponder his dilemma before acting. But this deserves separate treatment.

NOTES

1. Among the few essays devoted specifically to the third book of the *Aeneid*, I have found those of Lloyd, "*Aeneid* III" 133–51 and "Aeneas Legend" 382–400, especially valuable on matters of theme and structure. Cf. also Allen, "Dullest Book" 119–23, who sees book 3 marking the definitive break with the past as it slowly reveals the future. The conversion of Aeneas from Trojan to Roman is also a major concern of Semple, "Short Study" 225–40. Di Cesare, *Altar and the City* 61–76, gives a particularly sympathetic treatment of Aeneas, "the wanderer," in book 3. Ways in which the reader is forced to see Aeneas in book 3 because of his role as narrator are discussed by Sanderlin, "Aeneas as Apprentice" 53–56.

   The commentary on *Aeneid* 3 by Williams, *Liber Tertius*, is an informative guide. In general Williams sees the book as one "of low tension between the two intense books, II and IV" (p. 14; cf. p. 3). He argues that "the theme of book III is the gradual progress toward the desired goal [i.e., Rome], with difficulties and dangers countered by divine prophecies and encouragement" (p. 18).

2. Among other topics that *Aeneid* 3 shares with the *Odyssey*, aside from the obvious plots centered on adventure-ridden wandering, is an emphasis on eating—"That eating poem of the Odyssey" (*Tom Jones* book 9, ch. 5)—which can betoken need, yearning, fulfillment, or a combination thereof.

3. The most detailed examination is by Knauer, *Aeneis* passim, especially 181–209, on the relationship of *Aeneid* 3 and *Odyssey* 12.

4. The point is made by Quinn, *Critical Description* 394.

5. The importance of myrtle boughs in Greek foundation ceremonies is documented by A. Steier, *RE* 16.1.1181 s.v. *myrtos*.

   On the sprouting staff as marking the spot for a foundation, see Eliade, *The Sacred and the Profane* 27. Servius (on 3.46) refers appropriately to the sprouting cornel shaft in the legend of Romulus and Remus (cf. Ovid *M.* 15.561–64). See also Plut. *Rom.* 20.5ff.; Arnob. 4.3; schol. on Ovid *M.* (p. 720 Magnus).

6. The use of *procul* in the initial line of the episode (13) is emphasized by Halter, *Vergil und Horaz* 71. There are nine appearances of *procul* in *Aeneid* 3, a number equaled in other books of the *Aeneid* only by 8.

7. Aeneas' conduct here is sensitively defended by Reckford, "Some Trees" 67.

8. On Aeneas' *impietas* here see Nethercut, "Invasion" 88f.

9. To describe Aeneas' conduct Polydorus uses the word *laceras* (41): "Why, Aeneas, do you tear at my poor corpse?" are his first words.

10. The interconnection between the stops in Thrace and Delos is discussed by Jens, "Eingang" 194–97.

11. At no moment in the *Aeneid* are the wanderers more helpless and lost than here. The point is made and developed in relation to the evolution of the epic by Boyle, "Meaning of the *Aeneid*" 74–76.

12. In Apollonius Rhodius the name Strophades stems from the fact that the sons of Boreas there "turned back" after pursuing the Harpies (*Arg.* 2.296). The Harpies make their home on Crete (299). Their presence on the Strophades in the *Aeneid* is Virgil's invention.

13. As well as being a *pestis et ira deum* (3.215), the Harpies embody *malesuada Fames*, one of the abstractions at Hell's gate, ready to work on mankind (6.276). They are the hungry creatures who work their ill through hunger. They force Aeneas to leave his booty half-eaten (*semesam praedam*, 244) and then curse him with the desperate future need to eat his tables (*ambesas mensas*, 257).

14. "O gods, avert such a mishap and gently save those who are *pii*" (266), prays Anchises, quoted by his son and yet reflecting a certain authorial irony. The piety of respect for the rights of others has not much engaged the thoughts of the Trojans. There is a similar irony in Polydorus' cry to Aeneas, who is wrenching his buried body apart, *parce pias scelerare manus* (42).

The Trojan incursion into the territory of others is a prototype of one aspect of the Trojan absorption of Italy. At *Aen.* 8.146–47 Aeneas, in his suppliant speech to Evander, so much exaggerates the resistance he has received (. . . *gens . . . crudeli Daunia bello / insequitur*) that the reader tends to reverse matters and contemplate what violence the Trojan arrival brings that did not exist before.

15. Singleton, *The Divine Comedy* 224, commenting on *Inf.* 13.145, speaks of "the dominant theme of the canto, of rending, of tearing asunder by violence." Dante's borrowings here from *Aeneid* 3 prove that he has caught Virgil's tone in general and in detail. For further analysis of this canto see also Speroni, "Motif" 44–55.

16. It is curious that the eye of Polyphemus, which Achaemenides and Odysseus' other comrades pierce with a shaft, is later considered *Argolici clipei . . . instar* (637). Odysseus' vengeance against the Cyclopes is seen in parallel terms to Trojan vengeance against Greek.

17. Cf. Williams, *Liber Tertius*, on 294f. Galinsky, *Aeneas* 45, 112, has pointed out the evidence in the tradition that Aeneas met Andromache at the court of Neoptolemus. Virgil's novel change of setting, with Andromache freed from her Greek captors and restored to a Trojan husband, makes her narcissistic brooding on the past the more noticeable.

    On Andromache's escapism see Saylor, "Toy Troy" 26–28 and, on the episode in general, Grimm, "Aeneas and Andromache" 151–62.

18. Cf. *Aen.* 8.81–84. *Aen.* 3.390–92 = *Aen.* 8.43–45 and, with the change of *is* to *hic*, *Aen.* 3.393 = *Aen.* 8.46.

19. There is no mention of Rome itself. Though the reader learns of Rome and Romans at 1.7 and 1.33 and in Jupiter's speech at 1.234, 1.277, and 1.282, Aeneas first hears the name mentioned at 4.234.

20. Palinurus is named at lines 202 and 513, two hundred two lines before the end of Aeneas' narrative at 715. The pointed balance "surrounds" the Helenus episode and marks it as a new beginning.

21. *Rubescebat*: 3.521 and 7.25, two out of Virgil's four uses of *rubesco*. The only other appearance of the verb in the *Aeneid* is at 8.695 as Neptune's waters off Actium redden with blood.

22. Of the two other uses of *turritus* in Virgil, one is at 8.693, describing the *turritis puppibus* on which the Romans attacked the followers of Antony and Cleopatra at Actium.

23. Virgil's attempts at perspective, here and elsewhere, are treated by Reeker, *Landschaft* 40ff. He notes the personification of the Italian landscape but does not dwell on any idiosyncrasies in the description. Virgil's sense of depth and distance here is also touched upon by Andersson, *Early Epic* 82.

24. Williams, *Liber Tertius* 168, on 3.543.

25. They are *concordes animae* at 6.827. Virgil's only other use of *concors* is at *Ecl.* 4.47. By contrast *Discordia* and *discors* make fourteen appearances in Virgil's works, ten in the *Aeneid*.

    On horses in relation to a triumph see, further, Williams, *Liber Tertius* on 3.537; Gransden, *Aeneid* on *Aen.* 8.714; Ehlers, *RE* 2.13.504 s.v. *triumphus*.

26. Virgil apparently coins her epithet, and uses it, with great suitability, only here.

27. For a more detailed analysis of Virgil's description of Etna, see Reeker, *Landschaft* 62, 159.

28. Cf. especially lines 39–40:

    > gemitus lacrimabilis imo
    > auditur tumulo et vox reddita fertur ad auris.

    A tearful groan is heard from the mound and a voice in reply is carried to my ears.

    with 576–77:

    > liquefactaque saxa sub auras
    > cum gemitu glomerat fundoque exaestuat imo.

    And with a groan it tosses molten rocks to the skies and boils from its lowest depth.

29. The most recent treatment of the meeting with Achaemenides is by Römisch, "Achaemenides-Episode" 208–27. His analysis is especially penetrating on the many contrasts within this epi-

sode, for example, between the need to see the stars and the blackness of Etna (p. 210) or between man and monster (p. 222). He relates the name Achaemenides to *Achos* (p. 219).

Highet, *Speeches* 28f., dismisses the episode as derivative and unimportant.

30. On the proverbiality of the wealth of the Achaemenids, see Hor. *C.* 2.12.21, *dives Achaemenes* (cf. also *Epode* 13.8, *C.* 3.1.44). Horace uses *Persae* to mean *Parthae* at *C.* 1.2.22, 1.21.15, 3.5.4.

31. Anchises' patriarchal act is, of course, a grand gesture of unity. We must, however, not lose sight of the fact that shortly before the end of his final speech to his son in book 6 Anchises singles out for mention the destructive actions of Aemilius Paulus against Greece during the Third Macedonian War. He will overwhelm Argos and Mycenae, says Anchises,

> ultus avos Troiae templa et temerata Minervae.
> (6.840)
> having avenged his Trojan forebears and Minerva's defiled temple.

In spite of the reception of Achaemenides, vengeance and *clementia* will remain opposing principles in Roman history, even in Rome's evolving relationship with Greece. Mycenae still remains *saevae* in Ilioneus' words of greeting to Latinus (7.222).

32. Reasons for linking Achaemenides to Parthia are detailed by McKay, "Achaemenides Episode" 31–38, passim, who also discusses at length Augustus' careful policy of forbearance in this instance (p. 35).

33. At line 639 Achaemenides addresses the Trojans as *o miseri*, alluding to the communality of their menace from Polyphemus and reminding the reader that Aeneas had just described him as a *forma . . . miseranda* (591). We must also recall that in the opening episode of the book Aeneas and Polydorus are differentiated when the stronger harms the weaker:

> "quid miserum, Aeneas, laceras? iam parce sepulto, . . ."
> (3.41)
> "Why, Aeneas, do you tear at my poor corpse? Spare me now that I am buried, . . ."

Sparing comes only after intervention from the tomb.
Line 639 as a whole—

> "sed fugite, o miseri, fugite atque ab litore funem
> rumpite."

> "But flee, o poor creatures, flee and rend your cables from the shore."

—also looks back to Polydorus' double command to Aeneas:

> "heu fuge crudelis terras, fuge litus avarum."
> (3.44)
> "Ah, flee the cruel land, flee the greedy shore."

Singular imperative to Aeneas, unique perpetrator of hurt, is changed at the book's end to a plural embracing all the Trojans and, ultimately, Achaemenides himself.

34. There are important differences in the treatments of Polyphemus by Homer and Virgil. These have been well discussed by Glenn, "Virgil's Polyphemus" 47–59, especially 53–55. See also

Thaniel, "Note" 10–12; Römisch, "Achaemenides-Episode" 223, n. 18.

Resonances of the figure of Polyphemus later in the epic are also traced by Glenn, "Mezentius and Polyphemus" 129–55.

35. We also trace the movement of at least one other Greek from his homeland to Italy during the course of book 3, namely Idomeneus. At line 122 he has deserted Crete and by lines 400–401 he is besieging the Sallentine fields in southeastern Italy. Virgil there gives him the epithet Lyctius as remembrance of his Cretan origin.

36. Ortygia is named at lines 124, 143, and 154.

37. Cf. Williams, *Liber Tertius* 181, on lines 588f. On the parallels between the two passages, see Mackail, *Aeneid* Appendix B; Jackson Knight, "Pairs of Passages" 10–14; and Quinn, *Critical Description* 61 and 132–33, for a sympathetic treatment of Virgil's intentions.

38. The first four books of the *Aeneid* have often been viewed by critics as a group, the first, in other words, of three major divisions in the epic. This thesis has been notably defended by Pöschl, *Dichtkunst* 279, and Duckworth, "Trilogy" 1–10 (p. 4, nn. 13–15, for further bibliography). Newton, "Recurrent Imagery" 33, touches briefly on imagery in book 1 that will be elaborated in the fourth book.

39. Anderson, *Art* 42f., details further reasons why Dido might be moved by Aeneas' tale.

40. Dido is also *supplex* at 414 and *victam* at 434 (cf. 1.529 quoted earlier).

41. Venus first suggests the image at 1.673. It appears again at 1.719 and is reiterated strongly in simile at 4.668–71:

> resonat magnis plangoribus aether
> non aliter quam si immissis ruat hostibus omnis
> Karthago aut antiqua Tyros, flammaeque furentes
> culmina perque hominum volvantur perque deorum.

The heaven reechoes with great wails, even as though all Carthage or ancient Tyre were collapsing before an inrushing foe, and raging fires were swirling over the dwellings of men and of gods.

The intervening simile comparing the Trojans to predator ants is a careful segment of Virgil's design.

DAEDALUS,
VIRGIL,
AND THE END
OF ART

My text is Virgil's version of the story of Daedalus, from the opening of
Aeneid 6.[1] Aeneas confronts this tale on reaching Cumae in search of the
Sibyl. It is told in a series of tableaux on the doors of a temple dedicated to
Apollo by the artisan-sculptor himself after his safe arrival in Italy. This is
the only occasion in ancient literature where an artist is described as
constructing his literal, which in this case is also to say his spiritual, or
psychic, biography. As such I take it as a metaphor for the progress of any
artist, for his imaginative diary, as it were. My thesis will be that in certain
essential ways the tale of Daedalus, crafted by himself, sets up a typology
that is mirrored in the ethical artistry practiced by Aeneas from standards
set him by his father toward the end of the same book. After parading
before his son a host of future Roman heroes, most of them distinguished
for their military prowess, Anchises summarizes what he foresees as
Rome's special genius. It will not lie in any unique brilliance as sculptors
in bronze or stone, or as orators or astronomers, but in the accomplishments of the Roman people as governing warriors, in their moral usage
of political power:

> "tu regere imperio populos, Romane, memento
> (hae tibi erunt artes), pacique imponere morem,
> parcere subiectis et debellare superbos."
>   (6.851–53)
> "Remember, Roman, to rule peoples with might (these will be your
> arts), to impose upon them a custom for peace, to spare the hum-
> bled and war down the proud."

This is Roman "artistry" set up for Aeneas to model himself against in the
epic's second half.

But I would go still further in drawing analogies from the *vita* of
Daedalus and suggest that it reveals something, first, of the narrator's
spirit as he outlines Aeneas' progress, and then also of the intelligence of
the poet Virgil working within the demands of a strict generic tradition.
Aeneas who has himself, like Daedalus, just completed an extraordinary
journey, is not allowed by the Sibyl to meditate on even the most simplistic parallels between himself and the Cretan inventor. She brusquely
whisks her charge away from what she styles *spectacula*, sights presum-

ably purveying only aesthetic delight. But Virgil's reader, with his privileged, unheroic leisure for contemplation, is under the obligation to
respond not only—as Aeneas might have—to the sculptured encapsula-
tion of an artist's life but to what Aeneas does not know, to the emotions
of the artist in the crafting and of the narrator in the telling.

Here is the story as told by Virgil at *Aeneid* 6.14–37:

> Daedalus, ut fama est, fugiens Minoia regna
> praepetibus pennis ausus se credere caelo
> insuetum per iter gelidas enavit ad Arctos,
> Chalcidicaque levis tandem super astitit arce.
> redditus his primum terris tibi, Phoebe, sacravit
> remigium alarum posuitque immania templa.
> in foribus letum Androgeo; tum pendere poenas
> Cecropidae iussi (miserum!) septena quotannis
> corpora natorum; stat ductis sortibus urna.
> contra elata mari respondet Cnosia tellus:
> hic crudelis amor tauri suppostaque furto
> Pasiphae mixtumque genus prolesque biformis
> Minotaurus inest, Veneris monimenta nefandae,
> hic labor ille domus et inextricabilis error;
> magnum reginae sed enim miseratus amorem
> Daedalus ipse dolos tecti ambagesque resoluit,
> caeca regens filo vestigia. tu quoque magnam
> partem opere in tanto, sineret dolor, Icare, haberes.
> bis conatus erat casus effingere in auro,
> bis patriae cecidere manus. quin protinus omnia
> perlegerent oculis, ni iam praemissus Achates
> adforet atque una Phoebi Triviaeque sacerdos,
> Deiphobe Glauci, fatur quae talia regi:
> "non hoc ista sibi tempus spectacula poscit; . . ."

As tradition has it, Daedalus, fleeing Minos' kingdom on his swift
feathers, having dared to entrust himself to heaven, swam along this
unaccustomed path to the chill Bears and finally stood nimbly upon
the Chalcidic citadel. Restored here first to earth, he dedicated the
oarage of his wings to you, Phoebus, and built a huge temple. On
the doors was the death of Androgeos; then the Athenians were
ordered (o sad deed!) to offer as recompense the bodies of seven of
their children every year; there stands the urn with lots drawn.
Opposite this lies the land where Knossos was raised from the sea:
here is the cruel love for the bull, Pasiphaë placed secretly underneath, and the mixed race and two-formed offspring, the Minotaur,
a reminder of unspeakable passion—here is the toil of the house and

its inextricable maze; but indeed, Daedalus himself, who pitied the great love of the queen, undid the deceptions and tangles of the house, leading blind footsteps with a thread. You also, Icarus, would have a great part in so great a work, did grief permit. Twice Daedalus tried to fashion your fall in gold; twice your father's hand fell. Indeed they would have read all these things throughout with their eyes, were not Achates, who had been sent ahead, now present with the priestess of Apollo and Trivia, Deiphobe, Glaucus' daughter, who speaks thus to the king: "This hour does not demand for itself these sights; . . ."

The story divides itself into five parts: introduction (Daedalus' arrival in Italy), first segment of sculpture devoted to events at Athens, counterbalancing Cretan exploits, the story of Ariadne and the address to Icarus. There is a climactic heightening of emotion on the part of both artist and the narrator of his tale as the story progresses, leading in the final episode to the artist's inability to create. Let us watch this happening by examining each section in more detail.

At the start, through the phrase *ut fama est*, the narrator seems hyperconscious of putting things before us. By re-creating someone else's report and not, it would seem, inventing his own version of the Daedalus story, he distances us in time while apparently disclaiming any direct involvement on his part in the telling.[2] Yet even in this introduction the narrator betrays a certain empathy with his version of Daedalus which suggests a deep understanding of his subject's imaginative ways. Daedalus, as the Cretan vignette makes clear, is a dealer in duplicity, an inventor of hybrid objects that cater to the furtive in their recipients and in their turn create further hybrids—a fake beast enclosing a true human (Pasiphaë inside the replica of a cow) that begets a man-animal, the Minotaur. The narrator anticipates this proclivity even now in his own epic inventiveness. He replaces visual duplicity with verbal contrivance, exchanging the craftsman's dualistic artifact with the poet's ambiguous metaphor by seeing Daedalus, the human aviator, as swimmer through the heavens. The terrestrial creature, though airborne, is made poetically to deal (like Aeneas for much of the preceding story of his epic) with a watery element, and dedicate on return to earth the oarage of his wings.[3]

The narrator is a discerning critic of Daedalus' adventures in two other ways. One is a simple matter of rhetoric. By apostrophizing Apollo he, as it were, mimics Daedalus, claiming himself to share the emotion Daedalus felt on safe return to earth and voiced in gesture of thanks to Phoebus Apollo. But address to the god as Phoebus proves the narrator privy to the myth of Daedalus on a deeper level. Daedalus ends his adventuring on a spot sacred to Apollo, where Aeneas will hear prophecy of his, and Rome's, future through the god's mouthpiece, Deiphobe, the Sibyl. But

Apollo the sun god played an important role in Daedalus' recent life. By steering a course toward the chill Bears, Daedalus saved himself from the fate of Icarus whose wings melted as he drew too near the sun's heat. The artisan of hybrids, who turns himself and his offspring into birds, loses his son in the process of artistic experimentation.

But there is also a hint, in the verb *enavit* and the very phrase *gelidas Arctos*, of a certain insouciance on the part of Daedalus. By swimming free of danger toward northern cold he followed the proper procedures for survival, but his child Icarus either was not taught, or at least was not able to practice, them.[4] To put it another way, both Daedalus within this initial segment of the narrative and the narrator expounding his tale seem in different senses careless—and leave the reader thus far unaware—that more than one person was involved in this strange itinerary. Because there is no mention of Icarus and no hint of Daedalus' role as father, the reader remains with the impression, which the narrator's metaphors abet, that Daedalus thinks largely of his invention and the clever manipulation of it, not of its human consequences.

The narrator therefore gives us a foretaste of circularity in his rendering of the tale, preparing us for the address to Icarus at the end. But neither at the start nor at the conclusion of the episode is the actual death of Icarus mentioned, a fact which invites the reader to fill in the text, to exercise his own imagination re-creating and contemplating the most poignant incident in Daedalus' biography. In his role as father Daedalus is a double artistic failure, first incapable of completely imitating nature, then unable to mime the disastrous results of this inadequacy.

Though they now forthrightly continue the theme of sons killed or sacrificed, the initial sculptures proper, devoted to events in Athens, are treated as matters of fact, save in one respect. There is no word for the act of crafting and the only object mentioned, the urn, was not of Daedalus' making. The exception is the exclamation *miserum* (alas! dreadful!). From its placement in the middle of line 21 and therefore at the center of the three lines, it serves as emotional commentary on the whole segment. But to whom the emotion is imputed remains ambiguous. Is it that experienced by the suffering Athenians? Is it Daedalus' response as he contemplates the results of his handiwork (or, in his mind's eye, the events themselves), or Aeneas', examining the sculpture? Is it the reaction of the narrator sharing the same sensations, or of the reader being taught them in his turn? For one verbal moment, even in the most "detached" segment of Daedalus' tale, narrator, characters, and audience are united in empathy.[5]

The first Cretan segment is even more nominal, but now the list of characters and emotions concentrates specifically on Daedalus' art. His is an inventiveness which articulates subterfuge and doubleness, that tangibly fosters sexual perversity, and harbors its results, a man-bull, in a labyrinthine dwelling that is both *labor* and *error*.[6] It exemplifies the intensity of craftsmanship that imprisons the misformed product of human-animal passion in a maze symbolizing, like its contents, the troubling results of a "wandering" of the emotions. Pasiphaë's double "error" receives its artistic complement from Daedalus' tricky fabrication.[7] Thus far in his tale Daedalus' art is dangerous only for its receivers.

The second Cretan scene brings a series of abrupt changes. Though the labyrinth remains an essential part of the plot, we turn from one queen, Pasiphaë, to another, her unnamed daughter, Ariadne, and from a cruel love to another labeled simply "mighty." But the viewer-reader is also appropriately disoriented. We know from what follows that the Ariadne episode is part of the tableaux of sculptural reliefs. But Daedalus has suddenly, and Virgil brilliantly, led us from his *curriculum vitae* as guileful artisan to his role as apparently dispassionate reappraiser of the effects of that art. He becomes the undoer of his own trickery, an undoing we can hear in the sound of line 29:

Daedalus ipse dolos tecti ambagesque resolvit, . . .

Daedalus himself undid the deceptions and tangles of the house, . . .

Daedalus, who reprojects his artistic self through *se dolos*, the labyrinth's wiliness, now straightens its windings and lightens its darkening ways. But dispassionate is far too mild a word. Through poetry's magic Daedalus actually becomes Ariadne. She is the *regina* and she it was who, through Daedalus' gift of thread, directed the steps of Theseus out from the maze after killing the Minotaur.[8] Yet, according to Virgil-Daedalus, we find him *regens*, taking her emotional and physical role by linguistic sleight of hand. The reason for this empathy, as the artist unwinds his own artistry and forgoes his own self-made heritage of deception, is pity. Pity is the response that transforms the apparently aloof artistic deceiver into the emotional resolver of his own deceits. It is this response in himself that he would now monumentalize.[9]

His own poet-monumentalizer is equally forward. He puts no word of crafting into his own presentation. Nothing intervenes to prevent the reader from the stated actuality of Daedalus' experience.[10] By contrast to the preceding episode, then, this tableau is *vivant*. Frozen re-presentation yields to active experience, as we are made to share directly in the artist's suffering. We are Daedalus but, because he is one with his protagonist, we are Virgil as well, uttering through the power of words what cannot be expressed in sculpture.

Finally, we leave the triply fictive world of poet imagining artist crafting himself in art to look more simply at the artist's inability to create. We find him unable to bring to aesthetic completion the delineation in sculpture of an event which in itself, to the artist as experiencer, remained a subject of sorrow, rousing emotion unsatisfied and therefore incomplete. As an interested third party, Daedalus could be shown to share in Ariadne's feelings, ruling with her out of pity her lover's steps. The death of Icarus is a deeper matter. It is the death of a son from the misuse of his father's artistry and for which the father's artistic but duplicitous heroizing must bear some responsibility. As he did in the case of Ariadne, the narrator draws a lexical connection between artist and subject. But the artist who there rules the queen he depicts (*regina-regens*) now fails in his vocation. Because of Icarus' attempt to emulate his father as man-bird, he suffered a mortal fall, and the contemplation of this mischance (the Latin *casus* plays on both literal and figurative senses) caused his father's hands twice to fall as he attempted to monumentalize it.[11]

Here the empathy of the narrator, which has been building from the opening segment, is most fully expressed. As in the initial apostrophe to Phoebus Apollo, he seems to adopt the voice of Daedalus. There his cry was in thanksgiving. Here his words are uttered in sorrow. But in fact so strong is the narrator's involvement that he replaces Daedalus entirely so as to address Icarus directly in explanation of his father's artistic failure. In so doing, in replacing the sculptor-father, the poet's narrator becomes a Daedalian figure, bringing Icarus and his father's frustrating grief before us in the permanence of words.

We have therefore, in one of Virgil's richest poetic moments, a study in artistic incompletion that is extraordinarily complete as a poetic act. The incompletion, the tale within the tale, is Daedalus' and it results from a gradual heightening of his emotional participation. In the last three episodes of Daedalus' story as Virgil tells it, the only ones where the artisan is directly involved, we watch him first as aloof artificer of duplicity, constructing monsters to create further monsters. His empathy grows, and his characterization as artist disappears, as he shows himself (and is shown) pitying Ariadne and as a result unraveling his own artistic stratagems (which, I take it, is not only to show himself powerful over his own art but also, perhaps, even to admit fallibilities in that art). Finally he becomes the victim of *dolor*, of the spasm of grief for his lost son, and this distress results in his inability to create at all. Death renders this artist artless. Daedalus' final honesty, his deepest response to natural feelings, brings artistic barrenness as well as a final powerlessness. But this very gesture of unfulfillment becomes, through Virgil's narration of it, the perfecting element of a poet's holistic enterprise. One artist's failure through passion is the subject of another's successful finishing of his art.

My thesis is that this treatment by one artist of the spiritual biography of another serves as a paradigm of the Virgilian career and of the equally tripartite division of the *Aeneid* as a poetic entity, and that it is particularly enlightening for the reader probing the meaning of the epic's conclusion.

It is important for my argument to remember that the *Aeneid* begins and ends with acts sparked by *dolor*. At line 9 of the first book we find Juno, Aeneas' divine archenemy and emblem of irrationality, *dolens*, aggrieved, as she launches this hero, noteworthy for his *pietas*, into a sea of troubles. Sixteen lines later we are told in greater detail of the *causae irarum saevique dolores*, the sources of her wrath and fierce anguish that now spur her on to violence. In balance, eight lines from the epic's conclusion we learn of the *saevus dolor*, the fierce anguish which Aeneas experienced at the death of Pallas. Recollection of this event, aroused by sight of the belt Pallas had worn, now on the suppliant Turnus, who had killed him earlier in battle, drives Aeneas to a frenzy of rage (he is described as "set aflame by furies and terrible in his wrath"). In this paroxysm he slays his antagonist whose soul flees under the shades as the epic comes to its abrupt end. I have proposed elsewhere, from several angles, that Aeneas' final deed turns him into a Juno figure, in other words that he becomes a personification, not of his much touted *pietas* based on his father's injunction to *clementia* for the beaten down, but of its opposite, Junonian anger.[12] The subsequent pages will further defend this contention.

First, Daedalus and the Virgilian career, and Daedalus and the structure of the *Aeneid*. In two cryptic lines near the start of the second book of his *Georgics* Virgil in his own voice addresses his patron Maecenas:

> . . . non hic te carmine ficto
> atque per ambages et longa exorsa tenebo.
>   (*Geo.* 2.45–46)
> . . . I will not hold you here with a fictive song and through tangles
> and long beginnings.

This definition of casuistic poetry may apply to work Virgil anticipates for his later career, but more likely it is his way of looking back to his first work, the *Eclogues*. Certainly no other poems in Latin, with their many layers of symbolism and multivalent masquerades, could more justly claim the epithets fictive and ambiguous. The rich later history of pastoral poetry as a vehicle for necessary indirection of statement looks back in honor to its primarily Virgilian source.

As Virgil, Daedalus-like, leads his poetry out of the *ambages* of pastoral and into the greater openness and availability of didactic, his poetic voice moves from playful to serious and he from poet as implicit deceiver to poet as explicit pitier. His opening prayer to Augustus asks Caesar to nod approval to his bold beginnings

> ignarosque viae mecum miseratus agrestis
> ingredere . . .
>   (*Geo.* 1.41–42)

and having pitied with me the farmers who do not know their way, begin . . .

Pity creates poetry with the Daedalian power of Ariadne's thread, capable, through teaching, of directing those unsure of the path they tread. The immediate result, as the poet and his farmer set out on their interactive labors, is that new spring arrives, snow melts, and "the crumbling clod has broken itself up [*resolvit*]" under the power of the west wind (*Geo.* 1.44). Pity's poetry has also Daedalus' power to resolve nature's seasonal dilemmas and set the farmer firmly on his arduous road.

Last in the Virgilian career comes the poetry of *dolor*. The *Aeneid* seems the impersonal epic of one man's pious journey toward accomplishment, mirroring *in parvo* the future achievements of imperial Rome as it rises to unparalleled greatness under Augustus. But it is also, as we have seen and will further observe, a passion-ridden poem whose final deed of violence stemming from anguish and anger leaves open as many questions as it answers. It leaves dissatisfied the reader's expectations of praise for Aeneas' most memorable action as model for Rome's glorious enterprise to come, and instead completes a cycle based on *dolor*, that is, on an emotion founded in discontent and battening on deprivation. Like Virgil's history of Daedalus it is a brilliantly complete poem ending on premonitions of artistic incompletion.

For the *Aeneid* itself also has the rhythms of a Daedalian undertaking. As one of the most highly ordered of poems, the possibilities for imaginative structuring it offers to the reader are numerous. We gain pleasure, as we approach the epic in linear fashion, from sensing books grouped as pairs or trios, or from savoring a balance between the epic's halves, as they open out in clear echoes of book 1 in book 7. We may also acknowledge Virgil's grand chiasmus, where opening anticipates closure. We then focus centrally on the powerful linkage between books 6 and 7 which begins with address to Caieta, Aeneas' nurse, another in the host of those, especially prominent in the preceding book, who gain real death and dubious immortality for being in Aeneas' entourage.

I would also like here to reconsider what has long been observed as the *Aeneid*'s tripartite division.[13] We could distinguish the three movements as follows: books 1–4, which take us topographically and temporally from Troy to Carthage and revolve on Aeneas' meeting with Dido; books 5–8, as we move from Sicily, to Cumae, to Tiber mouth, which contain Aeneas' two great revelations of the future, from his father in the Underworld and on the shield of Vulcan; books 9–12, which deal primarily with the war for supremacy in Latium and, in particular, with Aeneas' confrontation with Turnus.

After the pattern Virgil has Daedalus establish for himself, the first segment of the *Aeneid* is rich with exemplification of deceit. As re-created

for us in Aeneas' words, the wooden horse, Troy's equivalent of Pasiphaë's cow, is, save for the shield of Aeneas, the single most memorable
artifact in the *Aeneid*, notable for its Daedalian duplicity and duality.[14] (It
is at once alive and dead, a wooden object, fashioned as an animal,
pregnant with a human brood. As objects both cow and horse are marvelous on the outside, deceptive on the inside. They can, even should, be
viewed as Virgil's epic can be read. Past a veneer of artificial charm—in
regard to the *Aeneid* the veneer is partially manufactured of our idealizing
expectations—lie, in all cases, terrible truths.) The second part of Aeneas'
narrative is also riddled with the monstral and the biform, with a plant
that drips with human blood, Harpies who are at once birds or maidens
or goddesses, Scylla (part human, part fish, part wolf), the man-mountain
Etna and the mountain-man Polyphemus.

But it is the story of Aeneas, especially as it merges with Dido's, to
which I want to call attention.[15] Venus, divinity of love and mother of
Aeneas, arrives on the scene in the disguise of the virgin goddess Diana.
She soon hides her son in a cloud, as he makes his way into Carthage, and
his beauty is said to be his mother's artifice (grace added by craftsmen to
ivory is the poet's simile, gold embellishing silver or marble) as he bursts
from its enclosure. But counterfeiting is once again her province, her
"new arts" (*novas artis*) in the narrator's words, as she replaces Ascanius
with Cupid in preparation for the temptation of Dido.

The pretendings of Aeneas, as orchestrated by Virgil, are more elaborate. The most patent example is his gift-giving. He offers to Dido
Helen's cloak and the scepter of Ilione, which is to say his presence brings
her, from Helen, illicit love leading to her city's symbolic razing by fire,
from Ilione, suicide. His relation to the sculptures on Juno's temple which
he sees in Carthage's midst is more subtle. They depict scenes from
Troy's fall which summarize Homer or intervene between the story line
of the *Iliad* and Aeneas' own tale. Aeneas and Achates take them as
evidence of Dido's sympathy for human suffering. The reader, aware of
their connection with Juno and her vengeful proclivities, looks at them in
other ways. Their great figure is Achilles. He appears directly in three of
their episodes, indirectly in three others, primarily as a killer, of Troilus,
Hector, Memnon, and Penthesilea. By the end of the epic, Aeneas will
become in part an Achilles, pitilessly killing his Latin Hector, Turnus.
The equation here is more understated. By continuing on the tale of Troy
in his narrative to Dido, Aeneas becomes active as well as passive, partici-
pant in events but their passionate recaller as well. His verbal artisanship,
in other words, takes up where the sculptures left off, yet also becomes
part of the seduction of Dido.[16] The destruction of Troy, which he suffers
as a character within his narrative, leads inevitably to the destruction of
Dido which his very act of narration helps to cause.

The lexical, symbolic, or imagistic continuation from the end of book

1, through Aeneas' narrative, to the masterful delineation of Dido's downfall in the fourth book needs only brief documentation. Cupid's fake words (*simulata verba*, 1.710) lead directly to the faking of the wooden horse (*simulant*, 2.17), which in turn anticipates Aeneas' attempts at dissimulation (*dissimulent*, 4.291), which Dido unmasks in her first words addressed to him after his decision to depart:

> "dissimulare etiam sperasti, perfide, tantum
> posse nefas . . . ?"
>   (4.305–6)
> "Did you also expect, treacherous man, that you could hide so great
> a wrong . . . ?"

It is an easy transition from the *doli*, the wiles of Venus and Cupid, in book 1, to the deceits of the Greeks in book 2 as executed by Sinon and the horse, to the deception of Aeneas that Dido uncloaks. The symbolic flames with which Venus plans to gird Dido become the destructive arson of Troy and then the triple fires of book 4—the metaphoric ardor of her love, her literal burning on the pyre, which, as we have seen, is visualized as the burning of Carthage, the queen as city demolished by a concatenation of circumstances.

It is not necessary to argue yet again the moral fine-points of a tragic adventure where ignorance and knowledge play intermeshed roles, and human weaknesses make its characters easy prey for divine machinations as well as self-deceptions. I want only to suggest that in detail and in general the constancy of deceit in the story line of *Aeneid* 1–4 finds its parallel in the exploits of Daedalus as artificer. The particularities and their consequences press the connection between Pasiphaë and Dido. Pasiphaë's love is *crudelis* and this is the adjective Dido twice applies to her absconding lover. Just as the Cretan queen's erotic adventure is based on a stratagem which is also a hiding (*furto*), so also, in the narrator's words, Dido ponders a furtive love (*furtivum amorem*), and it is against accusations of trickery (*furto*) from her that Aeneas must defend himself. Finally, the Minotaur, symbol of Pasiphaë's "unspeakable passion" (*Veneris monimenta nefandae*), has its more tangible counterpart in Aeneas' trappings and their marriage, "all the reminders of that unspeakable man" (*nefandi / cuncta viri monimenta*), which Dido will set aflame along with herself.

The generalities, on the other hand, center as we have seen on the artificers rather than on their products. They define Aeneas, and the narrator of his tale, as Daedalus figures. Both particular points of contact and more broad equations persist in the second segment of Virgil's scheme. Critics have remarked on the abruptness with which Ariadne is introduced into the narrative at line 28. She is not named and, though she was a princess, she was certainly not, at least not at that moment in her eventful life, a *regina*. This apparent discontinuity, however, is actually a brilliant transition when we pursue our projection of the plot of Daedalus' psychological progress on to the *Aeneid*'s triple divisions. For, if in the life of Daedalus we move from Pasiphaë to Ariadne, in the artistic development of the *Aeneid* we stay with Dido, who need not be renamed and who remains the poem's great *regina*.[17] The difference is that, in the second movement of the *Aeneid*, her *crudelis amor* (now become *magnum amorem*) is resolved. When Aeneas sees her in the Underworld, in the company of those "whom harsh love has gnawed through with cruel wasting" (*quos durus amor crudeli tabe peredit*), she scorns him, fleeing into a shady grove:

> . . . coniunx ubi pristinus illi
> respondit curis aequatque Sychaeus amorem.
> (6.473-74)
> . . . where her former husband Sychaeus responds to her sufferings
> and returns equal love.

Differentiation leading to suicide has yielded, in book 6, to reciprocation and balance.

Yet we have been readied for this denouement earlier. At the conclusion of book 4, as we prepare to leave the epic's initial third for its central articulation, we have Virgil's first, enormously moving example of pity for suffering leading to its resolution. The moment is Dido's death:

> Tum Iuno omnipotens longum miserata dolorem
> difficilisque obitus Irim demisit Olympo
> quae luctantem animam nexosque resolveret artus.
> (4.693-95)
> Then all-powerful Juno, who pitied her long suffering and difficult
> death, sent down Iris from Olympus to release her struggling soul
> and her entwined limbs.

At the end pity releases the troubled queen from her enmeshed body, which is to say from the deceits of what Anchises is soon to call the blind prison which confines us within the toils of our destructive emotions.[18]

There is another Daedalian resolution, centering on book 6, that belongs more exactly to Aeneas. The literal labyrinth of Daedalus' manufacture (*hic labor ille domus*) becomes now symbolic, but equally present, in the hero's effortful life as he faces the prospect of descending, alive, into the world of the dead and returning whence he came. *Hoc opus, hic labor est*, "this the task, this the effort," says the Sibyl.[19] As preparation for this undertaking, Aeneas must attend to the *horrendas ambages*, the fearful enigmas of the seeress' utterances which correspond to the palpable but no less devious windings (*ambages*) of the Minotaur's dwelling. The Daedalian "threads" that bring resolutions to Aeneas' quandary are manifold. They consist not only in a growing clarity to the Sibyl's words but in the person of the Sibyl herself who will serve as guide through the Underworld's paths. He is, however, given further assistance by a series of talismans, first, the birds of his mother, then the golden bough—a very Daedalian object, serving now to open out rather than close in, to undeceive instead of dupe—his chief passport, to which the birds direct his traces. Finally we have the words of the poet Musaeus to whom the priestess turns for help in the search for Anchises.

If deceit is the chief impulse behind Daedalus' initial fabrications, pity rules him in their undoing. Though Aeneas does address Dido in his first words to her as the only person to have taken pity on the Trojans' sufferings, it is a virtue noticeably absent from the first four books. Yet here once more it is our changing viewpoint on the figure of Dido that helps us make the transition from segment to segment. At 4.369–70 she speaks to her former lover as if he were already absent:[20]

> "num fletu ingemuit nostro? num lumina flexit?
> num lacrimas victus dedit aut miseratus amantem
> est?"

> "Did he groan because of my tears? Did he bend his eyes toward me? Vanquished, did he shed tears or take pity on the one who loves him?"

This, we remember, is exactly what Aeneas does do here in the Underworld, though she refuses to respond to his plea for words:

> prosequitur lacrimis longe et miseratur euntem.
>   (6.476)

Weeping, he pursues her for a distance and pities her as she goes.

Aeneas has now performed the great act of which Dido had earlier found him negligent. He himself has—at last, and too late—also pitied the queen's love (*reginae . . . miseratus amorem*).

He had come to this emotion, for the first time in the epic, in the fifth book, which opens the *Aeneid*'s second of three divisions. There, at the end of the footrace, Aeneas pities the unfortunate Salius who had slipped during the competition (5.350–54). It is an emotion that he must receive as much as offer during this middle segment of the epic. He pities the unburied who are forced to wait at length before crossing the Styx. Yet he is also himself subject to three notable acts of pity during these books, from Jupiter, who saves his fleet, from the Sibyl and her inspirer, to both of whom he must pray, and from the Tiber in book 8. For this reach of the epic is Aeneas' most extended period of dependence, which proves at the same time to initiate him, and the reader of his saga, into the most elaborate revelations of the future. Pity of Sibyl and of river god lead him, one, to his father, the other, to the site of future Rome. Anchises parades before him future Roman heroic greats and gives him his ethical commission. Evander's tour of Pallanteum anticipates the grand city to come, and the shield, which Venus brings to Aeneas at Caere, concludes book 8 with another series of visions into heroic action, the *enarrabile textum* of Roman history.

In details, then, and from a larger viewpoint, during the second segment of the epic Virgil has his hero put behind him the deceitful, artifice-ridden atmosphere of the initial quartet of books. He replaces it with a portrait of the artisan-hero as pitier. Aeneas undoes his own dissimulations, or those thrust upon him, while the mazy mysteries that lead him to Rome's future are tantalizingly unraveled for him by others who offer him their rich solace in turn.

The last third of the epic can be treated more briefly. Its plot is the war in Latium, but the narrator tells a singularly purposeless tale. The omniscient reader knows from occasional prophecies that Aeneas will become overlord of Latium and marry Lavinia. But the fullness of the narrative dwells on the relentless futility and unceasing loss that war engenders. It furnishes a catalog of deaths, especially those of the young whose lives have been cut off near their starts. We think immediately of Nisus and Euryalus, of Pallas and Lausus, of Camilla and finally of Turnus. The rampage of slaughter that Aeneas embarks on after Pallas' death, in which he kills with equal indiscrimination suppliant and priest, takes its last victim in his primary antagonist who is wearing Pallas' belt. Yet for all his *violentia* and pride our sympathies lie at the end with Turnus, not with the titular hero, with Turnus beaten down by Jupiter's minion Fury and by the inner furies which set Aeneas at the last ablaze.

One of the framing emotions of this last quartet of books, as it is of the epic as a whole, is *dolor*. We find it in Turnus near the opening of book 9 as he casts a greedy eye on the leaderless Trojans penned within their camp:

> ignescunt irae, duris dolor ossibus ardet.
> (9.66)
> His anger flames up, and resentment burns in his hardened bones.

Or, soon again, in a speech of exhortation to his colleagues:

"sunt et mea contra
fata mihi, ferro sceleratam excindere gentem
coniuge praerepta; nec solos tangit Atridas
iste dolor, solisque licet capere arma Mycenis . . ."
(9.136–39)
"I also have my fate against theirs, with the sword to cut down a
criminal race who snatched away my bride; this resentment does
not touch the sons of Atreus alone, nor is it allowed Mycenae alone
to take up arms . . ."

It is remarkable how much of the same language recurs in the counter-balancing moment of anger with which the epic concludes. Aeneas, in his final words, accuses Turnus of possessing *scelerato sanguine*, criminal blood. The reader could presume that a variation of the reason Turnus gives for his own *dolor*—that Lavinia, his Helen, has been torn from him—is applicable also now to Aeneas, poised to kill because of the *dolor* aroused by the death of Pallas. In any case, though the last appearance of *dolor* doubly rounds out the epic to a splendid rhetorical and psychological moment of closure, it is, in senses that transcend mere personal feelings, an extraordinarily unfulfilling, not to say devastating, emotion. Turnus asks for pity and Aeneas does hesitate, as if he were preparing to respond with sympathy and practice *clementia*.[21] For Aeneas to grant pity through clemency, though it might appear an unheroic act by Homeric standards, would be for Virgil to round out the poem spiritually. He does not—cannot, perhaps—allow himself the luxury.[22]

I would like, in conclusion, to look in more detail at reasons why *dolor* leaves Aeneas-Daedalus-Virgil with his (their, if you prefer) heroic-artistic-poetic fabrication unfinished. First Aeneas-Daedalus. The ethical artistry imposed on Roman might, pursuing its political ends, was summarized, as we have seen, by Anchises to his son near the end of their meeting in the Underworld. The nub of his command, which he addresses to Aeneas as *Romane*, ancestor of and paradigm for his distinguished race, is to remember to spare the suppliant and war down the proud. By the end of the poem proud Turnus has been battled into abject submission, but, for whatever deep-seated reason, Aeneas does not spare him. He does not, finally, recall his father's admonition. Instead, in the narrator's words, he drank in the reminders of his fierce grief (*saevi monimenta doloris*) and, in an access of fury and rage, buries his sword in his opponent's chest. *Dolor* initiates Aeneas' final act. In so doing it gives the lie to Roman pretensions toward clemency, toward an artistic morality that reincorporates an antagonist, abased but living, into the civic community. Aeneas' attack of *dolor* proves the impossibility of realizing in fact Anchises' exhortation. In this case to complete is to idealize, to idealize is to dream untruths.[23]

Second, we must pursue the analogy of Virgil, the creator of the
Aeneid, and Daedalus. We are not now concerned with Aeneas' emotions
as they undermine Roman political artisanship but with the imagination
that shapes such an ending. My thesis is that Virgil deliberately leaves his
poem incomplete, vis-à-vis the epic genre as he inherited it, as if the
Aeneid were to serve as one final, magnificent metaphor—one masterful
artistic symbol—for the incompletions in Roman, which is to say human,
life. Let me illustrate my point with brief reminders of the plot endings of
four other major epics of which three (the *Iliad*, the *Odyssey*, and the
Argonautica of Apollonius Rhodius) precede the *Aeneid*, while the other,
Statius' *Thebaid*, follows.

First the *Iliad*. The bulk of its last book is taken up with the reconciliation scene between Priam and Achilles, but its last moments are devoted
to the aftermath of the burning of Hector's body:

> And when they [the people of Troy] were assembled together, first
> they quenched with flaming wine all the pyre, so far as the fire's
> might had come upon it, and thereafter his brethren and his com-
> rades gathered the white bones, mourning, and big tears flowed over
> down their cheeks. The bones they took and placed in a golden urn,
> covering them over with soft purple robes, and quickly laid the urn
> in a hollow grave, and covered it over with great close-set stones.
> Then with speed heaped they the mound, and round about were
> watchers set on every side, lest the well-greaved Achaeans should set
> upon them before the time. And when they had piled the barrow
> they went back, and gathering together duly feasted a glorious feast
> in the palace of Priam, the king fostered of Zeus. On this wise held
> they the funeral for horse-taming Hector.
>   (*Il.* 24.790–804)

The completion of a life demarcates the completion of a poem. The
careful rituals of burial and feast, that bring the funeral of Hector to
conclusion with communal ceremony, are complemented by the perfection of the epic that describes them, by poetry's own exacting ritual.

The twenty-second book of the *Odyssey* finds its hero taking revenge
with bloody slaughter on the suitors of Penelope. But the ending turns
this thirst for vengeance around. Zeus says to Athene in heaven:

> "Now that goodly Odysseus has taken vengeance on the wooers, let
> them swear a solemn oath, and let him be king all his days, and let us
> on our part bring about a forgetting of the slaying of their sons and
> brothers; and let them love one another as before, and let wealth and
> peace abound."
>   (*Od.* 24.482–86)

Thus, as Odysseus is preparing to kill the suitors' relatives bent, in their turn, on revenge, Athene speaks to him, bringing the epic to end:

> "Son of Laertes, sprung from Zeus, Odysseus of many devices, stay your hand, and make the strife of equal war to cease, lest haply the son of Cronos be wroth with you, even Zeus, whose voice is borne afar."
> So spoke Athene, and he obeyed, and was glad at heart. Then for all time to come a solemn covenant betwixt the twain was made by Pallas Athene, daughter of Zeus, who bears the aegis, in the likeness of Mentor both in form and in voice.
> (Od. 24.542–48)

Forgiveness, reconciliation, a commitment to peace, and a statement by the narrator of an eternal past to assure it—these are the gestures with which the Odyssey ends. Reintegration of society betokens poetic wholeness, and vice versa. Content and imagination are one.[24]

The ending of the Argonautica is simpler still as the singer speaks in his own voice:

> For now I have come to the glorious end of your toils; for no adventure befell you as you came home from Aegina, and no tempest of wind opposed you; but quietly did you skirt the Cecropian land and Aulis inside of Euboea and the Opuntian cities of the Locrians, and gladly did you step forth upon the beach of Pagasae.
> (4.1775–81)

Just as the Argonauts bring their journey to completion by returning whence they started, so the singer, proclaiming direct control over the matter of his verse, brings his own poetic voyage to a parallel stop.

Unfortunately we lack the final lines of any pre-Virgilian Latin epics. We must therefore jump in our survey to silver Latin and in particular to Statius who, at the end of his only completed epic, the Thebaid, directly acknowledges his indebtedness to Virgil. He finishes with an address to his own book:

> vive, precor; nec tu divinam Aeneida tempta,
> sed longe sequere et vestigia semper adora.
> mox, tibi si quis adhuc praetendit nubila livor,
> occidet, et meriti post me referentur honores.
> (12.816–19)
> Live, I pray you: and do not put the divine Aeneid to the test, but follow it at a distance and always adore its traces. Soon, if some dark

envy still stretches a cloud over you, it will perish, and deserved honors will be offered you after my time.

The ending of the narrative proper, which precedes the speaker's *sphragis*, is equally important for our purposes. After the hideous carnage of civil strife and Theseus' killing of Creon (the equivalent moment to the end of the *Aeneid*), who had refused to allow the dead to be buried, the warring factions forge a treaty as the women rejoice in the Athenian leader's calming presence. The epic's plot ends with due display of mourning for the fallen and with some of Statius' most beautiful (and most Virgilian) lines. I could not tell, says the speaker, even if I had a hundred voices, of all the cries of grief:

> Arcada quo planctu genetrix Erymanthia clamet,
> Arcada, consumpto servantem sanguine vultus,
> Arcada, quem geminae pariter flevere cohortes.
> vix novus ista furor veniensque implesset Apollo,
> et mea iam longo meruit ratis aequore portum.
>   (12.805–9)
> With what lament the Erymanthian mother mourns the Arcadian, the Arcadian, who keeps his beauty though all his blood is lost, the Arcadian for whom the twin hosts equally wept. Scarcely would new inspiration or Apollo's presence complete the task, and my far-voyaging bark now deserves her haven.[25]

Though he gives them new turns, especially in his elaboration of the autobiographical "seal," Statius essentially clings to the closure patterns of his generic inheritance. In fact he combines elements from the endings of all three Greek epics—ceremonies of lamentation from the *Iliad*, the *Odyssey*'s call for forgiveness and reconciliation, and Apollonius Rhodius' self-projection as traveler, appropriately completing at once his poetic journey and the heroic voyage it had sung.

It is important to notice not so much how influential Greek epic remains upon Statius' conclusion but how clearly the *Aeneid*'s finale is absent as an imaginative force on this most Virgilian of poets while he wrote his *envoi*. Hence to my point. In terms of its Greek epic past and its Roman poetic progeny, Virgil's *Aeneid* is a strikingly incomplete poem.[26] Its ending is equivalent to Achilles' killing of Hector, to the death of the suitors in the *Odyssey* or of Creon in the *Thebaid*. No Iliadic mourning breaks the spell of Aeneas' inexorable bloodlust.[27] Reconciliations akin to the *Odyssey*'s are mouthed in heaven but form no part in human action, as victor kills suppliant. Turning to the end of the *Argonautica*, which has its spiritual kinship to the *Odyssey*'s conclusion, we do not find in the *Aeneid*

any equivalent satisfactions. No wife is given Aeneas in a marriage ceremony that might give the epic's quasi-tragic ending a comic twist. Nor is
there a speaking "I," proud of his accomplishment, who could at least
abstract us at the end from the lived experience of the violence his story
tells into the imagination that fostered it.

We will never know what Daedalian *dolor* within Virgil caused him to
leave his epic so generically incomplete. (The ancient lives tell us that at
his death Virgil had failed only to apply his *ultima manus*, his finishing
touch, to the poem, not that it remained deficient in any substantial way.)
But I have a suggestion. Critics have long since, and quite correctly,
sensed a parallel between Icarus and the many people who die as they
follow in the wake of Aeneas. I listed earlier the most prominent losses in
the last quartet of books and it is well to remember that books 2 through
5 all end with deaths, of Creusa, Anchises, Dido, and Palinurus. The
clearest parallel structurally, however, is with the death of Marcellus, the
son of Augustus' sister and his adopted heir, whose funeral is described at
the end of the sixth book.[28] It is as if the poet were saying that the Roman
mission cannot go forward without loss of life, that the reality of death
ever looms as a counterbalance to progress.

What critics have not stressed is the concomitant parallel between
Aeneas and Daedalus. To do so is to turn from deaths suffered as the price
of empire to placing responsibility for those deaths.[29] The artisan loses his
son from his overreaching. Aeneas loses Pallas but he also kills Turnus.
These deaths receive the final emphasis which is on causes as much as on
results, on the perpetrator as much as on its victims.

The conclusion of the *Aeneid*, then, doubly uncloaks the deceptiveness
of art. Aeneas cannot fulfill his father's idealizing, and therefore deceptive, vision of Rome, and Virgil, the artisan of his tale, cannot show him
as so doing. Aeneas' final killing of Turnus differs from Daedalus' loss of
Icarus essentially for being active instead of passive. Each demonstrates
nature's final, Pyrrhic, triumph over art.

We may be meant to think that, as he crafted the *Aeneid*, in the process
of writing, of practicing his own art, Virgil followed his own voyage of
self-discovery and came with full assurance to see *dolor*, the immediacy of
suffering, frustration, resentment, as an overriding presence in human life
and therefore in his creative life. His plot line, which mimes and re-
produces the artist's growing inwardness, suggests a paradox: when, in
the course of his experience an artist forgoes his natural role as trickster,
and relieves his art of duplicity, in favor of truth of expression, his artifact,
as his life's work, is an apparent failure. To idealize is to envision wholeness in self and society, to claim consistency in their patternings. It is to
twist the tragic divisiveness of life's irrationality into comic returns, reconciliations, renewals. But Virgil, by ending his epic with two consequen-
tial acts of resentment, the one resulting in violence, the other from

having to accept that violence, does not finally idealize. His final artifice is the sham of forging art.

In sum, Virgil does, idiosyncratically, complete the *Aeneid* just as he completes with growing emotion the tale of Daedalus' inability to create. This carefully, brilliantly flawed wholeness is perhaps his passionate way of saying that art's feigned orderings do not, cannot, claim to control the uncontrollable. For a poet of consummate honesty, the truths of nature, Virgil would seem to say, are ever triumphant over the soothing trickery of art, however seductively its practitioners pattern their wares. For the art that supplants deceit with honesty, that composes life's imperfections, that unthreads its own labyrinthine text, not piety, or even pity, is possible, only the final, perfecting deficiencies of anger and sorrow.[30]

NOTES

1. The most recent discussions of the Daedalus episode are by Pöschl, "Tempeltüren" 119–23, who sees it as exemplifying the failure of art when the artist confronts the truth of his suffering; Weber, "Gallus' Grynium" 45–76, for whom the sequence serves as model for a miniature epyllion; and Fitzgerald, "Aeneas, Daedalus" 51–65. Fitzgerald's important essay views the two major segments of the tale as illustrating the change from "a finished work of art" to "the narrative of Daedalus, unfrozen and released into history" (54). In his earlier discussion, Pöschl, *Dichtkunst* 244–46 (Eng. tr. 149–50), draws analogies between Aeneas and Daedalus. Both are exiles, both offer pity at crucial moments (Daedalus for Ariadne, Aeneas for Dido), both exemplify *pietas* (Daedalus' love for Icarus is parallel, according to Pöschl, to Aeneas' yearning for Anchises with whom he is soon to be reunited). See also Weber, "Gallus' Grynium" 60 n. 33.

   Such analogies are further developed by Segal, *"Aeternum I"* 617–57, especially 642–45, in his sympathetic analysis of these lines. For Segal Daedalus "foreshadows the sufferings of the individual in the *mythical*, not the historical world, sufferings which lead to no lasting fruition in history, hence no transcendence of death."

   The legend of Daedalus has been treated in depth by Frontisi-Ducroux, *Dédale*, and by Koerner, *Suche*, who draws analogies between Daedalus and the modern mind dealing with its labyrinthine past while at the same time drawn toward self-sufficient flights into the ahistorical and the novel. Cf. also the remarks on Daedalus as typifying "the artist and magician" by Kris and Kurz, *Legend, Myth, and Magic* 66–71.

2. The authoritative discussion of the phrase *ut fama est* is by Norden, *Aeneis* ad loc. The variations on tradition which it implies are numerous. Foremost is the connection of Daedalus with Italy. Writers of the generation before Virgil return Daedalus to earth either in Sicily (Dio. Sic. 4.78) or Sardinia (Sall. *Hist.* fr. 2.7 [Maurenbrecher] from, among others, Servius on 6.14). By having him aim directly for Cumae, Virgil emphasizes the parallel with Aeneas which will gradually grow clearer as the ekphrasis evolves.

   By feigning to repeat tradition unemotionally and then significantly varying it, the narrator claims control over the history of his subject. The poet does the same generically. Virgil's model for Aeneas' arrival at Cumae as prelude to his visit to the Underworld is the opening of book 11 of the *Odyssey* where Odysseus reaches the land of the Cimmerians and immediately conjures up the spirits of the dead. No ekphrasis intervenes (cf. Knauer, *Aeneis* 130, n. 1). Therefore, even where Daedalus seems as yet indifferent to, or even unaware of, his loss, the narrator-poet is very involved with the tale so as to mold Daedalus, to make the sculptor his own artifact, to impress his stamp of originality on his artisan-hero. If Daedalus deepens his emotional involvement in his subjects over time, as he sets about the crafting of his psychic biography, the narrator has a deep imaginative commitment from the start.

3. According to Austin, *Liber Sextus* on 18 (following Norden, *Aeneis* on 18f.), the dedication to Apollo "marks his gratitude for a safe landing and also his retirement from air-travel, in the manner of many Greek dedicatory epigrams." But these strange oar-wings are also an offering for passing safely through the god's province in which men do not ordinarily trespass. (Virgil's only other use of the phrase *remigium / remigio alarum* is to describe the means of Mercury's descent from heaven at *Aen.* 1.301. The repetition here suggests a momentary equivalence between god and mortal who ascribes to the supernatural.) The overreacher might be expected to pay a penalty for challenging Apollo in his territory. The passive *redditus* implies that throughout this stage of his adventures Daedalus has in fact been the god's subject. Virgil may portray him as flying *praepetibus pinnis*, but Horace, in an ode of which Servius twice reminds us (on 15 and 18), sees the means of his journey as *pinnis non homini datis* (*C.* 1.3.35). Perhaps the implication is that Phoebus Apollo does claim recompense, in the form of Icarus, for earth-bound man's sally into the skies, for momentary human arrogation of divinity. As god-man, the ultimate in spiritual hybridization, the Orphic artist, fulfilling for an instant his imagination's divine claims, suffers a profound human loss.

By forcing us even here to meditate on the negative demands of progress, Virgil reminds us that, in the unfolding epic story, it has not been long since Neptune exacted *unum caput* (5.815), one life for the safe completion of Aeneas' journey to Italy through the god's watery element.

4. *OLD* (s.v. 1b) would translate *enavit* here as "to fly forth," but it is more enriching within the context to take the meaning as a metaphorical example of the dictionary's first definition: "to swim out or forth; (esp.) to escape by swimming; swim to safety." But, since Daedalus escaped the danger and the (pointedly) unnamed Icarus did not, the reader should rightly sense ambiguities in *praepetibus* and *levis*.

The first is an augural word, discussed in detail in relation to these lines by Aulus Gellius (*NA* 7.6). It appears four times in Ennius (Gellius mentions two instances) and lends a tone of majesty to the description of the artisan's epic accomplishment. As a term in augury it means "propitious," the opposite (according to Gellius' source, Figulus' *Augurii Privati*) of *infera* which he defines as a low-flying, less auspicious appearance. Its etymology is from *prae-peto*, "forward-seeking." As Gellius (followed closely by Servius on 6.15) expounds the meaning, the word becomes closely complementary to *enavit*:

> idcirco Daedali pennas "praepetes" dixit, quoniam ex locis in quibus periculum metuebat in loca tutiora pervenerat.

> Therefore he called the feathers of Daedalus "propitious" because he had come from places in which he feared dangers into safe places.

The reader, wondering why the narrator does not have Daedalus here include Icarus in his daring, sees *praepes* as "well omened" (at least for Daedalus!), as "flying directly ahead" (without a concern for the tragic events occurring behind?), and as "lofty" (unlike Icarus who, after rising too high, fell into the sea?). *Levis*, then, while primarily defining Daedalus' nimbleness, hints at a certain fickleness as well. Physical dexterity (or artistic talent, for that matter) does not necessarily ally itself with stability of mind.

5. Even here Virgil may possibly be alluding to Aeneas' tale. The seven bodies (*septena corpora*) of sons sent to Crete each year by the Athenians are reviewed shortly later in the *septem iuvencos* (38), the seven bullocks and the same number of heifers which Aeneas must now present to Apollo and Trivia. As the two myths follow their parallel progress, human offering is replaced by animal but in each case sacrifice is essential.

6. The standard article on Daedalus' labyrinth and its resonances for Virgil is by Enk, "Labyrinthi Imagine" 322–30.

7. The language is close to *Aen.* 7.282–83 where the horses given by Latinus to Aeneas are described as coming

> illorum de gente patri quos daedala Circe
> supposita de matre nothos furata creavit.

> from the stock of those (steeds) which cunning Circe, stealing them from her sire, bred bastard from the mare she had mated.

Aen. 6.24 and 7.283 document Virgil's only uses of the perfect participle of *suppono* in a sexual sense, and *furata* (7.283) echoes *furto* (6.24). The connection is further secured by Circe's epithet *daedala*. Circe is prone to the same erotic supposititiousness and "thievery" as the Athenian artificer. This supposititiousness is both literal and figurative. To "put under" sexually is fraudulently to replace the usual with the unexpected. The resulting miscegenation is, in book 7, between mortal and immortal (in the animal kingdom), in book 6, between human and animal. In each case generic mixing, as performed by Circe and Daedalus and re-created by the latter in sculpture, is typically Daedalian. Circe's hybrid horses anticipate the figures on the armor of Turnus: a Chimaera on his helmet (7.785–86), which, like Circe's horses (*spirantis naribus ignem*, 281), spouts fire (*efflantem faucibus ignis*), and Io in the process of metamorphosis from human into animal, *iam saetis obsit, iam bos*. Hybridization and metamorphosis complement each other in both instances. The latter, especially metamorphosis down from a higher to a lower sensibility, typifies book 7 as a whole (lines 660–61, e.g., offer an example of the furtive "mixing" of god and mortal). I trace the book's patterns of metamorphosis in further detail in chapter 5.

On the association of Turnus and the Minotaur, see duBois, *History* 39f., part of a thoughtful discussion of Daedalus' sculptures.

8. It remains deliberately ambiguous whether *caeca vestigia* refer to the unseeing steps of Theseus or to the Labyrinth's dark path. Support for the former proposition comes from Catullus' reference to Theseus' *errabunda vestigia* (64.113) and from later imitations (cf. Austin, *Liber Sextus* on 30), for the latter from Virgil's earlier description of the Labyrinth with its dark walls (*caecis parietibus*, *Aen.* 5.589) and from the sentence structure whose logic suggests a sequence from *ambages* to *caeca vestigia*. In either case the artisan is directly involved, though his duplex activity lends different shades of meaning to *regens*. He becomes Ariadne and empathetically "leads" her lover to safety, or "straightens" the windings of his Labyrinth, unraveling the unravelable out of pity. *Inextricablis* (27), Varro's coinage to describe Porsena's Etruscan labyrinth (Pliny *HN* 36.91), helps define the Labyrinth's puzzlement and toils, and adds a further dimension to Catullus' parallel, *inobservabilis* (64.115, itself a coinage), whose point is absorbed into Virgil's *caeca*. Virgil's Daedalus first creates, and then solves, the problems of his "text."

The influence of Catullus 64 on the Daedalus episode as a whole, most recently treated by Weber, "Gallus' Grynium" 47, 50–51, deserves further study. It begins with similarities between the Argonauts and Daedalus through the primacy of their daring (there is a common emphasis on nimbleness, oarage, and swimming in both initial episodes), develops in close parallels between the poet's treatments of Androgeos (64.77–83; *Aen.* 6.20–22) and the Labyrinth (64.113–15; *Aen.* 6.28–30), and concludes with loss. In Catullus the loss is double. Ariadne loses Theseus, Theseus Aegeus. In Virgil Daedalus misses Icarus alone.

9. Perhaps the artist unravels his artistry, out of manifest pity, to abet the love of others for fear that it might bring doom on himself. At the least his uniting of two other lovers anticipates the loss of love in his own life. (For the relation of pity and fear, see Pucci, *Violence of Pity* 169–74.)

10. This point is valid for the ekphrasis as a whole. We are earlier made aware of the placement of sculptures (*in foribus*), of the dynamic interrelationship between episodes (*respondet*), of the specifics of location within a scene (*hic . . . hic*). The absence of a word for crafting in the Ariadne vignette is particularly telling. Because the Icarus scene could not be started, we assume that Ariadne's story, which precedes it, was brought to completion, but nothing in the narrative attends to this. Instead, while Daedalus implements the penultimate, and the second most emotional, episode in his artistic biography, the narrator of his tale shows him in the emotional act of unraveling his past art, not in the dispassionate formation of it. Even here, though we are led to presume one act of artistic fulfillment, emotion directly undoes the mind's creation.

11. Though Virgil on three occasions repeats *bis* in a line or between adjacent lines (*Aen.* 2.218, 6.134, 9.799–800), only once elsewhere does he employ it in anaphora at the opening of contiguous verses, 11.629–30, which is also the only instance where the two uses of *bis* contrast with rather than reinforce each other. The

context is the ebb and flow of war which in turn, if we look at the last four books as a whole, analogizes its futility.

The parallel with 6.134–35, where the Sibyl remarks on Aeneas' *cupido*

> bis Stygios innare lacus, bis nigra videre
> Tartara . . .

> Twice to swim the Stygian lakes, twice to see black Tartarus . . .

no doubt strengthens the bond between Daedalus and Aeneas. Though Aeneas does in fact complete his Underworld journey, where Daedalus fails to finish his sculpture, the verbal interconnection may be one of Virgil's several subtle ways in book 6 of questioning the success of Aeneas', or Rome's, enterprise. There is, however, a later moment in book 6 with an even richer correlation to lines 32–33. When Aeneas finally reaches Anchises, son tries to embrace father (6.700–701):

> ter conatus ibi collo dare bracchia circum;
> ter frustra comprensa manus effugit imago . . .

> Three time he there attempted to offer his embrace; three times the *imago*, grasped in vain, fled his hands.

The lines are repeated from book 2 (792–93) where Aeneas fails in his attempt to clasp the ghost of Creusa. Both events document the hero's inability throughout the epic to achieve emotional fulfillment (he does embrace his mother at 8.615 but at her insistence, not his). As critics note, Daedalus' inability to sculpt Icarus after two attempts may be modeled on Odysseus' triple attempt, and triple failure (*Od.* 11.206–8), to embrace the spirit of his mother (cf. Pöschl, "Tempeltüren" 121; Fitzgerald, "Aeneas, Daedalus" 63, n. 18). This, of course, was Virgil's model in the episodes of books 2 and 6 (the imitation, in the case of the latter, has most recently been noted by Austin, *Liber Sextus* ad loc.). But further potential meanings of this last anticipation in the Daedalus story of the later narrative of book 6 must not be overlooked. If Daedalus cannot perfect the loss of his son in art, can Aeneas finally fulfill the *pietas* owed to Anchises, especially given the strong need for *clementia* with which his father overlays his future loyalty?

It is noteworthy that the fall of Icarus is alluded to only by paranomasia in the word *casus*. The fall of Daedalus' hands, however, suggests that now, finally, the artisan experiences a version of his son's misfortune. Father becomes son. The son's physical fall is reiterated in the father's emotional collapse. Empathetically, literal death is the death of art.

12. I examine the reasoning behind Aeneas' actions at this crucial moment in chapter 8.

13. See especially Duckworth, "Trilogy" 1–10, revised and expanded in Duckworth, *Structural Patterns* 11–13.

14. The parallels between the wooden horse and Daedalus' cow and Labyrinth are noteworthy. In each case they include *doli* (2.44), accompanied by the supportive wiles of Thymoetes, Sinon, Epeos—the Daedalian *doli fabricator* (264)—and the Greeks (34, 62, 152, 196, 252), trickery (18, 258), and *error* (48). In both instances a hybrid animal produces a monstrous birth. Both the

cow and horse are mounted on wheels as they implement the subterfuge (Dio. Sic. 4.77, Apollodorus 3.1.4, for the cow; *Aen.* 2.235–36, for the horse). Daedalus' gift to Pasiphaë therefore resembles the Greeks' gift to Minerva, the *innuptae donum exitiale Minervae* (2.31), which the art of the goddess has helped produce (*divina Palladis arte*, 15). At this stage of his career and in this particular instance, Daedalus anticipates both duplicitous Greeks and crafty Minerva as they bring into being the *machina . . . feta armis* (2.237–38), the horse and its destructive brood.

15.   Allusions to deceit begin, in book 1, at 130 where Neptune becomes aware of the *doli* and *irae* of his sister Juno. Out of eighteen uses of *dolus* in the *Aeneid*, ten are in books 1–4.

16.   Dido, in this matter as in others, is an accomplice in her own downfall, asking, at the end of book 1 (750–52), for Aeneas to retell the known as well as the novel in Troy's demise, and reiterating the request as her tragic love deepens (4.77–79).

   Yet, whereas the sculptures of book 1 lead diachronically toward Aeneas' narrative, as he "sculpts" Troy's fall and manages Dido's death, and the shield of book 8 details Rome's future in linear progression, Daedalus' artistry analogizes the whole of the epic on several levels, offering a series of synchronic paradigms. The two longer ekphraseis, by dwelling, in the first instance, on Aeneas' response, in the second, on Vulcan's craftsmanship, retain a strong specific point of focus that the Daedalian sculptures, with their lack of concern with the crafter at work or the viewer reacting, carefully forgo.

   Aeneas' perception of the sculptures on Juno's temple is discussed, with great sensitivity, by Johnson, *Darkness Visible* 99–105. By contrast with the earlier episode, the narrator does not allow us to learn how far in his examination of Daedalus' sculptures Aeneas had proceeded (*quin protinus omnia perlegerent oculis, ni . . .* , 33–34), though we presume that his "reading" was near to completion. In any case only narrator and reader, not the poem's protagonists, know of Daedalus' final suffering. But perhaps a similar event will occur in Aeneas' life. At the moment in book 8 when Aeneas is about to set out from Pallanteum, taking himself and Pallas to war, we find him, and Achates, "pondering many hardships in his sad heart" (*multa . . . dura suo tristi cum corde putabant*, 8.522). To break his spell of contemplation Venus sends as sign a lightning bolt and resounding thunder (*iterum atque iterum fragor increpat ingens*, 527). Aeneas will not explain what *casus* (533) this betokens, only that he must go into battle. But he may already sense the loss of Pallas with its many ramifications of incompletion in his life. It is a *fragor* (493), three times heard in Avernus, which, in the fourth *Georgic*, signals Eurydice's death caused by the *furor* (495) of Orpheus. The reader schooled in Virgil's symbolic modes is prepared to await a parallel misfortune as the *Aeneid* draws to a close and Aeneas, potential artist of Rome, undoes his work by his own version of madness.

17.   Looked at within the bounds of books 1–4, the story of Dido shares common ground with that of Daedalus and, partially, of Aeneas. It begins with double artistic accomplishment—an extraordinary city being built with a magnificent temple at its heart, a disciplined civilization arising to bring order to the territory around it—and ends with a series of *dolores* (419, 474, 547,

679, and the death agony at 693; cf. the uses of *doleo* at 393 and 434). These destroy, literally, the queen and, symbolically, the city she had founded. Pöschl, *Dichtkunst* 246 and note (Eng. tr. 150 and 207 n. 17), recognizes the parallel between Ariadne and Dido *regina*.

18. The complex *resolveret* is simplified shortly later in *solvo* (703). For Dido here, as for Pasiphaë, passion creates the need for subterfuge, for *doli* (563), which only augment and finalize the *doli* of Venus and Juno that initiate her tragedy (95, 128) and of Aeneas who furthers it (296, the narrator's word). In Daedalus' artistic, which is to say psychic, life, *doli* precede *dolor*. For Dido *dolor* both anticipates and is precipitated by her resort to *doli* (see n. 17). The release of Dido from her entrapment, cares, and body, unmeshed at once (*me . . . his exsolvite* she cries to Aeneas' *dulces exuviae*, at 652), is the reader's release into the second third of the epic. Aeneas is the major Daedalian figure in Dido's life, but it is Virgil who frees her from his text.

19. Fitzgerald, "Aeneas, Daedalus" 63 n. 13, sees a probable connection between Labyrinth and Underworld. The link is strengthened by appeal to the Sibyl's definition of Aeneas' *labor*:

> sed revocare gradum superasque evadere ad auras . . .
>   (128)

> but to recall one's step and make one's way out to the breezes above . . .

Though Aeneas' "mad enterprise" (*insano . . . labori*, 135) works on the vertical plane while the Labyrinth presents a horizontal complexity, the parallels between the two adventures, where the hero must enter treacherous territory, engage in an arduous challenge or challenges, and return out alive, are suggestive. They are supported by the narrator's striking, ironic designation—and presumably Daedalus' depiction—of the Labyrinth as a *domus*. It will not be long before Aeneas will cross the *atri ianua Ditis* (127) and enter the *vestibulum* (273) in order to make his way *per . . . domos Ditis* (269).

Among the monsters Aeneas must soon thereafter pass by are *Scyllae biformes* (286). (Virgil's only two uses of the word are at 25 and here.) It will not be long before he crosses the *inremeabilis unda* of the Styx (425), an adjective used of the *error* of the Labyrinth at 5.591 and akin to the rare *inextricabilis* at 6.27. These difficulties past, Aeneas, as we shall see, continues his Daedalian enterprise with his pity for Dido and with his manifold inability to embrace his father.

20. Cf. also Dido's plea to Aeneas at 4.318—*miserere domus labentis*—and her later command to Anna, *miserere sororis* (435).

21. See n. 23.

22. If we pursue the analogy between Daedalus and Aeneas as we reach the poem's conclusion, we could say that in terms of life's terminations the two are successful. Each has reached a goal. Daedalus gains Cumae and constructs a notable artifact (*immania templa*), an awesome temple to Apollo. Aeneas, too, has come to Italy and defeated the enemy who, presumably, has stood in the way of his founding the Roman race. But to turn biographical completions into art, to make them appear as art, is for each a different, highly inconclusive matter.

23. By the end of his epic Aeneas could also be seen as an Icarus figure, the most palpable sign of his father's artistry, realistic proof of how idealizing are Anchises' notions of *clementia*. (We remember that it is Anchises, not Aeneas, who initiates the sparing of Achaemenides in the epic's third book.) Daedalus' *dolor*, yearning for his lost son, which may well include resentment and self-hatred also, results only in artistic incompletion. Aeneas' *dolor*, where loss is directly linked to furies' fires, to *saevitia* and *ira*, leads to a resentful, passionate killing with far more complex intimations of failure.

   Forgetful Aeneas is made to mimic careless Icarus with the forceful difference, of course, that Aeneas lives on. For him, in Virgil's richly ironic narrative, survival is the equivalent of over-reaching Icarus' plummeting into the sea, and this survival means the end of his father's art.

   The "celestial" plot of the *Aeneid* concludes with Jupiter yielding to Juno's demand that all things Trojan submerge their identity in the Latin present and future. What follows, therefore, up to the epic's last lines, is in fact the intellectual birth of Rome, as Aeneas becomes, according to his father's definition, *Romanus* (6.851). Two actions are paramount. First, Jupiter co-opts the Dirae to warn Juturna and her brother of the latter's impending death. Second, Aeneas kills Turnus. In the first deed heaven summons hell to motivate earthly doings for the last time in the epic but for the first, one could surmise, in Virgil's Roman history, as history's cycle starts anew. The second, Aeneas' concluding deed, becomes the initial Roman action. Motivated by inner furies, it betokens a continuum of passion and anger, portending the impossibility of any new aesthetic or ethical wholeness.

24. The case for the authenticity of the *Odyssey* from 23.297 to the end is argued persuasively by Moulton, "End of the *Odyssey*" 153–69.

25. His beloved Virgil is here on Statius' mind, but the Virgil not of the *Aeneid* but of *Georgic* 4 (525–27).

26. The abrupt conclusion of *De Rerum Natura* offers the closest parallel in earlier literature to the end of the *Aeneid*. I strongly support the view of Clay, *Lucretius* 251, that Virgil's "grim and unresolved" finale deliberately echoes both the style and tone of his great predecessor.

27. The reversals of the *Iliad* in the *Aeneid* deserve separate study. The *Aeneid* ends in one respect where the *Iliad* begins. Achilles' anger at the start of the *Iliad* turns to forgiveness at the end. The story of Aeneas, on the other hand, begins with the hero's suppression of *dolor* (1.209), for hardships experienced in the past, and ends with his outburst of *dolor* over the loss of Pallas. In at least one episode of the *Aeneid* the reversal directly concerns Achilles. In Pyrrhus' vengeful killing of Priam, Achilles' anger lives on. It too, of course, is an emotion that spurs on Aeneas to his final deed (*ira terribilis* is the narrator's characterization of Aeneas immediately before his final speech, 12.946–47). Is it mere coincidence that Helenus bestows the *arma Neoptolemi* (3.469) on Aeneas as his parting gift?

28. The parallel is developed with sensitivity by Segal, "*Aeternum II*" 34–72, especially 50–52. Cf. also Rutledge, "Vergil's Daedalus" 311, and Pöschl, "Tempeltüren" 120.

29. Fitzgerald, "Aeneas, Daedalus" 54, rightly notes that Daedalus' tale delivers him "from the past [that his artwork first encapsulated] into the painful and unfinished world of history." He pursues his insight by concluding that Aeneas, as Daedalus, is forced into a tragic history "that forfeits the comfort of closure."

30. The truth of Aeneas' emotions at the end of book 12, as in the Helen episode in book 2, leads to artistic inconclusions, in the first instance because the text (2.567–88) would be expunged by, and nearly lost because of, Varius and Tucca, in the second because it leads not to potential elimination but to aspects of incompletion. The first episode suggests, too early and too strongly, it might have been said, the truth of the hero's emotionality. The second cannot be argued away, though its author sought to destroy it as part of his whole epic. It forms a special complement to the first. Virgil stops at a moment of the greatest honesty, which demonstrates Anchises' model to be one based on wishful thinking while Aeneas' violent response to Turnus and the emotional thrust behind it speak the truth. This truth brings about, literally and splendidly, the end of art.

AENEID 7

AND THE

AENEID

I would like to deal here with the theme of metamorphosis in the *Aeneid*, specifically in the seventh book. In so doing I will touch again on a topic rightly of growing concern to Virgil scholars—the meaning of the final moments of the epic and some of the questions its hero's actions raise about Rome and human life.

At the end of book 6 of the *Aeneid*, Aeneas and the Sibyl, under the direction of father Anchises, issue forth from the Underworld through the ivory gate of Sleep. This is the gate, the poet tells us, whence the spirits send *falsa insomnia*, treacherous, misleading nightmares, to the world above. There had been no mention of *portae* at the entrance, only a *vestibulum* and *fauces*, *limen* and *fores* leading into the house of Dis. The way down is easy, the Sibyl predicted, but suffering and trial await the moment of departure. That there is no apparent *labor* in Aeneas' withdrawal adds to the effect of Virgil's words and forces the reader to ponder their symbolism for the books which follow.

We can divine something of his meaning by turning back to the description of the shapes Aeneas sees on first entering Hades. They lurk, ready to make their way to the earth above, where they must spend a great deal of their time. Among other equally hideous personifications we find, at the end of the list, *Bellum*, the furies in their iron chambers, and mad *discordia*, her snaky hair bound with bloody fillets.

It is not long before all these vices will have full opportunity for display. At 6.86–87 the Sibyl in her trance cries:

> . . . bella, horrida bella
> et Thybrim multo spumantem sanguine cerno.

> I see wars, frightful wars, and the Tiber frothing with much blood.

The vision soon becomes a reality. In the next book the priest who interprets the omens of the bees and Lavinia's flaming hair for Latinus agrees that she will be renowned in report and reputation (*illustrem fama fatisque*, 7.79). The signs also portend a *magnum bellum* for the people. And Juno, addressing the unfortunate girl in her thoughts, can gloat:

> sanguine Troiano et Rutulo dotabere, virgo,
> et Bellona manet te pronuba . . .
> (7.318–19)

> You will be dowered with blood both Trojan and Rutulian, maiden,
> and Bellona awaits you as bridal matron . . .

Blood will be shed by both sides in the ensuing gory "marriage" of peoples over which the goddess of war will preside.[1]

As for the Furies one need only refer to the devastating role Allecto plays in book 7 and the anonymous *Dira* in book 12. And *discordia*, which Allecto boasts of "perfecting" at 7.545, is but another name for *impius Furor* who for a brief moment is locked by Jupiter's words in the temple of Janus (1.293–96). Juno's more realistic thrusting open of the twin gates of War (*geminae Belli portae*, 7.607) releases an unstated Discord (and a host of warriors) whose effects can be immediately gauged.

There is another set of creatures who cluster at the entrance to Hell, on or around an aged elm. These consist, with one exception to be mentioned in a moment, of Centaurs, Scyllas, Briareus, the Lernaean Hydra, the Chimaera, Gorgons, Harpies, and Geryon. Aeneas would have attempted to kill them had not the Sibyl assured him that they were slender beings without flesh (*tenuis sine corpore vitas*) and that they floated around as specters of empty shape (*cava sub imagine formae*). Their lives are hollow and bodiless, and what form they have is only an image. Aeneas cannot kill them by a sword thrust which would act only against body. Their workings are more subtle. Many act on the spirit and take "physical" shape only in human natures gone sufficiently awry to serve as visible symbols for the mind's madness.

Aeneas would have been acquainted with two members of this catalog from previous experience. In the real-unreal transitional world of book 3 he knows enough of Scylla's threat to skirt the danger. Not so with the Harpies, who bring out the worst in him. He declares causeless war on their cattle (*inruimus ferro*, 3.223) and on them:

> . . . sociis tunc arma capessant
> edico, et dira bellum cum gente gerendum.
>
> (3.234–35)
>
> I then order my comrades to seize arms, and that war must be waged with the dread race.

Misenus, who is later killed for vying with a god, trumpets them into battle. Celaeno, *furiarum maxima*, sums up the event with a question:

> bellum etiam pro caede boum stratisque iuvencis,
> Laomedontiadae, bellumne inferre paratis
> et patrio Harpyias insontis pellere regno?
>
> (3.247–49)

Sons of Laomedon, is it even war in return for the slaughter of cattle
and slain bullocks, is it war you are preparing to offer and to drive
the guiltless Harpies from their ancestral kingdom?

Unnecessary slaughter of cattle leads to war against rightful inhabitants.
Celaeno curses them with hunger and Aeneas misremembers her words
as those of his father when the curse is fulfilled at 7.107–34.

The same pattern begins to rework itself when Celaeno's kindred fury,
Allecto, stirs up the Italian world in book 7. Madness seizes Iulus' hounds
and ambition their master, in the pursuit of Silvia's tamed stag. Italy has
been for some time at peace. The inherent strength of a wild though
pastoral people has been molded to the uses of civilization and prosperous, georgic living. Aeneas brings madness with him and, in rousing
opposition, renews a natural rudeness. But it is a rudeness in defense of
one's own, like the Harpies' care for their land. However distasteful the
external image they present, the treatment is undeserved.

In book 3 the Harpy-Furies are still *Odyssey*-like personifications of
emotion. The Trojans' violent action rouses direct retaliation. But Virgil
takes what appears a literal myth and gradually turns it into a figment of
the mind, with potency more latent. In book 6 Aeneas reacts in physical
fashion to the metaphysical, naturally enough from his past experience.
His attack, however, is only against the spiritual causes of anguish, somehow visible though only *imagines*. The curious fact is that Aeneas himself
is one of these. He leaves the Underworld as a *falsum insomnium*. Yet
Somnia vana stand ready at Hell's entrance, along with Grief, Suffering,
and a host of other monsters, to make facile way up to torture mankind.

These other creatures will soon enter directly into Aeneas' life. Of the
list quoted earlier (and with the exception of Scylla and the Harpies, who
appear in book 3), only one, Briareus, does not make some appearance in
book 7. Geryon is mentioned at 8.662 as the victim of Hercules. The fury
Allecto, who starts the war, is tainted with the Gorgon's poisons (*Gorgo-
neis infecta venenis*, 7.341). In the catalog of enemies who are to confront
Aeneas, Catillus and Coras are compared to Centaurs. Aventinus carries
the Hydra as shield device and Turnus' crest sports a Chimaera. Briareus
finds proper replacement in *saevus* Orion, who appears in a simile comparing the forces of Clausus to the waves of the Libyan sea (7.719). These
are the "monsters" whom Aeneas is to confront, and Virgil builds up
their prowess accordingly.[2] But we should not forget that Latinus was
ruling over cities quiet after long peace (*longa placidas in pace*, 7.46) before
Aeneas' arrival.[3] The full extent of the *falsum insomnium*, the nightmare
Aeneas himself conveys and the emotions he thereby arouses, awaits final
revelation only at the epic's conclusion. Aeneas is the source of Rome's
heroic lineage, yet he brings torments with (and in) himself as he leaves
the Underworld. The twin gates of Sleep and the twin gates of War have

their parallels. Some of the poet's intent, however, can be determined from the opening of book 7, to which we now must turn.

It begins on a particularly gloomy note—*tu quoque . . . Caieta*. No heroic invocation here. That occurs—if such it can be called—only after some thirty verses of intense symbolic revelation (the prayer to Erato) and then again after six hundred more lines where the goddesses of Helicon are called upon to help survey an Italy roused to war. The word *quoque* recalls that Palinurus and Misenus have recently died and given their names to nearby places. Caieta is noteworthy for being the nurse of Aeneas (*Aeneia nutrix*). She cherished Aeneas as Italy, *terra alma*, nourishes those who will oppose him. We are reminded that, in spite of the ending of book 6, Aeneas is alive as well as dead, that he is real as well as a dream, and that the process of his growth continues now into maturity. But we are given a careful message also in these opening lines. Everlasting fame (*famam*) is gained only at the price of death (*moriens*). Honor (*honos*) is balanced by a tomb (*sedem*), reputation (*nomen*) keeps guard only over bones (*ossa*)—if there is any glory in that, the poet adds.[4]

The warning, to Aeneas through Caieta, is that progress demands sacrifice and that reputation is bought by death. The oracle of Faunus soon makes the same point in an ambiguous utterance whose negative implications Latinus does not seem to grasp. The newly arrived Trojans are a race, the voice says, "who by blood will bring our reputation to the stars" (*qui sanguine nostrum / nomen in astra ferant*, 7.98–99 = 271–72). Blood is a price as well as a cause of renown.

Anchises, at the end of book 6, kindled in his son's mind yearning for coming glory (*incendit . . . animum famae venientis amore*, 6.889). Virgil now warns that any search for *fama* may mislead even to the point of bringing death. The reputation of the past, he later tells us, glides on scarcely even a slender breath (*ad nos vix tenuis famae perlabitur aura*, 7.646). For *fama* may become *Fama*, daughter of earth, a *monstrum horrendum, ingens* (7.181), ready to spread truth and falsehood with equal ease in Carthage. She is already loose in Italy at the moment of the Trojans' arrival (102ff.). This time, however, the actual revolution is accomplished by still more vigorous partisans. One of them, it must be noted, is Ascanius who, in pursuing Silvia's stag, is fired with a yearning of extraordinary praise (*eximiae laudis succensus amore*, 7.496).

Aeneas next passes by the shores of Circe. The adventure is not superfluous but serves as precursorial symbol for the whole book.[5] She is the daughter of the Sun but works by moonlight. She seduces by the senses. We see her groves, her proud house, her lights, and slender weaving. We listen to her songs and smell the cedar she burns. Yet we also hear the angry groans and roars of the men she has changed to animals and visualize the tension and incoherence in their beings. They rage (*saevire*) as she is wrathful (*saeva*). They have only the shapes of beasts (*formae*).

Who once had the visage of humans (*hominum ex facie*) now possess the features and frames of animals (*vultus ac terga ferarum*). They are men forced to adopt the characteristics of beasts. Circe signifies the power that causes and then effects such a hideous transformation, whatever the many emotional guises each example of her craft may assume.

The groaning of the beasts recalls a moment of more intensive, elaborate horror in book 6—Phlegethon, at whose gate Tisiphone presides, whence issue the moans of the tortured and the shrieks of whips. In book 7 the description is circumscribed:

> hinc exaudiri gemitus iraeque leonum
> vincla recusantum et sera sub nocte rudentum, . . .
> (7.15–16)
> Hence are heard the angry groans of lions, irritated at their bonds and roaring late into the night, . . .

The corresponding lines in book 6 introduce a lengthier roster of terrors:

> hinc exaudiri gemitus et saeva sonare
> verbera, tum stridor ferri tractaeque catenae.
> (6.557–58)
> Hence groans are heard, and savage lashings resound, then the creaking of iron and the dragging of chains.

"*Quae scelerum facies?*" (6.560) Aeneas first asks the Sibyl. She responds with example after example. Nevertheless, she concludes, even with a hundred tongues and a voice of iron she could not detail all the different types of crimes (*omnes scelerum . . . formas*, 6.626).[6] These are the actual shapes of crime as well as its instruments. Tisiphone guards those who have twisted themselves by misdeeds. Circe is a symbol of the power that transforms. The road branches in book 6 and Aeneas is guided toward the Elysian Fields. In book 7, though he appears to pass Circe by, his life takes a more realistic turn.

The intervention of Neptune apparently prohibits the pious Trojans from "suffering" such monsters, but Circe's influence penetrates the book. We hear of Picus

> . . . equum domitor, quem capta cupidine coniunx
> aurea percussum virga versumque venenis
> fecit avem Circe sparsitque coloribus alas.
> (7.189–91)
> . . . a tamer of horses, whom his wife Circe, seized by desire, made into a bird, stricken with her wand and transformed by her potions, and sprinkled his wings with colors.

The only way that Circe's lust can keep love is to transform it into bestial form, not elevate to divinity (as Homer's Calypso proposes to Odysseus). This *cupido* demands the perverse loss of human shape and lives by diversity of superficial texture alone (her multiform animals are paralleled in the variety of colors Picus assumes here). So at line 282 Circe is styled *daedala* because, as craftsman of eccentricities, she delights in a multitude of appearances.

Though now a bird, Picus had been an *equum domitor*. The same epithet is given to two of the warriors (Lausus, 651, and Messapus, 691) in the concluding list of the marshaled Italians. Circe herself also makes two appearances in the catalog. The grove of Angitia, we learn at 759, will weep for Umbro, the Marruvian. As Medea (or her sister—commentators differ) transplanted, she would be Circe's niece. Umbro was a priest and magician:

> vipereo generi et graviter spirantibus hydris
> spargere qui somnos cantuque manuque solebat,
> mulcebatque iras et morsus arte levabat.
> (7.753–55)
> who was accustomed to sprinkle sleep on the race of vipers and on heavy-breathing hydras by song and by touch, and who soothed their anger and alleviated their bites by his art.

But there are stronger vipers and hydras on the loose, stronger enchantments and deeper angers than he can control. He has no power against a Trojan wound. Virgil devotes to him the most poignant lines in the book, reminiscent of Orpheus weeping for Eurydice:

> te nemus Angitiae, vitrea te Fucinus unda,
> te liquidi flevere lacus.
> (7.759–60)
> For you the grove of Angitia, for you with its glassy wave, Fucinus, for you the clear lakes wept.

Finally among the followers of Turnus are those who work the *Circaeum iugum* (799). They could absorb her influence firsthand.

Cedarwood figures of early Latin heroes (the Trojans would know the smell from Circe's shores) and the admonitory statue of Picus ushered Aeneas' ambassadors into the court of Latinus. They took away with them another example of the goddess' handiwork:

> absenti Aeneae currum geminosque iugalis
> semine ab aetherio spirantis naribus ignem

illorum de gente patri quos daedala Circe
supposita de matre nothos furata creavit.
   (7.280–83)

For the absent Aeneas (he chooses) a chariot and twin horses of
etherial seed breathing fire from their nostrils and sprung from the
stock of those (steeds) which cunning Circe, stealing them from her
sire, bred bastard from the mare she had mated.

The novelty of fire-breathing horses, Virgil's usual symbol for war, horses
part divine, part mortal, would have appealed to the monster-maker
Circe. Aeneas would not realize the full implication of receiving such an
apt gift.[7] Virgil gives us a hint when he describes the quasi-allegorical
Chimaera Turnus wears on his helmet's crest as "breathing Etna's fires
from its jaws" (*Aetnaeos efflantem faucibus ignis*, 786). The kinship with
spirantis naribus ignem is inescapable.[8]

   I will anticipate later, more thorough investigation of the possibilities
of Circean metamorphosis by drawing attention to one detail in the
description of Picus' transformation. Circe accomplishes her act by po-
tions (*versum venenis / fecit avem Circe*, 190–91). The verb *verto* has many
special places in book 7, none more important than in the description of
the fury Allecto. Like the changes that she wreaks on people (or, more
exactly, the latent, devastating characteristics she draws to the surface),
she is a creature of varied shapes (*tot sese vertit in ora*, 7.328). The words
echo an ambiguity inherent in a remark Juno had just made—"I turned
myself to all resources (into all things)" (*memet in omnia verti*, 7.309).
Allecto alone is left. She has many fierce faces (*saevae facies*, 7.329), many
facades for the beast within us.[9] Her counterpart Circe, *dea saeva*, can
alter the faces of men with potent herbs. Allecto, too, makes use of subtle
medicines. She is stained with poisons (*infecta venenis*, 7.341) when she
first sets out against Amata. Her disease slips into the maddened queen
with damp venom (*udo veneno*, 7.354). She breathes in a viper's soul
(*vipeream animam*, 7.351) against which there is no recourse.

   The Tiber's mouth at which the Trojans now land would seem at first
a happy alternative to Circe's shores. Night turns into day.[10] The *vada
fervida* which swirl near Circe's shores give place to *lento marmore*, a calm,
sluggish sea. The similarity of the two descriptions seems to set one place
off from the other. Circe's *inaccessos lucos* (7.11) become the *ingentem
lucum* (7.29), which Aeneas enters happily. Her unceasing song (*adsiduo
cantu*, 7.12) yields to the bird calls which now soothe the air (*cantu*, 7.34).
The Tiber exerts its own form of magic charm, with deep groves and
gripping voices. Indeed it could be argued that it carries over into the
Italian landscape the very changeability that Circe can exercise. The sea
outside may be quiet, but the Tiber itself presents a different spectacle

more akin to Circe's swollen floods than not. It swirls down with rapid turnings (*verticibus rapidis*)—the importance of the latent metaphor is already apparent—and breaks forth (*prorumpit*) into the sea, as if its violence had been hemmed in or was at last spent.[11] It is not long before we contemplate the spectacle of all Italy gone wild after Juno breaks open War's iron gates (*rumpit*, 7.622). Aeneas may not sense this (he is *laetus* at the prospect of the stream), but Virgil gives us a careful warning by altering the attributes attached to the river from *amoenus* (30) to *opacus* (36). Things may be somewhat darker than they at first seem.[12]

The irony of the address to the muse of love poetry, Erato, when it finally comes (37) is that no creative love enters this world as a result of Aeneas' arrival. Nothing is ever said of any bond of affection between Lavinia and Aeneas whose alliance is a primary cause for the coming war.[13] Scrutiny of the uses of *amor* in the book is revelatory. We hear first of Amata's *miro amore* (57) for her would-be son-in-law, an emotion upon which Allecto plays to full effect. We learn of Turnus' *amor ferri* (461) and of the *insani Martis amore* (550) with which Allecto fires the Italians. This causes Virgil to exclaim *huc omnis aratri / cessit amor* (635–36). It was *eximiae laudis amore* (496), we remember, which causes Iulus to wound Silvia's pet.[14]

One aspect of his action deserves mention here. As he shoots at the stag, it is *perque uterum . . . perque ilia* (499) that Iulus' arrow flies. The shot does not kill but only emasculates the stag. But inside the animal exterior there are near human traits. It groans (*gemens*) and, in its grief, takes on the attitude of one in prayer (*imploranti similis*, 502). Circe's spirit alters men into beasts. In the wounded stag we may feel a more happy combination of wild and human that could stand for tamed Italy itself. It is Ascanius who is ambitious and his dogs who are maddened.

An obvious link between Turnus and the stag is only felt, not stated, in book 7 (the stag, for instance, is *forma praestanti*, 483, while Turnus, armed, is *praestanti corpore*, 783). In book 12, however, Virgil makes a direct equation of Aeneas with a *venator canis* (no trace even of the human Iulus here!) and of Turnus with a stag (12.749–55).[15] At the end of book 12 Turnus is killed, but by the middle of the book 7, Italy has begun to lose its manhood and the Trojans to absorb an uncontrolled vigor.

The love, then, over which Erato is called upon to preside, is perverse, not creative. Its beginnings are rooted in war, not peace, compulsion, not gentleness. If the *maior rerum ordo* to which Virgil alludes at line 44 is Rome, the remark is made with bitter stress—the rebirth of Aeneas is the "birth" of war. If it refers specifically to the catalog of horrors that follows in the next six books, it is a begetting that leads to funerals, not lives.

The metamorphosis of peace into war begins forthwith. Though Latinus had long lived in peace two omens now predict war—the sudden advent of a cluster of bees on the palace laurel and a mysterious fire on Lavinia's head. As usual with Virgil each omen prepares us for its later reformulation.

Bees in the fourth *Georgic* are notable for their energetic industry and warlike ways. The latter quality makes itself felt here. The bees arrive with a mighty shriek (*stridore ingenti*, 65) and take such dense possession of the laurel that the soothsayer unhesitatingly sees them standing for a new race which will have dominion on the topmost citadel (*summa dominarier arce*, 70). This overlordship apparently brooks no compromise. ·And the turn of georgic occupations into martial pursuits is a motif of the book as a whole. Worship of plowshares and sickle (635), the farmer's "weapons," gives place to arms of a more destructive sort. It is a *pastorale signum* (513) with which Allecto calls the countryside to war.

Camilla embodies both aspects. She carries a

> . . . pastoralem praefixa cuspide myrtum.
> (7.817)
> . . . pastoral myrtle with spear point attached.[16]

This is not so much a symbol of the Italian shepherds[17] (they too were at peace before the Trojans came) as it is the final emblem of the perversion of pastoral into violent, of love misguided into war, of Venus' myrtle into a weapon of Mars. Hunting gradually changes in the *Aeneid* from an occupation necessary to produce life's staples (book 1) to the unnecessary and inflammatory search for booty (books 3 and 4) to war itself, finally, as man tracks man, one predator after another.

The omen of Lavinia's burning locks is clearer still. The fire becomes metaphysical and takes many forms as the book progresses. We are told of Lavinia

> regalique accensa comas, accensa coronam
> insignem gemmis; . . .
> (7.75–76)
> With her royal locks afire, afire with her crown marked by gems; . . .

We then turn to the inner world of Amata and her matrons (*furiis . . . accensas pectore*, 392). This has been Allecto's work. So also is her power, via Iulus, on the local rustics (*bello . . . animos accendit agrestis*, 482). Of still wider influence she later boasts:

> accendamque animos insani Martis amore . . .
> (7.550)
> I will set afire their souls with love of insane Mars . . .

Turnus' transformation is visualized in terms of water frothing as fire is set beneath a cauldron (462–66). The water itself swirls like smoke as once again elements which could well stand for pastoral and war are combined.[18] From this moment on he is clearly associated with fire's power, as at 577–78:

> Turnus adest medioque in crimine caedis et igni
> terrorem ingeminat.

> Turnus is there, and in the middle of the accusation of slaughter and fire he redoubles terror.

There is a direct line from Lavinia, spreading Vulcan throughout the house (*totis Volcanum spargere tectis*, 77) to the Aetnean fires which Turnus' Chimaera sports (796). Lavinia, too, plays her part in letting slip "the dogs of war."

For further reinforcement of the omens' meaning, Latinus consults the oracle of his father Faunus:

> . . . adit lucosque sub alta
> consulit Albunea, nemorum quae maxima sacro
> fonte sonat saevamque exhalat opaca mephitim.
>   (7.82–84)

He approaches and consults the groves beneath lofty Albunea which, grandest of forests, resounds with her holy fountain and darkly breathes forth harsh sulfur.

From Circe's grove to the dark Tiber mouth to Albunea, the intensity grows. As in the case of Circe, the situation plays on the senses of hearing and smelling as well as sight. Like the Tiber's stream, this grove is *opaca*. But whereas Circe is charmed by burning cedar, Faunus presents his prediction of blood and dominion from a spot that breathes fierce sulfur (*saevam mephitim*). Circe, *dea saeva*, misleads by a presentable exterior. Faunus' words issue from an Acheron which exhales a ghastly odor.

Again the words are anticipatory. Juno we soon find calling on the Underworld since loftier aids have failed her in the task of hindering the Trojans:

> flectere si nequeo superos, Acheronta movebo.
>   (7.312)

If I cannot bend the gods above, I will set Hell in motion.

Her instrument, Allecto, purpose fulfilled, returns to Hell in the valley of Ampsanctus (563–71). This too has a dark grove and roaring stream (*torto vertice torrens*, 567—and we recall the Tiber, *verticibus rapidis*). There a cave lets forth the breath from fierce Dis (*saevi spiracula Ditis*)—all this the product of Hell's bursting jaws (*rupto . . . ingens Acheronte vorago / pestiferas aperit fauces*, 569–70). Allecto, the goddess with the many masks for herself and others, is the stench of Hell bursting forth. Faunus' utterance initiates this particular aspect of the evil. For whatever reason, Latinus allows the words to become public.[19] This in turn is responsible for starting *fama* on her way.

The next stage in the upheaval of Italy is the arrival on the scene of Juno, *saeva Iovis coniunx*, who with her pawn puts the power of Circe into operation. Virgil has already read us a lesson on the futility of ambition and search for reputation, but it is for the sake of these very goals (*honor*, 332; *fama*, 333) that she feels the need to act. Though Jupiter's vengeful wife might not have it so, this is the first step toward the fulfillment of Faunus' prophecy that the future Romans will see all things "turn" beneath their feet (*omnia sub pedibus . . . verti*, 101). It commences, ironically, with a further display of Juno's hatred and with her appeal to the multiform Allecto. So variable is the creature that at the moment of her attack on Turnus she puts off her menacing face and fury's limbs (*torvam faciem et furialia membra*, 415) to become an old priestess of Juno (*in vultus sese transformat anilis*, 415). She assumes her true form again when he treats her lightly (*tanta . . . aperit*, 448). But her metamorphoses are only aspects of the changes she effects in others—to release the pent up violence and irrational hatreds inherent in us all.

Among her many talents is the ability to turn brothers against each other and overthrow homes by hatred (*odiis versare domos*, 336). She sees in the maddening of Amata the perfect example of this (*omnem . . . domum vertisse Latini*, 407). Amata becomes a plaything, a top, in her hands, spun into action by twists of a lash (*torto verbere*, 378). Here the way was prepared because her victim was already enraged at the coming of the Trojans (345).[20]

Juno boasts of Allecto's power to bring the scourge and funeral torch under roofs (*verbera tectis / funereasque inferre faces*, 336–37).[21] Both these objects serve in the metamorphosis of Turnus which is her next accomplishment. She sounds her scourges, hurls a torch at him, and fixes under his heart smoking brands:

> . . . facem iuveni coniecit et atro
> lumine fumantis fixit sub pectore taedas.
> (465–67)
> . . . she hurled the torch at the young man and thrust the firebrands, smoking with dark glow, under his breast.

The deed echoes Juno's evaluation of Aeneas as a new Paris:

... nec face tantum
Cisseis praegnas ignis enixa iugalis;
quin idem Veneri partus suus et Paris alter
funestaeque iterum recidiva in Pergama taedae.
    (319–22)
... nor did only the daughter of Cisseus, pregnant from a torch, give birth to nuptial fires; no indeed, Venus' offspring will be just the same, another Paris and once again a destructive firebrand for a rebuilt Troy.

Juno's rage may be once more in the open, but it is the idea of Aeneas and what he stands for that Allecto "throws" at Turnus. As this fear "breaks" his sleep (*rumpit*, 458), sweat burst forth from his body (*proruptus*, 459). Love of the sword rages in him (*saevit*) as he makes to Latinus, the peace violated (*polluta pace*, 467).

Allecto's next victim is Aeneas' son. She maddens his hounds and, as we have seen, he is set afire with love of praise.[22] This emotion wells up inside of him, but the metaphor puts him squarely in the tradition of Amata and Turnus. The whole incident Virgil acknowledges to be that

... quae prima laborum
causa fuit belloque animos accendit agrestis.
    (481–82)
... which was first cause of the sufferings and which set afire the rustic minds with war.

Iulus has appeared once before in book 7 as the unwitting interpreter of the oracle of the "tables" to be eaten. The harpy Celaeno in anger had prophesied that the Trojans reach their destined land in such a state of hunger as to be driven to eat their tables. On reaching Italy they are indeed compelled to eat the crusts due Ceres. Virgil's words make clear that such action is profane. Yet it fulfills Celaeno's prophecy, as Iulus announces. To this Virgil comments:

ea vox audita laborum
prima tulit finem ...
    (117–18)
That voice, first heard, brought an end to their sufferings ...

This may be the end of one phase of Aeneas' *labores*, but Iulus' action in shooting the stag, as the verbal echoes make clear, is the beginning of another. Like the attack on the Harpies' herds, this is an unnecessary onslaught against the animal world. The Trojans are not fully blameless as they now themselves present a literal cause for war.[23]

Juno puts her *extremam manum* (572–73) to her plot as if this were some special work of art that deserved a final touch (we have heard twice before of Allecto's *ars* [338, 477]). The injured shepherds, Turnus, and Amata all stream in to force Latinus' approval for the war. He remains momentarily firm, like a cliff against which waves "bark" (*latrantibus undis*, 588) while the rocks "roar" (*saxa fremunt*, 590). The Latins, too, are "dogs," and we have heard before of both Amata and Turnus "roaring" (385, 460). But Juno (once more *saeva*, 592) wins the day. As his resolve breaks he curses Turnus:

> . . . te, Turne, nefas, te triste manebit
> supplicium votisque deos venerabere seris.
> (596–97)
> For you, Turnus, guilt, for you, sad punishment will remain, and you
> will beseech the gods with tardy offerings.

The goddess then breaks open the iron gates of War, a task Latinus refuses, and Italy arms for battle. These are the gates, Jupiter foretold in book 1, that will be closed at the coming of Augustus:

> . . . dirae ferro et compagibus artis
> claudentur Belli portae; Furor impius intus
> saeva sedens super arma et centum vinctus aenis
> post tergum nodis fremet horridus ore cruento.
> (1.293–96)
> . . . the gates of War, grim with tight fastenings of iron, will be
> closed; unholy Furor, sitting within upon fierce arms, bound with a
> hundred brazen knots behind his back, will roar dreadful from his
> bloody mouth.

Juno's action merely gives symbolic confirmation to what we already knew, that Discordia-Furor was at large.[24]

It was one of Augustus' proudest boasts, incorporated in his *Res Gestae*, that the temple of Janus was closed three times during his regime whereas in all Roman history up to his time this had happened but twice before (*Res Gestae* 13). In the same work he also gives his thoughts on war and peace (*Res Gestae* 3):

> Bella terra et mari civilia externaque toto in orbe terrarum suscepi
> victorque omnibus superstitibus civibus peperci. Externas gentes
> quibus tuto ignosci potuit, conservare quam excidere malui.
>
> I undertook civil and foreign wars on land and sea throughout the
> whole world, and as victor I spared all the citizens who survived. I

preferred to save rather than to cut down the foreign races that could be pardoned in safety.

The crucial *tuto*, "in safety," in the second sentence may be defended as sop to necessary expediency. The first statement is more open to doubt. We are dealing with times which Tacitus called a *pacem cruentam* (*Ann.* 1.10). In the same paragraph Tacitus, while talking of Augustus, raises a moral issue which has some bearing on the end of the *Aeneid*. It is morally correct, the historian says, to give up private hatreds in favor of public needs (*privata odia publicis utilitatibus remittere*). In Tacitus' eyes Augustus was in this respect constantly delinquent. What of Virgil's Aeneas? Is his killing of Turnus an example of private hatred or of public need?

The opening of the gates of War gives Virgil the occasion for listing Aeneas' opponents.[25] The catalog as a whole is a fascinating example of poetic artistry. I would like to dwell here only on the way Virgil describes the figure of Aeneas' archenemy:

> ipse inter primos praestanti corpore Turnus
> vertitur arma tenens et toto vertice supra est.
> cui triplici crinita iuba galea alta Chimaeram
> sustinet Aetnaeos efflantem faucibus ignis;
> tam magis illa fremens et tristibus effera flammis
> quam magis effuso crudescunt sanguine pugnae.
> et levem clipeum sublatis cornibus Io
> auro insignibat, iam saetis obsita, iam bos,
> argumentum ingens, et custos virginis Argus,
> caelataque amnem fundens pater Inachus urna.
> (783–92)

Among the foremost, with his handsome physique moves Turnus himself holding weapons and towers (over them) by a whole head. His lofty helm, with its crest of triple plume, sports the Chimaera breathing the fires of Aetna from its jaws; the more it roars and the wilder (it becomes) with its gloomy flames, the more the battles grow grim as blood is spilled. And marking the smooth shield in gold was Io, her horns raised up, now covered over with bristling hairs, now a cow, a strange device, and Argus, the maiden's guard, and her father Inachus pouring his stream from a carved urn.

Two pieces of his armor, crest and shield, are given the equal stress of four lines.[26] Each summarizes and anticipates much. The crest is topped by a Chimaera, roaring and wild, reveling in fire and the blood of battle. He is associated with three beasts at once, lion, dragon, and goat. The ambiguity of *vertitur* (and to a lesser degree *vertice*), to "be turned" as well as simply to "move," shows the power of Circe at work for the most impressive time in book 7. The Chimaera, the hollow image that frightens Aeneas on his way to Hades, is loose now as Turnus, Aeneas' dehumanized opponent.

The shield carries Io, *iam saetis / obsita, iam bos*—an even closer connection with the *saetigeri sues* Circe creates. In the myth itself Jupiter effected the transformation from human to beast as Juno does here through her power to enrage. To effect such a monstrosity is the *argumentem ingens*, as well as the engraving itself. It is a madness that derives from Juno and Greece, not Italy, as the association with Argos which runs through the book proves. At 286 Juno has set out *Inachiis ab Argis* when she sights the Trojans already established on the Latian shore. At 372 Amata, by then insane, boasts of Turnus' ancestry as

> Inachus Acrisiusque patres mediaeque Mycenae.

> Father Inachus and Acrisius and the midst of Mycenae.

At 6.89 the Sibyl styles him *alius Achilles*, a boast which he utters himself at 9.742. He is made to assume the ancient Greek enmity rediscovered as well as the native Italic wildness rearoused. Antagonism would come to Aeneas all the easier.[27]

But Virgil is more careful than to make Turnus the emblem of reason and order overthrown in favor of some Boschian grotesquerie. He associates Turnus with one more *argumentum ingens*, the belt of the dead Pallas that he dons:

> impressumque nefas: una sub nocte iugali
> caesa manus iuvenum foede thalamique cruenti.
> > (10.497–98)
> An unspeakable crime was imprinted upon it: on one wedding night a band of youth slaughtered foully and bloody wedding chambers.

The Danaids are also Argive, in direct line from Io. Turnus inherits their crime and elicits from Virgil a broader generality:

> nescia mens hominum fati sortisque futurae
> et servare modum, rebus sublata secundis.
> > (10.501–2)
> Mind of men, ignorant of fate and of their future lot and of how to preserve the mean when lifted up by success.

This is the pattern that Nisus, Euryalus, and Camilla follow. It afflicts mankind, whether Trojan or Italian. But there is always Hypermestra, the one Danaid who had the heroism to spare her husband and blot out a tradition of violence by the courage of restraint.

Aeneas kills Turnus at the end of the epic because he sees the belt of Pallas.[28] Turnus is even then fulfilling the curse of Latinus. As *supplex*, with knee bent, he entreats forgiveness and at the same time pays a penalty for rashness. He is symbol of a humbled race. Latinus had attached to him the guilt of a *nefas* and he now wears over his shoulder an *immensum nefas* that reminds his antagonist of a nearer act of violence. Aeneas kills him and offers him as sacrifice to Pallas. The verb *immolat* (12.949) is the same as Virgil uses to describe Aeneas' seizure of the sons of Sulmo and Ufens as human offering on the pyre of Pallas (10.519).[29] Turnus is the last victim of Aeneas' *saevus dolor*.[30]

The action results, one suspects, from what Tacitus could call a *privatum odium*. Aeneas' temper is not one to wrestle more than momentarily with his father's lofty sentiments to spare the humbled and beat down the proud (*parcere subiectis et debellare superbos*). That Turnus is *superbus* (and therefore deserves defeat) we have often heard. We have not yet seen Aeneas confronted with an ancient enemy at last cowed into submission. The moment is crucial to the *Aeneid* and Rome. Virgil's words calculate a mood of wrath, not magnanimity, of his hero. He is burned by rage and terrifying in his wrath (*furiis accensus et ira terribilis*, 946–47). Aeneas, as Virgil chooses to portray him, is now on equal spiritual footing with Amata (whose matrons are *furiis accensas*) and Turnus in book 7 (392).[31] Each succumbs to *ira* under the influence of *furor*. The difference is that in book 12 Aeneas has the help of Jupiter and the Dira in humbling Turnus and yet the advantage of Anchises' schooling in necessary generosity.

The Roman, his father had warned in book 6, pursues greater arts than bronze casting and sculpture, rhetoric or astronomy. He molds people to his rule and makes peace a custom. But the closing scene of the *Aeneid* is scarcely pacific. To practice one's arts on human beings and not on metal or stone requires greater control than Aeneas can muster. We would hope that the cycle of quasi-fraternal violence that runs through the last six books of the *Aeneid* might come to an end at its conclusion. Virgil is more realistic than to tell us so.[32]

One of the great points of value in the *Aeneid* is to serve as a reminder (to us certainly, to Augustus, if he was wise) of natural unrest in society which must be held in control. A certain turbulence is important in the creative individual as well as in mankind as a whole. But the forcing of individual irrationalities on society can do it fatal harm, especially when these disorders are imposed by its rulers themselves, or even offered by them as models.

The questions which linger at the end of the *Aeneid* are worth constant asking. Can, or better does, Furor remain suppressed as Rome goes about its supposed work of civilization? Can peace ever be made into a fixed tradition when any such "custom" is ever at the mercy of human caprice? By the end of book 6, through the intellectual guidance of his father, Aeneas has become the incorporation of the dream of Rome, the embodied founder of a myth. Yet Virgil, by having him exit by the gate of *falsa insomnia*, allies him with the *Somnia vana* and other monsters, the Centaurs, Gorgons, and Chimaeras that cluster around Hell's gate. In book 7 the creatures seem to be at large in the persons of Aeneas' opponents. Aeneas does "suffer" them ultimately. He sets them free. During the course of the last books, and especially at the conclusions of books 10 and 12, Aeneas undergoes a similar metamorphosis. From *pius*, faithful to his father's words, he becomes forgetful.[33] Circe, the beast-maker, and Juno, the arouser of Hell's fury, have the final say. The dream is proved false by the hero's actions. He becomes as much the representative of life's irrationality as Allecto, with her Gorgon's locks, or Turnus with a Chimaera for crest.

Daedalus, the brilliant artisan of Apollo's temple at Cumae, by overreaching is the cause of his son's death. Augustus, for all his accomplishments, will see Marcellus dead. Virgil's regular pattern leads us to expect that Aeneas will lose Pallas. By killing Turnus, however, he fails in the craftsmanship of empire, a deeper fault to suffer because self-inflicted. He is blind to Turnus as symbol of anything beyond momentary, individualistic concerns. By the middle of the sixth book Aeneas is purged of empathy with the past. Palinurus, Dido, and Deiphobus pass in final review emotions no longer relevant. Aeneas cannot even embrace his dead father who becomes a persona of the future.[34] He has become at last an original, originating being with a historical mission, the standard and emblem of a whole people. The birth of the hero is the birth of a city in book 8. Lavinia is only the Italian shores at last claimed and Iulus only the ancestor of a noble line. The propulsion of personal momentum now lies with Turnus and his confreres, in his love for Lavinia, in the wildness of Camilla. But the public espousal of the future, the parade of heroes watched and the glorious shield raised, cannot wholly eliminate private involvements and sufferings. In Aeneas' case these seem finally to triumph over any attempt to follow Anchises' philosophical exhibit.

In this version of the timeless conflict between moral stance and individual action, the latter wins, as is its wont. Aeneas, Virgil assures us with frequency, yearns for equity and peace. The *lacrimae rerum*, life's inherent tragedy, have left too many scars for immediate emotion to be a constant resort. As he tells Iulus before the final debacle, his son may learn of courage and suffering from him, not good fortune. There is a lofty, heroic side to Rome which Aeneas must embody. In any groping toward civilization there must also be a continuing search for honest justice and here

Aeneas—and Rome—pay the price for their humanity. Aeneas is no idealized fiction, finally purged of ignoble human emotions, an automaton operated only by an unreal impetus toward impossible goals. Personal passion gains full control of reason at the moment of final crisis.

Even were the epic to end with praise of Aeneas, as it clearly does not, we would still sense that the cycle of madness would begin again. That Virgil turned down so clearly the opportunity for a fraudulent appraisal of human existence is perhaps our greatest compliment to the poet and his poem.[35]

NOTES

1. At 423 Allecto, in disguise, can taunt Turnus that Latinus has denied him *quaesitas sanguine dotes*. There may be a pun in Virgil's address to Saturn as *sanguinis ultimus auctor* (49). Juno, prime cause of future bloodshed, is called *Saturnia* four times in book 7 (428, 560, 572, 622), more than in any other book. For explicit connections between blood and war, cf. lines 541–42, 554, 595.

2. It is curious that the four Trojan boats which take part in the race during Anchises' funeral games carry as emblems a *Pristis*, Chimaera, Centaur, and Scylla. The *Pristis* (or *Pristix*) was a sea monster which formed part of Scylla's makeup (3.427). The connection with future Rome is, in each instance, carefully stressed by the poet. Mythic experience switches to allegorical emblem which in future actions will become symbolic only.

3. As late as line 285 the Trojans bring peace back from Latinus to Aeneas (*pacem . . . reportant*).

4. For a more detailed treatment of Caieta, see Segal, *"Aeternum II"* 56ff.

5. In this respect the adventure of Circe parallels, out of many examples, the wooden horse in book 2, the *monstrum* of Polydorus in 3, the panels of Daedalus in 6. Though the time is night, the breezes blow and the moon gleams with sufficient brightness for sailing. It is untrue day, and travel is suspect (in book 3 we have examples of breezes falling at sunset while nightfall brings the end of journeying). The moon's light is borrowed from the sun and fickle (*tremulo*). Nocturnal breezes drawing toward Circe are wrongly seductive (cf. Horace's use of *aura* at *C.* 1.5.11 and 2.8.24).

6. *Saevus* is again an adjective much in evidence (557, 572, 577).

7. The gift Aeneas gives Latinus, *Priami gestamen* (246), also has its irony. The fate of Priam is transferred to Latinus, each an old ruler unable to control a kingdom heading toward ruin.

8. Though Aeneas' envoys apparently return with peace, they bring as gifts symbols of war (see commentators on *Aen.* 1.444, 3.539–43), and Circe is the medium of the change.

   The horses have two things in common with the portrait of Camilla at the end of the book. They are fleet of foot (*alipedes*, 277) and they are caparisoned in purple and gold (*ostro*, 277 and 814; *aurea, auro, aurum*, 278–80, *auro*, 816). It is her vanity that proves her undoing as she contemplates the accoutrements of Chloreus in book 11, where again purple (*ostro*, 772) and gold (*auro*, 771, *aureus*, 774, *auro*, 776, *auro*, 779) are prominent (see Small, "Vergil" 298). In accepting such a gift, Aeneas receives something of Camilla's superficiality and wildness as well as the possibilities of Circean metamorphosis.

9. Fraenkel, "Some Aspects" 5, speaks of the "private egoisms" at the root of the war.

10. The description is usually taken as idyllic (as, most recently, Kraggerud, *Aeneisstudien* 86: "eine Szene voll tiefer Freude"):

> iamque rubescebat radiis mare et aethere ab alto
> Aurora in roseis fulgebat lutea bigis.
>   (7.25–26)

and now the sea was growing red with rays, and from the lofty heavens Dawn was glimmering yellow in her rosy chariot.

Rubesco is used three times in the *Aeneid*. The other two occasions have bearing on 5.25. At 3.521 *rubescebat Aurora* begins the description of the first landfall in Italy (and Anchises' prediction of war). At 8.695 we find the sea red from blood (*arva nova Neptunia caede rubescant*).

A similar description of dawn occurs at 6.535–36:

> hac vice sermonum roseis Aurora quadrigis
> iam medium aetherio cursu traiecerat axem.

At this juncture in their conversation Dawn in her rosy chariot had now passed beyond the middle axis in her heavenly journey.

In book 7 Aurora gleams from a two-horse, not four-horse, chariot. The change may anticipate the *currum geminosque iugalis* (280) that Latinus sends to Aeneas. Aurora, as another daughter of the Sun, carries on Circe's influence. Aeneas' steeds are also bred by Circe of heavenly descent, a bastard combination of mortal and immortal.

11. Cf. the use of *vertex* at Hor. *C.* 2.8.22.

12. This dualism in the opening lines is analyzed by Reckford, "Latent Tragedy" 252–69. Williams, "Purpose of the *Aeneid*" 37, calls Allecto "a personification of man's own evil desires."

13. See Todd, "Virgil's Invocation" 216–18, and the comments of Reckford, "Latent Tragedy" 257 n. 15.

14. The only other mention of *amor* in book 7 is at 769 (Diana's strange affection for Hippolytus).

15. This point is made in an interesting article by Nethercut, "Invasion in the *Aeneid*" 82–95.

16. Throughout the *Aeneid* Virgil reveals a fondness for metaphors from nature twisted into contexts of war. In book 7 we may note *atra . . . late / horrescit strictis seges ensibus* (525–26); *florentis aere catervas* (804).

17. Such is the interpretation of Pöschl, *Dichtkunst* 275.

18. The relationship between this simile and 8.22–25 (and their respective settings) deserves further exploration. The latter simile has much in common with the description of the waters which swirl around Circe's land and of the goddess herself (e.g., *tremulo lumine*, 7.9, *tremulum lumen*, 8.22; *luna*, 7.9, *lunae*, 8.23; *solis*, 7.11, *sole*, 8.23). Circe is associated with both the sun and the moon at the opening of book 7. By 7.526–27 the sun gleams off the shields

of the newly armed rustics (*aeraque fulgent / sole lacessita et lucem sub nubila iactant*). By the start of book 8 Turnus, his allies, and the dangers they present have become the "constellations" which trouble Aeneas' mind (*tremulum labris . . . lumen aenis / sole repercussum*, 8.22–23).

19. According to Servius in a strong comment, Latinus thereby loses a reason *quo a se repelleret generos*.

20. The change in Amata is echoed in the alteration from *Turni hymenaeis* (344) to *Phrygiis hymenaeis* (358). This in turn becomes the "marriage" of Trojan and Latin at 555–56 which is closely conjoined to the *sanguis novus* that Juno realizes must stain the warriors.

21. She also sounds her whip against Turnus (*verbera insonuit*, 451). Tisiphone uses the same instrument at 6.558.

22. In one sense Iulus anticipates Allecto's efforts. We know that she is a goddess given to *iraeque insidiaeque* (326). Iulus is already at work chasing wild beasts *insidiis cursuque* (478) when Allecto arrives on the scene. *Ira* (508) aids in the result.

23. Of Allecto's part in the Iulus episode Servius remarks (on line 479) *studium mutavit in rabiem*. Here again the poet emphasizes the bitter uselessness of peace turned to war (536).

24. The "turning" of War's hinges (*cardine verso*, 621) is the final example of peace overturned by war.

25. Virgil's prayer to the Muses is *pandite nunc Helicona*. The Muses must fling open Helicon as if the mountain had gates. Juno releases Furor from the gates of War. It takes many shapes in the subsequent catalog of warriors.

26. For a different, more detailed treatment of these lines, see Small, "Arms of Turnus" 243–52. See also Williams, "Function and Structure" 152–53.

27. The phrase *ipse inter primos* is used of Pyrrhus at 2.479 and of Aeneas at 12.579. We might expect a further echo of Greek destructiveness in our first full description of Turnus. The metamorphosis of Aeneas into violent "Greek" is more subtle but crucial for our understanding of the epic's finale.

28. The most recent treatment of the final scene is by Williams, "Purpose of the *Aeneid*" especially 36ff. ("it is certain that the poem ends with our thoughts concentrated on the tragedy of Turnus, not the triumph of Rome"). A cogent expression of this new, more realistically honest evaluation of Aeneas is given by MacKay, "Hero and Theme" 157–66, especially 164–66.

29. The sacrifice is made ready at 11.81–82. The only other use of *immolo* in the *Aeneid* is at 10.541.

30. We have seen the frequent use of *saevus* in association with the enemies of Aeneas in book 7. It is curious how often the adjective is attached to the hero himself in book 12. Only at 12.406 and 609 is it connected with Turnus (at 406 *saevus horror* creeps nearer the wounded Aeneas as Turnus momentarily has the upper hand; at 629 Juturna tries to persuade her brother to bring *saeva funera* to the Trojans). These instances are 107 (Aeneas is *maternis saevus in armis*), 498 (Aeneas effects *saevam nullo discrimine caedem*), 849 (Jupiter, *saevus rex*), 857 (the Dira as an arrow armed with the venom *saevi veneni*), 888 (Aeneas speaks *saevo pectore*), 890 (Aeneas and Turnus fight *saevis armis*), 945 (Aeneas recalls his *saevi doloris*). Benario, "Tenth Book" 35, points out

that in the epic Aeneas alone (and he only at 10.878) is called *saevissime*.

It is curious, too, that Aeneas is called *heros* only until 12.502, yet Turnus is given this designation at 12.723 and 902. (This is not to make any specific defense of the "character" of Turnus who, at 10.443, can go so far as to wish Evander present at the death of his son.)

31. Can we speak of any character "development" in Aeneas when wrath and madness are the very vices to which he succumbs in book 2 (*furor iraque mentem praecipitat*, 2.316–17)? That the results of each encounter are pointless seems not to have suppressed the emotion. It is scant defense of the actual killing of Turnus to say (as Kraggerud, *Aeneisstudien* 23) that it, unlike a similar event in Troy, is just because done in accordance with fate. It is fate (if we can judge from Jupiter's final words—we would scarcely guess it from the context) for Juno to give up her *furor* and the two peoples to merge happily into one. Turnus' death is never once intimated to be fated, in spite of his own predictions.

32. Those who see in Aeneas a gradual development or perfecting of self-discipline (as, e.g., Austin, *Liber Secundus* xvi) or *pietas* (as Quinn, *Aeneid* 17 and 123) avert their thoughts from the thorough gruesomeness of the endings of books 10 and 12.

33. The word *pius* is stressed at the opening of book 7 (*pius Aeneas*, 5; *pii Troes*, 21). In book 12 Aeneas is called *pius* only until line 311. By the end he has come a long way from the dutiful son who supported his father on lowered shoulders (*subiecta colla*, 2.721). Someone else is now *subiectus* and Aeneas, for the worse, has freed himself from any spiritual *impedimenta*. He cannot bear the weight of his father's historical and moral revelation. The "dream" is false.

34. The words which describe the meeting (6.700–702) echo Eurydice's disappearance from Orpheus (*Geo.* 4.499–502). They are the same as *Aen.* 2.792–94, where Creusa leaves Aeneas. Anchises is like swift sleep, his story of future Rome is Aeneas' dream.

35. It is becoming a fashion to speak of the public and private aspects of the *Aeneid* as if they were somehow separable (their true interconnection is shown by Parry, "Two Voices" 66–68). I would agree that we must not overreact against the long-standing, debilitating view of the *Aeneid* as only a glorification of Augustan Rome. But in seeking a mean line between the horror and the glory we need not at the same time partition the poet's Muse. The "private" voice may on occasion offer the most desperately "public" of utterances.

UMBRO,

NIREUS,

AND LOVE'S

THRENODY

Among Virgil's most moving creations is the figure of Umbro, priest, magician, and soldier, who is sent by King Archippus as head of the delegation of Marsian troops who will join with others in aiding Turnus in his conflict with Aeneas. The passage occurs at *Aeneid* 7.750–60 and centers largely on the powerlessness of Umbro's spells, potent though they be against the limited universe of land vipers and water snakes, when confronted with wounds from the Dardanian spear thrust:

> Quin et Marruvia venit de gente sacerdos
> fronde super galeam et felici comptus oliva
> Archippi regis missu, fortissimus Umbro,
> vipereo generi et graviter spirantibus hydris
> spargere qui somnos cantuque manuque solebat,
> mulcebatque iras et morsus arte levabat.
> sed non Dardaniae medicari cuspidis ictum
> evaluit neque eum iuvere in vulnera cantus
> somniferi et Marsis quaesitae montibus herbae.
> (750–58)

And indeed there also came from the Marruvian people a priest, adorned with leafage and the fertile olive above his helm, who was sent by king Archippus—bravest Umbro, who was accustomed to sprinkle sleep on the race of vipers and on heavy-breathing hydras by song and by touch and who soothed their anger and alleviated their bites by his art. But he did not have the strength to heal the blow of the Trojan spearhead, nor did his sleep-bearing songs and his herbs sought on the Marsian mountains aid him against wounds.

The nub of Virgil's portrait is the tension between two types of hurt and two types of medicine. Snakebite can be healed by proper incantations and by the application of suitable herbs. The injuries which men inflict upon each other are of a different order and require a different level of sophistication and knowledge to cure, knowledge which the sorcerer Umbro does not possess.[1]

Virgil's language brings the two spheres of man and nature together, for both *cuspes* and *ictus* can refer to wounds inflicted by nature's creatures—*cuspes* to the sting of a scorpion or bee, *ictus* to the "blow" of a snake, spider, wasp, or hornet as well as, again, of a bee or scorpion.[2] In the case of Umbro the distinction between one type of assault and another comes about because he lacks force not so much against man in general but when facing a special Dardan hero who need not be named but who remains as prime a representative of the Trojans as Umbro is of the Marsi. His art, which can counterbalance nature, "lightening" the "heavy" breathings of snakes, cannot outface the reality of man's weaponry. His sacrality, by which he himself doles out mere sleep to the animal world, is unable to cope with death's deeper slumber, inflicted upon him from elsewhere. Human wrath, and the physical gestures that result from it, are of a different order than the menace of animals and take more than a wizard's charms, the quasi-Orphic songs for which the Marsi were famous, to mollify.[3] In the case of the *Aeneid* it is an emotion in the ascendant as the poem reaches its climactic conclusion, when the Dardan warrior scorns his antagonist's prayers and, *ira terribilis*, buries his sword in his opponent's chest, in the poem's final, particularized, display of fury.[4]

Virgil's use of hendiadys calls our attention to the beginning of the passage, as we behold Umbro "adorned above his helmet with foliage and the fertile olive." The olive is appropriate decoration for a priest as well as symbol for peace.[5] The irony of the latter in this context is supplemented by the words *fronde* and *felici*, which Virgil's figuration stresses. *Frons* implies growth and productiveness while *felix* has the double meaning of fertile and well omened. Neither Umbro's authority as a shaman nor the emblem of peace that he sports as crest will save him, for all his bravery, from a stronger warrior, with powerful auspices in his favor.

But it is on the concluding two lines of the episode that I would like primarily to dwell here. I will look first at their Virgilian background and its source in Hellenistic poetry. Then, after a brief reminder of the influence which this complex of passages in Virgil's trio of masterpieces exerted on later literature, I will turn back to Homer and suggest a neglected source in the *Iliad* for these lines and for the portrayal of Umbro as a whole.

The verses themselves are among Virgil's most astonishing creations:

> te nemus Angitiae, vitrea te Fucinus unda,
> te liquidi flevere lacus.
>   (759–60)
> For you the grove of Angitia, for you the Fucinus with its glassy wave, for you the clear lakes wept.

The tricolon (making use of triple apostrophe, in anaphora,[6] as well as asyndeton) gives special immediacy to a landscape which is represented in its sorrow by a version of the "pathetic fallacy" more focused around a carefully particularized setting than in any earlier example. We learn, here and now, as if the anticipated moment of dirge were vividly occurring before us, how the Marsian countryside will bemoan its central figure when death comes to him during the forthcoming war. As future blends with past, the merger conjures up a moment, which the narrator forces us directly to share, of mourning's ever present constancy as a sad afterglow of war in a world of groves and lakes that has lost its pivotal "you." Liquids dominate each line, with *n* permeating the first (twice in conjunction with an array of *us* that extends into the subsequent verse) and the alliteration of *l* prominent in the second.[7] Assonance of *e* is the chief unifying factor for both verses which, with the help of repeated *ts*, extends the sound of *te*, and the effect of grief, throughout each line. Line 760 is a powerful finale, first because it breaks off at the fourth-foot caesura, as if furtherance of lament, by the landscape or by its poet-designer, were impossible. We also note the paranomasia in *liquidi* which at once conveys both limpidity of texture (a confirmation of Fucinus' "glassy wave") and clarity of sound. The "pathetic fallacy" lends to the waters not only emotionality but the ability to utter their feelings in voice, and the plural *lacus*, the passage's last word, standing for one lake and its unique, sparkling wave specified in the previous lines, pits continued iterations of mourning against the abrupt cessation of the poet's words.

The imagining of nature's sad response to the momentary or eternal loss of a beloved figure on whom she depends or with whom she senses empathy, is a device Virgil utilizes from the start of his career. We find it in *Eclogue* 1 where, in words given to Meliboeus, the absent Tityrus is addressed by woods and fountains:

> Tityrus hinc aberat. ipsae, te, Tityre, pinus,
> ipsi te fontes, ipsa haec arbusta vocabant.
> (38–39)
> Tityrus was absent from here. You the very pines, Tityrus, you the fountains, you these bushes themselves were calling.

In the fifth *Eclogue* nature grieves for the demise of Daphnis (21–28) and rejoices in his deification (58–64) while in the last poem of the collection the landscape responds in sorrow to the amatory travails that have brought Gallus to the verge of pastoral (*Ecl.* 10.13–15). The fourth *Georgic* offers a particularly moving instance where the anguish of nature at the death of Eurydice (460–63) is immediately supplemented by Orpheus' own threnody to his beloved into which the speaker also directly draws us:

ipse cava solans aegrum testudine amorem
te, dulcis coniunx, te solo in litore secum,
te veniente die, te decendente canebat.
    (464–66)

He himself, solacing love's sickness on his hollow lyre, was singing
of you, sweet wife, of you to himself on the deserted shore, of you as
the day comes, of you as it departed.

Nature's poet, whose song later is said to soothe tigers (Virgil uses the
same verb, *mulceo*, as he does of Umbro quieting the rage of snakes)[8] and
to draw oak trees in its wake, supplements nature itself in lamenting the
loss of his wife. The quadruple repetition of *te* in anaphora is recalled at
the conclusion of the episode, after Eurydice has returned irrevocably to
Hades, in the poet's threefold repetition of her name, placed by the inner
narrator, Proteus, on the lips of Orpheus' head, torn from his body, and in
the streambank's complementing echo:

. . . Eurydicen vox ipsa et frigida lingua,
a miserum Eurydicen! anima fugiente vocabat:
Eurydicen toto referebant flumine ripae.
    (525–27)

His voice itself and his chill tongue were calling Eurydice, ah, hapless
Eurydice, as his breath fled: Eurydice the banks of the whole stream
reechoed.

The "pathetic fallacy" has its origins in Homer, at *Iliad* 17.426–28,
where the horses of Achilles are said to weep for Patroclus, and 19.362,
where Homer imagines the earth laughing at the flash of bronze. It is
given renewed impetus by the tragedians. Both Aeschylus and Euripides
speak powerfully of landscapes possessed by Bacchus' mesmeric dynamism.[9] But it is at the hands of the Hellenistic poets that the device
becomes standard, attached in particular to "pastoral" poetry. In Thyrsis'
song from the first *Idyll* of Theocritus, animals, both wild and tame, are
imagined mourning at the death of Daphnis (71–75). Likewise in the song
of Lycidas, which initiates the contest forming the central section of *Idyll*
7, Theocritus again incorporates a vision of nature's lament for Daphnis
(74).[10] The motif is absorbed by Bion in his *Epitaphios* for Adonis (31–38),
while Bion himself is the subject of a pastoral dirge by Moschus (3.1–24).[11]

In its context, then, the loss of Umbro is a double "death." On a literal
level we anticipate the demise of a personage upon whom the landscape
depends to mitigate its own inner self-threatenings. By his loss a major
manifestation of the vigor of the countryside of Italy seems diminished.
On the level of genre, the arrival of Aeneas into the course of Latian
history elicits from the narrator an example of pastoral lament embedded

into, which is to say in part controlled by, one of the most traditional of epic contexts, the catalog of heroes preparing for martial adventures to come. Virgil's mastery gives further assurance to the Hellenistic formalizing which had appropriated a rhetorical device of classical poetry for the particular purposes of pastoral. This combined inheritance, from Virgil himself as he further strengthens a Hellenistic generic development, has special importance for the seventh book of the *Aeneid*. One of the essential subjects of this extraordinary beginning to the epic's second half is the triumph of war over peace, of experience over innocence, and, generically speaking, of epic over pastoral, elegy, or their combination. Perhaps the most prominent individual manifestation of this conjunction in book 7 is the figure of Silvia's tamed stag. It draws to itself motifs from pastoral, as "nature" responds empathetically to man's emotions.[12] It is likewise closely associated with elegy. The personified animal is envisioned not only as a lover, emasculated by the arrows of Iulus, but as a designer of love elegy itself, adorned by his beloved with "soft garlands" (*mollibus sertis*, 7.488) and washed in an "untainted fountain" (*puro fonte*, 7.489), both emblems which the elegist Propertius, in one of the most comprehensive surveys of his *Dichterweihe*, associates intimately with the sources of his poetic power (3.1.3, 19). In hunting to its death this rich symbol, Iulus destroys not only the tranquillity of the landscape but its capability to inspire as well, when nature fosters man's creative impulses.

Metamorphosis from one mode to another is manifested climactically in the book's last line (817) where the warrior-virgin Camilla is said to carry a quiver

et pastoralem praefixa cuspide myrtum.

and pastoral myrtle with spear point attached.

Myrtle has regular associations with both Venus and the pastoral world. To imagine it capped with a spear point is to envision a final emblem for the transformation which Iulus' tracking of the stag had already helped achieve. This same doubleness was also apparent in the helmet of Umbro, which, as we saw, ironically sports the olive of peace. There is a kinship, too, between Umbro and Silvia's stag. The latter's story looks to a moment of fruitful union between man and the landscape and its denizens, before the landing of the Trojans brought with it Juno's fury and the resultant battling. The figure of Umbro incorporates song's enchanting potential to mollify nature's more violent moods, and his death, as the magic continues dazzlingly on, elicits from the inanimate a grief that corresponds to mankind's deepest utterance. The initial charm is obliterated, just as the final death is caused, by the same war which starts with the killing of Silvia's pet and continues on with Camilla, whose

spear grafts war's metallic hardness on to the pastoral affectiveness of
myrtle. In the cases of both Silvia and Umbro, the sources of song and
song itself, enlivened and particularized by a poet brilliantly drawing on
his generic inheritance of pastoral and elegy, cannot compete with the
force of arms, which is to say of epic's devouring inexorability. All that
remains is death, now or to come, and, in the case of Umbro, the futile
reecho of lament for the absent, forever lost beloved.

Sooner or later the subjects of these lamentations, from Tityrus in
Eclogue 1 to Umbro in *Aeneid* 7, disappear from Virgil's immediate text. We
think especially of the poet's presentation of Eurydice whose double
death, as we have noted, is mourned twice over by Orpheus. The first
occasion lures us into participating in the actual dirge itself, the second
stems from the moment of his own death. Both are built around the idea
of repetition, whether the reiterated *te* in anaphora, which reconstitutes
Eurydice for us in Orpheus' imagined lament, or the triple, useless, final
annunciation of her name. The force of these poetic presentations had a
profound influence on later poetry. Ovid's own description of the death of
Orpheus takes double advantage of Virgil's lines, with fivefold repetition
of *te* (*M.* 11.44–46), as nature grieves for her beloved's loss, and triple use of
flebile (*M.* 11.52–53), replacing Virgil's naming of Eurydice, to describe the
contents of Orpheus' last music. On two separate occasions Ovid uses
triple anaphora of the youth's name when he portrays Daedalus sorrow-
ing for his son, Icarus (*M.* 8.231–33, *AA* 2.93–95). Finally, in a stunning
reversal of Virgil's plot, Ovid from Tomi can address his wife in Rome:

> te loquor absentem, te vox mea nominat unam;
> nulla venit sine te nox mihi, nulla dies.
> (*Tr.* 3.3.17–18)
> I address you in your absence, you alone my voice calls by name; no
> night comes to me without you, no day.

Here it is the ill poet who, from the deathlike remove of exile, can call
upon his wife who survives in their homeland and who might herself
summon up the Orphic charm to have his living death countermanded.[13]

Subsequent to Ovid, Statius, at the conclusion of his *Thebaid*, presents
another powerful example of anaphoric lament where the name of the
departed is repeated three times. The subject is the Arcadian boy Parthenopaeus who had been killed in the epic's ninth book and whose
name underscores the virginal features of his pubescent beauty. His presentation throughout the epic is modeled in part on Virgil's Camilla, and
he, too, like Umbro, is associated with a particular landscape. For Parthenopaeus it is an Arcadia of prehistoric, preepic innocence where pursuing animals, not battling humans, is the rule. This sequestered world
cannot survive the arrival of war:

Arcada quo planctu genetrix Erymanthia clamet,
Arcada, consumpto servantem sanguine vultus,
Arcada, quem geminae pariter flevere cohortes.
   (St. *Th.* 12.805–7)
With what lament the Erymanthian mother mourns the Arcadian,
the Arcadian who keeps his beauty though all his blood is lost, the
Arcadian for whom the twin hosts equally wept.

In grieving for her son, the Erymanthian mother, Atalanta, chaste goddess of the hunt, sorrows for a past whose loss both sides, as the fratricidal
strife comes to an end, can join in lamenting. Following after Evadne and
Argia, hers is the ultimate of three dirges, recollection of which by the
narrator brings the poem virtually to a close. What follows is Statius'
first-person envoi to his poem. The epic action proper concludes with
threefold acts of mourning (the final one of which evolves in triple form)
which at once round off war and the poet's words which tell of it.[14]

Having looked briefly at the *Nachleben* of Virgil's anaphoric laments, let
us turn back to his portrayal of Umbro, to look again at its sources. We
followed the generic background of the "pathetic fallacy" from Homer to
Hellenistic poetry as a rhetorical source for Virgil's laments. It is time
now to trace the narrative background of these lines from *Aeneid* 7. The
figure of Umbro is the tenth in the list of Latin warriors (or groups of
warriors) who are preparing to join Turnus in his incipient campaign
against the Trojans. He is followed by Virbius, Turnus himself, and Camilla for a total of thirteen representations. It is natural for critics to look
back in their search for models, as Virgil himself did for inspiration, to the
double catalog in *Iliad* 2 of the heroes who came in their ships from
Greece to do battle and of the allies of Troy's defenders. The most
obvious original for a Marsian wizard-warrior about to succumb to an
enemy's spear thrust (impelled by Dardan energy newly revived on Italian soil) is the augur Ennomos who, Homer announces, could not ward
off death at the hands of Achilles as he slaughtered Trojans in the river (*Il.*
2.858–61).[15] But I would suggest that Virgil also turned to a figure in the
Greek catalog as he created his representation of Umbro and that much
of the dynamism of his lines arises from his conflation of different aspects
of the two Homeric portraits. From the tale of Ennomos Virgil drew the
notion of the wonder-worker's fallibility before superior might. From
Homer's delineation of Nireus, my second figure, he gleaned something
of the rhetorical brilliance that lies behind his characterization. I quote
Homer's sketch in full:

Νιρεὺς αὖ Σύμηθεν ἄγε τρεῖς νῆας ἐίσας,
Νιρεὺς Ἀγλαίης υἱὸς Χαρόποιό τ᾽ ἄνακτος,
Νιρεὺς ὃς κάλλιστος ἀνὴρ ὑπὸ Ἴλιον ἦλθε

τῶν ἄλλων Δαναῶν μετ᾽ ἀμύμονα Πηλείωνα·
ἀλλ᾽ ἀλαπαδνὸς ἔην, παῦρος δὲ οἱ εἵπετο λαός.
   (Il. 2.671–75)

Nireus from Syme led three balanced vessels,
Nireus son of Aglaia and the king Charopos,
Nireus, the most beautiful man who came beneath Ilion
beyond the rest of the Danaans next after perfect Achilles.
But he was a man of poor strength and few people with him.
   (Lattimore)

Homer distinguishes Nireus for two traits, his beauty and his weakness. The latter quality is both striking and anomalous in a context
detailing the extent and puissance of the forces marshaled by Greece to
back the Atreid claims. His feebleness may not be totally disconnected
from the fact that henceforth Nireus never reappears in the text of the
Iliad. We do not hear of his death nor even of his participation in any
fighting.

Nevertheless, brief though his appearance be in the epic itself, Homer's
presentation of Nireus initiated for him a career in later literature.
Though the author of the *Iliad* may have chosen to eliminate him from
the remainder of the poem, yet the very power of his five-line representation had an opposite effect. It caught the attention of subsequent readers
who, in writing of Nireus, replaced, or, perhaps better, reconfirmed what
was taken to be Homer's desire by preserving in memory a character
whom, save for his single moment, the epicist had banished from his
song. Something which he sensed in Homer's short narrative led Ovid to
refer to Nireus as "deeply adored by Homer of old" (*antiquo Nireus
adamatus Homero*, AA 2.109), to claim, in an almost offhanded aside, that
Nireus was his poet's lover. Homer could then be said at once to "kill" his
idol while at the same time depicting him with verbal magic sufficient to
reassure his immortality, at his own hands, and through the verbal means
of future authors seduced by Homer's brilliant design.

Two interrelated questions follow from what Homer's words seem to
have implied: first, how does Homer betray the affection for Nireus
which Ovid assumes and, second, what is there about the particular
rhetorical means that he utilized to trace the figure of Nireus which
caught the fancy of later writers?

A preliminary answer to the first question lies in the other characteristic besides feebleness with which Homer distinguishes Nireus, namely his
physical glamour. He is second in handsomeness among the Greek forces
only to unsullied Achilles. His mother is Aglaia (Beauty, Splendor) and
his father Charops, he of the sparkling eyes. This parentage implies a
double inheritance of attractiveness, for in later tradition (or perhaps
already even here) Aglaia is one of the Graces who claim Charis, an

abstract soon to be personified, as one of their major attributes.[16] This combination of physical winsomeness and personal charm—an inheritance of abstractions missing even to Achilles, most beautiful of all—especially when linked with Homer's implication of Nireus' vulnerability and his brief life-span is no doubt what drew Greek authors from Euripides, for whom he is κάλλιστος ᾽Αχαιῶν, to Quintus of Smyrna, who reiterates Homer directly and imagines into being Nireus' untold tale, to see him as the embodiment of beauty.[17]

For Horace, who is the first to mention him in Latin (at *Epode* 15.22 where he is said to be known for his *forma*), he is parallel to Ganymede, an epitome of adolescent, androgynous allure.[18] Propertius (3.18.27), with an ironic bow to Homer, links him with Achilles, acknowledging death's transcendent power over the latter's strength as over Nireus' beauty:

> Nireus non facies, non vis exemit Achillem.

> Handsomeness did not exempt Nireus, physical might did not exempt Achilles.

And the later Ovid (*e.p.* 4.13.16) takes note of his beauty, once again.[19] The references are few, yet Homer's Nireus, as received by later Greco-Roman authors, is like Ripheus' portrayal by Virgil as reevaluated by Dante. Ripheus makes a series of momentary appearances among the *Aeneid*'s cast as the most just man among the Trojans, dying as their city is destroyed (*Aen.* 2.339, 394, 426). His singular epithet, *iustissimus*, attracted the Florentine master sufficiently to imagine him, in one of the poet's most memorable acts of sorcery, not only redeemed but placed prominently in the eyebrow of the eagle of Justice in *Paradiso* 20.68. Likewise, because of the force of Homer's description, Nireus is in fact saved from death, with an ongoing grace that lives on in the words of later bards.

If Homer betrays his affection for Nireus by his characterization of him as beautiful, in his own person and because of his inheritance, he also reveals his feelings by the rhetoric of his portrait. This caught the ear of one of the ancient world's greatest theoreticians. At *Rhetorica* 3.1414 Aristotle is talking about asyndeton:

> Therefore an asyndeton produces amplification: Thus in "I came, I conversed, I besought," the hearer seems to be surveying many things, all that the speaker said. This also is Homer's intention in the passage [*Il.* 2.671–73, the initial words of each of which Aristotle quotes] for it is necessary that one of whom much as been said should be often mentioned; if then the name is often mentioned, it seems as if much has been said; so that, by means of this fallacy, Homer has increased the reputation of Nireus, though he only men-

tions him in one passage; he has perpetuated his memory, though he
never speaks of him again.

    (Freese)

Though he is nominally concerned with the working of asyndeton, Aristotle's attention seems primarily caught by the idea of reiterated naming
to preserve the unknown in memory, a procedure which to the philosopher betrays Homer's desire to gain immortality for Nireus in his poetry.
But if asyndeton and repetition of name point up Homer's insistence on
Nireus' continuity beyond his one Iliadic mention, anaphora argues perhaps even more strongly for the poet's intensity of feeling, especially
triple anaphora where the name Nireus begins three contiguous lines. In
a larger schema this threefold "naming" gives shape to the lamentations
at Hector's wake which conclude the poem. There three mourners give
vent to three dirges, each with its own triadic structure and each mentioning the name of Hector once (Andromache at 742, Hekabe at 748,
and Helen at 762) for a total of three namings.[20] Homer's compressed,
triple iteration of the name Nireus, then, suggests in concise form an
implicit love song that is equally an implicit dirge. He appears in fact to be
both mourning before the fact his beloved's disappearance and at the
same time Orphically charming him into life again because of the power
of repeated naming to maintain its object ceaselessly in memory.

    As in so much else, Homer here sets a formative pattern for later
authors. Triple anaphora, where, as in Homer, a name begins three
consecutive verses, is finely exampled in lines from a love poem of Ana-
creon:[21]

    Κλεοβούλου μὲν ἔγωγ' ἐρέω,
    Κλεοβούλῳ δ' ἐπιμαίνομαι,
       Κλεόβουλον δὲ διοσκέω.

I love Cleobulus, I am mad about Cleobulus, I gaze at Cleobulus.

Likewise repetition of the name of the deceased is an important component of ritual lament from Homer on. It is prominent in several poems
we have already mentioned, for instance Bion's *Epitaphios*, which begins
with the name Adonis voiced three times in the first two lines and which
soon proves itself at once both love song and threnody.

    It is this very union of love song and dirge that is central to the
Virgilian texts where use of anaphora to recall the beloved and employment of the "pathetic fallacy," in which nature mourns her lost lover,
complement each other. The roots of this combination lie in Homer's
powerful précis of the story of the beautiful but weak youth Nireus,
where naming monumentalizes absence and death while equally memo-

rializing affection. For inspiration in crafting his final example of ritual lament, as the landscape of Marsian groves and waters mourns the death of Umbro, its priest, magician and warrior, Virgil returned to two sources in the catalogs of *Iliad* 2. One—the figure of the helpless augur Enno-mos—energizes plot, the other, with deeper spiritual significance, sug-gested a rhetorical pattern whose influence he had already experienced. In the anaphoric figuration of Nireus, Homer's understated words and their deployment had, for all their brevity, offered model lines along which future amatory, threnodic, and pastoral poetry, or their intermix-ture, would proceed. In *Aeneid* 7 for one last time Virgil returns to this original theme with his own virtuoso variation.

Finally, a word on Statius. The dozen lines that follow on the lament for Parthenopaeus and conclude the *Thebaid* send the epic out into the world with a prayer that it not seem to rival Statius' cherished *Aeneid* too closely but only to offer it due reverence. This obeisance is certainly apparent throughout the appearances of Parthenopaeus up to the an-nouncement of Atalanta's dirge. But there are crucial details that belong to Homer and not to Virgil—the three women mourners,[22] a beautiful youth as the object of sorrow, the funeral lament as act of epic closure. Statius' public bow is to Virgil but his words also in themselves look to Homer, to the conclusion of the *Iliad* but also to a moment near its start where he projects into a multilayered career in later literature a feeble but handsome youth whom he banishes from his text. Statius in his own way, as had Virgil before him, carefully tugs the whole epic tradition together into his poem, extending Virgil but equally acknowledging and recon-firming the foundational text for them both.

NOTES

1. The passage is also discussed in some detail by Parry, "Two Voices" 107–23 (*Virgil* 107–23 especially 107–9 for analysis of *Aen.* 7.750–60), and Williams, *Tradition and Originality* 723–25. Cf. also Clausen, *Hellenistic Poetry* 86, for whom the episode illustrates "the passing of an older Italy." For the "catalog" of *Aeneid* 7 in general, the standard essays are Fowler, *"Gathering of the Clans"* 73–79; Williams, "Function and Structure" 146–53 (152 specifi-cally on the Umbro passage); Lesky, "Katalogen" 189–96, who notes (190–91) how the idea of magic links the Umbro episode with that of Virbius which follows.

2. For *cuspes* as sting of a scorpion, see Ovid *M.* 2.199, of a bee, Pliny *HN* 21.78. For examples of *ictus* as sting or bit see *OLD* s.v. 2b.

3. See, e.g., Hor. *Epode* 5.76 (*Marsis vocibus*) and 17.29 (*Marsa nenia*). According to Servius (on 7.750) Angitia in another name for Medea, niece of Circe (she received the name, the commentator continues, *quod eius carminibus serpentes angerent*). Her grove's weeping for Umbro therefore associates him with that potent goddess whose presence as metamorphic power plays an impor-tant role in *Aeneid* 7. The irony is that Circe's spell exerts, not

unexpectedly, a negative influence throughout the book, animalizing the human, whereas Umbro's incantations, which maintained their authority over what is already brutish, will have no effect against a stronger process of bestialization now taking place in Italian soil. (For Circe in book 7, see Segal, "Circean Temptations" 430, and my chapter 5.)

4. We hear of Umbro again only at *Aen.* 10.544. We are not told explicitly of his death and, in particular, whether it was at the hands of Aeneas. But the juxtaposition of line 544, which ends *veniens Marsorum montibus Umbro*, with the beginning of line 545, *Dardanides contra furit*, supports the hypothesis that the wielder of the *Dardania cuspes* (7.756) is none other than the chief Dardan hero himself.

5. In Virgil the olive is associated with peace at *Geo.* 2.425 and *Aen.* 8.116, with the priesthood or sacerdotal functions at *Geo.* 3.21 (= *Aen.* 5.774 with the change of *evinctus* for *ornatus*), *Aen.* 6.230, 6.808, 7.418.

6. Macrobius (*Sat.* 4.6.23) mentions 7.759–60, along with *Geo.* 4.465–66 and 4.525–27, in a discussion of anaphora: *nascitur pathos et de narratione.*

7. Williams, *Tradition and Originality* 724, remarks on how the final segment of the tricolon "makes a mainly onomatopoeic appeal with repeated l-sounds."

8. *Aen.* 7.755, *Geo.* 4.510. Cf. *Aen.* 1.153, *pectora mulcet*, in a simile of the furious anger of winds compared to a mob calmed by a man of *pietas*.

9. For detailed commentary see Dodds, *Bacchae*, on 726–27.

10. Examples of the "pathetic fallacy" to be found in post-Theocritan Greek literature are listed by Gow, *Theocritus*, on *Id.* 7.74.

11. For such a sensitive reader of Virgil, Henry, *Aeneidea* 3.611–12, allows himself several injudicious asides when comparing Moschus *Id.* 3.1–2 with *Aen.* 7.759–60. He speaks of "stiff inflexible Latin" in the hands of someone who "was himself too civilized, too Augusticized."

12. The episode occurs at 7.483–510.

13. Another example in Ovid of repetition of the beloved's name (Pyramus) occurs at *M.* 4.142–46, and Cephalus addresses Aura with threefold *tu* at 7.817–19.

14. With the exception of the quote from Ovid's *Tristia*, these post-Virgilian passages are discussed with great sympathy and insight by Jacoff, "Intertextualities" 131–44. Her essay centers on the triple repetition of Virgil's name in *Purgatorio* 30 and on its accompanying allusions to his poetry, as he leaves the poem to be replaced by Beatrice. Jacoff acknowledges, as I do here, the importance of the work of Ahl, especially "Statius' *Thebaid*," for the present reevaluation of the quality of that poet's work.

15. The connection is made by most commentators (e.g., Forbiger, Conington, Page, Fordyce, et al.) as well as Parry, "Two Voices" 109, and Fraenkel, "Some Aspects" 1–14, at 8, n. 14.

16. Aglaia is already one of the three Graces at Hes. *Th.* 945. For the association of χαροπός with χάρις, see Frisk, *Wörterbuch* s.v. χαίρω 1063–64. See also *RE* 3.2.2184 s.v. Charopos (Echer) with further references. Charis is the wife of Hephaestus at *Il.* 18.382.

17. Besides Euripides (*Iph. Aul.* 204–5) and Quintus of Smyrna (6.372–89, 7.8), Nireus is mentioned, among other Greek au-

thors, also by Lycophron (*Alex.* 1011–12) and Diodorus Siculus (53.2).

18. It is arguable that Horace is making explicit a trait that Homer leaves only suggested in the adjective ἀλαπαδνός. In fact the effect of Nireus' "history" in later literature, beginning with his evanescence from the remainder of the *Iliad* and extending to Statius' outright emulation of Homer's portrait, consists partially in a series of realizations of what in Homer are only hints.

19. To the list of Nireus' appearances in Latin literature, add also Hyg. *Fab.* 113.3.

20. On the triple role of the number three in the scene of mourning for Hector, see Alexiou, *Ritual Lament* 232, n. 14.

21. Fr. 359 Campbell = 5 Gentili, from "Herodian" *de figuris* (*Rhet. Gr.* 8.598.16 Walz).

22. It should be noted that, unlike *Iliad* 24 where the three laments are solely offered for Hector, here the objects of grief for the three women are all different.

PIUS AENEAS
AND THE
METAMORPHOSIS
OF LAUSUS

I shot him dead because—
Because he was my foe,
Just so: my foe of course he was;
That's clear enough; although . . .
THOMAS HARDY
The Man He Killed

My essay will review some aspects of the relationship between *pietas* and
the use of force in the *Aeneid*. The intimate cooperation between piety
and power regularly defines Rome and its founding hero. Ilioneus' sketch
to Dido of his absent leader is an early example:

> rex erat Aeneas nobis, quo iustior alter
> nec pietate fuit, nec bello maior et armis.
>   (1.544–45)
> Our king was Aeneas. No other was more righteous in piety nor
> more powerful in war and arms.

Dido herself bitterly demonstrates this collocation in her final soliloquy,
where *dextra* proves equally related to Aeneas' strength at arms and to his
faithless breaking of a compact:

> . . . en dextra fidesque,
> quem secum patrios aiunt portare penatis,
> quem subiisse umeris confectum aetate parentem!
>   (4.597–99)
> . . . behold the right hand and the pledge of him who they say carried
> with him the gods of his fatherland, who supported on his shoulders
> a father undone with age.

The Sibyl puts the conjunction summarily to Charon, presenting her
companion as:

> Troius Aeneas, pietate insignis et armis.
>   (6.403)
> Trojan Aeneas, outstanding for piety and arms.

Ilioneus, now introducing Aeneas to Latinus, can boast of his king's *dextram potentem* and allude again to *fides* and *arma* (7.234–35).[1]

But, as the epic progresses and words are replaced more regularly by deeds and definitions by exemplifications, this mating of abstract duty to gods, family, and patriotic mission with the physical means toward its validation becomes a more ambiguous union, shading into the use of force for questionable goals, often for the gratification of private feelings rather than the fulfillment of idealistic, public purposes. I would like to examine in detail one striking instance of Aeneas in power drawn from the tenth book, the death scene of Lausus, and then follow out parallel passages, ending with a brief look at Aeneas' final confrontation with Turnus.

We have learned from the seventh book of Lausus' personal beauty and of his prowess at taming horses and harrowing wild beasts (7.649–51),[2] but from the start we are prejudiced against his father Mezentius, the *contemptor divum* with a bent for the macabre torturing of his victims (7.647–48, 8.480–89). Yet in the tenth book the human, private image diverges from the public. Son remains faithful to father and, in a striking manifestation of *pietas*, shields Mezentius from the onslaught of Aeneas— *genitor nati parma protectus* (10.800). The reprieve is short-lived. The titular hero soon buries his sword in the side of the youth, as he himself is centered in the language, *per medium Aeneas iuvenem* (816).[3]

At this moment, when the reader is drawn to Lausus, protecting his father and wearing a tunic woven for him by his mother, Virgil seizes the occasion for an irony pointed against Aeneas. Before he wounds Mezentius and initiates the dissolution of one of the more poignant parent-child relationships in the epic, Aeneas is given his epithet *pius* (783), and as he prepares to wound Lausus mortally the poet has him shout:

> "quo moriture ruis maioraque viribus audes?
> fallit te incautum pietas tua."
> (811–12)
> "Whither do you rush, about to die, and dare deeds greater than
> your strength? Your piety deceives you in your folly."

Aeneas ironically interprets in negative terms the abstract that had always been his, symbolized in his rescue of his father and son from Troy and in his visit to Anchises in the Underworld. It becomes an impediment, making Lausus vulnerable to his opponent's *saevae irae* (813), and killing him. Virgil reverses our expectations by having Aeneas grimly see himself as an incorporation of a *pietas* that destroys in a particularly vicious manner because it kills the embodiment of a *pietas* that saves. And, as at the death of Turnus which concludes the epic, Aeneas takes no responsibility. What his maddened words would have the immediate—and dis-

tant—hearer believe is that not Aeneas but *pietas*, and his antagonist's
pietas at that, performed the deed. If Lausus had been *cautus*, the hero
implies, he would not have practiced *pietas* and would have escaped
death.

The final *tua* (812) therefore serves a double purpose. It shows Aeneas
shifting the cause for Lausus' death onto Lausus' own practice of Aeneas'
virtue. But it also reveals a half-conscious awareness that he himself
is blameworthy, while the reader is left wondering about the depth
of Aeneas' commitment to *pietas* elsewhere. How often, we ask, does
Aeneas adhere to or reject *pietas* for subjective, even self-serving, reasons?

For Aeneas to impute Lausus' defeat not to himself but to *pietas*
smacks of self-deception, fabricated to ward off the full implications of his
words and action. At moments of rage *pietas* and *arma* do not easily
blend. In the case of Lausus' death each destroys. Aeneas' arms, working
out a continued desire for vengeance, do the actual deed, but Aeneas'
abstraction, as practiced by Lausus and explained by Aeneas, abets the
negative impulse. Meanwhile the reader's disposition changes from understanding for Aeneas, about the sometimes violent task of establishing
Rome, to compassion for his victims. Though Mezentius despises the
gods, publicly abrogating an important form of *pietas*, he gains at the end
a measure of our sympathy.[4] When it comes to the practice of virtue in
the heat of war his son feels and displays both *amor* and *pietas*, while *pius*
Aeneas performs the greatest act of *impietas* by killing first the son who
protects, then his wounded father. His deeds in battle elicit our apprecia-
tion of Lausus, whose affection for Mezentius makes the latter less despi-
cable, but our respect is undermined for Aeneas who is brutalized by an
inability to respond sympathetically to his own supposedly characteristic
virtue in the operations of others. In moments of rage the merely physical controls his life, to suggest more similarity with than distinction from
Mezentius himself.

Then occurs one of the most beautiful and moving moments in the
epic. After lines of unremitting fury,[5] culminating in the death of Lausus,
we have a moment of quiet, as Aeneas contemplates the features of his
victim:

> At vero ut vultum vidit morientis et ora,
> ora modis Anchisiades pallentia miris,
> ingemuit miserans graviter dextramque tetendit,
> et mentem patriae subiit pietatis imago.
> (821–24)

But when the son of Anchises saw the face and features of the dying
man, the features pale in marvelous ways, he groaned deeply from
pity and stretched out his right hand, and the picture of paternal
piety entered his mind.

Epic diachronism yields to lyric depth and intensity. We enter a complex verbal world where reiteration of words, assonance, and alliteration force the reader to hear sound echo in sound, and where such interweaving and repetition linguistically mimic Aeneas' own pause to look, and look again, as the poet slows action to a stop. *Vultum vidit, modis miris, morientis,* and *pallentia* form unifying sound clusters, but it is the repetition of *ora* at the end of line 821 and the beginning of line 822 that especially causes the reader to follow Aeneas' own mental progress and momentarily choose contemplation over action, explanation over heedless, continued doing.[6] Line 822 adds nothing to plot, much to atmosphere. It is a golden line, brilliantly centered around *Anchisiades* which stands out, furthermore, as the longest word in lines 821–22 and the only one that lacks melodic intimacy with any of its neighbors.

As we savor this calming panel breaking the onrush of narrative, we watch, first, the metamorphosis of Lausus from living to dead, from body to spirit, from physical being to disembodied emblem. Virgil would have us think of those *simulacra modis pallentia miris* from among whom, Lucretius tells us, the ghost of Homer arose to enlighten Ennius (*DRN* 1.123). In the first *Georgic* Virgil draws on the same phrase to describe those images that appeared among the disquieting portents accompanying the death of Julius Caesar. Venus, in *Aeneid* 1, tells of the apparition in dreams to Dido of her unburied husband, *ora modis attollens pallida miris* (354), raising his face pale in marvelous ways.[7] As we join Aeneas in beholding Lausus' color paling and life giving place to death, we turn from surface to substance and examine through Aeneas' eyes the change in Lausus from literal to figurative. He alters from palpable enemy, to be killed both by and even at the expense of the hero's prime virtue, to a wraith that is symbol of that virtue, *patriae pietatis imago*, the personification of piety toward one's father. As war's wildness is momentarily subdued by thought, Aeneas appears to see beyond what his previous intensity had not allowed into human motivations that should be, but have not always been, a part of his thinking during his bout of killing. Contemplation and madness, *pietas* and slaughter would seem incompatible entities.

Pause in epic thrust for a moment of lyric intensity is thus a metaphor for the differentiation between history's relentless progress—the teleology of a brilliant Roman destiny personified in the conduct of its founding father—and the personal suffering this progress causes. The tale of Mezentius operates on both levels at once. Virgil imputes to Mezentius alone what seems to have been a common pattern of Etruscan behavior.[8] But by stressing the public odiousness of Mezentius' former conduct he makes more remarkable the private devotion of Lausus, faithful to his father even to the sharing of exile. Moreover, through his son's sacrifice the *contemptor divum* elicits a vivid demonstration of *pietas* which in turn forces *pius* Aeneas to become a killer of the pious. Larger abstract notions

of slaying barbarous enemies to rid the world of the primitive and the
bestial are constantly questioned by Virgil when focused against the
realities of human emotions, and the pause, Aeneas' and the reader's,
from linear action at Lausus' death is one of the most poignant examples
in the epic.

The transformation of Lausus is also the transformation of Aeneas. By
imitating him, Aeneas for a moment becomes Lausus' double. The
phrase *patriae pietatis imago* is equally his.[9] The Aeneas who buried his
sword into the body of Lausus has become *Anchisiades*, perceiving in
Lausus' saving conduct an emblem of his own behavior toward his father.[10] He no longer stands alone but becomes part of a relationship of
son to father, particular son to particular father. Although he will soon
proclaim, with a renewal of callousness, that Lausus' consolation is his
fall "by the right hand of mighty Aeneas" (*Aeneae magni dextra*, 830), that
right hand is at present stretched forward in a gesture not of violence but
of pity, perhaps even of supplication.[11] Pity now becomes the chief component of this late learning. Aeneas is *miserans* as he begins to speak, his
initial apostrophe to Lausus is *miserande puer* (825), and he defines the
youth's death as *miseram* (829).

There is another vehicle by which Aeneas not only commiserates but
verbally becomes Lausus, just as he suddenly remembers his own son-
ship. At the moment in the previous duel when Lausus rescues his father,
Aeneas has just wounded Mezentius with his spear and, "happy (*laetus*) at
the sight of Etruscan blood," has drawn his sword for the kill. This is
Lausus' reaction to the sight:

> ingemuit cari graviter genitoris amore,
> ut vidit, Lausus, lacrimaeque per ora volutae . . .
>   (789–90)
> As he looked Lausus groaned deeply from love of his dear father, and
> tears rolled down his face . . .

The phrases *ingemuit graviter* and *ut vidit* recur in close proximity at the
moment of Lausus' death, attached now to Aeneas, as he and we notice
the youth's features, deathly pale instead of tear-stricken.[12] For Aeneas,
after his mortal deed, to react in the same way as Lausus about the saving
of his father, is for the poet to fuse the two characters and to have Aeneas,
in the hiatus before he turns to kill Mezentius, share Lausus' emotion to
the point of linguistically merging with him as well.

That the conjunction is brief does not detract from its power, but the
reader is prepared by Aeneas' prior deed in the book not only for the
mood to be evanescent but to learn once again that such thoughts do not
influence his actions. One previous example from book 10, which will
turn our attention to earlier books of the epic, must suffice to illustrate

Aeneas' inattention to *pietas* in the heat of combat. In his bloodlust after
the death of Pallas he first secures eight victims to be offered alive as
sacrifice on the young hero's pyre. After that he slays Magus who is a
suppliant (*supplex*, 523), grasping Aeneas' knees. Magus' initial words are
well chosen to affect the reader, though they do not deter Aeneas who
twists their tone:

> "per patrios manis et spes surgentis Iuli
> te precor, hanc animam serves gnatoque patrique . . ."
>   (524–25)
> "I beseech you by the shade of your father and the hope of growing
> Iulus, save this life for a son and for a father . . ."

Magus' plea is a pastiche contrived from book 6. His first line recalls
Palinurus' prayer to Aeneas to lead him across the Styx:

> "per genitorem oro, per spes surgentis Iuli . . ."
>   (364)
> "I pray you by your father, by the hope of growing Iulus . . ."

The helmsman's request appeals to the gestures, if not the emotions, of
pietas:

> "da dextram misero et tecum me tolle per undas . . ."
>   (370)
> "Give your right hand to me in my misery and carry me with you
> through the waves . . ."[13]

Before Aeneas can reply, the Sibyl forbids any intervention.

The second line of Magus' speech reaches further back in book 6 to an
earlier prayer, of Aeneas to the Sibyl. His request is briefly put:

> ". . . ire ad conspectum cari genitoris et ora contingat . . ."
>   (108–9)
> ". . . May I be allowed to make my way to the sight and face of my
> dear father . . ."

And his plea follows readily:

> ". . . gnatique patrisque
> alma, precor, miserere . . ."
>   (116–17)
> ". . . kindly one, I beseech you, pity son and father . . ."

In the press of battle he denies the power of Magus' words that he had expected to be able to bring to bear himself, in proposing to the Sibyl his strange, pietistic adventure. In common with Lausus he shares love of a dear parent, but forgets its validity when passion has mastered him. In book 6, where Aeneas is a *supplex* (115) and the tangible efforts to carry out his mission have not brought the moral dilemma of the final books, he is introduced by the Sibyl to Charon as *tantae pietatis imago* (405). He incorporates in himself what he will see in Lausus after he has killed him, and rage has momentarily retreated before understanding and commiseration. When father and son do meet (670–702), it is again the gesturing of hands and facial expressions which are the manifestations that, in Anchises' words, *vicit iter durum pietas* (688). Anchises stretched forth both palms, weeping, and Aeneas attempts in vain to clasp hands with his father, as he too weeps. There is a shared emphasis on the features of each, the *ora* through which both demonstrate *pietas*, by which Lausus also showed his love for Mezentius and in which Aeneas too saw a symbol of piety.

Pietas, therefore, reveals itself regularly by facial and verbal gestures of supplication and affection. It is not incompatible with *arma* in a general definition of the Roman achievement that combines force with human understanding. Yet it remains unreconcilable with the maddened and the irrational, especially when the weapons of war are involved. This we know from the beginning of the epic. The first we hear of Aeneas, his sufferings in war and conveyance of gods to Latium—*pietas* and *arma* combined—are contrasted to the *saevae memorem Iunonis iram* (1.4–6). Immediately thereafter the hero who appears *insignem pietate* (10) is caught between an emotional queen of the gods (*dolens regina deum*, 9) and the narrator's amazed questioning that *tantae irae* (11) could persist among the immortals.[14] The contrast remains alive throughout the book and the epic. At lines 251–53, for example, Venus juxtaposes the anger of unnamed Juno and the *pietatis honos* that is due Aeneas for his fidelity. The contrast is summarized in the first simile of the epic. Juno has given her resentments full play and stirred up Aeolus and his winds against the Trojans. Neptune senses the confusion and rightly imputes it to *Iunonis irae* (130). Virgil compares his calming presence amid wildness untrammeled to a man *pietate gravem ac meritis* (151) who soothes a ferocious mob to which fury lends arms (*furor arma ministrat*, 150).

In the first book Aeneas is buffeted by the elemental nature of Juno and her creatures, with little power to resist. During the bitter night of Troy's fall, the subject of book 2, Aeneas can take a more active, if unproductive role. We therefore watch with interest the relationship between Aeneas' first acts of piety and his recourse to arms, and how the polarity between enlightenment of mind and dark lack of understanding often shapes this relationship. Here too *imagines* play an important role in helping Aeneas clarify the obscure, penetrate behind the facades of motivation and action, and, finally, move away from bouts of futile violence toward an acceptance of a future symbolized in the professions of *pietas*.

The first "image" in book 2 is Aeneas' dream of Hector:

> in somnis, ecce, ante oculos maestissimus Hector
> visus adesse mihi . . .
>   (270–71)
> In dreams, behold, most pitiful Hector seemed to stand before my
> eyes . . .

The sleeping hero cannot yet appreciate the meaning of Hector's wounds, which would be to remember his mutilation by Achilles. Hector's speech, therefore, has a twofold importance. It forces the reality of his loss on Aeneas and forewarns that his tragedy anticipates the general suffering of Troy's demise. Hector then pronounces the futility of reliance on arms and succinctly predicts to Aeneas his future, suggesting his first act of *pietas*:

> sacra suosque tibi commendat Troia Penates;
> hos cape fatorum comites . . .
>   (293–94)
> Troy commits to you its holy objects and its household gods; seize
> them as comrades of your fortune . . .

The vision of Hector allows Aeneas to face the truth of both present and future. At the same time Hector's wraith, by thrusting fillets, Vesta, and the everlasting fire into his hands, proclaims Aeneas as protector of Troy's gods in transition.

It is a part that wakened Aeneas is not prepared to accept. For a moment he seems aloof from the *furentibus Austris* that fan the flames and akin to a shepherd who comprehends a stream's rampage only through a distant echo.[15] Yet, forgetful of Hector's revelation and command, he plunges irrationally into arms:

> arma amens capio; nec sat rationis in armis . . .
>   (314)
> In madness I seize arms; nor is there sufficient reason in arms . . .

In his own words, *furor* and *ira* drive his mind headlong (316). The first "image" has proved wasted on Aeneas who takes up arms not in defense of *pietas* but under the sponsorship of the unthinking use of force that so often stands in the way.

The next revelation to Aeneas comes after the central episode of the book, the forcing of Priam's palace and the decapitation of the old king. Aeneas seems only a voyeur of this impious sequence of events as Pyrrhus kills first Polites before the eyes of his parents, then Priam himself. He makes no attempt to intervene or avenge the double murder, perhaps because he is meant to appreciate that the death of its aged leader betokens the downfall of Troy. After the appearance of Hector *armorum horror* (301) had increased to the point that it had wakened the sleeping hero. Now it surrounds him:

> At me tum primum saevus circumstetit horror.
> obstipui; subiit cari genitoris imago,
> ut regem aequaevum crudeli vulnere vidi
> vitam exhalantem, subiit deserta Creusa
> et direpta domus et parvi casus Iuli.
>   (559–63)

But then first dreadful horror surrounded me. I stood amazed; the vision of my dear father stood before me when I saw the king, his age mate, breathing forth his life from a cruel wound, deserted Creusa came before me, my plundered house and the fate of little Iulus.

Yet instead of rushing thoughtlessly into war Aeneas now allows the vision to develop a deeper significance. The hero responds to the sight of *pietas* affronted by becoming possessed with *pietas* of his own. It is no wonder that the description and especially the phrase *subiit cari genitoris imago* reverberate in the remainder of the epic. Anchises appears again a *cari genitoris* as Aeneas requests the Sibyl to visit his father in Hades (6.108),[16] and the phrase *subiit imago*, as we have seen, initiates Aeneas' realization that in Lausus he had killed an emblem of *pietas*, forced to die "because of love for his dear father" (*cari genitoris amore*, 10.789), and had himself become a deadly, not saving, manifestation of the same presumed virtue.

Yet, instead of implementing his new insight, Aeneas again yields to impetuosity and contemplates the killing of Helen.[17] Anger, not the spirit of filial duty, rules his thoughts:

> ". . . subit ira cadentem
> ulcisci patriam et sceleratas sumere poenas."
>   (575–76)

". . . anger overcomes me to avenge my falling fatherland and to exact punishment for her crimes."

As he admits, before he has a chance to turn words into deeds, *furiata mente ferebar* (2.588). He is the passive victim of insanity rather than the active pursuer of a more noble, less tangible, goal. What changes his mind is another vision:

> cum mihi se, non ante oculis tam clara, videndam
> obtulit et pura per noctem in luce refulsit
> alma parens . . .
> (589–91)
> When my kindly mother offered herself to my sight, never before so clear to my vision, and gleamed in pure radiance through the night . . .

With the appearance of Venus both the hero's parents replace Helen as the primary objects of his thinking. Her first words demand such recollection:

> "nate, quis indomitas tantus dolor excitat iras?
> quid furis? aut quonam nostri tibi cura recessit?
> non prius aspicies ubi fessum aetate parentem
> liqueris Anchisen, superet coniunxne Creusa
> Ascaniusque puer? . . ."
> (594–98)
> "My son, what great resentment arouses your ungovernable anger? Why are you raging? Or whither has your care for us gone? Will you not first see where you left your father Anchises spent with age, whether your wife Creusa and the boy Ascanius survive? . . ."

Useless vengeance against the past is replaced by renewed allegiance to continuity and, ultimately, acceptance of future destiny. The abstractions which polarize around this change are standard, with one exception. The resentment, anger, and rage that press Aeneas toward the unheroic urge to kill a woman, are countered now by an appeal to *pietas* defined specifically by the word *cura*. It is *nostri cura*, "care for us," love of Venus, that should have motivated Aeneas' deeds.

As will be the case when he is exposed to the deeper significance of Lausus' death, Venus' potency has the other extraordinary but complementary effect of allowing Aeneas, in pondering a course of action, to see beyond the superficial and observe larger forces at work upon humankind. *Tyndaridis facies invisa Lacaenae*, the (ironically) hateful features of Helen, had, according to Venus, impelled Aeneas to an equally superficial, negative waste of energy. Venus now dramatically unclouds her son's vision to allow him to look beyond appearance and watch *divum inclementia* at work. This is Virgil's only use of the abstraction in the *Aeneid*,[18] and it gives emphasis to an occasion where Aeneas can note the force of divine unforgiveness at work, in Juno, *saevissima* and *furens*, in Athena,

equally *saeva*, and in the father of the gods himself, urging on his colleagues. Presumably Aeneas, and we, at moments where we must scrutinize the symbolic meaning of events, would associate *inclementia* with
ferocity, and *clementia* with restraint.

The last "vision" occurs at the end of the book. Aeneas returns to his
father's house and persuades him, with the help of a series of positive
omens, to leave Troy. In the process of retreat, as Aeneas carries out his
first great act of *pietas*, shouldering his father and grasping Iulus by the
hand, Creusa is lost and Aeneas, *amens*, returns in quest. Her sudden
appearance to him parallels the previous epiphanies of Hector and Venus:

> infelix simulacrum atque ipsius umbra Creusae
> visa mihi ante oculos et nota maior imago.
> (772–73)
> The sad ghost and shade of Creusa herself appeared before my eyes
> and a vision larger than her wont.

Its potential is not dissimilar. Like Venus, Creusa chides Aeneas for his
indulgence in *insano dolori* (776). Then, expanding on the example of
Hector, she reveals to Aeneas the *res laetae* of the future, a kingdom and
royal wife. Her last words, however, center on a love that is intimate with
pietas: *nati serva communis amorem* (789). As she disappears, and Aeneas
attempts to hold her, Virgil uses three lines that he will repeat exactly in
book 6 as son greets father:

> ter conatus ibi collo dare bracchia circum;
> ter frustra comprensa manus effugit imago,
> par levibus ventis volucrique simillima somno.
> (792–94)
> Three times there I attempted to throw my arms about her neck;
> three times the vision, embraced in vain, fled my hands, kin to light
> winds and very like a swift dream.

Each figure is a crucial *imago* in Aeneas' life, a ghost that foretells the
future after a period of insecurity and search. Each exemplifies a melan-
cholic aspect of the life of the hero, unable to embrace those dear to him,
forced away from Dido for whom he does care, and allotted at the end of
the epic a *coniunx* thrust on him by fate. Yet each also is a creative
influence in disparate ways—Creusa, by calming his final act of *dolor* in
book 2 with a look at the future, Anchises by expanding that future in a
delusive vista where arms and piety, clemency and power seem to abide
in harmony.

Hence in book 2 as a whole we regularly find emotionality opposed to
reason, especially when directed toward long-range goals. Such moments

of irrationality are often centered on immediate gratification, understandable however morally misguided. Heedless action finds its counter-
poise in the words of Hector, Panthus, Venus, and Creusa, and the
thoughts and insights they arouse. The hero's display of aimless chauvin-
ism that follows his dream of Hector is not defended within his narration,
and his rationalization for killing Helen, argued in a soliloquy he quotes
himself delivering a moment before he almost performs the deed, Aeneas
himself qualifies as the product of a maddened mind (*furiata mente*).

It is inevitable that discussion of such polarities must focus on the
finale of the poem as Aeneas ponders the situation of the now suppliant
Turnus, and then slays him. How is Aeneas to see him, and how, as he
weighs alternatives, will whatever analysis he makes of his victim sway
him, as he hesitates?[19] Their differentiation (as well as commonality) is
made explicit by the poet's concentration on the eyes and right hands of
each hero, preceding and following Turnus' last words. Before he speaks
we watch Turnus—

> ille humilis supplex oculos dextramque precantem
> protendens . . .
>   (12.930–31)
> He, a suppliant, with eyes humbled, and stretching forth his right
> hand in prayer . . .

—and after, our attention focuses on the hero in power:

>   . . . stetit acer in armis
> Aeneas volvens oculos dextramque repressit . . .
>   (938–39)
> . . . Aeneas stood fierce in his armor, rolling his eyes, and held his
> right hand in check . . .

The eyes of Turnus are humbled, of Aeneas revolving in thought, as
victoriously he plots out the possibilities before him.[20] When Turnus
states that the Ausonians have seen him, conquered, stretch forth his
hands (*victum tendere palmas*, 936), he merely reinforces the contrast between his gesture of supplication and Aeneas' posture of strength, his
right hand momentarily restrained.

The gesture of supplication is one that Aeneas would have understood.
He had seen his father twice use it, first, as Troy falls, in asking Jupiter to
confirm the omen of fire on Iulus' head (*palmas tetendit*, 2.688), second
while greeting Aeneas in the Underworld (*palmas tetendit*, 6.685), when
last he saw him. He had employed it himself to Jupiter in prayer to save
the burning ships (*tendere palmas*, 5.686), and watched it in the suppliant
Liger in book 10 (*tendebat palmas*, 596–97).[21] The reader remembers it

from the hero's initial appearance in the epic, awed by the prospect of
death from nature and preparing to address those who die (to him) more
heroically at Troy:

> extemplo Aeneae solvuntur frigore membra;
> ingemit et duplicis tendens ad sidera palmas
> talia voce refert . . .
>   (1.92–94)
> Suddenly Aeneas' limbs were undone with cold; he groans and,
> stretching both hands toward the stars, speaks thus aloud . . .[22]

Line 92 closely resembles the description of Turnus, frightened by the
Dira sent by Jupiter to ensure his final defeat:

> Illi membra novus solvit formidine torpor . . .
>   (12.867)
> A strange numbness undoes his limbs in fear . . .

This spectacle is complemented shortly later by the prospect of Turnus
incapable of movement (*gelidus concrevit frigore sanguis*, 905), and imitated
most clearly in the next to last line of the poem as Turnus dies:

> . . . ast illi solvuntur frigore membra.
>   (951)
> . . . but his limbs were undone with cold.[23]

Matters have come full circle. Aeneas, once helpless before the elements, has now become the elemental power, abetted by Jupiter and his
Dira, before which Turnus must pray in supplication and which finally
destroys him. But the closest parallel between the two is suggested by the
previous words of Turnus:

> ". . . miseri te si qua parentis
> tangere cura potest, oro (fuit et tibi talis
> Anchises genitor) Dauni miserere senectae . . ."
>   (12.932–34)
> ". . . if any care of a sad parent can touch you, I pray you, pity the old
> age of Daunus (Anchises was also such a father to you) . . ."[24]

Virgil has graphically sketched Turnus' aging and debilitation in the lines
that lead up to the final duel. (Our growing sympathy for prideful Turnus
now suffering humiliation is not unlike our response to savage Mezentius
at the moment his vulnerability is shielded by his loving son.) Suddenly,
therefore, we find his prototype not in wounded Hector but in Priam

whose first, dramatic words to Achilles, as he comes to ransom his son's body, remind him of his father Peleus:

"μνῆσαι πατρὸς σοῖο, θεοῖς ἐπιείκελ' Ἀχιλλεῦ,
τηλίκου, ὥς περ ἐγών, ὀλοῷ ἐπὶ γήραος οὐδῷ . . ."
    (Il. 24.486–87)
"Achilles like to the gods, remember your father, whose years are like mine, on the grievous threshold of age . . ."

They would also serve to recall to Aeneas his own vivid display of *pietas*, searching out his father in the Underworld, and, as we have observed, his preliminary position as suppliant, craving pity from the Sibyl:

"quin ut te supplex peterem et tua limina adirem,
idem orans mandata dabat. gnatique patrisque,
alma, precor, miserere . . ."
    (6.115–17)
"Nay he also in prayer gave me commands that as a suppliant I seek you out and approach your threshold. I pray, kindly one, pity both son and father . . ."[25]

First introduced in the epic as a new Achilles, Turnus becomes now not only Priam before Achilles but also Aeneas before the Sibyl.[26] He should appear to his victor as a figure of Aeneas himself, as he appeals to an *imago* Aeneas should well remember. Instead of following the pattern of book 10 where he saw Lausus as an emblem of *pietas* only after he has killed him (and only then does he become *Anchisiades*), Aeneas has a chance to be affected by words, ideas, and memories, to pity before rather than after a deed, even to spare, combining force with generosity, not madness. He could show that he also has absorbed what the reader has learned from the conclusion of book 10.

The phrase *parentis cura* and its association with two fathers, Anchises and Daunus, should also cast Aeneas' thoughts back to the past. The reader associates the phrase with Aeneas' love for Ascanius (1.646) and, as Andromache reminisces, with Ascanius' for his lost mother (3.341). Aeneas might hear again Venus' question after he has nearly killed Helen:

". . . aut quonam nostri tibi cura recessit?
non prius aspicies ubi fessum aetate parentem
liqueris Anchisen . . . ?"
    (2.595–97)
"Or whither has your care for us gone? Will you not first see where you left your father Anchises spent with age . . . ?"

Remembrance of both parents, the *cura parentum* for which *pietas* should provide the motivation, contrasts with the *dolor, ira,* and *furor* that, in Venus' words, Aeneas has just displayed by his desire for vengeance against Helen. It is not, however, Turnus as image of *pietas* or even as representative of Aeneas himself that moves the hero to act at the epic's end. Turnus' words do in fact cause him to delay, to experience a moment of detachment, which means at least the possibility of *clementia,* of words taking precedence over deeds. What impels Aeneas to kill is the sight of Pallas' baldrick worn by Turnus. It serves as a *saevi monimenta doloris* (945) which drives Aeneas mad, *furiis accensus et ira / terribilis* (946–47). It is not *pietas,* and the moderation both Venus and Anchises see in its practice, but *ira* that holds the hero in thrall as he embarks on his final action. The clarity of broadened vision that Aeneas is allowed in book 2, when he beholds divine *inclementia* about its devastating work, and that is offered to him so brilliantly as action pauses for the double figuration of Lausus' death, is once again, and for the last time, obscured.[27]

NOTES

I would like to thank Professors Christine Perkell, Kenneth Reckford, and Charles Segal for their helpful comments.

1. Cf. also 6.769, 6.878–79, 11.291–92. The practice of *pietas* and the production of *arma* are linked in Venus' request to Vulcan (8.383): *arma rogo: genetrix nato.*
2. Only Turnus is more handsome.
3. This point is made by Benario, "Tenth Book" 33.
4. The reader's sympathy for Mezentius grows as the book nears its conclusion, for his self-understanding, and for his realization of how his earlier misdeeds have affected his son whose loyalty he has nonetheless retained. We hear of his *canities* (10.844) only after Lausus' death.

    Leach, "Blindness of Mezentius" 83–89, notes well the change in Mezentius which Aeneas is unable, or unwilling, to perceive.
5. For an examination of Aeneas' conduct earlier in the book, viewed against its Iliadic background, see Farron, "*Furor* and *Violentia*" 204–8.
6. *Ora* is also repeated effectively at 6.495–96, as Aeneas contemplates the mutilated features of Deiphobus. Virgil uses the same verb, *subeo,* to describe Aeneas' imagining of piety at 10.824 and the carrying of his father at 2.708. Cf. also 2.560 and 4.599.

    Virgil repeats the name Lausus prominently when we first hear of him (7.649–51). *Esset* ends both lines 653 and 654; the first use is connected with *patriis imperiis;* the other has *pater* as subject. Lausus and his father Mezentius are linguistically and emotionally intertwined from the start. I cannot agree with Jones, "Mezentius" 53 (cf. 51), that Mezentius is "effectively isolated from his son." The personal allegiance of Lausus, in spite of his father's conduct, remains significant.

    For a sensitive treatment of 10.821–24, to which my analysis is indebted, see Johnson, *Darkness Visible* 72–74. Professor Johnson carefully elucidates Virgil's originality by comparison with his

Homeric models, especially the lamentations of Priam and Achilles that begin at *Il.* 24.507.

7. Cf. also the priest at the oracle of Faunus who *multa modis simulacra videt volitantia miris* (7.89).

8. Virgil's treatment of Mezentius is analyzed by Burke, "Role of Mezentius" 202–9. His departures from tradition in dealing with Lausus and Mezentius are touched on by Heinze, *Technik* 172–73, 179, and 213. Mezentius' exile is a Virgilian invention which proves that, for Virgil at least, the Etruscans were capable of responding to cruelty before the arrival of Aeneas. His death at the hands of Aeneas is original with Virgil whom Ovid (*F.* 4.895–96) follows. Tradition has him either slain later (Cato *Orig.* fr. 9–11P, noted by Servius on *Aen.* 1.267, 4.620, 6.760, and 9.742) or making peace (Livy 1.3.4; D.H. 1.65.5; Dio Cassius fr. 3.7 Melber [from Tzetzes on Lyc. *Alex.* 1232]). Aeneas' killing of Lausus is likewise an alteration of tradition which has him dying also in a subsequent battle against Ascanius (D.H. 1.65.3). Virgil's use of tradition in molding his characterization of Mezentius is treated by Sullivan, "Mezentius" 219–25, who plots analogies with the Ajax of Homer and Sophocles, and Glenn, "Mezentius and Polyphemus" 129–55, who finds Virgil's principal model in the Polyphemus of the *Odyssey*.

9. The phrase is similar to one used of Iulus at 9.294 (*animum patriae strinxit pietatis imago*). Though Iulus is responding to Euryalus' concern for his mother, the words more strictly refer to the *pietas* he bears his absent father, and vice versa.

10. The power of *Anchisiades* here is discussed by Benario, "Tenth Book" 33. Virgil uses the patronymic on five other occasions, 5.407, 6.126, 6.348, 8.521, and 10.250. In each case there are reasons to remember the father-son relationship.

11. I will turn to the phrase *palmas tendere* in a moment. The words *tendere manus* are directly associated with *amor* at 6.314.

12. Alliteration draws the reader's attention from *cari*, *genitoris*, and *amore* to *ora*, and prepares for the latter's repetition at 821–22.

    The effect of first-person narrative is particularly powerful at 10.790–93. This witness of emotional involvement is congruent with the detailed knowledge the narrator evinces of Lausus at 10.832 (*comptos de more capillos*). This sudden specificity suggests more than the difference between death's dishevelment and life's order.

13. Cf. also 2.721–23 and 2.804. At 4.274 Mercury reminds Aeneas of *Ascanium surgentem et spes heredis Iuli*. When Aeneas acts against Magus he is no longer helpless before fate.

14. An instance of the distinction between anger and piety, outside of book 1, occurs at 5.781–88 where the *ira* (781), *nefandis odiis* (785–86), and *furoris* (788) of Juno are contrasted by Venus with the *pietas* (783) of Aeneas.

15. *Furentibus Austris* (1.51) helped Aeolus threaten the Trojan fleet in the epic's opening episode.

16. The phrase *cari genitoris* is also used at 1.677 of Aeneas in relation to Ascanius-Iulus.

    The parallel between 2.560 (*genitoris imago*) and 10.824 (*pietatis imago*) is noted by DiCesare, *Altar* 174.

    A *genitoris imago* is twisted at 4.84 where Dido is misled by the image of Aeneas in the features of Ascanius, a delusion that

commenced in book 1 when Cupid had adopted the same features. It is an *imago* empty of significance. An *imago* of Anchises,
however, and mention of Ascanius at 4.351–54 are among the
causes of Aeneas' departure from Carthage.

Aeneas accused his mother of deluding him *falsis imaginibus*
(1.407–8). Throughout the epic, when *imagines* matter most,
they often betoken personal lack of fulfillment, *pietas* without its
final symbolic seal.

17. The Helen episode lacks the final Virgilian polish, but *Aeneid* 2 is
not whole without it. Venus' reminder to Aeneas of Anchises,
Creusa, and Ascanius at 596–98 makes little sense unless some
event has intervened to make the hero forget his perception of
them at 562–63. A prior encounter with her is the logical way to
explain Venus' allusion to Helen (601), the first of two creatures
(the other is Paris) whom Aeneas would be prone to blame but,
according to his mother, should not.

Beyond the level of plot, there are other imaginative factors
that suggest the intimacy of the Helen passage with its context.
Both share the polarities of seeing and nonseeing, insight and
blindness. There is the common notion of fire as analogy between physical and human, exterior and interior worlds. But
such themes deserve separate analysis.

18. Virgil's only other use of *inclementia* is in relation to death (*Geo.*
3.68). By the epic's end the *inclementia* of the gods against Aeneas
and Troy has become the *saevitia* of Jupiter and Aeneas against
Turnus.

19. I will deal in the next chapter with the importance of hesitation
throughout the epic and especially in connection with the
poem's final moments.

20. I follow the Oxford Classical Text of Mynors at line 930. If, with M
and several later manuscripts, we read *supplexque*, then *humilis*
would modify not *oculos* but *ille* and *supplex* (see Williams, *Aeneid*
ad loc.). Dido is also seen *volvens oculos*, worrying through her
course of action against Aeneas (4.363), as is Latinus, pondering
acceptance of the Trojans (7.251). We are told that Aeneas *oculos
volvit*, contemplating Vulcan's shield (8.618). See also 4.643 and
7.399, where madness is part of a process of decision, and cf. 1.482
and 6.469 where fixed eyes betoken decisiveness of mind.

21. Before Aeneas kills Lucagus and then Liger, his brother, he is
called *pius* (10.591). Liger prays for mercy by appeal to Aeneas'
parents. Aeneas' reply ends *morere at fratrem ne desere frater* (600).

22. Mezentius, when he sees the lifeless body of Lausus, *ambas / ad
caelum tendit palmas* (10.844–45), a curious gesture for a despiser
of the gods.

23. Virgil uses the same line of Aeneas responding to Mercury's
command for withdrawal from Carthage (4.280) and of Turnus'
facing the Dira (12.868). Here too the early Aeneas maintains
kinship with the later Turnus.

24. Turnus' words to Aeneas are similar to ones Latinus had addressed to Turnus at the start of the book (12.43–45). Turnus'
gradual change from pride to humiliation is the book's process
also.

25. There are other words common to Aeneas' speech in book 6 and
to Turnus in 12, among them *genitor* (6.108) and *senectae* (6.114).

It is apt that the Sibyl's reply first apostrophizes Aeneas as *sate sanguine divum,* / *Tros Anchisiade* (6.125–26).

26. Aeneas, at his ugliest moment of rage in book 10, is also patterned after Achilles (with *Aen.* 10.557–60 compare *Il.* 21.122–27).

27. Virgil tells us something about Aeneas', and human, nature by having piety most operative in the epic when the hero is downtrodden, apprehensive of the future, and without arms, least available and useful when power is assured and compassion possible without harm to his "mission." The end of the epic offers Aeneas a last, grand opportunity to unite the *pietas* of affection and the *dextra* of power. It is unfortunate, but not unexpected, that he fails. Aeneas gradually loses his power at arms in book 2 as Troy's fortune ebbs away. The regaining of weapons in book 8 and their application in books 10 and 12 show little ultimate difference from their use in book 2 where *pietas* and the associates of *furor* remain at loggerheads. It is the latter who win at the epic's end, as Aeneas' actions could be seen to negate what his mission sets out to affirm.

THE HESITATION

OF AENEAS

Though with their high wrongs I am struck to the quick
Yet, with my nobler reason, 'gainst my fury
Do I take part: the rarer action is
In virtue than in vengeance: they being penitent
The sole drift of my purpose doth extend
not a frown further . . .
SHAKESPEARE
The Tempest 5.1.25–30

My title may at first seem paradoxical. Heroes are not supposed to hesitate but rather to forge ahead in dogged pursuit of their goals. We think of Achilles ruthlessly bent on the killing of Hector, to avenge the death of Patroclus, or of Odysseus aiming for Ithaca, Penelope and home, through a variety of difficulties. Aeneas, too, has a goal which is gradually clarified for him in the course of the epic, first to reach Italy against great odds, then to battle his way to supremacy in Latium and become thereby the founder of Rome. The first six books see him more the passive hero, unwilling to leave Troy, suffering destiny as it comes. In the second half of the epic, following on the revelations of Rome's future delivered by his father in the Underworld, we find him seizing a more active role, fighting with those who oppose his fated domination of Italy and, at the conclusion of the epic, killing Turnus, their leader.

But there is one moment of hesitation, at the climax of this inexorable sweep of events, which I think worthy of more consideration than it has received. It occurs at the very end of the epic, in the middle of the final scene.[1] You will recall the details. Aeneas casts his spear against Turnus and wounds him in the thigh. The victim falls to his knees, stretches his hands in prayer—Virgil calls him humbled and a suppliant—and asks for mercy and an end to hatred. Aeneas hesitates but, after seeing on Turnus' shoulder the baldrick of his protégé Pallas, whom Turnus earlier killed in battle, he becomes enraged, cries out that his deed will be Pallas' vengeance, and kills his opponent. The last words of the epic concern Turnus' life fleeing indignant down to the shades.

Something of the intensity Virgil gives this moment of pause within the finale of the *Aeneid* can be divined by a brief comparison with the scene in the twenty-second book of the *Iliad*, in which Achilles finally meets and slays Hector.[2] That Virgil doubtless had this moment in mind as he wrote the climax of his own epic makes the distinctions between the two episodes of vital importance to any criticism of the poet's meaning.

First, one general point: the *Iliad* continues on for two more books, concluding only after Achilles has received Priam with honor and allowed the father to redeem the body of his son. By watching Achilles eat with the parent of his foe and through pity embrace again a semblance of humanity after the wildness of his blood vengeance, the poet's audience experiences a catharsis parallel to what his protagonist suffers. Virgil allows his reader no similar distancing but ends unquietly and abruptly with his hero's deed of violence.

Second, by contrast with the two addresses at the end of the *Aeneid*, there are no less than nine brief speeches by the protagonists during the duel in *Iliad* 22. Let me summarize. As soon as Hector decides he must face Achilles or appear a coward, he promises Achilles that he will treat his body kindly, should he win the combat. Achilles replies that there are no compacts between men and the lions they track. Hector then speaks twice—to Achilles in the hope that his spear will hit its mark, then, when it has missed, to himself, with the prayer that he may die heroically. At this point Achilles wounds Hector fatally in the throat and gloats that he will be the prey of dogs and birds. Hector begs that his body be returned to his family but Achilles once again announces that dogs will eat his corpse. Hector then dies after predicting Achilles' death and the spoken parts of the episode end as Achilles avows acceptance of death when Zeus wills.

Virgil, more compact than his great predecessor, as I said allots his heroes only one speech each, after Turnus is forced to face Aeneas, Turnus first, Aeneas in reply. The wounding of Hector in the throat occurs in the middle of the heroes' interchanges and is immediately pronounced to be fatal. Achilles has already carefully scouted the armor of Patroclus to locate its vulnerable spot. Virgil has Aeneas wound Turnus in the thigh. The wound is not mortal, and, though there has been an exchange previous to Turnus' facing of Aeneas, only after the physical act do the heroes speak in a situation which in any sense parallels that of the *Iliad*.

In itself this is a curious way for the poet to conclude his epic of Rome. We might expect Aeneas, who now is in total control of events, backed by Jupiter and the fates, to kill his opponent outright, and his poet to reassure his reader first of the justice of the act, then of the future glory of Rome that Aeneas' necessary removal of his prime enemy will now confirm. He does none of this. Instead, by having Aeneas gravely but not fatally wound Turnus, Virgil creates a sudden unexpected moment of tense drama which in its intellectual ramifications projects the greatest single difference with his Homeric prototype.[3] To illustrate this we must look in detail at Turnus' words to his victorious foe:

> "utere sorte tua. miseri te si qua parentis
> tangere cura potest, oro (fuit et tibi talis

Anchises genitor) Dauni miserere senectae
et me, seu corpus spoliatum lumine mavis,
redde meis. vicisti et victum tendere palmas
Ausonii videre; tua est Lavinia coniunx,
ulterius ne tende odiis."
   (12.932–38)

"Indeed I have deserved [my fate] nor do I pray it away," he says.
"Use your lot. If any care of a sad parent can touch you, I pray you,
pity the old age of Daunus (Anchises was also such a father to you)
and return me, or, if you prefer, my body bereft of light, to my
people. You have conquered and the Ausonians have seen me, conquered, stretch forth my hands. Lavinia is your wife. Do not press
further in your hatred."

A series of alternatives had been offered by Homer to his protagonists all
of which are based on the assumption of the death of one hero. As Hector
says, the hero takes a life or his own life is taken; he slays or is slain. After
his death, at least in this particular situation, he can either be ransomed
by his family and given decent burial, or ignominiously fed to birds and
dogs. The alternatives that Turnus proposes presume not death but a
possible avoidance of death. Aeneas can kill or not, as Turnus sees his
situation. He can practice *clementia* and return Turnus alive to his father,
if he so chooses. It is no wonder that Turnus mentions Anchises to
Aeneas. The last words father had uttered to son in the Underworld, as he
outlined the Roman mission and the abstracts which were to govern
Rome's role as imposer of peace on a restless world, were "spare the
subjected and war down the proud" (*parcere subiectis et debellare superbos*,
6.853). Proud Turnus has been humbled. Now is the moment to see
whether he will be spared, to see whether Aeneas can practice a most
difficult virtue and abjure physical action and the personal response of
hatred, for a grander vision that relies on restrained power, not on an
individualistic, often blind, use of force.

   There is another important difference between Achilles' slaying of
Hector and the death of Turnus which I will return to later but would like
to mention briefly now, centering on the way the authors handle the
question of motivation. Throughout *Iliad* 22 there is little doubt that
Hector will die. The reason for Achilles' relentless pursuit is constantly
before the listener—his desire for vengeance for the death of Patroclus
whose armor Hector is wearing. What should motivate Aeneas is not all
that clear. Evander, in book 11, verbalizes what could be one important
reason behind Aeneas' action. As the Trojans prepare to leave the funeral
of Pallas and return to Aeneas, Evander gives them a message for their
leader whom, though absent, he addresses in the second person: "Your
right hand," he says to Aeneas, "is the reason that I linger in this hated life

after Pallas has been slain. It is your right hand which you see owes Turnus both to son [i.e., Pallas] and to father [Evander himself]" (11.177–79).

But we must remember that this is what Virgil presents as Evander's motivation for the final killing, not necessarily as Aeneas' own. If in fact vengeance extracted from Turnus because of Evander for the death of Pallas were foremost in Aeneas' mind, then there would be no need for him to pause. A brief word and a brisk act would be sufficient to finish off Turnus and the poem. Instead, though only for a moment, Virgil has his hero stop and turn his eyes—a revelation of inner doubt and uncertainty. "He held back his right hand," says Virgil, "and now, even now, the speech [of Turnus] began to bend him as he hesitated" (12.939–41). Turnus' humbled eyes and right hand outstretched exemplify the suppliant at Aeneas' mercy whose only weapon is words and the fleeting authority of his strengthless position. Aeneas' right hand is restrained for an instant from the use of force while the motion of his eyes betrays his pondering of alternatives. For a moment the double emphasis in the poetry on the eyes and hands of each hero suggests the mutuality of a shared humanness as much as the disparity separating victor from vanquished. Were Aeneas to spare his suppliant, both would remain alive.

Aeneas is now in a situation he has never been in before. The decision before him concerning the treatment of a suppliant is unique. Although his previous killings in books 10 and 12 can be uneasily defended as a necessity for the establishment of his settlement to assure Rome's future, after Turnus' speech Aeneas can no longer use his mission as justification for or cause of the use of force. For one thing Turnus is defeated theatrically and publicly. In one line (936) he announces his loss as both inflicted and endured, active for Aeneas (*vicisti*), passive for himself (*victum*).[4] Second, he acknowledges the end of a major, in his eyes perhaps the major, cause for war: *tua est Lavinia coniunx.*[5] That he is destined a *regia coniunx* Aeneas heard already in book 2 from Creusa (2.783). That she is Lavinia he learns from Anchises (6.764). More specifically, the Sibyl, in looking ahead to the war, sees her as another Helen—

> causa mali tanti coniunx iterum hospita Teucris
> externique iterum thalami . . .
>   (6.93–94)
> The cause of such a trouble for the Trojans [is] again an alien bride
> and again a foreign marriage.

—and the poet himself reiterates the initial phrase in direct connection with *Lavinia virgo* at 11.480. Presumably the forfeiting of Lavinia by Turnus should mean the end of the evil for both heroes and their adherents. Therefore the position in which Aeneas finds himself and the hesitation to which he briefly yields are new to him and to the events of the epic.

War can no longer be extended by an appeal to the need for self-preservation. Since battling should not provide Aeneas with a rationale for action,
he, and we, must look elsewhere for motivation when we analyze the
various conflicts and tugs of responsibility that could seize Aeneas in the
moments after Turnus' speech.

Before continuing our examination of the epic's ending it is well to
pause and examine the pattern of Virgil's other uses in the *Aeneid* of the
verb to hesitate (*cunctari*). Hesitation is different from delay in that the
latter often indicates postponement of a decisive choice, retreat from a
crisis of doing, even abstention from commitment. Hesitation defines the
moment before two possible actions, as a choice is made. It denotes a
moment of pondering, even of contemplation, a turning inward to pause
for thought before voicing and implementing a course of behavior to be
seen by, and often tangibly to affect, others. We would expect a wise
hesitation to abort any temptation toward premature or rash activity, and
at times even to exchange the easy potentiality of physical response for
the often more difficult wisdom of a rational restraint that works its
public wisdom through words alone.[6]

Hesitations in the *Aeneid* divide roughly into two categories which
could be called active and passive. The latter regularly betoken a final
yielding to the inevitable, following upon a last resistance to a higher
power whose ultimate potency or authority is indisputably assured. This
kind of hesitation can also be seen on occasion as the last assertion of
individuality against a greater power that might obliterate the integrity of
the self. Here are a few scattered examples. In book 5 the helmsman
Palinurus hesitates and clings to his rudder even though his doom of
death by water is unavoidable (5.856). The personified golden bough in
book 6 hesitates before Aeneas' tugging, an event strange in itself—and
much discussed by scholars—because the Sibyl had earlier maintained
that the bough would follow easily the touch of those fated to pluck it
(6.211).[7] Perhaps it is a last, thoughtful resistance to Roman might or even
a premonition that the implementation of the Roman mission would
have its less than idealistic moments. The ninth book finds the Tiber
hesitating in terror before the omen of the ships turned to sea nymphs,
even though Turnus makes light of the event (9.124). Finally Turnus
himself is said by Virgil twice to hesitate at the instant before Aeneas
throws his fateful spear (12.916, 919). Virgil does not follow Homer's
treatment of Hector who thinks out loud and decides that not to fight is
the path of cowardice. At this crucial moment Turnus makes no active
decision. He is still faltering when Aeneas hurls his weapon, looking only
for a way to bring *fortuna* to his foe. The latent power in Aeneas' own
hesitation some twenty lines later is thus cast the more into relief.

Then there are hesitations of a second sort, at which the waverer seems
master of his or her own destiny (though not necessarily conscious of the

significance of nonaction). Dido before departing on the fateful hunt with Aeneas is *thalamo cunctantem*, lingering on the threshold (4.133).[8] To desert her marriage chamber is symbolically to abandon her vow to the ashes of Sychaeus never to marry again, and to embark on a new, unfortunate love. It is an understandable enough decision, yet both she and the narrator define it as a *culpa*.[9] Book 8 shows Vulcan hesitating before making love to Venus (8.388). Whether or not he understands its implication, his decision to yield to Venus seals his commitment to forge arms for her son, Aeneas, to mate *arma virumque*, and therefore to help cause the moral dilemma of the ending which only a victory in arms could bring. Of particular interest is Virgil's mention in book 6 of Fabius Maximus, who gained his epithet Cunctator from the tactics of his campaign against Hannibal during the Second Punic War. He receives a place of honor in the *Aeneid*, coming last in the gallery of future Roman warriors which Anchises displays before his son in the Underworld.[10] It is important that a campaigning general known as a hero for a decision not to fight should appear only lines before Anchises utters his famous *sententia* to his son about sparing the beaten and warring down the proud. You restore the state by lingering, says Aeneas' father.

The position in which Virgil places his hero at the end of the *Aeneid* is not dissimilar. Aeneas is poised to spare or not to spare, to yield to words and practice *clementia* or to resort to physical violence and kill. Virgil leads his reader to believe that Aeneas is moved by Turnus' plea and will in fact spare him. But something suddenly twists Aeneas toward an opposite course of action. He notices on his enemy's shoulders the baldrick of Pallas whom Turnus had slain in book 10. Inflamed by furies and terrible in his anger, as Virgil puts it, he kills his opponent, claiming Pallas as the doer of the deed. "Pallas sacrifices you with his wounds," he shouts, "Pallas extracts punishment from your criminal blood" (12.948–49).

I will examine the logic of this and the rest of Aeneas' brief speech in a minute. It is important to remember here that at the moment in book 10 when Turnus kills Pallas and puts on his sword belt Virgil does something he rarely does elsewhere in the epic: he comments with an aside. "O mind of men," he says, "ignorant of fate and of future lot and how to preserve the mean when uplifted by success. A time will come for Turnus when he will wish Pallas bought back untouched at a great price, and when he will hate those spoils and the day" (10.501–5). The belt has engraved on it the murder of the sons of Aegyptus by the Danaids, an act of reprisal for what had been done to their father by Aegyptus himself. It continues a vendetta. Though Virgil does not say that Turnus will suffer death for his action but merely late learning, we assume that a heavy doom is his lot. It is important to add, however, that Aeneas now also absorbs the symbolism of the scene Turnus has donned and kills in a burst of passionate vengeance.

Earlier in this century it was customary to analyze Aeneas' action more in terms of what the reader wished Virgil had said than through the poet's actual words. The evil had been humbled. It was only right and proper, the argument went, that he be eliminated so as not to thwart the progress of the new golden age which Aeneas will found on Italian soil as prototype for its reestablishment by Augustus at the end of the civil wars.[11] To use the terms of structuralism, Aeneas' deed was the triumph of culture over nature, of sophisticated over primitive. It exemplified righteous indignation unleashed in the service of civilization, the defensible use of force—and here I paraphrase other words of Anchises to his son—to establish a custom for peace. In brief it was a model of the Roman mission to maintain law by power. Turnus' death was a necessary sacrifice for the future of Rome.

When it was pointed out that there was nothing in the text to bolster such a view, that Virgil in fact focuses attention only on his hero's blind rage, those seeking to defend the morality of Aeneas' action reminded us of Aeneas' sense of duty toward Evander.[12] Though Aeneas never alludes to Evander's words, critics of this persuasion urge that his loyalty toward both Evander and his son Pallas offers sufficient reason to vindicate an act of vengeance. Aeneas is visualized as punishing Turnus for Evander's sorrow at the death of his son for whom Aeneas in part assumed responsibility and who could therefore be seen as playing the role of son to Aeneas. Two forms of *pietas* could thus be said to rest in conflict as Aeneas acts. The first is *pietas* toward his father who in the Underworld had preached *clementia* to his son in his last words and who, toward the end of book 3, had offered a prime example of his philosophy by accepting into his company without menace Achaemenides, a Greek companion of Odysseus who had been abandoned by his leader to the mercy of a variety of terrors on the island of Sicily. The second, as we have seen, is *pietas* toward a different father and a surrogate son.

The first form of *pietas*, pressing no doubt the harder decision, argues the nonviolent course of forgiving an enemy in order to reintegrate in peace a split society and not pursue divisive hatred further, which only breeds further hatred. Such is Turnus' proposal. It rests on a son's memory of his father, on words alone and their inner effect. The second, based on force and more personal in orientation, is triggered by something visible and therefore more immediately explainable. It relies on the traditional perquisites of heroism to kill an enemy. Turnus had once in the past killed someone to whom the now victorious hero was obligated by that bond which unites protector and protected. Hector killed Patroclus so Hector must die. Turnus killed Pallas so he too is doomed. The presence of Evander in the background here makes the difference and, according to Virgilian criticism as early as Servius,[13] puts a certain seal of duty on the decision of Aeneas to kill.

The problem is that here again Virgil fails to admit any such motivation on Aeneas' part. We would expect that if *pietas* toward Evander were a primary concern to Aeneas he would kill Turnus, who is at his mercy, without further ado save perhaps for a brief mention that he got what he deserved for the hurt resulting from his slaying of Pallas. Instead Virgil has Aeneas hesitate and nearly yield to the argument of Turnus' words. A leap forward in civilized treatment of a defeated enemy nearly occurs as Aeneas seems to weigh aggression and compassion, hatred and forgiveness, in the balance. Julius Caesar's much touted *clementia* would have been a model for the latter in Virgil's thinking.[14] Killing in the heat of vengeance, however, is an act hallowed in behavior patterns apparently natural to mankind and, one need scarcely add, well documented from Homer to the present day. Aeneas proceeds as we might expect, however much otherwise than we might hope.[15]

That *pietas* toward Evander cannot claim a part in Aeneas' thoughts as he hesitates is apparent from a closer examination of Virgil's words. Aeneas notices the gleam of Pallas' belt on Turnus. (We learned in book 10 that it was incised *multo auro*, with much gold.) Then

> ille, oculis postquam saevi monimenta doloris
> exuviasque hausit, furiis accensus et ira
> terribilis: "tune hinc spoliis indute meorum
> eripiare mihi? Pallas te hoc vulnere, Pallas
> immolat . . ."
> (12.945–49)

After he had drunk in with his eyes the memorials of his savage grief and the spoils, inflamed by furies and terrible in his anger: "Are you, clothed in the spoils of my own, to be snatched from me? Pallas, Pallas sacrifices you with this wound . . ."

Virgil's description and Aeneas' words point to someone caught up in intense personal emotion.[16] They point to a man seized by passion to the point of irrationality, not to someone soberly weighing alternative responses to *pietas* before performing the climactic action of his career— and of Virgil's epic. *Dolor*, *saevitia*, and *ira*, passion, ferocity, and wrath, are not abstractions that ordinarily carry weight in the reactions of a judicious, thoughtful individual. No one *furiis accensus*, fired by furies, is acting contemplatively. The verb of Aeneas' final question, *eripiare* ("Are you to be snatched from me"), furthers the impression of madness. There is in fact no opponent who might do the seizing. Aeneas is imagining nothing other than his own possible instinct for *clementia*, a nonviolent abstraction implementing only a mental act which the hero, in his wildness of mind, now perverts into a physical creature bent on grabbing from him what seems rightly his.[17] Private grief and private possessiveness—hence his double emphasis on "mine" and "me"—now rule his actions. *Clementia* and the thoughtfulness of hesitation are forgotten.[18]

Aeneas' final excuse furthers the notion that he is acting irrationally. By imputing his deed to Pallas and shunting off elsewhere inspiration for his action, Aeneas is already adopting an irresponsible stance.[19] Aeneas' last phrase addressed to Turnus, suggesting that Pallas now "exacts punishment from your criminal blood" (*poenam scelerato ex sanguine sumit*, 949), betrays still further irrationality. Though *violentia* is characteristic of Turnus and though the narrator singles out his lack of *temperantia* in the killing of Pallas, still Turnus is in no way guilty of *scelus*.[20] Jupiter does not disagree with Juno when, with some irony, she styles Turnus' blood *pio* (10.617), and Turnus himself, at 12.648, calls his soul *sancta* to Juturna.

Matters had not always been thus. I would like now to turn back into the epic and look briefly at three further examples of hesitation which have bearing on the poem's finale and on Aeneas' behavior there. The first involves Aeneas himself and occurs in book 4 as part of the exchange of words between Dido and himself. The Carthaginian queen had already pleaded with him to stay and he has replied that he makes toward Italy not of his own free will. At this point there is a pause and Dido moves her eyes about, *volvens oculos* (4.363), as does Aeneas at the epic's end. She too is debating a course of action. She could without a complaint let him go to fulfill his destiny. She could kill him, for ever since his arrival at Carthage the Trojans have been at her mercy. She chooses a way in-between, relying on words but anticipating violence. She curses her former lover, praying that he will pay the penalty for his deeds by running aground on rocks and promising that she will pursue him no matter where he goes, even when she has become a shade after death.

Sympathy for her suffering urges the reader to side with Dido abandoned by her lover for a future about which he himself is still unsure. Nevertheless Virgil treats her as if her stance revealed a certain irrationality. The words the poet uses are important for they echo his portrayal of Aeneas as he kills Turnus. He styles her *accensa* (4.364), afire, as she begins her speech, and has her comment on herself in an aside at its center: *heu furiis incensa feror*, "alas I am born along set aflame by furies" (4.367). She is the passive victim of a madness that will soon show itself in ways more physical than words.[21] It is small wonder that Aeneas, whether out of fear for himself or for her, reacts with awe at this negative phenomenon. As she departs Virgil has him "hesitating with fear [*metu cunctantem*] and preparing to say many things" (4.390–91). Aeneas here suffers the type of hesitation that must be endured before a power over which the viewer has no control. His words, were they to be uttered, would have little chance of affecting the irrational force who, as Virgil puts it, "breaks off her speech in its midst and, sick, flees the open air" (4.388–89).

My second further example of hesitation concerns Turnus and occurs in book 7. He has just been confronted by Juno's pawn, the Dira Allecto, who under the disguise of Juno's aged priestess Calybe, has been attempting to rouse him up to do battle with the Trojans. When he replies that her care should be for the statues and the temple, that war was the concern of men, she burns in anger and reveals herself as a Fury, hissing with hydras and twisting flaming eyes. In response we find him, like Aeneas before Dido, "delaying and seeking to speak further" (*cunctantem et quaerentem dicere plura*, 7.449).[22] But the Fury works her will and changes him into a madman. "Love of weaponry and the criminal insanity of war enrages him," says the poet as final commentary on the Fury's metamorphic authority to turn rational to irrational and peace to war (7.461).

Turnus is the second of Allecto's three victims in book 7. I would like to call attention in passing to certain details in Virgil's description of her power over Amata whom she had attacked before Turnus. Once again the subject of fury becomes furious herself "raging maddened through the huge city without order [*sine more*] in her behavior," notes Virgil (7.377).[23] In a bacchic frenzy she sweeps her daughter, who in her mind was to have married Turnus but now in the new dispensation will be espoused to Aeneas, out of the city along with other mothers who are caught up in her wildness. These mothers Virgil calls *furiis accensas*, inflamed by furies, while Amata herself shortly later at the end of the episode he styles *fervida*, blazing (7.397). It is important to note that the only other place in the epic where Virgil uses the verb *accendo* with *furiis* is to describe Aeneas at the end of the epic, *furiis accensus* as he prepares to kill Turnus. It is probably no accident that the final adjective the poet allots his hero, in the next to last line of the poem, is also *fervidus*, burning with wrath (12.951). The sight of the belt of Pallas has the same effect on Aeneas as the snaky madness with which Allecto alters her prey and subverts a whole landscape. It changes a hero, whose power is now fully confirmed and who is briefly forced into the process of weighing alternatives, leaning toward clemency when he has the opportunity to kill, into a maniac, a terrifying addict of physicality and personal impulse.

This leads me to my final example of hesitation, which is only a reminder. Before Aeneas casts his fateful spear at Turnus, Virgil twice in four lines sees the soon to be wounded hero as *cunctans*. I will quote the first instance in context. "He beholds the Rutulians and the city," the narrator says, "and hesitates from fear [*cunctaturque metu*] and trembles that death looms over him" (12.915–16). Again, as so often in Virgil, one context resonates to another. The only other occasion that Virgil uses the verb *cunctor* with *metus*, fear, is at the moment we examined a minute ago when Aeneas confronts the raging figure of Dido. There are many allusions to book 4 in 12 which urge a parallel between events in the lives of

Turnus and Dido, both victims of a higher, more fatal power than they can master. None is more potent than the present example, which suggests several important points: that the role of Aeneas has been reversed from victim to inflicter of fate, that Turnus is now in the former role of Aeneas, cowering before the irrational, and, finally, that Aeneas stands for an instant like Dido, enraged, the pawn of Jupiter and the Dira he sends from his throne to terrify Aeneas' enemies.[24] Aeneas is also already the victim of rage. Before the final conflict he speaks *saevo pectore*, from a fierce heart, and Turnus characterizes his taunting words as *fervida*, anticipating the epic's concluding lines. By his last action this anger has risen to an irrational pitch.

It is dubious, then, if we ponder the power of Virgil's vocabulary closely, to rest the difference between Aeneas the hesitator and Aeneas the killer on the distinction between two forms of *pietas*. His deed could be seen, in fact, as the final *impietas*, since he forgets his father's last utterance, remains unmoved before the idea that Turnus' father might suffer, and kills a suppliant before the eyes of his people, especially after the suppliant has offered logical and reasonable terms for peaceful community. I suspect that the change in Aeneas is more faithfully explained by putting before and after in terms verging on objective and subjective, if someone bent on slaughter in hand-to-hand combat can be called detached. Aeneas first grapples with the inference of words. The hesitating hero, pondering the *clementia* that Turnus proposes, for an instant mulls over an abstract principle which, if espoused in statesmanlike fashion, would have wide-ranging public repercussions. The belt of Pallas and what it represents, tangible reminder of Aeneas' devotion to his protégé, which at the same time sports figures bent on a particularly vivid example of revenge, switches matters about, or, better, drives the hero's fury to its highest pitch. He who has already been *acer in armis*, fierce in arms, now uses his weaponry for one last deadly gesture.

In the *Aeneid* the sighting of gold's gleam is a frequent cause of misfortune, usually endured rather than inflicted. For instance, both Nisus and Euryalus, heading for Aeneas on the site of Rome but waylaid by greed for slaughter and treasure, and Camilla, fleetest of warrior maidens but mesmerized by the brilliance of the armor of Chloreus, find in gold their undoing. The baldrick Turnus wears is no exception. It is the unlucky emblem both for what Turnus suffers and for what Aeneas perpetrates. Tangible though it is, its vision elicits a highly impassioned reaction from Aeneas based on private, personal emotion.[25] As Virgil sees Aeneas' action, a moment of restraint in the midst of ferocity yields to the hero's most intensely subjective response and to a form of narcissism which, because Aeneas sees himself acting as surrogate for a vengeful Pallas, never is made to reach out beyond individual self-gratification to any larger concerns.

For Virgil to acknowledge so directly such a human weakness on the part of his hero at the poem's most impressive moment in no way diminishes the universal stature of the *Aeneid* as a masterpiece. In my view it enhances it. The relationship between arms and men in history, between human energies and the means by which these energies are deployed before or upon our fellow men, remains a theme of some consequence in Western literature. At the moment when Rome turned from republic to empire and began to cement its position as the world's foremost power with strength and breadth of authority hitherto unexampled in Western history, it is no wonder that the reality as well as the idealism that come with wide dominance should have been much on the mind of its greatest poet.

The idealism is touched upon at prominent moments throughout the epic, most notably in the speeches of Jupiter that frame the epic in books 1 and 12, in Anchises' lengthy survey of future heroes in book 6, and in the shield of Vulcan given to Aeneas in the eighth book. Jupiter in the first book can pronounce, saying that "To these [Romans] I place neither boundaries of power nor limitations of time; I have given *imperium* without end" (1.278–79). Of the reign of Augustus he is equally reassuring for "Then rough ages will grow mild with wars put aside: hoary Trust and Vesta, Romulus with his brother Remus will give laws; the dread gates of War will be closed with iron and tight bolts" (1.291–94). And Anchises can claim, also of Augustus, that "Here is the man, here indeed, whom you hear often promised to you, offspring of a god, who will again found the golden age in Latium through fields once ruled over by Saturn" (6.791–94).

These particular grand excursions into the future, which often have their own negative sides,[26] are accomplished by prophecy and by the ekphrasis of the shield, by words and by artistic design. But there is a myriad of smaller, often subtler ways by which Virgil foresees Rome's later destiny even in the doings of Aeneas by drawing direct verbal analogies between the two temporal spheres. We may take the phrase *stans celsa in puppi* as a ready example. It is used in three places in the epic—of Anchises as he first sights Italy in book 3 and explains the omen of the four white horses, of Aeneas in book 10 arriving to do battle, holding the blazing shield in his left hand. In between, enshrined on the shield, is the figure of Augustus at the battle of Actium, also "standing on the lofty poop" as he drives Italians into battle against Antony and Cleopatra. The Trojan past, the founding hero, and the raiser of Rome to unparalleled grandeur in a restored golden age are thus linked through clear verbal reminiscence. Recent critics have shown with what care for minute detail Virgil makes these interconnections between the ancient past and his Augustan present.[27] This is true throughout the poem but especially in book 8 as Evander and Aeneas examine the site of future Rome.

This temporal thrust forward, expounding history's linear horizon-
tality by ideological echoes of one time in another, abets that aspect of
the epic which suggests a teleology of accomplishment for Rome. At the
end of a certain period Rome's manifest destiny will become apparent on
the apocalyptic occasion of Augustus' rise to prominence. What Aeneas
began Augustus will solidify into the assured greatness of Rome. If there
is a cycle here, as the golden age is renewed, it is a cycle with a positive
conclusion. The presumption remains that this new perfected era will be
stable and enduring.[28] This idealistic view of Rome, which Virgil at
chosen moments in the *Aeneid* carefully supports, is based on the developmental possibilities of human rationalism. As Troy changes to Rome and
literature makes a chronological jump from Homer to Virgil, we presume that civilization advances from more primitive states to more sophisticated ones. We presume also a parallel ability of human ethics to
evolve in the direction that Jupiter and Anchises outline, with brother
living happily with brother instead of initiating civil conflict, with war put
aside and Furor imprisoned.[29] This is to intimate—and here I focus on
one small point—that *clementia* will supplant undue violence in human
relations.

But, countering this linear inevitability of a grand historical design,
Virgil constructs an opposite force which we might call the sphere of
private, personal reaction to events. I am urging more than a variation on
what Adam Parry, in a brilliant article some years ago, called "The Two
Voices of Virgil's *Aeneid*."[30] Parry outlined with great sensitivity the suffering Virgil so movingly shows always resulting from history's lurching
forward. Every book of the *Aeneid*, from 2 through 6, ends with a death.
Readers have always found Dido's suicide particularly moving, but it is
the funeral of Marcellus at the end of book 6 which is perhaps most
striking for the contrast it generates with its context. All the glory that
culminates in Augustan Rome cannot avert the death of Augustus' young
heir. The thoughtful reader finds a parallel in the myth of Daedalus and
Icarus, subject of sculpture adorning Apollo's temple at Cumae where
Aeneas lands at the start of the book. Daedalus may make his way from
Crete to Italy and in the process conquer an element hitherto untamed
by man, but by so doing he loses his son, Icarus.[31] This balanced intertwining of progress and hurt continues unabated through the last six
books. We think of the deaths of Nisus and Euryalus, of Pallas, Lausus,
and Camilla. We may even find the arrival of death to Turnus of some
poignancy, in spite of his past arrogance and propensity for *violentia*—a
noun Virgil associates four times with him and with no other character in
the epic.

Rather than dwelling on any alternation of progress and suffering, I
have been trying to call attention to another recurrent, more cyclic pattern of behavior and its expression in the epic which centers on the deeds

of the very persons who make history. I am thinking particularly of those in authority who impose hurt on others rather than suffer it themselves. I refer to the community throughout the poem of those negative though natural human characteristics which with unfortunate frequency exhibit themselves in the users of power. Aeneas' action at the end of the epic is an example of prime importance because of its position. Turnus attributes *odium*, hatred, to his opponent,[32] but in Virgil's authorial description, we remember, he is a prey to furies' flame, terrible in his anger, a model of those who act under the impulse of *saevus dolor*, which could be called an amalgam of ferocity, anguish, and its concomitant resentment. This cluster of abstractions, or various combinations of them, recurs regularly in the poem. Virgil says of Dido and her madness that she "conceived furies, overwhelmed by anguish" (*concepit furias evicta dolore*, 4.474). This is a strikingly effective way to show the mutation Aeneas has caused in her life. Instead of a child to seal their relationship, she conceives only the insanity of suicide. Turnus himself is often said to rage. In one line of book 9 we hear of the *irae* and *dolor* that burn him as he contemplates the Trojan camp (9.99).

Only once does Virgil comment positively on such motivation as a spur toward action. In the eighth book Evander, while detailing for Aeneas the help he will receive from the Etruscans in his imminent warfare, elaborates the reason why they have turned against their former leader Mezentius. Among the unspeakable carnage and bestial deeds he perpetrated, he used to join dead bodies with living, "putting hands together with hands, faces with faces." In response Etruria rose up, states Evander, *furiis iustis*, with justifiable rage. This reaction is confirmed by the words of the soothsayer he goes on to quote who in turn speaks of the *iustus dolor*, the just indignation that leads them against their enemy, and the *merita ira*, the deserved wrath that Mezentius inflames in them.[33]

"Just" and "merited" are positive accolades not given elsewhere in the epic to *dolor* and *ira*. When we first meet these abstractions, at the opening of the epic where they motivate Juno's vendetta against the Trojans, they stand alone or are negatively characterized. Virgil first pits her indignation (she is called *dolens*) against the *pietas* of her adversary and dwells on the enormity of her wrath. Shortly later he refers in more detail to the causes of her angers and to her *saevi dolores*, her ferocious resentments, inflamed by which—again we have the passive participle *accensa*—she pursues the Trojans over the seas. Juno's conduct seems archetypal for that personal irrationality that opposes an idealistic version of future Rome and its founding father, giving battle only under duress and practicing in its aftermath a *clementia* learned from instinctive filial piety. But Virgil reveals to us something else at the very end. He demonstrates that his hero shares characteristics with his vengeful goddess. Aeneas too can react with unrestrained violence under the pressures of those same abstractions that have ruled Juno from the start in her disruptive attempt to prevent a Trojan settlement in Italy and the foundation of Rome.

Jupiter's words part way into book 1 and toward the end of book 12 preach the peaceful glory of Rome to come, but the actions of Juno and Aeneas provide the epic's outer frame. It is their vengeful behavior that introduces the reader to the epic's action and brings it forcefully to a close.[34] If nothing else the finale, then, reminds us not only of the suffering that any progress brings but of the humanness of all those who wield arms. In the emotional world of Aeneas, Roman everyman, as styled by his father in the Underworld, now responding to the potentiality of full authority in arms at last achieved, an understandable, though unfortunate, impulse toward personal gratification triumphs over a rarer, wiser instinct of more universal validity. In this respect his action does speak out to humanity in general more movingly than any of the so-called Augustan segments of the poem, idealistic visions as they regularly are of future dreams, not verifiable studies of lived emotions in the process of implementation. Aeneas' final deed reminds us of the essential perversity of power even in the hands of those who could with some truth lay claim to have established the most orderly society that the world had yet known.

NOTES

1. For a survey of recent literature on the epic's conclusion, see McKay, "Recent Work on Virgil" 1–92, to which add now especially Johnson, *Darkness Visible* 114–34, and the essays in *Arethusa* by Segal, "Art and the Hero" 67–83, especially 81–82, and Stahl, "Aeneas" 157–77 passim with my "Introduction" 7–15, especially 7–10.

2. The two scenes in *Iliad* 22 and *Aeneid* 12 are compared in detail by West, "Deaths of Hector and Turnus" 21–31. Van Nortwick, "Aeneas, Turnus and Achilles" 303–14, has recently offered a timely, carefully argued warning against overly rigid linkage between characters in the two epics, especially in the standard equations of Achilles with Aeneas and of Hector with Turnus. See also Putnam, "Introduction" 10.

3. This tense pause for contemplation of words before action also differentiates the epic's closing scene from one of its closest comparable moments earlier in the narrative, Aeneas' killing of Mezentius at the end of book 10. Each hero speaks during the course of the scene, Mezentius before he hurls his spear from horseback (878–82), Aeneas, with sword drawn over his fallen foe (897–98), and Mezentius again, praying that his body be buried with that of his son, out of reach of his foes' vengeance. But there is nothing parallel to the dialectic between thinking and doing that so enlivens the epic's finale.

4. At 12.190–91, Aeneas suggests a reasonable solution to the problem of hierarchy, that both races be considered *invictae* and live together under ever-enduring compacts. Part of his dilemma at

the end, at least when seen idealistically, is how to conquer and not totally defeat at one and the same time.

5. The importance of Lavinia to Turnus is a specific theme in his speeches in book 12 (she is mentioned at 17, 80, and 937). The meaning of the *coniugium* for the war is a constant subject of the last four books (e.g., 9.138, 9.600, 9.737, 10.79, 10.649, 11.105, 11.217, 11.355–71, 11.440, 11.472, 12.657, 12.805, 12.821).

6. I was reminded recently of the *Aeneid*'s conclusion when reading one of the last essays (dated August 1967) of the late Ernest Becker, *Angel in Armor* 159–91. On pp. 186–87 he writes, "only *ideally* are motives words: ideally one would hope to place his primary reliance on the free flow of symbols that would guide his choices, and allow him to weigh them before acting. But this is ideal. Actually, man acts, and then masks his action in the automatic justification of words."

Save for the fact that the (in some ways irresponsible) justification precedes his final action, these words could apply to Aeneas' final deed, especially in the light of the symbolism suggested by Turnus. Since after Turnus' speech his commitment to Rome can no longer provide a rationale for action, Aeneas' hesitation is all the more crucial as he, and we, balance his conflicting obligations and their varying motivations.

7. The most important discussion of the golden bough, and one of the major articles devoted to the *Aeneid* is Brooks, "Discolor Aura" 260–80. See also d'Arms, "Virgil's *cunctantem*" 265–68, and the attempt to mitigate the paradoxical use of *cunctantem* there by Avery, "Reluctant Golden Bough" 269–72.

8. The repetition of *thalamo* at 392 is significant, the moment when Dido is carried back into her bedchamber after her first denunciation of Aeneas.

9. 4.19 (Dido to Anna), 4.172 (the narrator).

10. In connection with Fabius, Virgil uses the gerund *cunctando* for the only time (6.846). In thus dwelling on the series of delays by which Fabius gained his reputation he is following the lead of Ennius *Ann.* 370–72V 3rd ed. The latter's lines are preserved by Cicero in *De Off.* 1.84, where Fabius' tactics offer an *exemplum* of one who preferred the safety of the state over individual reputation, and in *De Sen.* 10, where his *patientia* is a counter to Hannibal, *exsultantem iuveniliter.* Cf. also Cic. *Ad Att.* 2.19.2 = 39.2SB, Macr. *Sat.* 6.1.23, and Servius on *Aen.* 6.845. (Ennius' line remained well remembered, e.g., by Livy, 30.26.7, and Ovid, *F.* 2.240–42.)

Seneca (*De Ira* 1.11.5) elaborates Virgil's point, seeing delay as the polar opposite of anger, passion, and vengeance:

> Quo alio Fabius adfectas imperii vires recreavit quam quod cunctari et trahere et morari sciit, quae omnia irati nesciunt? Perierat imperium, quod tunc in extremo stabat, si Fabius tantum ausus esset quantum ira suadebat; habuit in consilio fortunam publicam et aestimatis viribus, ex quibus iam perire nihil sine universo poterat, dolorem ultionemque seposuit in unam utilitatem et occasiones intentus; iram ante vicit quam Hannibalem.

> How else did Fabius restore the broken forces of the state but by knowing how to loiter, to put off, and to wait—things of

which angry men know nothing? The state, which was standing then in the utmost extremity, had surely perished if Fabius
had ventured to do all that anger prompted. But he took into
consideration the well-being of the state, and, estimating its
strength, of which now nothing could be lost without the loss
of all, he buried all thought of resentment and revenge and
was concerned only with expediency and the fitting opportunity; he conquered anger before he conquered Hannibal.
(Basore)

11.   Northrop Frye, *Return of Eden* 13, for instance, writing in 1965,
      can say, "The first six books of the *Aeneid* have a similar quest
      pattern [to that of the *Odyssey*]; the next six, the account of the
      struggle of Aeneas with the Italian warlords, also has the struc-
      ture of romantic comedy, full of compacts, ordeals and other
      traditional features of comic action, and ending in success, mar-
      riage and the birth of a new society."
12.   As, e.g., Otis, *Virgil* 351 and 380.
13.   Servius on *Aen.* 12.940.
14.   We recall the words Sallust puts in the mouth of Caesar at *Cat.*
      51.12–14 (and there is no reason to doubt that Sallust intended to
      make the words as authentic as possible):

      qui demissi in obscuro vitam habent, si quid iracundia deliq-
      uere, pauci sciunt; fama atque fortuna eorum pares sunt: qui
      magno imperio praediti in excelso aetatem agunt, eorum
      facta cuncti mortales novere. Ita in maxuma fortuna minuma
      licentia est; neque studere neque odisse, sed minume irasci
      decet. Quae apud alios iracundia dicitur, ea in imperio su-
      perbia atque crudelitas appellatur.

      If the humble, who pass their lives in obscurity, commit any
      offence through anger, it is known to few; their fame and
      fortune are alike. But the actions of those who hold great
      power, and pass their lives in a lofty station, are known to all
      the world. So it comes to pass that in the highest position
      there is least freedom of action. There neither partiality nor
      dislike is in place, and anger least of all; for what in others is
      called wrath, this in a ruler is termed insolence and cruelty.
      (Rolfe)

      It is important to note that Sallust's Cato, in his response to
      Caesar advocating death not leniency for the conspirators, three
      times accuses the senate of hesitation (Sall. *Cat.* 52.25, 28, 31), as if
      by such a reaction they were supporting the *clementia* of Caesar.
15.   It is ironic that, at the moment when empire is consolidated in
      the defeat of Turnus, Aeneas suffers his greatest loss. I am not
      referring only to his remembrance of the loss of Pallas, which, to
      Aeneas, apparently is not outweighed by the defeat of Turnus,
      the gaining of Lavinia, and the assurance of empire. The *Aeneid*
      presents a cycle of loss as well as of emotional response. The
      more impersonal "gains," which could elicit the more abstract
      rejoinder of nonkilling, are offset by the more easily understood,
      if less morally defensible, response of physical retribution, of
      power used in the service of individual desire. The primary
      difference between the beginning of the epic and the end is that
      Turnus is placed in the role of victim, while Aeneas, in reacting
      to loss, changes from passive sufferer of someone else's vendetta

to active perpetrator of vengeance for his own needs. Rome is achieved at the expense of compassion, even in the epic's titular hero who himself has been so often dependent on the pity of others. Victory would seem to enhance rather than nullify *superbia*. The killing of Turnus would no doubt offer final proof to Aeneas that he has at last reached full authority. It is for the reader to analyze the concomitant losses (or perhaps even to speculate on what would have been won or forgone if Turnus had been spared).

16. By ellipsis of the introductory verb the narrator abets the hero's briskness of emotion.

17. Even on the surface level of plot it is irrational to ask if Turnus will be stolen away. He is alone, helpless, and immobile.

18. Virgil never uses the noun *clementia* or the adjective *clemens*. He (apparently) coins the word *inclementia* at *Geo.* 3.68 and uses it only once again, at *Aen.* 2.602 of the *inclementia divum* whom Aeneas can perceive ransacking his city.

19. The verb by which Aeneas imputes responsibility for the killing of Turnus to Pallas, *immolat* (949), is an important choice. Aeneas has Pallas see Turnus as a sacrificial victim. The usage would be quite different if in third-person narration Virgil had given the verb to Aeneas (twice in book 10, at 519 and 541, the first as direct reaction to the death of Pallas, Virgil does exactly that). The critic might then impute to the narrator rich possibilities of meaning in Aeneas' deed whereby, for instance, Turnus becomes the necessary "sacrifice" to end the epic and prosperously found Rome. That Aeneas, as he prepares to kill Turnus, imputes the verb to Pallas, forces the reader to scrutinize what Aeneas would see as Pallas', as well as Aeneas' own, motivation for such an action. One suspects that larger notions of Roman destiny would not have been at the forefront of Pallas' (as they apparently are not of Aeneas') thinking.

20. *Violentia* is associated with Turnus at 11.354, 11.376, 12.9, and 12.45. With 12.949 (". . . *poenam scelerato ex sanguine sumit*") we should compare 11.720 where Camilla closes with Ligus *poenasque inimico ex sanguine sumit*. There are two interrelated differences between the passages. In noting the change from *inimico* to *scelerato* we should also emphasize that the first occurs in third-person narrative, the second as part of the words of Aeneas. The choice of *scelerato* is Aeneas', not the narrator's, and should be analyzed accordingly. Could it be that Aeneas' imputation of *scelus* to Turnus is his own way of twisting responsibility away from his own potential *scelus* in killing a suppliant who had appealed for *clementia*? (The *dictum* of Mezentius, *nullum in caede nefas*, at 10.901, is only partially applicable as an indictment of Aeneas' words.)

Latinus' words at 7.595–97 are also to the point:

"ipsi has sacrilego pendetis sanguine poenas,
o miseri. te, Turne, nefas, te triste manebit
supplicium, votisque deos venerabere seris."

"Poor creatures, you yourselves will pay the penalty for this with your criminal blood. For you, Turnus, guilt, for you sad punishment will remain, and you will beseech the gods with tardy offerings."

Turnus' posture at the end of the epic is an example of a *triste supplicium* already before Aeneas kills him. (For *poenae* referred directly to Turnus, cf. 8.538.)

21. Though she is passive, Dido's use of the first person, *feror*, especially as part of an aside within her speech, proves that she understands and acknowledges her victimization by furies. Hence one difference between Aeneas *furiis accensus* and Dido *furiis incensa* lies precisely in the Carthaginian queen's self-realization. Aeneas' condition, not admitted by himself in the brief words that follow, is within the narrator's description. Dido's indictment of Aeneas we learn directly from her. For whatever reason (and I have offered several), Aeneas is never allowed to stand back and contemplate himself.

22. Cf. the similar phraseology used of Tarquitus, suppliant before Aeneas at 10.554–55.

23. Cf. Dido at 4.300–303.

24. This interconnection suggests an interesting example, given one of the most prominent places in the epic, of the way Virgil can have us see characters and their deeds from two opposing viewpoints. At 12.806 Jupiter commands Juno *ulterius temptare veto*, forbidding any further disruption of Aeneas' destiny on his wife's part. The only other time Virgil uses the comparative adverb is at 12.938 where Turnus prays to Aeneas *ulterius ne tende odiis*. Jupiter and Turnus would seem to be equated as voices of moderation, opposing further violence, and Juno and Aeneas to be the impetuous forces needing restraint. It is curious, then, that even before Turnus has uttered his final plea, Jupiter must make use of a Fury to help Aeneas, himself soon to be *furiis accensus*, dispatch Turnus, as if Jupiter and Aeneas must make common cause with a wildness long associated with Juno!

25. The interrelationship of visual and mental images in the *Aeneid* is a subject worth further study. Aeneas' emotion here is sparked by the visual reminder of visual contact, by a tactile object as referent for a being once equally palpable. Turnus himself, appealing for *clementia* by allusion to *pietas*, does not arouse *dolor* and *ira* in Aeneas. It is only the sight of the belt that does. I treat a different alternation in books 2 and 10 between *imagines* and bouts of futile action in the previous chapter.

26. One thinks especially of Anchises' description of Brutus (6.817–23) who expelled Tarquinius Superbus but is himself possessed of an *animam superbam*, who gains consular *imperium* and with it *securis* called *saevae*, who puts his sons to death, preferring *amor patriae* and *laudum cupido* to a father's love. The "reader" of the shield does not soon forget Tullus' bloody vengeance against Mettus Fufetius (8.642–45). On the pessimism of book 8 in general, see Wiesen, "Pessimism" 737–65.

27. Cf., e.g., Binder, *Aeneas und Augustus* passim.

28. It should be noted, though, that decline from a golden time into more decadent eras is a major point of Evander's anthropology at 8.325–27.

29. We are allowed to forget momentarily Jupiter's primary association with the Iron Age, explicit throughout the *Georgics* (especially at 1.129–35) and implicit at *Aen.* 8.319–20, where Saturn and Jupiter are differentiated. If exiled father refounded a golden age in Latium, what of the morality of his omnipotent son?

30. Parry, "Two Voices" 107–23.

31. This balancing structure of book 6, where suffering and loss constitute the outer frame, spills over into the epic as a whole where anger and violence constitute its extreme limits.

32. *Odium* is a key word of Juno and Allecto in books 1 (688) and 7 (298, 327, 336). Cf. Jupiter's *dictum* to the gods at 10.14. The time for *odia* will be when Rome fights Carthage (as Dido implies at 4.623), not now. The word is also associated with Mezentius at 10.692, 853 and 905, where it is the cause of *furor* against him (in the last two instances acknowledged by himself). Only at the end does it characterize Aeneas, in Turnus' words.

   In the second *Epistle* of his book 1, published a year or so before his friend's death, Horace offers a pertinent definition of *odium* as part of a concatenation of abstractions much on Virgil's mind as he wrote the end of the *Aeneid*. It is discussed in chapter 9 but is worthy of reiteration here:

   > . . . qui non moderabitur irae,
   > infectum volet esse, dolor quod suaserit et mens,
   > dum poenas odio per vim festinat inulto.
   > ira furor brevis est . . .
   >   (*Epi.* 1.2.59–60)

   Cf. also Tacitus' pronouncement at *Ann.* 1.10:

   > . . . fas sit privata odia publicis utilitatibus remittere.

33. The poet himself supplies the phrase *iustae irae* to describe the motivation of Mezentius' attackers at 10.714. It is important to remember that the reason *iustus* and *merita* are applied to his people's resentment against Mezentius is not because he has killed but because of the sordidness with which he treated the bodies of his victims. His previous behavior despised the gods and human dignity at once. For further discussion of these uses of *iustus* and *merita*, see Putnam, "Introduction" 14–15, n. 8. There I make the point that it is strange, and crucial, that Virgil qualifies *dolor* and *ira* positively when qualification is least required or expected. What, then, of a significant moment like the end of the epic when we await some moral designation by the author and none is forthcoming?

34. The reader's expectations also play a vital role as the poem's finale works its way out. Because generic tradition leads us to expect that victor will kill vanquished, we are all the more startled by Aeneas' pause for reflection and, in one sense, relieved when he finally succumbs to the traditional enemy-friend distinction and relinquishes any momentary inclination toward a wider spirit of community.

ANGER, BLINDNESS,
AND INSIGHT
IN VIRGIL'S
AENEID

> [Philosophia] ab animo tamquam ab oculis caliginem
> dispulit, ut omnia supera infera, prima ultima media
> videremus.
>
> [Philosophy] dispersed the darkness from the eyes as it
> were of the mind, so that we saw all things above,
> below, things first and last and in between.
>
> CICERO
> *Tusculan Disputations* 1.64

Since the time of Servius and, I have little doubt, from the moment of the
Aeneid's publication, it has been a critical option to debate the morality of
Aeneas' final killing of Turnus in terms of *pietas*. Aeneas' deed, as the
fourth-century commentator presents it to us, is the aftermath of his
inner struggle between *pietas* owed to his father and *pietas* demanded of
him by Evander.[1] His father, at the climax of the poem's most densely
ideological moment, had asked of him, as *Romanus*, exemplar of behavior
for a great civilization to come,

> parcere subiectis et debellare superbos.
>   (6.853)
> to spare the humbled and war down the proud.

We presume that remembrance of these paternal *dicta* causes the hero's
moment of hesitation, a pause to ponder instead of to act. But Evander,
the argument runs, also exerts a stringent form of moral pressure
through the commanding words which his legates convey to Aeneas after
the death of his son, Pallas, at the hands of Turnus:

> "quod vitam moror invisam Pallante perempto
> dextera causa tua est, Turnum gnatoque patrique
> quam debere vides."
>   (11.177–79)
> "Your right hand is the reason that I linger in this hated life now that
> Pallas has been slain, (your right hand) which you see owes Turnus
> to son and to father."

What is owed by Aeneas to Pallas and Evander is usually postulated to be Turnus' death. Virgil carefully reminds us of the king's expectations during the epic's final moments by focusing attention on the right hands of his two protagonists—Turnus' stretched forth in prayer (*dextram . . . precantem / protendens*, 12.930–31), Aeneas' source of power restrained for an instant of thought (*dextram . . . repressit*, 12.939). Sight of Pallas' belt on Turnus rouses the hero to make his choice and Evander, so Servius would have it, wins the day as Aeneas plunges his sword into his enemy.

Virgil leaves any inner reasoning on Aeneas' part for his readers to infer from the text. But as we contemplate the hero's resolve to kill we might remember the only other occasion in the text where duty to Evander and Pallas stimulates Aeneas to action, that is, immediately after the son has been killed by Turnus:

> . . . Pallas, Evander in ipsis
> omnia sunt oculis, mensae quas advena primas
> tunc adiit dextraeque datae.
>   (10.517–18)
> Pallas, Evander, all stands before his eyes—the board whereto he then came first, a stranger, and the right hands pledged.

Loyalty to Evander, Servius' triumphant *pietas*, now produces some extraordinary results in the life of our precedent-setting hero. It first drives him to take eight prisoners as human sacrifice on Pallas' pyre. He then rejects the prayers of the suppliant Magus, though the latter appeals directly to his *pietas*:

> "per patrios manis et spes surgentis Iuli
> te precor, hanc animam serves gnatoque patrique."
>   (10.524–25)
> "I beseech you by the shade of your father and the hope of growing Iulus, save this life for a son and for a father."

He next kills a priest, Haemonides, and soon thereafter, following the model of Achilles, can boast, as he rolls forward the still warm, headless corpse of Tarquitus,

> "istic nunc, metuende, iace. non te optima mater
> condet humi patrioque onerabit membra sepulcro:
> alitibus linquere feris, aut gurgite mersum
> unda feret piscesque impasti vulnera lambent."
>   (10.557–60)
> "Lie now there, you terrible one! No loving mother will lay you in earth, nor load your limbs with ancestral tomb: you will be left to

birds of prey or, sunk beneath the flood, the wave will bear you on, and hungry fish will suck your wounds."[2]

As his rampage nears its end Virgil compares him to the giant Aegaeon, antagonist of Jupiter, the Olympian (10.565–68).[3] He thus forces his readers to question not only the quality of the piety which Evander and Pallas elicit from their guest and which urges him to action but also any Olympian rationality on his part, both as he reacts to Pallas' death in book 10 and as he performs the epic's ultimate deed.

Pietas may be said to offer justification for Aeneas' final action but its nature and even its presence are left for the reader to ponder or debate. What Virgil makes explicit is that Aeneas, readying himself to kill after seeing the belt of Pallas on Turnus, is caught in the throes of fury and anger—

> ille, oculis postquam saevi monimenta doloris
> exuviasque hausit, furiis accensus et ira
> terribilis . . .
>   (12.945–47)
> He, after he had drunk in with his eyes the memorials of his savage grief and the spoils, inflamed by furies and terrible in his wrath . . .

My essay takes Aeneas' anger as its subject. Since his emotionality has been studied recently by Karl Galinsky who finds his action "unequivocally moral" when scrutinized in terms of the Greco-Roman philosophical tradition in which Virgil was schooled, I would like first to explore the evidence for such a positive verdict.[4] I will then turn to an examination of what the Virgilian texts themselves say about someone set aflame by furies and terrifying in wrath. Next, tracing a dialogue between poets who were also friends, I will propose that book 1 of Horace's *Epistles*, the first segment of his most philosophical work, written as Virgil was giving his final years to the epic, offers stringent commentary on the *Aeneid* and especially on its last episode. Finally, I will turn back to the poem itself and to the hero's concluding frenzy, to observe how blindness and insight, madness and clarity of thought interact at crucial moments in the poem.

First the Hellenic background. In summarizing his argument Galinsky states that "in the best tradition of Aristotle and Plato, he [Aeneas] is both compassionate (πρᾶος) and impassionate (θυμοειδής)."[5] Galinsky is aware that Plato regularly conjoins anger with the irrational elements as well as that the Greek philosopher's treatment of anger is more than once a subject of discussion in the *Tusculan Disputations* where Cicero strongly espouses the Stoic point of view which finds all anger indefensible. At 1.20, for instance, Cicero distinguishes between *ratio*, the soul's "sovereign part," which Plato lodged in the head, and *ira* and *cupiditas*, which, resided, respectively, in the breast and below the diaphragm.[6] Later in the same book he elaborates on the division between *aegritudines, irae libidinesque*, on the one hand, and *mens* on the other (1.80).[7] In book 4, in still greater detail, Cicero writes of the soul as described by Pythagoreans and then by Plato

> . . . qui animum in duas partes dividunt, alteram rationis participem faciunt, alteram expertam. In participe rationis ponunt tranquillitatem, id est, placidam quietamque constantiam, in illa altera motus turbidos cum irae tum cupiditatis contrarios inimicosque rationi.
> (4.10)
> . . . who divide the soul into two parts: to the one they assign a share in reason, to the other none; that which has a share of reason they make the seat of peacefulness, that is, a consistent state of quiet and tranquillity; the other part they make the seat of stormy emotions both of anger and desire which are contrary and hostile to reason.[8]

Twice, however, in the *Laws* Plato says that a law-giving citizen can be at once gentle and spirited. He first makes the point at 731b:

> θυμοειδῆ μὲν δὴ χρὴ πάντα ἄνδρα εἶναι, πρᾶον δὲ ὡς ὅτι μάλιστα.

> Every man ought to be at once passionate and gentle in the highest degree.

Shortly later (731d) he elaborates the same point in regard to the anger one feels against someone who in his behavior remains "obstinately perverse" (ἀπαραμυθήτως πλημμελής):

> διὸ δὴ θυμοειδῆ πρέπειν καὶ πρᾶόν φαμεν ἑκάστοτε εἶναι δεῖν τὸν ἀγαθόν.

> Wherefore we affirm that it behooves the good man to be always at once passionate and gentle.[9]

I will leave aside the question of whether or not Turnus is ἀπαραμύθητος, when he is the one who had just used words in a vain attempt to reason with Aeneas, not vice versa. Rather I would take note of the point, implicit in the first passage, explicit in the second, that Plato is talking about the contemporaneity of passion and gentleness in his good citizen's reasoned response to the unrepentant evildoer. Both qualities must be exercised together to reach a considered judgment. In the case of Aeneas' reaction to Turnus we may, granting him every benefit, find him having a moment of gentleness as he hesitates, but πραότης can scarcely be characteristic of one preparing to act *furiis accensus*.[10] Aeneas' moment of hesitation might suggest that, for this brief span, he is πρᾶος, but even allowing that such a pause betokens an instant of mildness, nevertheless the immediately subsequent violence undercuts any notion of the permanence of gentleness in Aeneas' spiritual makeup. He is, finally, not "at once passionate and gentle."

πραότης figures importantly also in Aristotle's description of anger. In his initial definition, πραότης (Cicero's *lenitas*) is the defensible mean between the evil extremes of ὀργιλότης (called a κακία), which Cicero terms *iracundia*, and ἀοργησία, the *lentitudo* of Cicero.[11] Shortly later Aristotle expands on this same definition, with specific qualifications as to how the πρᾶος should act:

> . . . for "gentle" really denotes a calm temper [ἀτάραχος], not led by emotion [ὑπὸ τοῦ πάθους], but only becoming angry in such a manner, for such causes and for such length of time as principle may ordain, although the quality is thought to err on the side of defect, since the gentle-tempered man is not prompt to seek redress for injuries but rather inclined to forgive them [οὐ γὰρ τιμωρητικὸς ὁ πρᾶος, ἀλλὰ μᾶλλον συγγνωμονικός].[12]

If Aeneas does possess an inclination to forgive it is certainly not his ruling emotion as he prepares to kill Turnus. ὀργιλότης controls his thinking, not πραότης, *ira*, not *lenitas* or the *clementia* to which it might give form.

For all his eclecticism in other matters, throughout his *Tusculan Disputations* Cicero endeavors to refute the Peripatetic position on the emotions and unhesitatingly to accept that of the Stoics.[13] There can be no limit to the excesses to which the passions will be prone, once allowed at all (4.41). All passion is disorder (4.43) and *ira* is no exception. I have earlier shown how Cicero connects *cupiditas, aegritudines*, and *libidines*.[14] Thrice in a two sentence stretch in book 3 he twins the species *iracundia* with its genus *libido*, and proceeds to link it directly with *timor* and *dolor* (3.11). At 4.16 *ira* and *odium* are conjoined and at 4.52 *ira* is defined as a form of *insania* while at 4.77 it serves as companion of *furor*.[15] Cicero is at pains to list Greek and Roman heroes who, though under severe pressure, have never acted out of *ira* (the catalog includes Hercules, the Stoic hero par excellence, and, no doubt with due modesty, the author himself, twice over!).[16] Perhaps his most telling pronouncement about the incompatibility of wisdom and anger occurs in the third book (19):

> Sapientis autem animus semper vacat vitio, numquam turgescit, numquam tumet; at irati animus eius modi est: numquam igitur sapiens irascitur. Nam si irascitur etiam concupiscit; proprium est

enim irati cupere, a quo laesus videatur, ei quam maximum dolorem
inurere . . .

But the soul of the wise man is always free from defect and never in
an inflamed, never in a swollen state; but this is the condition of the
angry soul; therefore the wise man is never angry. For if he is angry
he is also covetous. The covetousness peculiar to the angry man is
the desire to stamp the brand of uttermost pain upon the person by
whom he considers himself injured.

But Cicero has a still more focused definition of *ira* / *iracundia* to
which he recurs four times in the *Tusculans* and which has specific value
for anyone pondering the force exerted by Stoic values, especially as
voiced so powerfully by Cicero two years before his death, on Virgil as he
wrote his epic and, in particular, its final lines. The formulation first
occurs at 3.11, *sic enim definitur iracundia, ulciscendi libido* (for the definition
of wrath is lust for vengeance). This phrasing is varied at 4.21 where, in a
list of five definitions of *ira*, we find that the vice is synonymous with a
"lust of punishing the man who is thought to have inflicted an undeserved injury" (*libido poeniendi eius, qui videatur laesisse iniuria*) and that
inimicitia is *ira ulciscendi tempus observans*, watching an opportunity for
revenge, while at 4.44 Cicero recurs to his initial wording (*est enim ira, ut
modo definivi, ulciscendi libido*).[17] But it is the question he phrases at 4.79
that is most apropos to our discussion:

quo modo autem, si naturalis ira, aut alius alio magis iracundus esset
aut finem haberet prius, quam esset ulta, ulciscendi libido aut quem-
quam poeniteret quod fecisset per iram?

How, moreover, if anger were natural, would either one man be
more irascible than another? or how would lust for vengeance come
to an end before it had exacted retribution? or how would anyone
repent of what he had done through anger?

Correct thinkers, and doers, like Alexander the Great, can, according
to Cicero, restrain themselves from anger's lust for revenge. Though
Aeneas, at the end, claims to pass the responsibility for extracting *poena*
from Turnus on to Pallas—

        ". . . Pallas te hoc vulnere, Pallas
immolat et poenam scelerato ex sanguine sumit."
  (12.948–49)
"Pallas, Pallas sacrifices you with this wound and exacts punishment
from your criminal blood."

—he is still the actor, acting out of anger. To him, in his wildness, his previous instant of hesitation had almost cost him the object of his vengeful fury:

> . . . "tune hinc spoliis indute meorum
> eripiare mihi?"
>   (12.947–48)
> "Are you, clothed in the spoils of my own, to be snatched hence from me?"

Whether we miss in his last deed any appearance of πραότης or question the absence of *clementia*, Aeneas' action is morally dubious. If Aeneas were to respond to his opponent from innate πραότης, then he should forgo all notion of vengeance. If, on the other hand, we allow any justification to his proclamation of revenge, then his deed should be performed totally without emotion, especially without anger. The reader, however, is disappointed of any reasoning on the hero's part of why moderation in whatever manifestation should not in fact rule his response to Turnus' final plea.

Cicero can again serve as the best of commentators, and here I quote at length:

> His aut subtrahendi sunt ei, in quos impetum conantur facere, dum se ipsi colligant—quid est autem se colligere nisi dissipatas animi partes rursum in suum locum cogere?—aut rogandi orandique sunt, ut, si quam habent ulciscendi vim, differant in tempus alius, dum defervescat ira.
>   (*TD* 4.78)
> Either the victims of angry men's attempted onslaught must be withdrawn from their reach until of themselves they gain self-control (but what is it to control oneself except to bring together the scattered parts of the soul again into their place?) or, if they have any power of taking revenge, they must be begged and entreated to put it off to another time, until their anger cools down.

Aeneas exclaims on how his victim might have been snatched from him, after furies and anger had kindled in him the impetus to act. Cicero, by contrast, warns that the prey of men who are in the throes of anger, the visible spark of their emotionality, must be withdrawn from their clutches until their anger wanes or, as he shortly later puts it, *ardor* has yielded to the persuasions of *ratio*. Virgil allows his hero's victim no such opportunity as Aeneas follows his very un-Stoic course of anger and revenge.

Before we proceed to watch Horace commenting on the *Aeneid*'s conclusion, it is well to pause and ask whether or not we can validly apply

Cicero's intensely Stoic interpretation of anger to the end of the *Aeneid* or, better, whether Virgil himself would have wished us so to do and whether his contemporary readers would have likewise understood him as doing so. The core philosophical document of the poem, Anchises' disquisition to his son in the Underworld on the origin of the universe and on the future of Rome, demands that the answer be positive. It has long been recognized how much Anchises' initial description of the evolution of nature, especially human nature, owes, first to Plato (and through him to Orphism and Pythagoreanism) and then to the Stoics. The soul, imprisoned in corporeal emotionality, must, on the body's death, undergo a period of purgation whence it either rejoins its original ether or enters once again into a body's decadent limbs. The chief political virtue that Anchises' speech promotes is *clementia*, which Seneca would later define as "restraining the mind from vengeance when it has the power to take it, or the leniency of a superior toward an inferior in fixing punishment" (*temperantia animi in potestate ulciscendi vel lenitas superioris adversus inferiorem in constituendis poenis, Cl.* 2.3.1). Anchises' advice takes both practical and apothegmatic turns. The practical is a plea, in anticipation, to Julius Caesar to end his civil war against Pompey:

> "tuque prior, tu parce, genus qui ducis Olympo,
> proice tela manu, sanguis meus!"
>   (6.834–35)
> "and do you first, do you spare, who draw your descent from heaven; cast the weapons from your hand, o my blood!"

The apothegmatic is the strategically placed command we have already quoted, addressed to his son as incipient Romanus:

> "parcere subiectis et debellare superbos."
>   (6.853)

Cicero would have concurred that a speech which begins with the Stoic view of the *spiritus* and the *igneus vigor* that informs the universe ends also with a very Stoic exhortation to restraint, especially when bringing peace through war and when assuming a position of superiority over the humbled proud.

    At the poem's conclusion Virgil has his reader, if not his hero, face squarely the force of Anchises' imperative as Aeneas prepares to act. Proud Turnus has now been beaten down, for there is no doubt that Virgil, during much of the last four books, would have us see Aeneas' foe as an incorporation of *superbia*. For instance, the narrator breaks into the story, after Turnus robs the body of Pallas of its sword belt, to remark on the victor's lack of moderation (10.501–2), and soon thereafter, as Aeneas

begins to track his foe, the reader remains unsure whether he is entering
the thoughts of Aeneas or of the narrator of his tale as the hero begins his
task of warring down the proud:

> proxima quaeque metit gladio latumque per agmen
> ardens limitem agit ferro, te, Turne, superbum
> caede nova quaerens.
> (10.513–15)

With the sword he mows down all the nearest ranks, and fiercely
drives with the steel a broad path through the host, seeking you,
Turnus, proud from your new-wrought slaughter.

Whether the reader's sympathy for the doomed hero is meant to grow
during the course of the epic's final book or whether he is still in his last
moments to be remembered as the personification of *violentia*, a characteristic which Virgil allots only to him, should make little difference to
those analyzing Aeneas' action.[18] For, as Turnus prepares to utter his final
plea to Aeneas, the narrator affirms that Aeneas has at least fulfilled the
second part of Anchises' *dictum*. We now find Turnus

> . . . humilis supplex oculos dextramque precantem
> protendens . . .
> (12.930–31)

a suppliant, with eyes humbled and stretching forth his right hand in
prayer . . .

The haughty have been made to supplicate, the prideful have been
brought low. Since Turnus' position now fleshes out half of Anchises'
command and since his subsequent words remind Aeneas directly of his
father, these last words have particular power especially as they in turn
conclude with a prayer, "press not your hatred further" (*ulterius ne tende
odiis*, 12.938).

The very fact that Turnus can be viewed as paradigm for the prideful,
defeated in war, might well be meant to invest his words with special
authority as he reminds Aeneas of the other half of his father's injunction,
which is to say of the fact that *clementia* is as possible for Aeneas in fact as
it was essential for his father in words. In Turnus' eyes Aeneas is guilty of
continued *odium* which he should now forswear (we recall Cicero's definition of *odium* as *ira inveterata*). The question is, as we observe Aeneas,
ira terribilis, prepare to kill his foe, whether or not Turnus' eyes should
also be those of Virgil's readers.

Let us now turn from Cicero whose *Tusculan Disputations* were written
and presumably published when Virgil was twenty-five, to Horace and

specifically to the first book of *Epistles* which the poet released in 20, the year before his friend's death and on which he was working as Virgil brought his epic to a close.[19] Many things caught Horace's eye and ear as he read or heard his friend recite from his poem in progress.[20] One instance is the beginning of Anchises' speech to his son on the destructive emotions to which the flesh is heir and which can be purged only after death. After speaking of our earthly limbs and moribund bodies he adds:

> hinc metuunt cupiuntque, dolent gaudentque, neque
> auras dispiciunt clausae tenebris et carcere caeco.
>   (6.733–34)
> Hence their fears and desires, their griefs and joys; nor do they discern the breezes, pent up in the gloom of their dark prison.[21]

Horace makes use of the same list of negative emotions, in exactly reverse order, when commenting on the sources of our misplaced yearnings, our tendency to "admire" too much:

> gaudeat an doleat, cupiat metuatne, quid ad rem
> si, quidquid vidit melius peiusve sua spe,
> defixis oculis animoque et corpore torpet?
>   (*Epi.* 1.6.12–14)
> Whether a man feel joy or grief, desire or fear, what matter it if, when he has seen aught better or worse than he expected, his eyes are fast riveted, and mind and body are benumbed?[22]

Horace, as Virgil, is commenting on the origins of our emotionality, on the baggage of bodily "diseases" (*corporeae pestes*) which weigh down the soul and drive us to act out our lives in spiritual darkness (*Aen.* 6.737).

But Horace is interested, too, in the most crucial moment of emotionality in the epic where Anchises' abstractions, his philosopher's exhortation toward an ethics of moderation in the use of force, are put to the test as Aeneas prepares to kill. Horace's meditation takes place in *Epistles* 1.2, a poem devoted to the study of epic as source book not for entertaining adventure but for the ethics of behavior.[23] The great imaginative literature of the past, in this case the works of Homer, can teach us, begins Horace, what is beautiful or ugly or useful more plainly and clearly than the Stoic Chrysippus or the Academic Crantor. The *Iliad*, in Horace's précis, is the story of the interaction of lust and anger, just as *amor* (6, 13), *libido* (15), and *ira* (13, 15) are interwoven in Horace's text. Paris' love for Helen, Achilles' devotion to Briseis and his reciprocated anger at Agamemnon: because of these and the intrigue, guile and crime that accompany them

Iliacos intra muros peccatur et extra.

> (*Epi.* 1.2.16)

within and without the walls of Troy all goes wrong.

The *Odyssey*, in Horace's contrastive view, provides a useful example of the capabilities of courage and wisdom. If the *Iliad* shows two peoples subjected to the folly of kings, the *Odyssey*, in the person of its titular hero, differentiates between one man's wise judgment and the foolish greed of his followers or of our own overinclination to yield to indulgence of the flesh as if we were reincarnations of Penelope's suitors or the courtiers of Alcinous. Horace sums up his thoughts on reviewing Homer with a reminder that there is nothing better than a good book to cure us of envy and passion.

Horace is not done with allusiveness for he now turns quite directly to Lucretius[24] and, then, perhaps, also to the line from *Aeneid* 4 that we saw him varying in *Epistle* 6:

> qui cupit aut metuit, iuvat illum sic domus et res
> ut lippum pictae tabulae, fomentam podagram . . .
>
> (1.2.51–52)

To one with fears or desires, house and fortune give as much pleasure as painted panels to sore eyes, warm wraps to the gout . . .

After a further comment on envy's power to torture, Horace turns to anger and its consequences:

> qui non moderabitur irae
> infectum volet esse, dolor quod suaserit et mens,
> dum poenas odio per vim festinat inulto.
> ira furor brevis est.
>
> (1.2.59–62)

He who curbs not his anger will wish undone that which vexation and wrath prompted, as he hastens with violence to extract punishment for hatred unavenged. Anger is short-lived madness.

Horace may have had in mind the comment of Cicero on the angry man's belated desire to render undone what his immoderate impulse for vengeance had urged him to perpetrate (*TD* 4.79). Otherwise the commonality of situation between Horace's victim of anger and Aeneas, guilty of *odium* (in Turnus' eyes, probably in Anchises', perhaps even in ours), remembering his *saevus dolor*, and finally, at the moment of action, *furiis accensus et ira terribilis*, is noteworthy.

Horace takes us in his poem from a summary or reasons why contemplation of the *Iliad* and *Odyssey* is valuable for a student of ethics to a bow to Lucretius and his notion that philosophy, not external trappings, rids mind and body of suffering. From there, as if to complete his survey of epic by allusion to his friend's masterpiece now being finished as he himself also was writing, Horace, through his addressee Lollius, puts us in the same situation as Virgil places Aeneas at the end of his epic. Virgil does not comment on his hero's emotionality or its result. Instead Horace does it for him and for us. The *animus*, here the source of passions, chief of which is *ira*, is metaphorically parallel to a horse or dog, a creature of base instincts to be reined in with bridle or curbed with chain:

> . . . animum rege; qui nisi paret,
> imperat: hunc frenis, hunc tu conpesce catena.
> (1.2.62–63)
> Rule your spirit. Unless it obeys, it commands. Control it with reins, control it with a chain.[25]

Unless we make the creature obey, it dominates our actions. Horace's implication for Aeneas' conduct is clear. The hero is allowing some bestial aspect of his nature to rule his behavior as he kills, not the soul's higher claims. Anger, not reason, the animal, not the celestial part of his being, governs him as, *fervidus*, he performs his final deed.

But there is no better guide to helping us adjudicate what might have been Virgil's appraisal of someone whom he posits as acting on the remembrance of *saevus dolor* to become, in the next moment, "set aflame by furies and terrible in his wrath" than by examining his own usage of *dolor*, *ira*, and *furiae* (or the *furor* such inner "furies" adumbrate). Only in one context are these emotions given a positive accolade and that is where the figure of Mezentius is concerned. As an example of the unspeakable killings he had effected, we recall "how he . . . even joined dead bodies with living, putting hands together with hands, faces with faces" (8.485–86). Evander, whose words these are, finds that Etruria reacts "with just furies" (*furiis . . . iustis*) and the Etruscans' seer proclaims their "just grief" (*iustus dolor*) and the "deserved anger" (*merita ira*) by which Mezentius inflames them (8.494, 500–501). Finally the narrator himself pronounces on the "just angers" (*iustae irae*) of those who do battle with the villainous warrior (10.714).

This is Virgil's unique bow to a non-Stoic acceptance of anger and it is accomplished with careful circumspection. The two other characters in the poem with whom Mezentius' ugly conduct associates him, Polyphemus and Cacus, are equally distinguished for their subhuman nature.[26] Of Virgil's six uses of *efferus*, two are applied to Mezentius.[27] The phrase *dentibus infrendens*, at 10.718, clearly implies a symbiosis between Mezentius and the wild boar to which he has just been compared.[28] The

revenge of his people against Mezentius is richly motivated, long contemplated and executed by customary heroic procedure, as Mezentius himself admits (10.900–902). It would be defensible by Peripatetic standards
of behavior. By contrast, Aeneas' final anger against Turnus, aroused in a
flash from a sudden vision which triggers a briskly executed killing,
would not find support from the ethical dogmata of any ancient philosophical school, least of all the Stoics.[29] But in this case as in all other
instances where Virgil uses *dolor*, *furiae* (or *furor*), and *ira*, we have no
authorial accolades, only context to help us appraise the poet's meaning.

Aside from the epic's concluding lines the reader confronts Aeneas'
anger on two other occasions in the poem. The first is where he contemplates the killing of Helen in book 2:

> "exarsere ignes animo; subit ira cadentem
> ulcisci patriam et sceleratas sumere poenas."
> (2.775–76)
> "Fires blazed up in my heart. Anger overcomes me to avenge my
> falling fatherland and to exact punishment for her crimes."

These are Aeneas' words to Dido, and they describe a state of mind and
an impulse to act which Aeneas himself shortly later qualifies as maddened (*furiata mente ferebar*, 2.589). His own self-judgment is confirmed
by Venus in her first words after her epiphany to her son:

> "nate, quis indomitas tantus dolor excitat iras?
> quid furis? aut quonam nostri tibi cura recessit?"
> (2.594–95)
> "My son, what great resentment stirs your ungovernable wrath?
> Why are you raging? Or whither has your care for us gone?"[30]

There is no doubt that we are meant to sense a negative judgment in
Venus' rebuke, one which contrasts Aeneas' anger, desire for vengeance
through the extraction of punishment for (or is it through?) crime, and
fury with the love and clarity of vision which Venus projects.[31]

We also have a history of Aeneas reacting against and then succumbing
to anger in the last book itself, the final instance being both its culmination and its conclusion. We first find him addressing those embroiled in
battle after the augur Tolumnius had broken the truce:

> "quo ruitis? quaeve ista repens discordia surgit?
> o cohibite iras!"
> (12.313–14)
> "Whither are you rushing? What means this sudden outburst of
> strife? O curb your rage!"[32]

Before beginning his brief plea for restraint Virgil allots Aeneas his traditional epithet for the last time:

> At pius Aeneas dextram tendebat inermem . . .
> (12.311)
> But good Aeneas was stretching forth his unarmed hand . . .

Both the final use of the epithet and Aeneas' gesture are carefully chosen
by Virgil. We are reminded that from the beginning of the epic Aeneas'
pietas and anger, specifically the anger of Juno, are incompatible entities.[33]
Moreover, the next time that we find someone described in a similar
posture—and it is the last and climactic instance in the epic—occurs at
the end with Turnus, *dextram . . . precantem protendens*, about to make his
final plea to Aeneas (12.930–31). That prayer, as we have seen, by reminding Aeneas of his father, appeals to his *pietas*. It also for a moment staves
off anger (Turnus' word is *odium*, the narrator's *ira*), as Aeneas would
wish to do here. The roles, and abstractions, at the end are reversed, with
Turnus in the posture of *pius* Aeneas and Aeneas, first, in Turnus' eyes, a
victim of hatred and, finally, in the narrator's and ours, "terrible in his
wrath."

   In between we have a double instance of Aeneas' anger as Messapus
attacks him. First we are told that "then indeed his wrath swells" (*tum
vero adsurgunt irae*, 12.494). Then Virgil elaborates:

> iam tandem invadit medios et Marte secundo
> terribilis saevam nullo discrimine caedem
> suscitat, irarumque omnis effundit habenas.
> (12.497–99)
> Now at last he plunges into the midst, and down the tide of war
> terribly awakes grim indiscriminate carnage, flinging loose all the
> reins of passion.[34]

For Aeneas to let loose "all the reins of his anger" is to give the beast or
beasts of revenge full sway.[35] That Virgil means us to visualize this conduct in a negative light is clear, first, from the preceding line: rational
anger (and, as we saw, Virgil's epic offers only one instance of wrath
which the narrator deems justifiable) is certainly not possible when all
"distinction" (*discrimen*) yields before savagery. Second, for negative uses
of the metaphor elsewhere in Virgil we need only mention the uncontrolled chariot of *impius* Mars, at the end of the first *Georgic* (1.511–14), the
reins that Aeolus will fail to apply to his horse-winds in book 1 of the
Aeneid (1.63), or the destructive fire in book 5 that rages "with loosened
reins" (*immissis . . . habenis*, 5.662).[36] The animal energy of anger must be
kept under tight control, that is, according to Horace, be made subject to

moderatio, and not be given the freedom to follow where *dolor* and *furor* lead.[37] Far from defending his hero Virgil is here preparing us for the ferocity (*saevitia*) (and perhaps even for an unspoken lack of *discrimen*) that renders Aeneas *ira terribilis* in his last outburst.

Let us turn now to what it means, in Virgil, to be subject to "furies," or, specifically in the case of Aeneas, to be *furiis accensus*. The Virgilian corpus offers fifteen instances of *furiae* at work, ranging from animals maddened by love and plague (*Geo.* 3.244, 511) to a series of human victims—Ajax frenzied for having violated Cassandra (*Aen.* 1.41), Orestes "driven by the madness of his crimes" (*scelerum furiis agitatus, Aen.* 3.331), the maddened mothers aroused by the Fury Allecto (*Aen.* 7.392).[38] Aside from Aeneas, two of the epic's major protagonists are caught by *furiae*. The first is Dido. She is so characterized in her own words as her second speech to Aeneas becomes more and more disjointed: "alas, I am borne along set aflame by furies" (*heu furiis incensa feror*, 4.376).[39] And shortly later the narrator, after she has been compared to Pentheus and Orestes, finds her ready for suicide

> . . . ubi concepit furias evicta dolore
> decrevitque mori . . .
>   (4.474–75)
> when, overwhelmed by anguish, she conceived furies and resolved to die . . .[40]

Virgil has prepared the way. At line 91, when Juno notices that Dido's reputation no longer stays her madness, which is to say that her standing as ruler, which would offer her immortality, has yielded to love's destructiveness, she can announce to Venus

> ardet amans Dido traxitque per ossa furorem.
>   (4.101)
> Dido is on fire with love and has drawn the fury through her bones.

And thus also the poet will conclude her tale, seeing her as

> . . . misera ante diem subitoque accensa furore . . .
>   (4.697)
> hapless before her day and set aflame by a sudden madness . . .

As in the case of the earlier allusions to her *furiae* / *furor*, we are reminded of how closely Virgil's words anticipate Aeneas, *furiis accensus*. Each is driven by inner furies to maddened action. The one is directed against the self and results in a suicide that ends a life before its time is up. The other is projected outward against an enemy become suppliant.[41]

The second protagonist of the *Aeneid* who is subject to *furiae* is Turnus himself. As in the case of Dido, we hear of them twice, both occasions in the epic's last book. The first comes after a verbal attack on Aeneas as a eunuch Phrygian "whose curled hair drips with myrrh." The narrator immediately pronounces that "he is driven by these furies" (*his agitur furiis*, 12.101) and compares him to a bull preparing for battle. The second occurrence, to which I will return, joins "love driven by furies" (*furiis agitatus amor*, 12.668) with shame, madness, and courage to form a complex of abstractions which motivates Turnus as the epic draws to a close. As to his *furor*, he himself puts it most strongly in words addressed to his sister, anticipating death from the madness about to catapult him into the final conflict:

> ". . . hunc, oro, sine me furere ante furorem."
> (12.680)
> "with this madness before the end, I pray, allow me to rage."

At crucial junctures earlier Virgil has prepared his readers for this final outburst. In book 7, after Allecto has roused him to do battle—

> saevit amor ferri et scelerata insania belli,
> ira super . . .
> (7.461–62)
> love for the sword rages in him and the criminal madness of war, anger above all . . .

—he is compared to a cauldron within which water seethes (*furit*, 7.464). And book 9, which essentially belongs to Turnus, brackets him between an initial outburst of *ira* and *dolor* and a rage that nearly proves his undoing:

> sed furor ardentem caedisque insana cupido
> egit in adversos.
> (9.760–61)
> but rage and the mad lust of slaughter drove him blazing on the foe in front.[42]

As in the case of Dido, Virgil suggests no reason why Aeneas' motivation and conduct at the end should be interpreted in a different light from that of Turnus, the victim over time of his own inner demons as well as of Furies sent by Jupiter and Juno.

Finally we have a double use of *furiae* in the eighth book, attached both to Hercules, hero of many labors, stopping at the future site of Rome on his way to Greece with the cattle of Geryon, and Cacus, stealer of eight animals from the herd and in the epic second only to Mezentius for ugliness of conduct.[43] As he prepares to act Cacus' mind is "wild with furies" (*furiis . . . mens effera*, 8.205). In response to this villain Hercules likewise rages. We are told that "his anguish furiously blazed forth with black gall" (*furiis exarserat atro / felle dolor*, 8.219–20) when he notices the theft. Then as he pursues his revenge he is called "raging in his mind" (*furens animis*, 8.228).[44] Since the adventure occurs where Rome will be founded and is readily perceived as a cut-and-dried account of good versus evil, Hercules' behavior is regularly appropriated as a model for Aeneas, hearing the tale from Evander's lips as he embarks on his campaign in Latium which ends in the death of Turnus.[45]

But Virgil, as often throughout his epic, does not leave matters so simply. There is, first, the question of motivation. We would expect Hercules, the great eliminator of monsters from the world, to go about his work of purgation immediately on arrival at Rome. The villain must be removed to leave Pallanteum at peace. Instead he only acts when eight of his beautiful cattle have been stolen. It is personal "anguish," not some impersonal Stoic desire to rid the universe of malfeasance, that set him on his angry course.[46]

Second, there are special touches to Evander's characterization of Hercules that give the reader pause. We find him, for instance, "gnashing his teeth" (*dentibus infrendens*, 8.230), a trait that, as we have seen, Virgil gives elsewhere only to the monstrous Polyphemus and to the arch-villain Mezentius.[47] Another troubling note is the juncture of black gall to qualify the anguish that burns Hercules along with "furies." Hercules is the prey of μελαγχολία which Cicero closely links with the *furor, iracundia, timor*, and *dolor* that we find in the tragic actions of Alcmaeon, Ajax, and Orestes (*TD* 3.11).[48] Pliny the Elder makes the connection succinctly: "but in black gall [lies] the cause of madness for man" (*sed in felle nigro insaniae causa homini*, HN 11.193).[49] And the only other figure in whose spiritual makeup Virgil regularly mixes *furor* and *insania* is Turnus.[50]

Finally we have a careful lexical conjunction of hero and victim. Both of course are prey to *furiae*.[51] Both are associated with blackness and with pride.[52] The fact that Virgil, through Evander, makes no distinction between the "furies" of Cacus and of Hercules, and that there are other links in common, offers the reader little encouragement to distinguish between the rage of monster and of monster-killer in action. Since Hercules, as he is made to appear by Virgil, also has attributes that link him with Mezentius and Turnus, we would be incautious to consider the *furiae*, through whose intervention Hercules' anger blazes up, the only positive manifestation, other than Etruria's indignation against Mezentius, of inner furies at work in the *Aeneid*. Rather Hercules joins the epic's roster of, among others, Cacus, Dido, and Turnus who act irrationally, who themselves become monsters, under the pressures of *furiae*. Aeneas, at the epic's conclusion, must be classed no differently.[53] Cicero, in a passage to which I have several times referred, calls our attention to a characteristic which in Virgil often qualifies the behavior of those caught by fury, namely *caecitas*, blindness of mind. After alluding to the writers of the Twelve Tables with whom he is in agreement for not allowing any-one *furiosus* to hold property, Cicero adds "frenzy they regarded as a blindness of the mind in all relations" (*furorem . . . esse rati sunt mentis ad omnia caecitatem*, TD 3.11). It is informative to watch what we presume from Cicero—that madness is accompanied by moral blindness while the complement of rationality is clarity of vision—become experiential in Virgil's text.

We take the linkage for granted at the moment of Dido's death, for example, when, after the furies of rage against Aeneas and, ultimately, against herself have subsided

> quaesivit caelo lucem ingemuitque reperta.
> (4.692)
> she sought light in heaven and groaned as she found it.[54]

This "light" is not only the brightness of day, which she had earlier resolved to leave (4.631), but the clearness of vision that comes to "wan-dering" eyes soon to be at rest (4.691).[55] Her posture is not unlike our last look at Mezentius, villain who at the end draws our sympathy for the deep affection offered him by his son, now about to beg his haughty victor, Aeneas, to ward off from his corpse the *odia* and *furor* of his countrymen. He speaks only

> . . . ut auras
> suspiciens hausit caelum mentemque recepit . . .
> (10.898–99)
> when with eyes turned heavenward he drank in the sky and regained his mind . . .

To "watch the breezes" and "drink in the heavens," as the Latin puts Mezentius' posture literally, is to recover one's mind. It is to share, for a final moment, in the higher aspects of the soul, as described by Anchises in book 6, namely to rejoice in its heavenly origin (*caelestis origo*, 730) and not fail to "discern the breezes" (*auras dispiciunt*, 733–34) as do those caught in the body's darkness and blind prison (*tenebris et caeco carcere*, 734).

We can observe the contrast more directly still in the figure of Turnus, frozen, as he nears the final conflict, into torpor by a conglomeration of abstractions (*pudor, insania, furiis agitatus amor, virtus*) which carefully mixes positive and negative. This moment of catalepsy passes only

ut primum discussae umbrae et lux reddita menti . . .
(12.669)
when first the shadows scattered and light returned to his mind . . .

Only after a return of "brightness" to his thinking after a moment of
madness and fury is further action possible.

Finally we have the figure of the titular hero. Aeneas, in his narration
to Dido of Troy's demise, includes himself among those who, "blind with
fury" (caeci . . . furore, 2.244), allowed the wooden horse to breach the
city's gates.[56] And in the battle that soon begins, as furor is added to their
spirits, the emboldened Trojans are compared by Aeneas to wolves driven
blind (caecos) by their bellies' ferocity (2.355–57). But the most astonishing
example in the epic of rage yielding to understanding, of clarity and
insight following on a moment of moral blindness, is allotted by Virgil to
Aeneas describing himself poised to kill Helen. We have looked earlier at
the way Aeneas' fury is described, in words given to himself and his
mother. It is with her apparition and above all with her explanatory
response to her son that I am here concerned. The epiphany occurs
immediately after Aeneas' soliloquy on rage, presumably in order to
prevent words turning to deeds:

> [. . . et furiata mente ferebar,]
> cum mihi se, non ante oculis tam clara, videndam
> obtulit et pura per noctem in luce refulsit
> alma parens . . .
> (2.588–91)
> [I was borne along with my thoughts frenzied] when my kindly
> mother offered herself to my sight, never before so clear to my
> vision, and gleamed in pure radiance through the night . . .

In the course of her calming speech she performs a magic action whose
ramifications will take us, in conclusion, into Virgil's most essential
thoughts about human nature. Aeneas should not resent Helen, says his
mother, or even Paris. It is the "inclemency of the gods" (divum inclementia) that is destroying Troy. To understand, in fact to observe this, Venus
allows her son an instant of perception, of seeing-through, not allotted to
the human eye:

> "aspice (namque omnem, quae nunc obducta tuenti
> mortalis hebetat visus tibi et umida circum
> caligat, nubem eripiam) . . ."
> (2.604–6)

> "Behold (for I will tear away all this cloud which now, drawn over your sight, dulls your mortal vision and surrounds you in dark mist) . . ."

The cloud that clogs Aeneas' vision can be particular or general. Venus' "now" can, of course, refer to the present moment, to Aeneas' mistaken vendetta against Helen. But the veil of his imperception can also be interpreted in wider terms, with one example standing metonymically for the whole series of moments that we call a human life, an individual's history of existence. Virgil expounds this wider view of blindness through the mouth of Anchises in a passage to which I have referred before but which I will quote again in fuller detail. Father is expounding to son the origin of the soul:

> igneus est ollis vigor et caelestis origo
> seminibus, quantum non noxia corpora tardant
> terrenique hebetant artus moribundaque membra.
> hinc metuunt cupiuntque dolent gaudentque neque auras
> dispiciunt clausae tenebris et carcere caeco.
>   (6.730–34)
> Fiery is the vigor and divine the source of those seeds, so long as harmful bodies do not check them nor earthly limbs and mortal frames dull them. Hence their fears and desires, their griefs and joys; nor do they discern the breezes, pent up in the gloom of their dark prison.

These passages, which include the only two appearances of the verb *hebeto* in the Virgilian corpus, complement each other.[57] The first documents a specific moment of blindness, here in the life of Aeneas, that could stand for any such instance in a person's emotional *vita*. The second, embedded in a segment of the poem which Virgil privileges almost before any other for its transcendent richness and sweep, generalizes on the sources of this emotionality. For Aeneas, caught up in the passionate swirl of Troy's final hours, a black cloud dulls the vision. For the ordinary human, for Aeneas and for us, the soul, in Anchises' formulation, would be heaven-bent, fulfilling the fiery, etherial nature of its consistency, were it not for the earthly limbs that blunt its higher aspirations. Aeneas' individual action, contemplated in book 2, becomes generalized in the impulse of everyman, as sketched in Anchises' essential psychology, whose soul is imprisoned in the body's passionate dark dungeon.

Venus' words to her son, as she prepares to uncloud his mortal vision, will lead us back also into another extraordinary moment in Virgil's poem and offer further illustration of my connection between fury and moral blindness. The lines are quoted by Macrobius (1.2.19), in his commentary on the *Somnium Scipionis*, as one of two texts used to explain why Virgil has false dreams depart from the Underworld through a gate of ivory while the trustworthy exit through a gate of horn.[58] After referring to Porphyry on Homer and then the lines I quoted previously from *Aeneid* 2 Macrobius directly offers his own commentary:

> Hoc velamen cum in quiete ad verum usque aciem animae introspicientis admittit, de cornu creditur, cuius ista natura est ut tenuatum visui pervium sit; cum autem a vero hebetat ac repellit optutum, ebur putatur, cuius corpus ita natura densetum est ut ad quamvis extremitatem tenuitatis erasum nullo visu ad ulteriora tendente penetretur.

> If, during sleep, this veil permits the vision of the attentive soul to perceive the truth, it is thought to be made of horn, the nature of which is such that, when thinned, it becomes transparent. When the veil dulls the vision and prevents its reaching the truth, it is thought to be made of ivory, the composition of which is so dense that no matter how thin a layer of it may be, it remains opaque.

Macrobius' analysis forces us to confront the two basic questions which any interpretation of the conclusion of *Aeneid* 6 must face: why do Homer and Virgil give the gates of dreams their particular constituency—ivory for the false, horn for the true—and why does Aeneas pass from the Underworld through the gates of ivory, bringing with him, as he takes the first steps toward establishing Rome, the implications of a nightmare's mendacity?

The two most recent critics of this astonishing passage have sought to find the difference between the twin gates of Sleep in terms of rough and dark for horn, smooth and brightly shining for ivory, but Macrobius' suggestion of transparency for horn, lack of translucence for ivory has powerful implications for Virgil's text.[59] Venus in book 2 can supernaturally snatch away the human veil from Aeneas' clouded, which is to say morally imperceptive, thinking. Nevertheless, four books later, as the hero proceeds, not unlike a newly born soul, into the world above to set out on the treacherous road of living, he embodies an aspect of falsity that comes from the inability, finally, to perceive through or beyond the immediately emotional, to acquire wisdom, if such were possible, from his mother's miraculous "unveiling" of truths ordinarily obscured.

Tertullian, some two centuries before Macrobius' commentary was written, had already succinctly glossed Homer's description of Sleep's gates in a manner that reinforces Macrobius' interpretation (*De Anima* 46.2). His words also add a detail of some significance to any reading of the poem which argues, as I do, that the end of book 6 and the conclusion of the epic richly complement each other:

> Homerus duas portas divisit somniis, corneam veritatis, fallaciae eburneam; respicere est enim, inquiunt, per cornu, ebur autem caecum est.

> Homer shared dreams between two gates, horn for truth, ivory for falsehood; for transparency, they say, is a property of horn, but ivory is opaque.

It is on Tertullian's use of *caecus* that I would like to dwell. I have translated the adjective as "opaque," that is, untransparent, but it must also mean here "blind." And this "blindness" partakes at once of the literal and the figurative, the physical and the spiritual. Those associated with it, be they false dreams or a hero who, at the moment of his most ominous *rite de passage*, shares their entranceway to the world of the living, become, like ivory, impenetrable and unpenetrating, deceptive to the viewer and at the same time imperceptive of true value. The connotations of Tertullian's epithet for the ivory of the gate of false dreams help us also further to appreciate Anchises' description of human emotionality. If Venus' words to her son urge us to connect the cloud that blunts her son's powers of understanding with the earthly limbs that Anchises knows to dull our souls' higher instincts, so the *caecitas* that Tertullian associates with ivory and we, Virgil's readers, perforce link with Aeneas as a false dream, blind while brightly blinding, connects him with another aspect of the soul, trapped, as Anchises likewise observes, in the body's dark prison (*carcere caeco*) of emotionality.

This blindness we have seen Aeneas himself, in book 2, twice associate with fury, first when he styles himself and his colleagues *caeci furore*, second when he characterizes his rage to kill Helen, a rage against which Virgil counterposes Venus' clear and clarifying vision. It is a rage, as we have seen, that in book 10, drives Aeneas to take eight humans for sacrifice, kill a suppliant and a priest, and offer, to a body he has just beheaded, the epic's most jarring curse.[60] It is rage, we have also seen, that in the case of Hercules, instead of helping to raise his heroism to an appropriate level of renown, demeans his accomplishment by equating him with rather than differentiating him from his inglorious opponent.[61]

The same holds true for Aeneas' conduct at the end of the epic. It is not without care that Virgil balances the halfway mark of his epic with its finale by having Aeneas, who leaves the Underworld like a false dream through the gate of ivory, at the end kill his suppliant victim while he himself is *furiis accensus*. In spite of the attempts at exoneration by Servius and his followers, Virgil's words have Aeneas act not from implicit *pietas* but under the direct impulse of furies. Instead of eliciting accolades of praise, Virgil's language should arouse in his readers the deepest suspicions about the ethical quality of his hero's final deed. As Virgil brings his poem to its powerfully inconclusive, brilliantly calculated ending, he allows no light to dawn in his hero's inner vision, to bring illumination after vengeful rage. On the contrary, as we imagine Aeneas burying his sword under his opponent's chest and Turnus' soul fleeing in indignation under the shades below, we, too, are left to ponder the open-mindedness of anger and hatred, the nonfinality of a fury that is delimited only through the confining registrations of a poet's extraordinary words.

NOTES

I am grateful to Martha Nussbaum for many helpful comments.

1. Servius on 12.940:

> omnis intentio ad Aeneae pertinet gloriam: nam et ex eo quod hosti cogitat parcere, pius ostenditur, et ex eo quod eum interimit, pietatis gestat insigne: nam Evandri intuitu Pallantis ulciscitur mortem.

> The whole thrust looks to the glory of Aeneas: for both from the fact that he ponders sparing his enemy, he is shown to be pious, and from the fact that he kills him, he bears the mark of piety: for out of consideration for Evander he avenges the death of Pallas.

The distinction between the *pietas* of Aeneas and the *furor* of Turnus is a major focus of the interpretation of the *Aeneid* by Otis, *Virgil* 93–94, 220–36, 249, 391, et al. Aeneas' *pietas* has again been recently invoked, as excuse for his killing of Turnus, by Clausen, *Hellenistic Poetry* 100.

2. Cf. *Il.* 21.122–24 (Achilles to Lycaon).

3. Williams, *Technique and Ideas* 180, narrows too severely the forcefulness of Virgil's analogy by limiting it, somehow, to the eyes of the frightened Latins alone. After what has immediately preceded, any reader, and not only the immediate sufferers of Aeneas' onslaught, would find the comparison valid. Aeneas incorporates not Jovian order but the sheer physical brutality of those who opposed it. If this is unexpected because, "The reader can be trusted to have grasped the poet's conception of Aeneas by now" (Williams, ibid.), then the shock of having this previous impression questioned or even shattered may be exactly Virgil's point.

4. Galinsky, "Anger of Aeneas" 323.

5. Ibid. 342. "Compassionate" is not among the translations offered for πρᾶος by Liddell-Scott-Jones ("of persons, *mild, gentle, meek*").

6. Cf. Plato *Tim.* 69.

7. Cf. Plato *Rep.* 439d–e and *TD* 2.47, 2.58, 3.7.

8. Cf. also 2.47. Elsewhere (*TD* 1.20) Cicero acknowledges Plato's tripartite division of the soul (*Rep.* 435b–c, 504a, 580d).

9. Plato does not make any further distinctions here about the behavior of his lawgiver, e.g., whether or not he is to be at once impassioned and mild to the same person in the same respect.

Cf. *Rep.* 376a on the anger of dogs, fierce to strangers, fawning to persons they know.

10. If Aeneas' hesitation is evidence for a moment of rationality ("a glimpse of the hero's essential humanity"—Clausen, *Hellenistic Poetry* 100; cf. also Otis, *Virgil* 381: "Aeneas is still a man who takes vengeance in blood, who can be driven to ferocity by the very recollection of Pallas. But this too is an aspect of his humanity"), what does this say of the subsequent enraged killing? Should we not expect humanity to be most operative at the moment which Virgil chooses to serve as our last remembrance of his hero, released into future consciousness as Turnus' soul is dispatched to the shades below?

11. *NE* 1108a4–9 (and cf. *TD* 4.43). On the difference between *ira* and *iracundia*, cf. *TD* 4.27.

12. *NE* 1125b33–1126a3, but the whole passage from 1125b26 on is pertinent.

13. Cf. 4.38–43 as well as 54 and 79.

14. At 2.58 *dolor*, *ira*, and *libido* are linked.

15. Cf. also 4.21.

16. On Cicero himself, 4.52, 4.55; on Hercules, 4.40. I will discuss below Virgil's non-Stoic version of the hero.

17. Cf. also the definition of *odium* as *ira inveterata* (4.21).

18. The most sympathetic treatment of Turnus is by Johnson, *Darkness Visible* 114–20. Those who emphasize Turnus' inhumanity could well remember the still more brutal and repugnant deeds of the titular hero in book 10, some of which I have listed previously. The argument that Turnus deserves death for cruelty displayed on the battlefield could be turned with still greater justice against Aeneas himself.

19. Cf. *Vita Donati* 35 for Virgil's wish to devote three further years to emending his poem and then the remainder of his life to philosophy.

20. Restudy of the relation of the first three books of *Odes*, published most probably in 23, to the *Aeneid* would be valuable. In connection with this essay, ode 3.11, a eulogy of Hypermestra's *clementia* vis-à-vis the conduct of her murderous sisters, is of particular importance. Her punishment, the ode finds her imagining, is to be put in chains by her father (46):

> quod viro clemens misero peperci.

> because in mercy I spared my pitiable husband.

In dealing with the *Odes* as well as *Epistles* 1 we should not dismiss the hypothesis that Horace could have influenced Virgil or even that there was a symbiosis, dissolution of whose constituent parts would be as fruitless as it would be hazardous.

21. Virgil arranges the four Stoic *genera*—φόβος, ἐπιθυμία, λύπη, ἡδονή —in their logical order of association with future (bad and good), and present (bad and good) circumstances, a sign of the strict Stoic credentials of the passage.

22. The borrowing is all the more significant because the Epicureans had no such *genera*.

23. The first part of Horace's *Epistle* has recently been addressed by Cairns, *Virgil's Augustan Epic* 85–88, in connection with a discussion of concord and discord in the *Aeneid*.

24. With lines 47–49—

> non domus et fundus, non aeris acervus et auri
> aegroto domini deduxit corpore febris,
> non animo curas.

> Neither house nor acreage, neither heap of bronze or gold
> removed fevers from their owner's sick body or cares from his
> mind

—compare, as do most critics, *DRN* 2.34–36:

> nec calidae citius decedunt corpore febres
> textilibus si in picturis ostroque rubenti
> iacteris, quam se in plebeia veste cubandum est.

> nor do fiery fevers withdraw more quickly from the body if
> you toss on embroidered pictures and blushing purple than if
> you must lie on a poor man's blanket.

See also lines 45–46 where Lucretius further discusses the releasing of the mind from cares.

25. Cf. also Plato *Phaedrus* 246–47 (and, for a further Latin example, Plautus *Trin.* 310).

26. With 8.485–88, cf. 3.618–38 passim and 8.193–97.

27. 8.484, 10.898 (spoken by Aeneas).

28. The phrase is also given to Polyphemus and Hercules. (On the association of the latter with Polyphemus and Mezentius see n. 47.) Because of this careful complementarity of man and beast I take the received order of 10.714–18 as valid.

29. It is a point worth further study that the specifics of Aeneas' final bout of anger—the sight of the *balteus* of Pallas, the remembrance of the youth's death and of Aeneas' consequent suffering, the need for and act of revenge on the prostrate figure of Turnus—are traced over a poetic space of only ten lines, mimicking the abrupt dispatch of the events themselves, and well exemplify the cognitive structure of anger for the Stoics as for Virgil here. (See, e.g., *TD* 3.75 for Zeno's notion of the "freshness" of evil.) Aeneas, who should be self-controlled, tellingly reveals his domination by an external object and by the emotions which it arouses, so much so that, as I have already observed, he can even deflect responsibility for his angry act on to Pallas himself, the possessor of the sword belt and the catalyst of Aeneas' emotionality. Colish, *Stoic Tradition* 225–52, treats Virgil's Stoicism in detail, with some salient pages (246–52) on non-Stoic aspects of Aeneas' conduct.

30. I take the so-called Helen passage (2.567–88) to be, in gist, genuine for many reasons. The most simple and compelling is that the lines which follow, wherein Venus chides her son for his behavior, make no sense unless motivated within the debated lines. It is impossible to read lines 566 and 589 as contiguous and make any claims for continuity, even on the most immediate level of plot development.

31. I will return to this episode. Elsewhere, Putnam, *Poetry* 151–52, I have suggested the close resemblance between the nexus of words which Virgil has Aeneas use to describe his emotionality here and those which he gives the narrator at the end of the epic, which we have been examining. Professor Galinsky, "Anger

of Aeneas" 344 and n. 62, feels that the connection cannot be pressed, especially as an argument against Aeneas' conduct, because "his *furor* in book 2 . . . was misguided, [whereas] his *furor* at the end of the epic is not: both the divine will, as indicated by the *dea dira*, and Aeneas' own inclination are in concord."

The *dea dira* is a manifestation of Jupiter's hatred (cf. especially 12.849–52 and Turnus' words at 895) but is dispatched by him specifically only to eliminate Juturna from battle. We hear no more of her once Turnus has been subdued (she last appears at 914 before Aeneas throws the spear that wounds but does not kill). But the private *furiae* that set Aeneas aflame before he actually kills are generated from within. Since they have no connection with Jupiter's *Dira* it seems far more likely that Virgil also means Aeneas' sudden anger to be connected not with Jupiter's enmity toward Turnus but rather with a further, empowering extension of the hero's inner furies, released not by some supernatural agency but by his impassioned self. Virgil could have had Aeneas say to Turnus: "Jupiter kills you for your villainy." Instead, while Aeneas lays the responsibility for the actual killing on Pallas, the reader knows that Aeneas acts from the memory of the *saevus dolor* of personal hurt, not out of any role as surrogate for the king of the gods.

32. The book begins, however, with Aeneas *saevus in armis* (107), arousing himself to anger (*se suscitat ira*, 108) in preparation for the single combat with Turnus that the treaty specifies.

33. Cf. 1.10–11 and the elaboration of Juno's *irae* and *saevi dolores* at 1.25, 5.781–83, and the simile at 1.148–53 where the *pietas* of Neptune, who to a degree is a figure of Aeneas, contrasts with the *saevitia* and *furor* of the winds. At 6.405–7 the *ira* of Charon is posed against the *pietas* of Aeneas.

34. 12.497–99 is quoted by Galinsky, "Anger of Aeneas" 340, but without its full context. The phrase *nullo discrimine* recurs strikingly at 770 where the narrator applies it to the Trojans' lack of discrimination in cutting down a wild olive sacred to Faunus. Both anger and insensitivity imply or proclaim the absence of the capability of making proper judgments (Cicero [*Planc.* 9] groups *discrimen* with *consilium* and *ratio*).

35. See 8.485–86 (quoted earlier).

36. Servius on *Aen.* 12.499, refers to 1.63 and Ennius' phrase *effundit irarum quadrigas* (= #534 Skutsch, *Annals*, who reads *effunde* for *effundit*). Cf. also Varro *Men.* 177B–H.

37. The primary excuse that the narrator allows Aeneas to present for his access of anger is the breaking of the treaty (496), the same he offers shortly later (582) when preparing to attack the peaceful city of Latinus ("untouched by such a war") at the instance of his "most beautiful mother" (554, 558–59).

38. *Aen.* 7.392 is the only instance, it is important to note, other than 12.946, where *furiae* and *accendo* are joined. Five lines later (7.397) Amata is called *fervida*, the final adjective Virgil allots Aeneas (12.951; cf. also 12.894). Other than 8.494 (the *furiae iustae* of Etruria) and the examples I discuss here, there remain the *furiae* of Cassandra's ravings (10.68) and of winds (10.694), though these are also metaphoric of the *furiae* raised against Mezentius.

The *Furiae* themselves appear as a group at *Geo.* 3.37; *Aen* 3.252, 6.605, 8.669.

39. After her final curse she is called *aegra* (389). Cf. Turnus at 12.46: *aegrescit . . . medendo.*

40. The irony of the childless, loveless Dido impregnated by furies has often been remarked upon.

41. Dido's *furor* is also mentioned at 4.433, her *dolor* at 4.19, 4.474, 4.547, 4.693, 5.5, and 6.464 (Aeneas' word), her *ira* at 4.532 and 4.564.

     Galinsky, "Anger of Aeneas" 344, sees the allusion to 4.697 at 12.946 as a "reminder of the grief to which she came because of Aeneas." But the verbal parallels suggest that the characters are also complementary in their actions and reactions.

42. Cf. 9.66 and the phrase *ira saevit* within the simile at 62–63.

43. With 8.195–97 cf. 486–89, quoted previously.

44. In connection with Aeneas in book 12 (894, 951) we should note Hercules' subsequent characterization as *fervidus ira* (230).

45. It is often so taken, most recently by Galinsky, "Anger of Aeneas" 339. The Greek hero's yielding to fury is "all with the poet's approbation because Hercules has justice on his side." The "episode is a mythological paradigm for Aeneas' battle with Turnus" (ibid.). (Cf. also Thornton, *Living Universe* 162, "The fight of Hercules with Cacus was, of course, one of the exemplary battles of a great hero against evil, and Hercules rages in the zest of his rightful warrior's anger." Her comment forms part of an appendix on *ira* and *furor*.) Since much the same vocabulary occurs at the end of the epic, Aeneas, so the argument runs, is justified in his rage for revenge against Turnus-Cacus. According to Galinsky (ibid. 338), Virgil is also pointedly throwing down the gauntlet to the Cicero of *Tusculan Disputations* 4, for whose Stoic Hercules anger would be impossible, by suggesting that in fact his wrath here is righteous. But the argument, of course, could be reversed to claim that Hercules, who should behave in a Stoic manner and serve thereby as a paradigm of moderation and reason for Aeneas, does not so conduct himself and should therefore in fact be condemned by the reader. (Nor, in the treatment by Lucretius at *DRN* 5.22–54, does Hercules gain at all from the comparison to Epicurus.)

     Galinsky (ibid. 339) notes that the Arcadians allude to Hercules' *ratio* when confronting the Lernaean Hydra, but the word, as used at 8.299, means "plan of action," not "reason" or "rationality."

46. In spite of the long disquisition of Frazer, *Fasti*, on Ovid *Fasti* 1.550, drawing parallels between Virgil's story and Indian epic, the Roman reader, along with most commentators, would have thought of Hermes' pilfering of the cattle of his older brother, Apollo, as told in the *Homeric Hymns to Hermes* where, in the end, Apollo forgoes his anger (495).

47. Cf. 3.664, 10.718, and my n. 28.

48. Elsewhere *fel* is linked to *invidia, malignitas, ira* (TLL s.v. 422 72–79, 423 45–53) and *insania* (423 32–38).

     Hercules is introduced as "the greatest avenger, prideful for the slaughter and spoils of triple Geryon" (*maximus ultor, / tergemini nece Geryonae spoliisque superbus,* 201–2). The only other instance in the epic where notions of revenge and pride are juxtaposed is at 6.817–18 where we are shown the "proud spirit of Brutus the avenger" (*animam . . . superbam ultoris Bruti*)—one of the poem's most trenchant ambiguities with Brutus receiving the attribute of the tyrant he had killed. Even before he acts, Hercules is visualized as the incorporation of haughty vengeance. Virgil gives us reason enough so to characterize Aeneas as he kills his suppliant at the epic's end.

49. Cf. also Seneca *Oed.* 358; Silius *Pun.* 11.548; Rutilius 1.448.

50. See 7.461–64, 9.760, 12.667–68.

51. Cacus at 205 (where the greater manuscript authority rests with *furiis*), Hercules at 219 (and cf. *furens*, 228).

52. Blackness—Cacus: *atros ignes* (198–99), *nebula atra* (258), *domus atra* (262); Hercules: *atro felle* (219–20). Pride—Cacus: *foribus superbis* (196); Hercules: *superbus* (202).

53. Aside from Galinsky's essay, the most recent treatment of Aeneas' *furiae* is by Cairns, *Augustan* 83–84. He also bases his argument for a favorable view of Aeneas' final rage on the fact that *furiae* against Mezentius are labeled *iustae* and on the analogy with Hercules: "So the *furiae* of Aeneas and Hercules are virtuous, while the *furor* of Turnus is evil" (ibid. 84 and n. 72 for bibliography of earlier treatments of the same parallel. His judgment is concise: "It is . . . highly significant that in 12.946 Aeneas is fired by *furiae* and not by *furor*, since *furor* is beyond the moral pale, but this is not the case with *furiae*"). It is a matter worthy of consideration by those who argue for the justice of Aeneas' final fury that the only occasion in the epic on which Virgil gives a positive attribute to *furiae* and *ira* is in connection with the behavior of Mezentius where the reader least needs help in evaluating their quality. Where we crave some authorial interpretation most, in the cases of Aeneas and Hercules, no guidance is forthcoming. Or, put another way around, when we least need authorial clarification, when the evidence most obviously justifies an approach based on anger, the action garners open approval as if to say that only villainy of such blackness can elicit in response an anger worthy to be considered valid.

54. Pease, *Liber Quartus* ad loc., comments: "Light typifies life, and is contrasted with the oncoming darkness of death." I would suggest that the contrast was rather with the preceding darkness of fury, from which light brings relief. Cf. Skutsch, *Annals* on Ennius *Ann.* 484.

55. For the association of "wandering" with misguided passion, compare, e.g., Silenus-Virgil's address to Pasiphaë (*Ecl.* 6.52): *Tu nunc in montibus erras*. From this point of view, the meaning of Dido's ferocity to Aeneas in the Underworld, as she wanders with her first husband among the suicides (*Aen.* 6.450–76), is worth further discussion.

56. Cf. Lucretius' picture (*DRN* 4.1153) of men so blinded by desire (*cupidine caeci*) as to attribute to women characteristics which they lack.

57. Virgil has a single use of *hebeo* at 5.396.

58. Macrobius quotes *Aen.* 6.896 at 1.3.3. Virgil's full description of the *Somni Portae* is at 6.893–99.

59. Roughness and imperfection: Macdonald, *Burial-Places* 51–52; brightness and deceptive brilliance: Edgeworth, "Ivory Gate" 145–57, especially 157. Edgeworth (ibid. 145, n. 2) has an up-to-

date bibliography, to which now add Gotoff, "Difficulty of the Ascent," and West, *Bough and the Gate.*

60. At 12.945 the sight of Pallas' belt serves as *saevi monimenta doloris,* a reminder of the "fierce anguish" that motivated his conduct in book 10. There Virgil uses first *furit* (545), then *desaevit* (569), to distinguish his behavior.

61. To urge an analogy between Aeneas' victimization by *furiae* in book 2 and at the end of 12 forces many questions into the open, one of which should be asked here. If Venus' clarifying magic in book 2 reveals the "inclemency of the gods" (*divum inclementia*) at its destructive work, how might Aeneas, were he allowed to peer through the veneer of his rage, see himself? As a further instrument of *divum inclementia*? Or, with more suitable particularity, as exemplifying lack of the very *clementia* which his father had urged on him in the Underworld?

WRATHFUL AENEAS AND

THE TACTICS OF *PIETAS*

IN VIRGIL, OVID,

AND LUCAN

My purpose in this essay is to trace certain aspects of the influence of the *Aeneid*, and especially its conclusion, on Ovid's *Metamorphoses* and the *Pharsalia* of Lucan. My primary interest lies in the concepts of *ira, clementia*, and *pietas* and in their interconnection and evolution during the course of the three poems. After illustrating how the anger of Jupiter, which serves to bound the *Metamorphoses*, finds a source in the *Aeneid's* finale, I then turn to Lucan to examine the forms of piety that serve as moral touchstones for the behavior of his epic's protagonists and primarily of its central character, Caesar. My thesis is that the corruption of *pietas*, which Lucan attributes to Caesar, where the abstraction is now based on force, is lavished on a single mortal who plays the part of a god and in particular of Jupiter, and defined by lack of restraint and the omnipresence of anger, finds its imaginative impetus in the conduct of Aeneas as his epic draws to a close.

First a word on Virgil's treatment of the concept of *clementia*, which lies at the heart of how we evaluate Aeneas' final actions. In the Roman Republic, as Sallust and Livy document it for us, decisions to practice political *clementia*, the disposition to pardon or spare an opponent who has been subdued, lay with the whole of the Roman people.[1] We hear regularly in the historians of the *clementia populi Romani*, on several occasions coupled with *fides*, the mutual trust that is a natural companion to any compact, however cynically bestowed by stronger on weaker, based on leniency. Under Caesar *clementia* becomes notoriously the "virtue" of one man with the power to spare someone at his mercy.[2] After Caesar clemency rests with the whim of the emperor. Its negative complement, as so often utilized by Ovid when describing the impulses that lead the gods to exert the force of metamorphosis, is *ira*, the wrath that abandons rightfulness for reprisal.

Virgil never uses the word *clementia* but he does, of course, offer a striking definition of the term at one of the epic's climactic moments, incorporated in the words of Anchises to his son, preparing to leave the Underworld:

> "tu regere imperio populos, Romane, memento
> (hae tibi erunt artes), pacique imponere morem,
> parcere subiectis et debellare superbos."
>   (6.851–53)

"Remember, Roman, to rule peoples with your might (these will be your arts) and to impose a custom for peace, to spare the humbled and war down the proud."

Two facts should be noted in this representation. The first, observed by critics from Servius on,[3] is that for Virgil *clementia* is realized in a context of *pietas*, of visible loyalty between father and son, and of the unspoken respect that operates reciprocally between men and gods. The second is the importance of the apostrophe *Romane*. Aeneas is addressed not only as one standing for many but as the epitome of Republican Roman moderation, emblem of a state that could, or perhaps better, should be gentle when it has achieved dominion over its antagonists.

We have also been taught from the beginning of the epic that *pietas* is antonymous to a series of negative abstractions including *ira, dolor, saevitia*, and various manifestations of *furor*. Jupiter early on predicts a time when *Furor impius*, Madness that lacks piety particularly because it is a source of war against internal, not external, enemies, will roar vainly from its prison (1.294–95).[4] In this utopian refashioning of Roman history and of human nature, Trust (*Fides*) and Vesta, goddess of hearth and home, will hold sway along with Remus and his deified brother as Rome's bloody beginnings are swept from memory (1.292–93). Elsewhere in the epic, those who have resort to *arma impia* are in death relegated *ad impia Tartara* (6.612–13, 543), and in the story's foreground, as the last book commences, Latinus bemoans the fact that he had once laid hold of *arma impia*, abandoning Turnus to espouse the cause of Aeneas, which is to say of fraternal strife (12.31).

What we are witnessing, then, as the last half of the epic unfolds (and as critics have long since remarked) is a prototype of civil war, climaxing in Aeneas' killing of Turnus. The titular hero's final deed has its defenders. Servius sees him acting out of piety toward Evander because he is avenging Turnus' slaying of his son Pallas, and David Quint has recently taken this argument still further by interconnecting piety with vengeance, as Augustus did so often in his aesthetic propaganda.[5] This led first to the temple of Apollo, opened in 28 B.C., with its door scenes of the god in the process of two acts of retaliation, and culminated in his forum with its centerpiece, the temple of Mars Ultor, dedicated in 2 B.C.

But Virgil is not Augustus, and his poem, for all its bows to the emperor and his accomplishments, is richly multidimensional, especially where the moral problematics of war are concerned. In scorning his father's command to spare a suppliant, Aeneas behaves impiously. In revenging Pallas' death he may act out of a *pietas* of which Virgil's words make no mention. Instead Virgil has Aeneas in the end take up the role of savage Juno and of Furor on the loose (12.946–47). If this is piety, it is for Virgil at best a highly debased variety, one we will see permeating the text of Lucan. But before we turn to the later authors, I would like to look more closely at details I have not discussed before in Virgil's concluding scene. These will help us make the transition to Ovid and to the *Pharsalia*.

As helpless Turnus debates a response to his triumphant foe, Aeneas prepares to hurl his *telum fatale*, the spear that will bring destiny to his opponent (12.919). Virgil compares the weapon, directly or indirectly, to three other entities, catapult stones, a thunderbolt, and a whirlwind:

> murali concita numquam
> tormento sic saxa fremunt nec fulmine tanti
> dissultant crepitus. volat atri turbinis instar
> exitium dirum hasta ferens orasque recludit
> loricae et clipei extremos septemplicis orbis;
> per medium stridens transit femur.
> (12.921–26)

Never do stones hurled from a siege engine roar so loudly nor do such crashings burst from the thunderbolt. The spear flies like a black whirlwind, bringing dread destruction, and lays open the rim of the corselet and the outermost circle of the sevenfold shield. Whizzing, it passes through the middle of his thigh.

Lines 921–23 are striking in several respects. The adjective *muralis* and the noun *crepitus* are used here for the only times in the Virgilian corpus, and the sentence they demarcate, that is from the third-foot caesura in line 921 to the same position in 923, is dispensable. Virgil could have gone from *intorquet* to *volat* without any unseemly interruption in either meaning or meter. Its presence thus lends it particular purpose, especially when juxtaposed with what follows.

The first comparison associates Aeneas' spear and, therefore, extending the figuration, the hero himself with rocks hurled against a city's walls. The image is focused and expanded in lines 924–25. The weapon is said to "unclose the edges of [Turnus'] corselet" (*oras . . . recludit / loricae*). Now *recludere* can mean to open the gate of a fortification,[6] and *lorica*, in the terminology of siegecraft, has the sense of breastwork or parapet.[7] Turnus, attacked by Aeneas' spear, is metaphorically akin to a rampart or city under final siege, its walls about to be breached. These specifics suggest deeper connotations for Aeneas' role in the epic, at least as we are made to visualize it at the poem's close. It has not been long since we have seen Aeneas play the part of incipient city-destroyer when his "most beautiful mother" (*genetrix pulcherrima*, 12.554) puts into her son's mind the impulse to destroy the city of Latinus, which he notices "untouched by the engulfing battle and at peace without requital" (12.559). Aeneas proclaims that, unless the residents accept his bridle and confess themselves conquered (12.565)

eruam et aequa solo fumantia culmina ponam.
   (12.569)
I will overthrow [the city] and place its smoking rooftops on a level
with the ground.

The hero who starts off his adventures retreating from the ruins of his
smoldering homeland has now incipiently become both the literal and
figurative destroyer of cities. Virgil is at pains to connect the two events.
When he places Aeneas, *ipse inter primos*, himself among the first to make
their way under Latinus' walls (12.579), he connects him with Pyrrhus,
ipse inter primos, breaking into Priam's palace at the heart of Troy (2.479).
By the end Aeneas has reversed roles to become, first, the son of Achilles,
who ruthlessly demolishes a city and slaughters the king at its center, and
then Achilles himself, killing Hector, his suppliant foe. Virgil concludes
his poem, of course, with analogy to *Iliad* 22. We end with the deed of
violence and without the reconciliation, ransom, and funeral games with
which Homer brings closure to his epic. But Virgil's vision has a still
bleaker side. In killing Turnus Aeneas kills a version of himself, brother
murdering brother, in a prototypical scene that leads not to dreams of
harmony and order but to civil war and the constancy of human violence.

It is likewise not accidental that Virgil uses the same verb, *condere*, for
Aeneas' foundation of Lavinium from which, in the course of time,
would spring "the defensive walls of lofty Rome" (*altae moenia Romae*),
and for the burial of his sword under the breast of Turnus, in the epic's
antepenultimate line.[8] In one sense the besieging and death of Turnus do
not merely overwhelm cities but make only those foundations based on a
tradition of bloodletting—in spite of Jupiter's tendentious optimism—
capable of survival into the Roman future. Instead of Aeneas' marriage
with Lavinia and its resultant union of opposing forces we have a passional killing with all the further instances of anger and revenge that this
inaugurates.

The death of the city also recurs as a major motif of book 4. Dido, too,
is a builder—

   urbem praeclaram statui, mea moenia vidi . . .
      (4.655)
   I have established a splendid city, I have beheld my walls . . .

—but in her dying to a degree she destroys her accomplishment as well.[9]
The cries of grief at her death are

   non aliter quam si immissis ruat hostibus omnis
   Karthago aut antiqua Tyros, flammaeque furentes

culmina perque hominum volvantur perque deorum.

(4.669–71)

as if all Carthage were collapsing at the inrush of foes, or ancient
Tyre, and raging flames were roiling through the rooftops of men
and of gods.[10]

I need not review the several parallels between Dido's actions in book 4
and Aeneas' at the finale of his epic that, to a reader who sympathizes
with her tragedy, grant her a special form of requital. The Carthaginian
queen, in the grip of the furies, kills herself with Aeneas' sword and in the
process calls down on Rome the eternal enmity of a foreign power.[11]
Aeneas, set aflame by the furies, becomes a Dido who kills not herself but
another, and who, in the process, initiates a pattern of civil, not foreign,
war. Aeneas only indirectly effects the death of his former lover. In mer-
cilessly killing Turnus he now takes direct responsibility for a death
whose consequences Virgil and his generation would have well understood.

If the comparison of Aeneas' spear to catapult stones links him to
Pyrrhus and Dido and his final action to the ambiguity of Rome's foundation myth, the assimilation of thunderbolt (*fulmen*) and whirlwind (*turbo*)
carry other related connotations. Let me take *turbo* first. To illustrate its
particular force we must turn back to an earlier moment in book 12.
Jupiter and Juno have reached their problematical compact when the
king of the gods decides to send down one of his twin Dirae in order to
drive Juturna away and leave him helpless as he enters the final combat.[12]
In obedience to his command

illa volat celerique ad terram turbine fertur.

she flies to earth and is borne on a swift whirlwind.

Virgil compares her to an arrow, armed with the venom of savage poison
(*saevi veneni*), which a Parthian or Cydonian has whirled (*torsit*), a shaft
against which there exists no cure (*telum immedicabile*), which shrieks
(*stridens*) as it leaps through the shadows (12.855–60).[13] The close relationship between this passage and the moment, quoted earlier, when
Aeneas brandishes his *telum fatale* is remarkable and carefully plotted.
This weapon, too, is a *telum*, now fate-laden; it flies (*volat*) through the air
like a whirlwind, black instead of swift (*atri turbinis*), and it shrieks (*stridens*) as it passes through the thigh of Turnus.

Aeneas' spear brings *exitium dirum*, dread destruction, with it, but the
adjective *dirum* cements the connection between Aeneas' weapon and
the Dira who wings her way from the throne of the chief of the immortals to lay Turnus low. Aeneas, in wielding the instrument of Jupiter's

will, becomes the principal god, embodiment of omnipotence and, it would seem, of fate itself. The link has already been forged by one feature of the earlier description. As Jupiter prepares to send forth the Dira, he is called "savage king" (*saevi regis*, 12.849), and the adjective, as we have seen, is picked up in simile, applied to the "savage poison" (*saevi veneni*, 12.957) of the Dira arrow. It is not coincidental that at the next appearance of Aeneas we find him preparing to address Turnus, in the narrator's words, "from his savage breast" (*saevo pectore*, 12.888). Turnus replies to Aeneas' brief speech saying that he is frightened not by his opponent's fervid words but by the fact that the gods and especially Jupiter are his enemies, ironically not realizing that Jupiter and Aeneas act as one during the opening segment of the final scene. Nor do we lose sight of Aeneas' savagery as the ending looms for, while he changes from Jupiter-Fury to victim of furies and at last killer, it is *saevus dolor*, we recall, that forms a major motivating element for his ultimate deed.

The final concatenation of emotions in which savage resentment is conspicuous relates Aeneas closely to the antipietistical, jealous, vengeful Juno of book 1. It brings the epic full circle and completes the spiritual reversal of its hero suggested in book 2 and elaborated more openly in the rampage of book 10. Aeneas' intimacy with Dira-Jupiter also creates another bond between him and his initial archenemy. When Virgil assigns the phrase *terras . . . petivit* to Jupiter's fury heading earthward (12.860), he echoes the same words he had used in book 7 (*terras horrenda petivit*) to describe Juno's parallel descent to stir up the fury Allecto "from the dwelling of the dread goddesses" (*dirarum ab sede dearum*, 7.323–24). The intimacy of the two passages is further suggested by the correspondence between the two furies themselves (though she is unnamed, Allecto could also be the servant of the *saevus rex* as well as of *saeva Juno*). Both, for instance, are described as *sata Nocte* and both have close connections with serpents.[14] But it is the link between Jupiter, Juno, and Aeneas that such a parallelism suggests that is of particular importance to study of the epic's end. Jupiter and Juno may swear a compact that purports to assure a peaceful, pious Roman future but as the epic concludes both divinities, as figures of fury, converge on Aeneas himself. The second half of the epic likewise, therefore, folds in on itself when Juno, that *saeva Iovis coniunx* (7.287), also enters into the spirit of Aeneas as he readies himself for his momentous final action.

If the significance of Aeneas' spear allies it most closely with Jupiter and his negative power, its equation with the *fulmen* reconfirms the close association. There is no more perspicuous emblem of the king of the gods than the thunderbolt, and throughout the epic its presence, directly or metaphorically, lends great force to its possessor. When, for instance, in book 4 Aeneas regains control of himself and his destiny, he uses a sword like a thunderbolt (*ensem fulmineum*) to cut his ship's hawsers, escape from Carthage, and pursue his illustrious destiny (4.579–80). When Turnus, in book 9, is at the height of his power, "he sends gleaming flashes of lightning from his shield" (*clipeo . . . micantia fulmina mittit,* 9.733). And, earlier in book 12, Aeneas, according to the words of Saces to Turnus, "flashes with lightning on his armor" (*fulminat Aeneas armis,* 12.654), as he threatens to destroy Latinus' city.[15]

At special moments both heroes become superhuman as they draw to themselves the potency of Jupiter and, for an instant, share his formidableness. But there is also a negative aspect to the last instance I cataloged, one that spills over into the final analogy between *telum* and *fulmen,* between terrestrial Aeneas and his celestial counterpart. Aeneas, as he nears the end of his epic career, both calls on Jupiter as he initiates preparations to raze Latinus' city—*Iuppiter hac stat*[16]—and metaphorically, in the eyes of others, follows the god's behavior as he proceeds to their implementation. This violence and its association with the king of the gods is operative in the spear-thunderbolt as well as in the catapult stones that destroy city walls. But there is a specific, crucial twist to this negativity, which I will turn to Seneca and then to Virgil himself to help elucidate and illustrate.

At a delicate moment in his argument, during the first book of *De Clementia,* Seneca co-opts the gods as exemplars for the behavior of his *princeps.* In words that are as much a model for their tactful flattery as for their pedagogical value, the philosopher urges his protégé Nero, to whom the dialogue is dedicated, to imitate the *clementia,* the forgiving gentleness of the gods, not their recourse to *fulmina,* that is to the ways of violence and brutality. Though the lecture is couched in vague terms— both the gods and *fulmina* are left plural—the specific aptness of an analogy between himself and Jupiter would not have been lost on the young emperor.[17]

The dilemma in which Aeneas is placed by Virgil could well have been an inspiration for Seneca's thoughtful words. He now has the full potency of Jupiter behind him. His weapon is a thunderbolt and his unique, quasi-divine mastery of his situation is unchallenged. The suppliant Turnus, his pride beaten down (thus far Aeneas follows Anchises' injunction), asks for mercy, offering Aeneas the opportunity to spare his beaten foe or to resort to force. Elsewhere in these essays I have discussed the rationale for Aeneas' action, that is to say what it means to respond in fury to a complex moral situation. Here I would like to point out that Virgil, though he never uses the word *clementia,* does offer one example of its opposite, *inclementia,* at work, an example apt for the understanding of the poem's conclusion.[18] This occurs in book 2, during Aeneas' description of Troy's downfall. At one terrifying moment Aeneas is allowed to see through (in words allotted to Venus) the cloud that blunts his mortal vision. What he observes is a manifestation of *divum inclementia* (2.602),

the gods at work destroying Troy. With Aeneas we notice first, and not
unexpectedly, Neptune, given the same verb, *eruere*, that Virgil allots
Aeneas threatening to demolish Latinus' city:

> fundamenta quatit totamque a sedibus urbem
> eruit.
> (2.611–12)
> He shakes the foundations and overwhelms the whole city from its
> bases.[19]

There follow Juno (*saevissima* and *furens*, 2.612–13) and Pallas Athena
(likewise *saeva*, 2.616). At the place of climax comes Jupiter himself:

> ipse pater Danais animos virisque secundas
> sufficit, ipse deos in Dardana suscitat arma.
> (2.617–18)
> the father himself supplies spirit and successful strength to the
> Greeks, he himself rouses up the gods against the arms of Troy.

Neptune tears up the city, Juno and Athena lend fury and savagery, and
the father of the gods is the energizing capstone in this configuration of
celestial ruthlessness at work.[20]

Many points, therefore, urge upon the reader a close parallelism between Jupiter and Aeneas as the epic nears its conclusion. Whirlwind and
thunderbolt lend him the god's fury and destructive force. But catapult
and its stones, too, add a further, boldly metaphoric dimension to Virgil's
portrait. Jupiter, in books 1 and 12, can imagine a Roman future without
civil war, but the final truth of the poem's foreground deliberately leaves
an opposite impression. When Jupiter chooses to practice *inclementia*, it is
as a city destroyer, in company with Neptune and the savage fury of Juno
and Pallas. This power is now concentrated in the figure of Aeneas, and
the battle of gods against a city is confined to a climactic confrontation of
two men, the one burdened with supreme Jovian potential, the other
humiliated and craving mercy. As the analogies suggest, Aeneas will opt
for *inclementia* and for the *saevitia* and *furor* that accompany it. In thus
emulating the violent side of Jupiter, in choosing the *fulmen* over *clementia*, the way of force over the way of mercy and leniency, Aeneas fails his
father and undermines one of the bases of Roman political power. The
founder of the literal city is its spiritual ravager as well.

Anchises' pronouncement in book 6 is the ethical center of the poem.
It establishes a major norm for Roman behavior, the combination of
power with moderation and restraint. As we move out from this core to
the periphery of the poem we notice again how the epic's initial actions

are reviewed as it reaches its closure. Juno's display of antipietistical wrath and resentment, as she rouses Aeolus against the Trojans, is echoed by Aeneas' reaction as he kills the suppliant Turnus.[21] Jupiter's *inclementia* toward Troy likewise finds a condensed analogue in the mercilessness with which the hero exercises omnipotence against his humiliated antagonist. Aeneas' metaphorical ascent to divinity, his final spiritual collocation with the chief of the gods and his consort, finds him, ironically, in fact at his least pious. Aeneas' human father propounds an ethical amalgam of strength and gentleness to his Roman, everyman son. As his son rises to unique power, the omens that he or the Rome he grows to exemplify can master the use of force according to the standards of his father are ill boding.

There is circularity in the poem's structure but also tremendous forward thrust as well. Book 6 may establish standards for a Roman hero's conduct and book 12 may offer impressive evidence that its implementation will be a challenging enterprise, but it is book 10 where Anchises' rules are first put to the test and which presents situations that offer criteria against which to measure other aspects of the poem's conclusion not yet touched upon. I discussed in the previous essay the important connection between the rampage on which Aeneas embarks after Turnus' killing of Pallas and his final act of violence. Here I am interested in the linkage between the two books set up by the duel between Pallas and Turnus and by the adversion to *clementia* that arises in its course. First let us look at Pallas' grizzly plea to Hercules before the fight begins:

> cernat semineci sibi me rapere arma cruenta
> victoremque ferant morientia lumina Turni.
>   (10.462–63)
> May Turnus watch me strip the bloody armor from his half-dead
> limbs and may his moribund eyes withstand a victor.

The particular horror of this petition lies in how Virgil evokes the point of view of the victim, caught in a limbo between life and death and made, twice over, to observe what is happening to him. But the general points are clear: Pallas prays to be the conqueror (*victor*), and with his victory he presumes the death and despoliation of his victim. None of this is to be. Instead Pallas is killed by Turnus who offers him burial and then, pressing the corpse with his foot, snatches Pallas' sword belt from the body and "exults in the spoils [*spolio*] and rejoices in their possession" (10.500). The event elicits one of Virgil's rare narratorial asides:

> nescia mens hominum fati sortisque futurae
> et servare modum rebus sublata secundis!

Turno tempus erit magno cum optaverit emptum
intactum Pallanta, et cum spolia ista diemque
oderit.
(10.501–5)

Mind of men, ignorant of fate and future lot and of how to preserve
the mean when lifted up by success! The time will come for Turnus
when he will yearn that Pallas be bought back untouched, for a great
price, and when he will hate those spoils and the day.

The meaning of the initial lines, emphasized by the repetition of *spolio-
spolia*, seems clear enough. Turnus has gone too far in his treatment of
Pallas by ripping off and claiming for himself the sword belt. But the
word *dies* seems to call in question the whole event itself, at least in
Turnus' future eyes. And this leads to the ambiguity of *emptum*. Are we to
think of Turnus as somehow buying back Pallas (from the dead?). Perhaps, but more likely because more usual, is the possibility of ransom not
by Turnus but by Evander. Virgil's narratorial voice takes a special moral
turn here. Students of the epic are used to the idea, promulgated from
Iliad 24 on, that dead heroes can be ransomed back from the enemy, and
in the preceding book of the *Aeneid* Nisus, before setting out on his fatal
night adventure, prays that, should he meet death,

sit qui me raptum pugna pretiove redemptum
mandet humo . . .
(9.213–14)

Let there be someone who might commit me to the ground, pulled
out of the battle or ransomed at a price.

More germane still is the story of Adrestus in *Iliad* 6 who, clasping the
knees of Menelaus, begs to be taken back alive to the Greek camp and
ransomed by his father from his store "of bronze and gold and iron
wrought with toil" (*Il.* 6.37–65). Menelaus is about to agree with his
petition and hand Adrestus over to his squire to lead away when his
brother runs up and dissuades him, cursing with death all Trojans, even
the unborn.[22] It is a way of thinking with which the narrator agrees,
characterizing Agamemnon as one "advising properly" (αἴσιμα παρειπών).

Virgil's editorial moralizing offers a different counsel. It suggests that
Pallas, after his confrontation with Turnus, instead of being killed and his
corpse pillaged, would not only be available for ransom but should also
be *intactus*, untouched, which is to say undespoiled and perhaps, as in the
case of Adrestus, even unwounded.[23] Virgil, in other words, at least in a
situation crucial to how we interpret Aeneas' action at the end, urges that
a double form of moderation hold sway in personal conflicts on the
battlefield and, in particular, that clemency replace vengeance as the

operative principle of martial heroism. As we turn to the epic's final conflict we find that the high standards that the narrator sets in book 10 are already partially undermined. Turnus does not remain *intactus* nor will he be ransomed (though such may be the suggestion of his prayer at 935–36). Nevertheless his first wound, in the thigh, is not mortal and leaves Aeneas the option to practice *clementia*.

There follows from here to the end a dialogue between acts of conquering and acts of wounding. First Turnus, already wounded, twice announces to his victor that he has been conquered:

> . . . vicisti et victum tendere palmas
> Ausonii videre . . .
>   (12.936–37)
> You have conquered and the Ausonians have seen me, conquered, stretch forth my hands.

His recourse to both active and passive voices may be Turnus' emphatic way of saying that conquering, by the winner, and being conquered, the position of the defeated, offer a sufficient consummation for Aeneas to expect in his victory.

But Aeneas notices the belt of Pallas on Turnus and with sight comes memory of another wounding, of Pallas

> . . . victum quem vulnere Turnus
> straverat . . .
>   (12.943–44)
> . . . whom, conquered, Turnus had laid low with a wound.

The implication is that, in the case of Turnus' final confrontation with Pallas, conquering and the act of fatal wounding are sequential, not contemporaneous, actions. During that crucial chain of events there was a moment, we are allowed to imagine, between winning and final wounding, when Turnus might have practiced *moderatio*. Aeneas is now in the same position vis-à-vis Turnus, and Virgil develops a whole scene, which he does not introduce into the Pallas-Turnus duel, where the words of the defeated move the victor to pause and ponder. But memory of Pallas and the fatal brew of emotions it arouses deflect Aeneas from *clementia* to vengeance and to the final, this time deadly, *vulnus* (948).

In sum, Pallas pridefully prays to kill and despoil a dying man with no thought of sparing. Turnus kills and despoils Pallas, and it remains for the narrator's ex post facto aside and for a hint at the end that conquering and death are separate entities to suggest that his conduct could, or should, have been otherwise. Only to Aeneas does Virgil allot the opportunity to respond both in a manner opposite to Turnus and, as complement to the forgoing, in accordance to his father's dictates of restraint toward the prideful in their moment of subjugation. That he conforms to the pattern set by the words of Pallas and the deeds of Turnus suggests that, as we look ahead to the Roman literary and historical future beyond the *Aeneid*, a precedence of vengeance will hold sway at the highest echelons of power and that action based on negative emotionality will regularly win out over words of restraint.

There is one final detail from the epic's conclusion to be discussed. As we might expect from him at a moment when every particular is given weight, Virgil has us look closely during the closing lines at physical aspects of his heroes. During the last thirty-four lines of the poem we watch the thigh and knees of Turnus as he suffers his first wound, his hands twice, as he prays for mercy, the shoulder where he wears Pallas' baldrick, the chest under which he receives his final blow and, at the last, his limbs undone with chill. Aeneas hurls his spear with the help of his whole frame (*corpore toto*) and represses his right hand, as he absorbs the import of Turnus' brief speech. The eyes of both heroes are mentioned four times, once those of Turnus (930), three times those of Aeneas (920, 939, 945).

It is on the middle instance of this last trio that I would like to pause. Turnus has just spoken:

> . . . stetit acer in armis
> Aeneas volvens oculos dextramque repressit;
> et iam iamque magis cunctantem flectere sermo
> coeperat . . .
> (12.938–41)

Aeneas stood, fierce in his armor, rolling his eyes, and held his right hand in check, and now, now, [Turnus'] speech began to bend him the more as he hesitates.

This is the last in a series of instances throughout the epic where rolling the eyes signifies that a character has not made up his or her mind about his circumstances and is still pondering what course of action to pursue. We find verbal parallels to Aeneas' situation at three other moments. The first is Dido's response to the speech of Aeneas in which he announces his desire to embark for Italy:

> Talia dicentem iamdudum aversa tuetur
> huc illuc volvens oculos . . .
> (4.362–63)

As he speaks such words she has all the time watched him askance, rolling her eyes this way, that way.[24]

How will she treat him, her gesture asks? How will his pronouncement affect her own life?

The second parallel finds Latinus *volvens oculos* after hearing the words of Ilioneus telling of the arrival of Aeneas and the Trojans (7.251). Are these the people, we sense Latinus asking, who are to fulfill Faunus' prophecy? Should he accept them and what will be the consequences? Finally we watch Aeneas receiving the iconic shield from his mother and learn that "he rolls his eyes across the individual details" (*oculos per singula volvit*, 8.618). What do these scenes mean, we expect Aeneas to imagine, and what does his "acceptance" of them betoken for his and Rome's future?[25]

The opposite of this fretfulness and, at least momentary, uncertainty is to be found in the phrase *fixos oculos*, which occurs in two places. The first occasion is during the scene, which forms part of the murals on Dido's temple to Juno, showing Athena's lack of generosity toward the women of Troy. I quote the vignette in full:

> interea ad templum non aequae Palladis ibant
> crinibus Iliades passis peplumque ferebant
> suppliciter, tristes et tunsae pectora palmis;
> diva solo fixos oculos aversa tenebat.
> (1.479–82)

Meanwhile the Trojan women were making their way to the temple of unjust Pallas, their hair loosened, and in suppliant fashion they were carrying a peplos, sad, their breasts beaten by the palms of their hands. Turned away, the goddess was holding her eyes fixed on the ground.

As her unmoved eyes prove, Athena presumably receives the gestures of suppliancy only to manifest herself as adamant against their appeal.

The second appearance of *fixos oculos*, in a similar verbal context, takes place in book 6 after Aeneas has appealed to Dido for some form of understanding. Setting again is important and remarkable:

> talibus Aeneas ardentem et torva tuentem
> lenibat dictis animum lacrimasque ciebat.
> illa solo fixos oculos aversa tenebat
> nec magis incepto vultum sermone movetur
> quam si dura silex aut stet Marpesia cautes.
> (6.467–71)

With such words Aeneas was soothing her spirit, burning and gazing fiercely, and was summoning tears. Turned away she was holding her eyes fixed on the ground nor was she more moved in her features than if hard flint or a crag from Marpessus stood there.

In an astonishing version of metonymy, Dido's mind gains its own powers of vision. Her thinking is projected outward in the way she sees and no doubt is seen. This visual signing is given particular force by the allusiveness of line 469. It recalls Dido herself in book 4, *aversa . . . volvens oculos*, as she prepares to respond to Aeneas, but it even more startlingly recollects the spectacle of unbending Minerva in book 1. In book 4 Dido, though enraged, is still visibly unsure of her future direction. In book 6, though now a suicide stationed among the victims of love, she has, through Virgil's analogy with Minerva, regained her posture of regality and, in a powerful reversal of roles, manifested to Aeneas the implacability she had sensed in his own previous conduct (6.471).[26]

In focusing the force of these passages on the lines from the epic's conclusion, my purpose is to examine the various relationships between words or gestures and actions that they propound. Before Aeneas acts we find him rolling his eyes, unsure of his response as the *sermo* of Turnus begins to bend him. He is for a moment parallel to Latinus after listening to Ilioneus, or to himself contemplating his strange shield. His fallen antagonist has similarities to the suppliant Trojan women in book 1, to Dido in book 4, or to the Aeneas of book 6 who tries to soothe his former lover in the tradition of Neptune, embodiment of calming piety in the epic's first simile.[27] But, as again we come full circle, *sermo* in the end does not finally win out over *furor* as Aeneas yields not to verbal persuasion but to anger's more potent manipulations.[28]

The similarities between Turnus at the conclusion of the epic—first stretching out his hands in supplication (*tendere palmas*, 12.936), then with his limbs undone with cold as life ebbs away (*solvuntur frigore membra*, 12.951)—and Aeneas at the beginning—his limbs undone with cold (*solvuntur frigore membra*, 1.92) in terror at the storm raised by Juno and Aeolus and stretching forth his hands to the stars (*tendens ad sidera palmas*, 1.93)—though often remarked upon, deserve remembering here. Turnus at the end becomes the earlier Aeneas, helpless before Juno's savagery. But the hero is saved by the intervention of Neptune whose statesmanship is metaphorized as soothing words. Aeneas at the end becomes by contrast a Juno who wins the day, victim of fury over whom speech has finally no power, who carries all with her by force. Dido, too, has another victory as once again our hero adopts the characteristics of his most salient victim. In both fury, as we saw, and now mercilessness Dido and Aeneas become one. Just as *clementia*, by sparing life, restores dignity to the individual and a sense of integrity to society as a whole, so *inclementia* not only fosters a continuum of vengeance and violence, it likewise abases both winners and losers so that all finally share in the same degenerative spiritual destiny.

If *clementia*, as practiced by Caesar, takes a supposedly communal

virtue and turns it into an individual right where stronger can magnanimously if whimsically offer pardon to weaker, then the ending of the
Aeneid goes a stride further. It adumbrates the negative side of one-man
rule, as harbinger of the political ethics of emperor and empire, and turns
fully away from the presumed consensus on which the Republic was
based. Private emotionality is not now subsumed into the larger exigen-
cies of community but controls the dynamics of the hero's action. His
primary emotion is anger as Aeneas, *ira terribilis*, undergoes the change
from ponderer of clemency to killer of his foe.[29]

As we turn from Virgil to his successor at epic, Ovid, and from the
Aeneid to the *Metamorphoses*, we find that anger now is a ruling principle
of divine action and therefore a major cause of metamorphosis. In the
first book it is the "savage anger of Cupid" (*saeva Cupidinis ira*, M. 1.453)
which causes Apollo to fall in love with Daphne. Book 2 finds "the wrath
of divinity" (*ira numinis*, 2.659) changing Ocyroe into a mare. The wrath
of Diana is the downfall of Actaeon in the major action of the third book
(3.252), and the fourth book opens with a warning that Bacchus will
exercise the "savage anger of his scorned divinity" (*saevam laesi . . .
numinis iram*, 4.8) against the daughters of Minyas.

The pattern extends throughout the poem. But in one striking way
Ovid absorbs and expands the metaphorical suggestion at the end of the
Aeneid that its hero is behaving like Jupiter. The first and last instances of
divine anger at work in the *Metamorphoses* are both attributed to the king
of the gods. In the first we find him exercising his wrath against Lycaeon
and making the latter's name come true by turning him into a wolf
(1.166). At the end of the poem, in the *sphragis* ("seal") through which the
poet's apparent "I" proclaims its immortality, he boasts that his work can
withstand even the *ira Iovis* (15.871). Here, too, the Virgilian hints that
Aeneas is in some measure an allegory for Augustus come to the fore.
From the beginning of his poem, where Ovid calls Jupiter's dwelling the
Palatia, the Palatine, of heaven, we have been prepared for the human-
divine complementarity, and its conclusion leaves no doubt of Ovid's
boast: whatever revenge Augustus-Jupiter may take on his mortal person,
his poem will survive well beyond the temporality allotted to the emperor or even to Rome itself (1.176).[30]

Several details are interesting in the lines that open the final seal:

> Iamque opus exegi, quod nec Iovis ira nec ignis
> nec poterit ferrum nec edax abolere vetustas.
> (15.871–72)
> And now I have finished my work which neither the anger of Jupiter,
> nor fire, nor sword nor gnawing age will be able to destroy.

As critics have long since pointed out, Ovid is alluding here and in what follows to the final poem of Horace's first lyric collection:

> Exegi monumentum aere perennius
> regalique situ pyramidum altius
> quod non imber edax, non aquilo impotens
> possit diruere aut innumerabilis
> annorum series et fuga temporum.
>   (*C.* 3.30.1–5)
> I have finished a monument more lasting than bronze and loftier than the pyramids' royal mass, which neither gnawing rain nor violent north wind nor the uncountable linkage of years and flight of time can destroy.

Horace goes on to draw an analogy between his poetry's endurance and priest with vestal climbing the Capitolium, presumably to worship at Jupiter's grand shrine. Lyric continuity finds its counterpart in the orderly performance that religion demands.

Ovid replaces this analogy with the simple *Iovis ira*, but this difference joins with others to create a picture that contrasts with Horace's. The lyric poet's brilliance survives the hazards that elemental nature offers a tangible memorial of human accomplishment. Ovid's opus surmounts not only the effects of age but the threats of human and divine (or, better, human posing as divine) violence. The poem itself tells us something of what this means. Similar phraseology is used of Ajax:

> Hectora qui solus, qui ferrum ignesque Iovemque
> sustinuit totiens, unam non sustinet iram,
> invictumque virum vicit dolor . . .
>   (13.384–86)
> He who had so often alone withstood Hector, withstood sword and fire and Jupiter, does not withstand anger only, and resentment conquered the unconquered man.

Or there are the Sibyl's opening words to Aeneas, requesting her aid to visit his father:

> "magna petis," dixit, "vir factis maxime, cuius
> dextera per ferrum, pietas spectata per ignes."
>   (14.108–9)
> "You ask great things," she said, "o man mightiest for your deeds, whose hand was tried by the sword, whose piety by fire."

Ovid's extraordinary poem is in fact a type of Aeneas who, unbowed by the savagery of Troy's fall, sweeps inexorably toward Rome. It is also refigured in Ajax but this time an Ajax who, instead of yielding to inner turmoil and suffering metamorphosis into a flower, prevails not only over human destructiveness but over the metamorphic power of superhuman irrationality. Virgil's Aeneas may make his extraordinary way out of Troy toward Rome, but in Ovid the text is the hero, at once containing and replacing warrior and exiled man of piety who triumph over fire and sword. And yet in replacing it also surpasses. Both the *Aeneid* and the *Metamorphoses* begin and end with anger. In the first the *ira* of Juno is finally absorbed by Aeneas, in the second the anger of Jupiter bounds the poem's subject matter. Ovid's poem is victorious over both, and in a sense over the *Aeneid* itself, by controlling the emotion Virgil makes finally paramount, and over the anger of Jupiter-Augustus with its power to alter a human life but not to surpass or suppress the enduring product of its imagination.

We have heard earlier in the poem's last book, from the lips of Jupiter himself, that no force, not even "the anger of the thunderbolt" (*fulminis iram*) can threaten the fixity of the "records of things," which is to say can alter fate (15.811).[31] Ovid's poem, his words to be ever spoken or read, are part of *fata*, above the menace even of consummate wrath. Ovid rephrases this notion, as well as much of the material of the "seal" of his masterpiece, in *Tristia* 3.7, addressed to his stepdaughter Perilla. Let anyone, he says, finish his life with "the savage sword" (*saevo ense*). Over his *ingenium*, his imagination, Caesar has no power, or over his *fama*, which will cause him to be read as long as Rome (or perhaps we should now say the Latin language and its genius) holds sway (*Tr.* 3.7.47–52).[32]

The poem's "seal" shares, as does Horace's grand ode, much in common with the epitaph, hardy symbol of death but also of a life completed and of deeds summarized to survive into the memory by reading.[33] It is a steadying token, at least here, of the imagination's invulnerability. But it serves also as a reminder that violence, which is the handmaiden of anger, is at the heart of Ovid's version of metamorphosis. Metamorphosis for its human victims leads regularly partway toward death just as the results of metamorphosis, a new myth, a new naming, lead partway toward immortality. One horrific form this survival takes, within the poem's story line, is in tales such as those of Io and Philomela where bestialized or brutalized humans communicate even though they cannot speak. But I am thinking more particularly of tales such as those of Myrrha who becomes at once a tree and a *nomen* (10.502), or Ajax who changes to a flower and to a *littera inscripta* (13.397–98).[34] Ovidian naming is the residue, not the commencement, of existence, the immortal essence after lives have been led, not their summoning into being. It is the digest of individuality, uniqueness generalized, the paradigms, reaffirmed on a different level of experience, so as to become the public property we call language. Nouns and letters are small particles, myths themselves only somewhat grander fragments, of that totality which forms Ovid's omnipotent texturing of self and selves become changeless.

If violence is central to Ovidian metamorphosis, poetry is the medium of reparation and restructuring through the forcefulness of words. A poem on metamorphosis postulates the permanence of the poet in writing, his bulwark against the changes his words reduplicate. And, though he himself may suffer metamorphosis through Augustan wrath, Ovid has the final, subversive joke: by spoofing the pseudoapotheosis of Julius Caesar; by noting, at the climax of his poem, that Augustus, for all his formidability, is subject to that same day (*illa dies*) that will carry off only the mortal part of Ovid; by incorporating Rome itself into a world of process and flux; and, above all, by surmounting anger with a form of permanence strong enough to resist its fragmentative power (15.868, 873).

This combination of subversiveness and permanence points up major differences between the *Aeneid* and the *Metamorphoses*. The *Aeneid* postulates a holistic vision of Rome, an appearance of ordered grandeur now and to come, that shatters, finally, through negative, human emotionality. Its chronological, historical thrust toward the manifest destiny of glorious Augustan Rome yields, finally at the end, to circular self-enclosure and to paradigm founded on the omnipresence of wrath. Angry, jealous Juno becomes angry, jealous Aeneas. The poem's periphery takes over and makes the center's moralizing problematical, questioning its validity. But the frame is also climax and dramatic conclusion as well, projecting an endless chain of hatred and revenge. The brilliance of the *Aeneid* allows us to keep in balance throughout its course ideal and real, imagined and experiential, programmatic and free-spirited, art and nature, even future and present, but Virgil leaves scant doubt that passion, man's irrepressible, angry need to destroy himself, wins the day at the end.

The framing of the *Aeneid* depends on anger, not on the singing "I" of the poem's famous first line. By contrast Ovid's poem takes us from the initial punning definition of his *carmen perpetuum* (1.4) on which he is embarking, a poem that is at once seamless and both embracing and outlasting all time, to the conclusion's proud boast that the "I" behind his work, his immortal part, will be borne, *perennis* beyond time, above the stars, and, according to the next line, that the *nomen* that comes to him from the composition of the *nomina* making up his poem will be imperishable (15.875–76). Looking at the two poems in terms of content, we could say that the singular spiritual chaos, the disintegrative anger, with which the *Aeneid* ends, without any relieving editorial statement, is splintered, in the *Metamorphoses*, into a multitude of private emotional articulations, which are held together directly by the poet's presiding genius alone.

It is a plausible conclusion that, as the Augustan age progressed from Virgil's death in 19 B.C. to A.D. 8, the year of Ovid's exile, life itself, at least spiritual life, became less cohesive, more subject to dissolution and alienation whether self-generated or imposed from without, and that words alone remained an ordering principle in an existential world where all patterns of order, whether ethical, scientific, or historical, possessed at best momentary validity as subjects of flux. The only systematization possible for life is the poet's, not his personal time-ridden *vita*, but the artistic imagination whose organization of words, whose Arachne's web of a book, survives his physical, exilic metamorphosis. Once more Ovid's imagination gets the better of the emperor, for cohesiveness is the privilege of poet, not politician.

Ovid, the mortal, is not so lucky. If the opening lines of the *Metamorphoses* refer to the ever-endurance of his song, they also contain a punning reference to his misfortune, as he prays to the gods

> prima . . . ab origine mundi
> ad mea perpetuum deducite tempora carmen.
>   (1.3–4)
> bring down my continuous song from the first beginnings of the
> world to my present time.

Perpetuum refers to both the unbroken poetic text and its endurance. *Ad mea tempora* looks to two aspects of time alone, the present existence of the poet in the Augustan era, that is, in the concluding temporal focus of the poem, and the particular misfortune that the poet's time-bound mortal frame suffers from the wrath of Jupiter.[35] Ovid thus subtly brings his poem also full circle on the note of physical suffering and mortality as well as of spiritual immortality. And no better definition of the metamorphosis that exile wreaks on Ovid himself is provided than by the poem itself, in Venus' curse upon the Cerastae:

> "exilio poenam potius gens impia pendat
> vel nece vel siquid medium est mortisque fugaeque.
> idque quid esse potest, nisi versae poena figurae?"
>   (10.232–34)
> "Rather let this impious race pay the penalty either by exile or by
> death or by some punishment in-between killing and exile. And
> what else could that be than the punishment of a changed form?"[36]

Ovid's relegation to Tomis participates in all the aspects of Venus' prayer. It illustrates a perfect metamorphosis. As an exile Ovid is still himself but not himself, alive and yet dead, changed and yet quintessentially the same. What remains after the event, aside from the mortal Ovid living on a few more years, is the powerful poetry of exile. To this we must turn for a final glimpse of the emperor and *ira*.

With the *Tristia* and the *Epistulae ex Ponto* Ovid returns to elegiac verse and with it to the world of the immediate responsiveness of the speaking "I." And as he leaps into contemporary, subjective experience all masks of allegory are dropped. Augustus is directly given the symbols of Jovian omnipotence. Beginning at *Tristia* 1.1.72 we hear of the thunderbolt from the Palatine that consigned Ovid to a world where Latin was scarcely spoken, and on other occasions in both collections of poems we see Augustus as wielding almighty power.[37] But it is the anger of Augustus that permeates these poems. Syme takes note of five instances each of *ira dei* and *numinis ira*, of seven occasions where *principis ira* is mentioned and of nineteen of the more specific *Caesaris ira*.[38] *Tristia* 1.5 alone makes use of *numinis ira*, *Iovis ira*, and *ira dei* in connection with Augustus' wrath and *Tristia* 3.11 dwells three times on *Caesaris ira*.

In response, and as assurance of his loyalty, the poet can furnish evidence of his *pietas*:

> nec pietas ignota mea est: videt hospita terra
> in nostra sacrum Caesaris esse domo.
> (*e.p.* 4.9.106–7)
> nor is my piety unknown: a foster land sees in my house a shrine to Caesar.

But as primary counteractive principle to *ira* we find scattered references to the emperor's *clementia*, and from time to time the two abstractions confront one another as Ovid rephrases his pleas.[39] At *Epistulae ex Ponto* 3.6.7–8 the poet's voice exclaims to an anonymous friend:

> quanta sit in media clementia Caesaris ira,
> si nescis, ex me certior esse potes . . .

> If you are ignorant of how great can be Caesar's clemency in the midst of his anger, you can glean sure knowledge from me.

But the instance on which I would like to dwell, in concluding this inquiry into Virgil and Ovidian anger, is to be found in the course of *Tristia* 2, the poet's powerful meditation on his misfortune, addressed in large measure to the emperor himself. Fallen is his house, though dear to the Muses,

> atque ea sic lapsa est, ut surgere, si modo laesi
> ematurverit Caesaris ira, queat

cuius in eventu poenae clementia tanta est,
    venerit ut nostro lenior illa metu.
vita data est, citraque necem tua constitit ira,
    o princeps parce viribus use tuis.
    (2.123–28)

yet so fallen that it can rise again, if only the wrath of injured Caesar grow to relent, Caesar whose leniency in the resulting penalty is such that the penalty is milder than was my fear. Life was given me, and your wrath halted this side of killing, o princeps, you who have used your strength sparingly.

Ovid's own poetic past is apparent in these lines. The phrase *laesi Caesaris* looks back to a reference earlier in the same poem to the emperor's "injured godhead" (*laeso numine*, 2.108). This in turn recalls the description of Bacchus' metamorphic power (*saevam laesi . . . numinis iram*—"the savage wrath of an injured divinity"), which we noted at the start of *Metamorphoses* 4 (8). And allusion to a wrath that stops short of killing echoes Venus' telling definition of metamorphosis as a grim amalgamation of exile, life and death. But the spirit of Virgil broods equally over these lines. The final apostrophe to Caesar, exclaiming on his lenient use of power, reminds us of Anchises' authoritative pronouncement to his son, as embodiment of future Roman power, to practice gentleness toward the defeated. In this light Ovid's relegation is a macabre version of "sparing the suppliant" where the poet of metamorphosis himself suffers a particularly ugly form of change, surviving in exile, all but beyond the world of the living.

The responsible agent is a god-human whose divinity has been vexed. We think of Bacchus in *Metamorphoses* 4 but above all Ovid urges remembrance of angry Juno at the opening of *Aeneid* 1, *numine laeso* (1.8), and his purposes are several.[40] The goddess persists at the end of the *Aeneid* but she also continues her career in the figure of the Augustus that Ovid creates in his exilic poetry whose truncated clemency is at best parodic of Anchises' standard-setting version. In the *Metamorphoses* the words of the poet triumph over exile and anger. In the world of the *Tristia* and the *Epistulae ex Ponto*, Ovid constructs the portrait of himself as pious wanderer, victim of unfortunate circumstances for which he deserves forgiveness. In other words he is partly reliving the *Aeneid* with the devastating proviso that, except in the imagination's hopeful fancies, there are no future visions, no Rome to gain or regain, only death for the protagonist away from the center.

The *Metamorphoses* unmakes the idealizing aspects of the *Aeneid* in one way, the exilic poetry in another. The one says that Augustan Rome is as much subject to disintegration as any other entity and that its leader is victim of, as well as victimizer through, anger. The other reinforces the suggestion of the *Aeneid*'s conclusion that anger lives on as a destructive force in Roman and therefore in human life. Aeneas, part Jupiter, part Augustus, kills Turnus without clemency, as harbinger of civil violence and the tyrannical aspects of unique rule. For Ovid's Augustus, with all pretense finally aside, anger still remains paramount, but its effects are more subtly hurtful, preserved immortally while they maim their immortalizer with death-in-life. The *Metamorphoses* exposes, with splendid irony, the futile continuities and expected hierarchies of religion, history, and politics, and claims that only art and the ever changeable universe of which it tells can survive. The horror of the exilic poetry is the knowledge, unfolded in poem after poem, that this fluctuating, discontinuous, arbitrary world of human foibles and ambitions can in fact partially twist, corrupt, even suppress the artist and therefore his mind's life.[41] Augustan *ira* does have a strong final say, but it is appropriate that we learn of it, and therefore still control it, through "letters," which, fragmentary cries of help though they be, remain, like the *Metamorphoses*, to be read and to foster now the *nomen* and the myth of mutant Ovid himself.[42]

Lucan makes explicit his debt to, and role as continuator of, Ovid from several angles near the beginning of his *Pharsalia*. After introduction and ambiguous invocation to Nero as surrogate Muse,[43] he initiates his narrative proper with the following line (67):

fert animus causas tantarum expromere rerum . . .

My mind moves me to set forth the causes of these significant events.

He proceeds to anticipate a return to the chaos with which Ovid had begun, the dissolution of order and form after a period of shaping—the theme, on one level of interpretation, of the *Metamorphoses*. His potential evidence, for instance, that "all the stars will clash in a jumble of stars" (*omnia mixtis / sidera sideribus concurrent*, 1.74–75)[44] is but a larger celestial echo of the horrors that civil war can perpetrate on the human race when, in the poet's opening words, "standards confront hostile standards" (*infestis . . . obvia signis / signa*, 1.6–7).

Nature's grand collapse into disorder mimics man's, and Lucan's salient source of inspiration is the initial lines of Ovid's grand enterprise:

In nova fert animus mutatas dicere formas
corpora . . .

My mind moves me to tell of shapes changed into new bodies . . .

The final book of the *Metamorphoses* offers abundant evidence for the aphorism that stands at the head of Lucan's undertaking—the inability of lofty ventures to endure for long (*summis . . . negatum / stare diu*, 1.70–71).[45] Ovid only leads us to the possibility of Rome's collapse. Lucan makes its dissolution his theme. On a literal level such a suggestion is of course impossible—Caesar and Pompey precede Augustus' rise to power and anticipate by several decades the reign of Nero—but allegory here too works its magic, obliterating distinctions between Republic and Empire and allowing power per se to be the focal factor of existence. Caesar is the central figure of Lucan's poem and with him, not with Pompey, he confounds his creative immortality (9.980–86). Caesar, too, as Lucan portrays him with a bow toward Nero, is a study in debasement. If *inclementia* and *ira* rule the end of the *Aeneid*, setting a pattern for the Latin poetic future, and if *ira* permeates the *Metamorphoses* as instrument of change, it is Caesar's corruption of *pietas*, reinforced by his pervasive anger, that remains perhaps the major ruling principle of the *Pharsalia*.

Here the moral background is set by allusion not to Ovid but to Virgil and in particular to the *Aeneid*. To illustrate this we must turn in more detail to Lucan's opening lines:

> Bella per Emathios plus quam civilia campos,
> iusque datum sceleri canimus, populumque potentem
> in sua victrici conversum viscera dextra
> cognatasque acies, et rupto foedere regni
> certatum totis concussi viribus orbis
> in commune nefas, infestisque obvia signis
> signa, pares aquilas et pila minantia pilis.
> (1.1–7)

I sing of wars worse than civil through the fields of Emathia, of right given to crime, and a powerful people with its victorious right hand turned against its own inwards, and kindred lines of battle, and, after the compact of rule was broken, the struggle of the shaken world with all its might toward universal crime, and standards confronting hostile standards, eagles matched together and javelins threatening javelins.

This brilliant example of epic's normative seven-line opening owes much not, as we might expect, to the initial lines of the *Aeneid* but to two other Virgilian passages on which Lucan built, here and elsewhere. The first is the powerful indictment of civil war with which *Georgic* 1 concludes. We find ourselves, where Lucan begins, on the plains of Thessaly which each poet chose to imagine as the setting for both the battles of Pharsalus and Philippi:

> ergo inter sese paribus concurrere telis
> Romanas acies iterum videre Philippi;
> nec fuit indignum superis bis sanguine nostro
> Emathiam et latos Haemi pinguescere campos.
> (1.489–92)

Therefore Philippi again saw Roman battle lines clash against each other, with spears matched together; nor was it unseemly to the gods that Emathia and the wide fields of Haemus twice grow rich with our blood.

As the diatribe continues we watch "the many faces of crimes" (*multae scelerum facies*, 1.506), pruning hooks forged into swords, and, in place of honor, the war god at work:

> vicinae ruptis inter se legibus urbes
> arma ferunt; saevit toto Mars impius orbe . . .
> (1.510–11)

Neighboring cities take up arms, the laws between them broken; unholy Mars rages through the whole world . . .

Lucan has availed himself of, and masterfully condensed, much that Virgil offers, whether it be the Thessalian setting with which he opens, lines of battle with the bitterly "balanced" accoutrements of civil strife, or compacts broken in a world at war. (Virgil's *ruptis legibus* have become in Lucan the fractured bond of the first triumvirate while *toto orbe* turns into the all-embracing might with which the world is shaken.)

Equally interesting is what Lucan elides. All this horror occurs, according to Virgil, because of the death of Julius Caesar when the sun pitied Rome and, in its darkness, forced the "unholy races" (*impia saecula*) to fear everlasting night. The only hope lies in the new Caesar, Octavian, and it is for his help that the poet prays to the gods of Rome. Lucan, of course, can have none of this, especially no saving Caesar, for the first Caesar is his villain-hero and what follows is above all Caesar's tale. Nor can *Mars impius* appear too quickly. Only the course of his poem will show that in a world without divinities Caesar takes over their omnipotence. In so doing there is no more suitable model for him to embody than the god who without prejudice takes delight in all wars, especially one with the godless impiety of brother killing brother as its essence.[46] Ovid undermines his divinities by his constant, parodic anthropomorphism and by defying, through co-optation, their metamorphic anger. In Lucan Caesar replaces the gods, who become now distant, untouching and untouched by human affairs. We will be watching closely the abstractions that rule his usage of power.

The second Virgilian passage that was in Lucan's mind as he wrote his introductory lines occurs in book 6 of the *Aeneid* as Anchises in the Underworld shows to his son the ghosts of Caesar and Pompey during his survey of future Roman greats:

> illae autem paribus quas fulgere cernis in armis,
> concordes animae nunc et dum nocte prementur . . .
> (6.826–27)
> Also those whom you see gleaming in equal arms, souls in agreement now and while they are submerged in darkness . . .

As he alludes to himself (and anticipates Lucan) Virgil enriches the punning in *paribus armis*. To the ironic complementarity of equal and civil we find in *Georgic* 1, he now adds the particular balance between Caesar and Pompey as father-in-law and son-in-law. While *concordia* reigns in death, so does the spiritual equilibrium that the piety of kinship engenders. Once life and *discordia* have set in, *par* takes on the more sinister meaning, only suggested here, that becomes a basis for Lucan's poem. Against the war, battle lines, and destruction (to paraphrase Virgil) to come, Anchises can only pray, as he apostrophizes his heirs and especially Julius Caesar:

> ne, pueri, ne tanta animis adsuescite bella
> neu patriae validas in viscera vertite viris;
> tuque prior, tu parce, genus qui ducis Olympo,
> proice tela manu, sanguis meus!
> (6.832–35)
> Youths, do not grow accustomed in your hearts to such wars and do not turn the force of your strength against the inwards of your fatherland; and do you, first, do you spare, who draw your descent from heaven, cast the weapons from your hand, o my blood!

These verses particularize what Virgil leaves in general terms in the famous lines with which Anchises concludes his speech. Caesar should spare (*parce*) just as Aeneas-Romanus should practice leniency toward the subjected (*parcere subiectis*). Together the passages set the moral standard for future Roman political behavior: spare the defeated and, above all, have no recourse to civil war.

What Lucan draws from the passage, however, is not the idealizing hope that Rome be spared civil strife but the reality of what would in fact occur. The end of the *Aeneid* allegorically projects civil conflict into the Roman future. Lucan's poem proves its vivid immediacy, and from Virgil he draws the powerful physicality of its presence as he turns Anchises' alliterative prayer—

> neu patriae validas in viscera vertite viris

—into the equally alliterative truth, which his poem elaborates, of a people "with its victorious right hand turned against its own inwards" (*in sua victrici conversum viscera dextra*).[47] The image and its variations remain central in the course of the epic.[48] It recurs most frequently in the seventh book as the battle on the field of Pharsalus between the two former relatives finally unfolds. At 7.350 it is Pompey's foolish prayer that

> ipsi tela regent per viscera Caesaris, ipsi
> Romanas sancire volent hoc sanguine leges.

> [The gods] themselves will guide our spears through Caesar's inwards, they themselves will wish to confirm Roman laws with this blood.

The wish is empty because Caesar, not some vague celestial divinities, is the redoubtable *numen* of Lucan's world. At 490–91 the narrator comments,

> . . . odiis solus civilibus ensis
> sufficit, et dextras Romana in viscera ducit.

> The sword alone satisfies the hatred of citizens, and leads their right hands toward Roman inwards.

But it is Caesar's army, we soon learn, which has the power to drive its weapons *ad viscera* (500), and Pompey's must endure the blow (501–2): "one army suffers, the other inflicts, civil warfare" (*civilia bella / una acies patitur, gerit altera*).

The image has been Caesar's from the beginning of the poem. At 1.376–78, in a telling illustration of what it means for a partisan to follow Caesar's impious arms, his soldier Laelius, presumably to hearten his chief, makes the bald promise:

> pectore si fratris gladium iuguloque parentis
> condere me iubeas plenaeque in viscera partu
> coniugis, invita peragam tamen omnia dextra . . .

> If you order me to bury my sword in the breast of my brother or in my father's throat or in the inwards of my pregnant wife, I will nevertheless carry everything through though my right hand be unwilling.

And it is Caesar who, as book 7 runs its course, draws the conceit twice more to himself. The first finds the narrator commenting that Caesar, scouting for victims, passes by the lowborn Roman soldiers in favor of more significant prey, the senators fighting on the side of Pompey:

> scit cruor imperii qui sit, quae viscera rerum,
> unde petat Romam, libertas ultima mundi
> quo steterit ferienda loco.
>   (7.579–81)

He knows where the blood of the empire runs, the inwards of its statehood, [he knows] whence to attack Rome, where liberty, making its final stand on earth, must be struck.

Second, after the battle has run its course, he addresses Caesar directly:

> tu, Caesar, in alto
> caedis adhuc cumulo patriae per viscera vadis,
> at tibi iam populos donat gener.   ·
>   (7.721–23)

You, Caesar, on the lofty heap of slaughter still stride through the inwards of your fatherland but your son-in-law now offers you nations.[49]

Lucan advances a variation on this Caesarian theme in the brilliant simile that initially fixes Caesar in our mind. We first meet Pompey getting along in years, susceptible to flattery, a shadow, in the poet's arch paranomasia, of his great name (*magni nominis umbra*, 1.135). In simile he is an ancient oak, mighty in size and garlanded with the trophies of respect, but standing upright now by sheer weight alone. Caesar follows, fierce and untamed, carrying his arms "where ambition [*spes*] and anger [*ira*] called him" (1.146). And, in a typically Lucanian turn, we learn that "he never spared a rash recourse to the sword" (*numquam temerando parcere ferro*, 1.147), meaning that Caesar practiced a perverse *inclementia*, that there was no inclination toward restraint on Caesar's part when the unchecked use of power was feasible.

I return in a moment to Caesarian *ira* and *clementia*. Let us first look at the simile that forms the counterbalance to Pompey's venerable oak:

> qualiter expressum ventis per nubila fulmen
> aetheris inpulsi sonitu mundique fragore _
> emicuit rupitque diem populosque paventes
> terruit obliqua praestringens lumina flamma:
> in sua templa furit, nullaque exire vetante
> materia magnamque cadens magnamque revertens
> dat stragem late sparsosque recolligit ignes.
>   (1.151–57)

Even so lightning, driven forth by winds through the clouds, flashed out with the din of the stricken heavens and the crashing of the firmament, and broke the daylight and terrified frightened peoples, dazzling the eyes with slanting flame; it rages against its own temples, and, since no solid matter forbids its march, it spreads far and wide great destruction as it falls, great as it returns and gathers again its scattered fires.

There are many details in this elaborate analogy which catch the attention—the crash of the sky that anticipates the *fragor* which would soon assail the heavens at the battle of Pharsalus (7.478), the military metaphor in *exire* announcing that Caesar is unstoppable, the double expropriation of Pompey's adjective so soon after the play on his name, with Caesar's verbal control anticipating his military superiority. There is even an allusion to a complementary moment in the *Aeneid*, for much of the simile's vocabulary, and in particular the phrase *dat stragem late*, echoes the simile at *Aeneid* 12.451–55 where Aeneas, cured of his wound and ready for the final combat, is compared to a cloudburst, instilling fear in the hearts of pitiable farmers who apprehend the ruin it will bring.[50]

Pompey is a time-ridden tree, withstanding collapse by weight alone. Aeneas and Caesar, as conceived by their poets, are forces of nature against which there is no recourse. But they have in common a symbol still more important, the thunderbolt. At the end of his epic, as we have seen, Aeneas, through the power of his weaponry and, finally, through the manner of his action, absorbs the essence of the king of the gods. Caesar, as Lucan first puts him before us, becomes forthrightly the thunderbolt itself. Since the *fulmen* is personified, raging against its own temples, he becomes at once Jupiter and his weapon, supreme divinity and that divinity's manifestation of power. Virgil's skill drew parallels for us between god and supreme mortal. Lucan manipulates the gods out of existence and replaces their lord with Caesar himself, omnipotent and filled with rage.

In this respect the phrase *in sua templa furit* and its qualification of Caesar gain particular importance.[51] The chief representations of Jupiter throughout the poem are as Tonans, whose weapon is the thunderbolt and whose cult temple was located on the eastern brow of the Capitolium,[52] and Latiaris, Jupiter of Latium worshiped on Mons Albanus. Caesar is at pains to associate himself with both Jovian manifestations in his first speech of the poem, responding to the vision of Rome herself, in mourning at his approaching march across the Rubicon. He begins:

> . . . "O magnae qui moenia prospicis urbis
> Tarpeia de rupe Tonans Phrygiique penates
> gentis Iuleae et rapti secreta Quirini

et residens celsa Latiaris Iuppiter Alba . . ."
    (1.195–98)
"O god, the Thunderer, who from the Tarpeian rock looks out on
the walls of the great city, and Trojan household gods of the Julian
race and the mysteries of Quirinus snatched away and Jupiter of
Latium, whose site is lofty Alba . . ."[53]

We will return to the irony of Caesar's appeal to household gods,
whether his own or those of others. Here I would like to point out that
one of the portents the narrator soon lists to illustrate the imminence of
civil warfare involves Alba Longa and the thunderbolt:

emicuit caelo tacitum sine nubibus ullis
fulmen et Arctois rapiens de partibus ignem
percussit Latiare caput . . .
    (1.533–35)
A thunderbolt, silently without any clouds, flashed forth in the heavens and snatching its fire from regions of the north, struck the
capitol of Latium.

That the omen refers specifically to Julius Caesar is confirmed by the
previous associations of Caesar with the thunderbolt, by his address to
Jupiter Latiaris and by the specificity of the phrase *Arctois rapiens de
partibus ignem*. Three times earlier in the book Caesar has been associated
with the north. He reminds his own men of "their blood shed in fields of
the north" (*cruor Arctois . . . diffusus in arvis*, 1.301). Laelius, his surrogate,
recalls how his hand not too long since "broke the Rhine, frothing with
its northern eddy" (*fregit . . . Arctoo spumantem vertice Rhenum*, 1.371), and
report goes out that tribes "uprooted from their territories in the north"
(*finibus Arctois . . . revolsos*, 1.482) are following Caesar in his onslaught on
Rome.[54]
    The action of the *fulmen*, in striking Latium at its religious core, em-
phasizes the truth, as Lucan would have it, both of Caesar's impiety and
of his destructiveness. The impiety says that, since he has hubristically
arrogated the power of Jupiter to himself, the sacred spaces of Latium
have henceforth no meaning, as he prepares to turn his energies against
them. The injuriousness takes us back once more to the phrase *in sua
templa furit* and to its intense irony. Caesar may become all-powerful
Jupiter but his actions are not only violent, they are ultimately self-
destructive. In raging against his own temples he is a Jupiter who exemplifies a powerful people that turns its suicidal right hand "against its
own inwards" (*in sua viscera*). And, of course, his own *viscera* will be the
receiver of the final wound.
    Caesar's rage, as we will see, permeates the poem. So does the fear that

the *fulmen* also arouses, and it figures in the first occasion where the narrator watches the difference between true *pietas* and its debased version on which Caesarian ethics is founded. Caesar has just delivered his first speech of exhortation to his men:

> . . . pietas patriique penates
> quamquam caede feras mentes animosque tumentes
> frangunt; sed diro ferri revocantur amore
> ductorisque metu.
>   (1.353–56)

Love of their country and the gods of their fatherland break their minds, though wild from bloodshed, and their swollen spirits; but they are called to order by dread love of the sword and by fear of their leader.

True piety, toward country and gods, is replaced by passion for martial violence and terror before Caesar. Fear figures also in a later definition of Caesarian piety as Scaeva urges on his leader's battered, fleeing troops in the early stages of the Pharsalian campaign. "Whither," he cried, "has a fear, disloyal and unknown to all Caesar's weaponry, driven you?" (*"Quo vos pavor,"* inquit, *"adegit / inpius et cunctis ignotus Caesaris armis?"* 6.150–51). Caesar must rely on *pius pavor*, terror based on adulterated *pietas* offered to him alone, to succeed in his campaigning.[55]

But the essential foundation for Caesarian piety is loyalty based on the sword's force. Vulteius puts it succinctly to his hard-pressed men in Illyria. His company, if given the chance, would have surpassed all records for "trustworthiness and military loyalty maintained by the sword" (*fides servataque ferro / militiae pietas*, 4.498–99). The key word here is *ferro*, referring to the sword by which Caesar's troops maintain their power or, more archly, by which Caesar consolidates his power over them. The theme is varied throughout the poem. At 5.272–73 Caesar's mutinous soldiers acknowledge what their life has been like:

> imus in omne nefas manibus ferroque nocentes,
> paupertate pii.

> We make our way to every crime guilty through our hands and through the sword, pious through poverty.

However seductive the rationalization for evildoing, their *paupertas* has made the soldiery pious toward Caesar and militarism, not toward some higher value.[56]

The link between one-man rule and the despotism of the sword is put concisely by the narrator at 4.577–79:

> ... sed regna timentur
> ob ferrum, et saevis libertas uritur armis,
> ignorantque datos, ne quisquam serviet, enses.

... but kingdoms [i.e., tyrannical rulers] are feared because of the sword, and liberty is corroded by ferocity of arms, and men are ignorant that swords are given them lest anyone suffer slavery.

And the link between impiety and autocratic rule is made most clearly by Pothinus to Ptolemy, each an alter ego of Caesar:

> facere omnia saeve
> non inpune licet, nisi cum facis. exeat aula
> qui volt esse pius. virtus et summa potestas
> non coeunt; semper metuet, quem saeva pudebunt.
>   (8.492–95)

It is not permissible for you to act savagely in all situations without requital unless when you are so acting. Let him leave the palace hall [i.e., kingly rule] who wishes to be pious. Virtue and supreme power are not compatible. He will always live in fear on whom savagery brings shame.[57]

This is the Caesarian enterprise: tyrannical ambitions based on power and force, with the fealty of his supporters attached to himself alone instead of to the state as a whole and to any higher loyalty it might elicit.

The impiety of Caesar runs as a continuous thread through the poem, from the *non pia classica* (1.238) that blare war's beginnings at the people of Ariminum to the *inpia bella* (7.171) of Pharsalus, to the "unholy throng" (*inpia plebes*, 7.760) of soldiers that waged the first fight and the *inpia signa* (7.838) of the victor. It forms a regular contrast with the true *pietas* that Pompey both offers and arouses in others. Caesar's manifestations of higher piety are, of course, a sham. At 9.1056 the editorial voice addresses him, with the accusation that he lacks *vera pietas* toward the dead Pompey. The same irony is operative at 9.1094–95 where Caesar claims that Pompey's spirit will hear his *voces pias*, especially given the fact that shortly before the narrator has apostrophized Caesar, charging that he acted "through a war based on crime" (*scelerato Marte*, 9.1047).[58] Caesar cannot even act piously toward the remains of his former son-in-law (8.316), and even his affection for Cleopatra is based on a pretense of honest devotion (*titulo pietatis*, 10.363).

In fact a primary worry for Caesar as he campaigns is that true *pietas*, for gods, for family, and for the larger *patria*, will undermine the monomaniacal constancy of his troops toward him. The first crisis occurs as the partisans of the two armies face each other in Spain, but the major challenge comes as the two leaders themselves clash. As they prepare for battle, various omens bolster their "wicked desire" to go after the throats of their fathers and their brothers' breasts (180–84), but, before the fight commences, Caesar himself must reaffirm this criminality, with a direct bow to a threat more troubling than anything Pompey could muster:

> sed, dum tela micant, non vos pietatis imago
> ulla nec adversa conspecti fronte parentes
> commoveant; voltus gladio turbate verendos.
>   (7.320–22)

But while their weapons gleam, no consideration of piety, no sight of your parents, brow against brow, should move you; maul with the sword the features that deserve reverence.

Caesar's concern becomes a reality when fathers and brothers finally confront each other:

>   omnia torpor
> pectora constrinxit, gelidusque in viscera sanguis
> percussa pietate coit . . .
>   (7.466–68)

Numbness froze every breast and chill blood gathered toward their inwards from the shock to piety.

But the impasse does not endure for long and the momentary seizure of *vera pietas* gives way to what Caesar would have expected:

>   . . . quis pectora fratris
> caedat et, ut notum possit spoliare cadaver,
> abscisum longe mittat caput, ora parentis
> quis laceret nimiaque probet spectantibus ira
> quem iugulat non esse patrem.
>   (7.626–30)

. . . one person smites the breast of his brother and hurls into the distance the head he has chopped off, so that he might rob the kindred corpse, one man maimed his father's face to cause onlookers to believe, from his excess of anger, that the person he killed was not his father.

If Caesar's *pietas* is corrupt and corrupting, his famous *clementia*, at least in the hands of Lucan, is equally degenerate.[59] His liking for peace is a sham and in fact the Massilians are punished because they sought peace (3.370). In the fighting at Corfinium Caesar spares Domitius for the very reason that he wants to be killed.[60] In the presence of Pompey's head, gift of Ptolemy, Caesar seems to utter an apothegmatic version of his fabled leniency when he says to the king's minion:

> . . . peius de Caesare vestrum
> quam de Pompeio meruit scelus; unica belli
> praemia civilis, victis donare salutem
> perdidimus.
>
> (9.1065–68)
>
> Your crime has done more disservice to Caesar than to Pompey. We have lost the one reward of civil war—to grant life to the defeated.

But the narrator has already informed us that the tears Caesar shed at sight of Pompey's features were forced (*lacrimas non sponte cadentes*, 9.1038) and that his subsequent words were as dissembling as his grief was false (9.1062–63).

The difference between Caesarian words and deeds, where clemency is concerned, is illustrated on the field of Pharsalus. Give victory, prays Caesar to the gods while addressing his men, to "whoever does not consider himself obliged to draw the savage sword against the defeated" (*quicumque necesse / non putat in victos saevum destringere ferrum . . .* , 7.312–13). Good Virgilian sentiments for Caesar to utter but, as Anchises apprehended in his prayer to *sanguis meus*, no more practicable, or even possible, for him to implement than for Aeneas. This is the narrator's view of the aftermath of battle:

> Caesar, ut Hesperio vidit satis arva natare
> sanguine, parcendum ferro manibusque suorum
> iam ratus ut viles animas perituraque frustra
> agmina permisit vitae.
>
> (7.728–31)
>
> Caesar, when he saw that the fields were flooded sufficiently with Italian blood, now thought that the sword and the hands of his soldiers should be restrained, and allowed survival to worthless lives and troops whose death would be of no gain.

This is clemency based on utility, not on any generosity of spirit. It serves the expedient purposes of one man, not any larger, altruistic design to which the individual is subservient.

This leads to the one instance where Lucan seems to allow Caesar to break his hypocritical mold and practice genuine *clementia*, namely his pardoning of Pompey's soldiers after their defeat during the campaigning in Spain.[61] But this is the exception that proves the rule for, after their spokesman's request that they not be forced to join the army of the conquerors, the narrator comments:

> . . . Caesar facilis voltuque serenus
> flectitur atque usus belli poenamque remittit.
>   (4.363–64)

Caesar is easily prevailed upon, with features unclouded, and ex-
cused them from military service and from any punishment.

Flectitur suggests that, in this instance, Caesar is being turned from what
would be his ordinary course of action and that here, for once at least in
Lucan's text, Caesar will truly act out of his vaunted leniency. But the
phrase *voltu serenus* adds a further innuendo to any interpretation. The
history of its parallels in Latin literature takes us from a first-person
Catullus resolutely accosting and observing the courtesans in the portico
of Pompey's theater *voltu sereno* (55.8), to the "calm features" of Horace's
Cleopatra as she dares to view her fallen kingdom and commit suicide (*C.*
1.37.26). In the *Aeneid* Virgil has Aeneas marvel at the wounds that defile
the *serenos vultus* of his phantom Hector, looking back (in his dream) to a
time when Hector's prowess was undaunted (2.285–86). And, in a further
Virgilian variation, there is Dido bent on self-destruction but hiding her
plans from her sister with features that beam forth hope (*spem fronte
serenat*, 4.477). All these examples look to situations where the heroic
protagonist acts, or acted, with firm self-assurance. Caesar, with consummate self-interest, can easily respond to Afranius' pleas for leniency because to offer it would bring him no serious threat.

But another Virgilian text adds a further twist to Caesar's apparent
moderation. Early in *Aeneid* 1 Venus addresses Jupiter, in prayer for her
tempest-driven Trojans. In response the king of the gods kissed his
daughter

> vultu quo caelum tempestatesque serenat . . .
>   (1.255)

with the features wherewith he calms the heavens and its storms.

Caesar can react magnanimously to the defeated because he is a type of
Jupiter, the fearless supreme being who can, on this one occasion, lay
aside his thunderbolt in favor of the sky god's calm features—when, to be
sure, it suits him, for, as Cleopatra and Dido teach us, a calm visage can
often mask designs of darkness.

We have looked at Caesar's *inclementia* and, since we touched again on
his quasi-Jovian omnipotence, it is well to remember that for Virgil the
final impiety is human craving for divinity. Early in book 6 we find *pius*
Aeneas mourning for the newly dead Misenus who challenged the gods
with his song (172), and as the book progresses we find among the
tortured in Hell not only those "who followed impious arms" (*qui arma
secuti impia*, 612–13) but the Giants and Titans who rose against the

Olympians (580–84), and Salmoneus who attempted to copy "the fires of Jupiter" (*flammas Iovis*) and "the storm clouds and inimitable thunderbolt" (*nimbos et non imitabile fulmen*) (585–94). Lucan's Caesar, as we have seen, becomes the thunderbolt and, by implication, king of the gods, but this initial parallelism merely sets the tone for his gradual, impious assumption of divinity. I will touch on a few of the grander manifestations of this arrogation throughout the epic.

Book 5 contains two powerful sequences, Caesar's quelling of the mutiny of his troops and his nocturnal adventure into the stormy Adriatic. Lucan is at pains for the reader to see the two episodes as complements. The *murmur* (255) and *minae* (261) of the unhappy soldiers become the murmuring (571) and threats (578) of heaven against Caesar and his boatman. The *tumultus* (300), the *rabies* (359) of the men, and their fury (304, 319) find counterparts in the *tumultus* (592) and *rabies* (603) of heaven and the fury of the wind (*vento furenti*, 578). The first threat Caesar surmounts by meeting the negative energy of his men with a more overwhelming version of the same. The *ira* they manifest (256, 294, 303) becomes the anger that prompts his words, and the wildness that lies behind their threats—Caesar does not even wait to respond "until their anger has lost its savagery" (*dum desaeviat ira*, 303)—is countermanded by "his fierce voice as he threatens" (*saeva sub voce minantis*, 364). At 315 the narrator addresses him as *saeve* and when his speech is over labels him a *saevus dux* (369–70).

In the later episode, as Caesar, virtually alone, challenges the elements, his antagonist has a more formidable arsenal, more akin to the Caesar-thunderbolt itself. *Saevitia* now belongs to the opponents, to the sea (568, 692), and to the "savage fury of the winds" (*furori / ventorum saevo*, 586–87). Nevertheless Caesar still triumphs, but this time the victory is not of superior anger over inferior but of Caesar over the gods. "What effort the gods take," cries Caesar, with sublime disdain, at the height of the storm, "to bring me to ruin."[62] In vanquishing elemental nature he vanquishes the gods themselves and in besting the gods he becomes the unique god.[63] As Caesar says to the boatman:

> . . . Italiam si caelo auctore recusas,
me pete.
(5.579–80)

If you refuse a course toward Italy under the guidance of heaven, seek it under my authority.

Caesar possesses an *auctoritas* that is loftier than heaven's. This raises one of the poem's most pointed ironies. Lucan, for all his loathing of him, carefully links his destiny with Caesar, as we have seen (9.980–86). Caesar defeats the gods, Lucan eliminates them from his poem. In the place where Virgil addresses the muse—*Musa, mihi causas memora . . .* (*Aen.* 1.8)—Lucan has *Quis furor, o cives . . .* (1.8). Civil war is his muse, Caesar (and Nero) his inspiration. Neither could exist nor gain immortality without the other.

Another extraordinary moment where Caesar proves the superiority of his *numen* over that of heaven occurs in the third book and this time Caesar's ever present *ira* becomes of paramount importance. In fact no book is more permeated by Caesar's violence. It is aroused first by Metellus attempting, verbally, to bar the conqueror from looting the temple of Saturn: "these words fired the victor with great anger" (*his magnam victor in iram / vocibus accensus,* 3.133–34). Caesar's response is another cynical example of mock clemency: "no office will make you worthy of my anger" (*dignum te Caesaris ira / nullus honor faciet,* 3.136–37), as if only the noblest accomplishments bring a deathblow that is truly worthy of Caesar's wrath! When the tribune fails to yield, Caesar's anger intensifies:

> acrior ira subit: saevos circumspicit enses
> oblitus simulare togam . . .
> (3.142–43)

His anger grew sharper still. He looks around for his savage swords, forgetful to put on a pretense of peace.

But it is only as the book progresses that anger and impiety combine, in the episode at Massilia. The Massilians try first to stave off his "untamed fury" (*furorem indomitum,* 3.303–4), holding out an olive branch and attempting to calm matters through words. The effect is only to bring more obviously to the fore his *ira* and *dolor* (357), and to urge him on to an act of destruction as gratuitous as Aeneas' sally against the city of Latinus. He may be on the move toward Spain, says Caesar, but he still has time to do away with Massilia (*Massiliam delere vacat,* 3.360). It is during the preparations for the subsequent siege that Caesar gives orders to his soldiers to hack down a grove that stands in the way of his military preparations. Lucan describes at length the sacredness of the place and therefore the reluctance of the troops to profane its majesty. Caesar is the first to seize an ax and his men follow suit. Though they remain fearful, nevertheless they obey, for, in Lucan's telling phrase,

> . . . sed expensa superorum et Caesaris ira.
> (3.439)

They weighed the wrath of the gods above and the wrath of Caesar.

The anger of Caesar is both more imminent and more potent than any parallel manifestation from heaven. No harm comes to him from desecrating the numinous grove because Caesar himself is a higher *numen* and his panoply of anger, savagery, resentment, and fury is more immediately telling than anything Lucan's invisible gods could offer. The Massilians rejoice because they act on the naive assumption that when the gods are so injured (*laesos deos*) they avenge the insult. Lucan may mean us, as we think of the natural response of the Massilians, to remember the opening reaction of Juno to her affronted divinity in the *Aeneid* (*numine laeso*, 1.8). For them, as for Virgil's epic world, the gods are still vital, proximate creatures, directly affecting human affairs. For Lucan the gods are remote and drained of effectiveness while it is Caesar who is the new Juno, ruling events with her initial and continuing combination of *ira*, *dolor*, and *saevitia*. Caesarian impiety with its wrath is the controlling divinity of the *Pharsalia*.

As we turn in conclusion to book 7 and to the epic's focal battle we find that Caesar does in fact call gods to his side, at least in Lucan's imagination. In good Junonian fashion he appeals to the evil spirits of the Underworld:

> (At tu quos scelerum superos, quas rite vocasti
> Eumenidas, Caesar? Stygii quae numina regni
> infernumque nefas et mersos nocte furores
> inpia tam saeve gesturus bella litasti?)
>   (7.168–71)
> (But you, Caesar, what gods of wickedness, what furies did you correctly invoke? To what deities of the Stygian kingdom, to what crime of Hell and madnesses submerged in night did you make due sacrifice, about to embark so savagely on a war of impiety?)

If any divinities can support Caesar's heinous endeavors, they are the lower creatures of the Underworld, especially the Eumenides whom Virgil conjoins with Bellum and Discordia (*Aen.* 6.279–80). Lucan's words purposefully recall the opening of Erichtho's invocation to the nether powers in the previous book:

> "Eumenidas Stygiumque nefas Poenaeque nocentum . . ."
>   (6.695)
> "Furies and Stygian crime and Punishments of the guilty . . ."

Caesar may call on the Underworld but, through Lucan's parallelism, he becomes a type of the witch herself, able to manage at will the powers of evil for her own nefarious purposes. Just as book 5 found him the superior of nature at its wildest, so here he not only petitions the nether powers, he appropriates their energies as well. Or, better still, as the book progresses and the battle grows in intensity, Caesar becomes madness itself and his troops but a self-extension.

The climax of the *impia bella* occurs when at last the brothers and
fathers of Caesar's men are the opponents:

> hic furor, hic rabies, hic sunt tua crimina, Caesar.
> (7.551)
> Here, Caesar, is your madness, here your frenzy, here your wicked-
> ness.

Lucan editorially exclaims that he cannot bear to tell of the license allowed this civil battling (*bellis civilibus*, 7.554), but he forges ahead, first, to
entitle Caesar "the frenzy of his troops and the goad of their madness"
(*rabies populis stimulusque furorum*, 7.557), and then, at the height of the
endeavor, to reinstate Caesar fully in the divine pantheon:

> . . . quacumque vagatur
> sanguineum veluti quatiens Bellona flagellum
> Bistonas aut Mavors agitans si verbere saevo
> Palladia stimulet turbatos aegide currus,
> nox ingens scelerum est . . .
> (7.567–71)
> Wherever he roams, like Bellona shaking her bloody scourge, or like
> Mars urging on the Bistones, when with fierce whip he goads on his
> chariot's steeds, terrified by the aegis of Athena, there is a mighty
> darkness of villainy.

The similes come alive in what follows as Caesar urges on laggards
among his soldiers "by a blow from the butt end of his spear" (*verbere
conversae . . . hastae*, 7.577). The phrase *verbere saevo* also recalls for us the
second Caesarian simile of the epic where he is compared to a lion who
gathers together all his anger (*totam iram*) and goads himself "by the whip
of his fierce tail" (*saevae . . . verbere caudae*, 1.207–8).[64] But it is the comparison of Caesar to Bellona and Mavors, female and male divinities of
battle merged into one consummate Warrior, that gives the passage its
special point. Lucan is carefully thinking back to one of Virgil's most
brilliant moments where, on the shield of Aeneas, in the confrontation
off Actium, the gods take sides. Cleopatra has her monstrous deities and
barking Anubis. Octavian and the Romans have Neptune, Venus, Minerva, and Apollo:

> . . . saevit medio in certamine Mavors
> caelatus ferro, tristesque ex aethere Dirae,
> et scissa gaudens vadit Discordia palla,
> quam cum sanguineo sequitur Bellona flagello.
> (8.700–703)

In the middle of the struggle Mars rages, chiseled in iron, and the grim Furies from the heavens, and Discord in torn robe makes her way rejoicing, whom Bellona follows with bloody scourge.

When Lucan wishes further to divinize Caesar, at the peak of his glory on the field of Pharsalus, he does not pursue the analogies he has already suggested with Jupiter or Juno, nor does he initiate any equation between his hero and the gods who support the winning, Augustan side (from whose number Jupiter and Juno are conspicuously absent). Rather he identifies him with Roman gods who are nevertheless common to all combatants. Caesar, in his grandeur, is the epitome of War itself, with all its bloody fury and destructiveness.[65] As the book and its battle evolve and we learn how Caesar's *ira* continues on insatiate (7.802),[66] Lucan allows us to enter his victor's mind:

fortunam superosque suos in sanguine cernit.
(7.796)
He sees fortune and gods who are his in bloodshed.

But his re-creator has done him one better. Caesar has no need for gods who delight in blood. He has himself.

Let me end with one further Virgilian allusion. In the lines after he has been compared to Mars and Bellona we find Caesar himself at work:

ipse manu subicit gladios ac tela ministrat
adversosque iubet ferro confundere voltus.
(7.574–75)
He himself supplies swords with his hand and provides spears, and orders them to mangle the faces of their foes with the iron.

The words *tela ministrat* hark back to the phrase *furor arma ministrat* in the *Aeneid*'s first simile (1.149–51), where, we recall, the rage of a mob and the weapons supplied by fury are counterbalanced by the soothing words of a man "venerable for his piety" (*pietate gravem*). Lucan's Caesar is now Furor itself, but on this occasion there is no *pietas* to set matters aright. Rather we have the opposite, as the impieties of human aspiration toward divinity and of civil war meld with the essence of Junonian animosity to form an irresistible creature we call Caesar, Virgil's *impius Furor* in person, on the loose.

One of the remarkable features of the opening of the *Iliad* is the amount of anger that courses through its lines—of Achilles against Agamemnon, of Agamemnon against Chryses, of Apollo against Agamemnon, of Agamemnon against Chalcas. This anger reaches a climax in book 22 as Achilles kills Hector. It is with the tonality of such anger that the *Aeneid* ends. Turnus' final speech to Aeneas deliberately echoes Priam's speech of appeal to Achilles in *Iliad* 24,[67] but the actual ending, in all its violence, reverts to the duel of book 22. It thus brings the *Aeneid* to closure not on any note of reconciliation, or even with the sense of community that the double celebrations for Patroclus and Hector generate, but with the idea of anger and vengeance with which the epic began still paramount.

In this essay I have been tracing anger, first, as a crucial ingredient in the final figuration of Aeneas, then, in its influence on the two immediately successive Roman epics, Ovid's *Metamorphoses* and the *Pharsalia* of Lucan. My thesis argues that, in killing instead of sparing Turnus, Aeneas denies the higher *pietas* of allegiance to a father who preaches the nonviolent sparing of a defeated foe and who would have Julius Caesar, his descendant and spiritual heir, throw away his arms rather than use them against Pompey. Instead Aeneas opts for the lower piety of anger and revenge, based on the Junonian remembrance of hurt, which throughout the emperor's career played such an important role in Augustan propaganda and iconography.[68] In this tension between ideal and real, between the Rome for which Anchises hopelessly wishes (and that Turnus offers in ethical microcosm to Aeneas) and the Rome that Aeneas and Augustus put into practice, lies the epic's extraordinary dialectic. For Aeneas at the end is an inchoate Julius or Augustus Caesar. He has sole power and that power smacks of divinity. His spear shares the strength of Jupiter's thunderbolt and Fury. It is capable of destroying cities.

The special force of this moment when Aeneas, in full glory of omnipotence, opts for anger rather than moderation and stasis, was not lost on Virgil's successors. We have traced this anger at work in Ovid's Jupiter-Augustus and watched it personified in Lucan's Caesar when all masks are off (and all gods dispensed with) as the emperor storms through his poem with the grandly impious force of divinity and wrath combined. And we have observed how Lucan, by allowing Caesar's gratuitous anger to permeate his epic, heightens the sense of moral impropriety that Virgil gives to his hero's final deed. At least Aeneas has a reason for anger. Caesar's is as volitional as it is ubiquitous.

Only with Statius' *Thebaid*, in the next generation, do we get at least some forms of conciliation, in the plot itself and in the poet's concluding *sphragis* that looks back on his Virgilian model with a public modesty that scarcely hides the rivalry lurking just below the surface. Clemency, in the figure of Theseus, does at last seem to work, and acts of mourning bring a closure that deliberately leaps back beyond Virgil to recall the Iliadic past common to both poets. And with the proposition that leniency might to some degree be practicable after all, classical Latin epic comes to its powerful, allusive ending. It is a "sealing" that Virgil did not allow himself.

NOTES

1. Roman *clementia* is mentioned twice by Sallust (*B.J.* 33.4; *Hist.* fr. 55.1), frequently by Livy, e.g., 33.12.7 (where see Briscoe, *Commentary*, on its commonplace nature). Cf. the general survey by Gernentz, *Laudes Romae* 129–37 ("De Romanorum in subiectos clementia") and, for Virgil in particular, Eggerding, "Parcere subiectis" passim.
2. For Caesar's clemency, see the discussions of Treu, "Clementia" passim; Earl, *Politic Thought* 101–2; Weinstock, *Divus Iulius* 234–43; and Wickert, "Forschungen" 67–70.
3. On 12.940.
4. We find aspects of *dolor, ira,* and *saevitia* all associated with Juno in the poem's initial twenty-five lines and opposed to Aeneas' *pietas* (10). *Furor* and *pietas* form a polarity in the epic's first simile (148–53).
5. See Quint, *Epic and Empire*, 78–79.
6. Cf., e.g., 9.675.
7. The ambiguity is absent at 10.477 where a spear "makes its way through the rims of a shield" (*viam clipei molita per oras*).
8. 1.5 and 7 (and cf. 1.258–59 and 1.264), and 12.950.
9. Cf. 1.340 et al.
10. Cf. 4.682–83.
11. 4.646–47 (*ensem . . . recludit / Dardanium*).
12. For analysis of the compact, see Feeney, "Reconciliations" passim, and O'Hara, *Death* 30–31, 149.
13. Cf. also *stridorem* (869).
14. 7.331, 12.860; 7.375, 12.848. It is well to note again here that Aeneas, at the end *furiis accensus*, is made to correspond with Amata and her fellow mothers made *furiis . . . accensas* (7.392) by Allecto's machinations.
15. Cf. also *Geo.* 4.560–61 where Caesar "thunders at the deep Euphrates" (*ad altum / fulminat Euphraten*), playing Jupiter as victoriously he "gives laws through willing peoples."
16. The tag is Ennian (*Ann.* 232 Skutsch).
17. *Cl.* 1.7.1–3 (and cf. 1.26.5), quoted by Feeney (*The Gods in Epic* 222) in an examination of Augustus' anger as illustrated in Ovid.
18. Virgil's only other use is at *Geo.* 3.68 where he speaks of the *durae . . . inclementia mortis.*
19. Cf. 12.569, quoted earlier. With *sternit . . . a culmine Troiam* (2.603), the accomplishment of *divum inclementia,* cf. Aeneas' boast, later in the same line of book 12, that he will level the rooftops (*culmina*) of Latinus' city.
20. It is one of the curiosities of Virgil's description of the shield of Aeneas that Jupiter nowhere appears during the scene of the battle of Actium. But sandwiched among Mavors, Discordia, and Bellona—that is, in the midst of the divinities that share in the horrors of war on whichever side—are *tristes ex aethere Dirae* (8.701). The emissaries of Jupiter are there as he is too, therefore, vicariously, bringing impartial fury to all contenders, whether Roman or Egyptian.
21. Let us recall again Servius' note (on 12.940) that Aeneas shows himself pious (toward Anchises) by the thought of sparing Turnus, pious also because "out of consideration of Evander he avenges the death of Pallas" (*Evandri intuitu Pallantis ulciscitur mortem*). By this reasoning the final, triumphant piety would

offer just cause for revenge. But two details of the plot line itself tell strongly against this line of reasoning. First, there is no mention of Evander. The narrator shows Aeneas motivated by personal, private response alone. Second, Turnus directly names *Anchises genitor* (12.934) to Aeneas in his prayer for mercy. The reader's mind, and perhaps Aeneas' also, for a moment, returns to the words of book 6.

22. His words, especially lines 57–60, touched the imagination of Horace who attributes their sentiment to Achilles (*C.* 4.6.17–20).

23. I will deal elsewhere with the sexual connotations of *intactus* especially in relation to the ekphrasis on Pallas' sword belt, which tells of the murder of the sons of Aegyptus by the Danaids on their wedding night.

24. Cf. Aeneas at 331–32, with *immota lumina*, assured of his purposes by the warnings of Jupiter.

25. Cf. the phrase *lumina volvit* used of Pallas at 10.447, pondering what to do in the face of the proud commands and huge physical presence of Turnus.

26. Cf. 4.366.

27. With 6.468 (*lenibat dictis animum*) cf. 1.153 (*ille regit dictis animos*).

28. We note that *sermone* follows one line after *fixos oculos* in book 6 as it does after *volvens oculos* in book 12.

29. The phrase *ira terribilis* is divided between 12.946 and 947, the climax in a powerful series of enjambments in these last lines.

30. On the anger of Augustus-Jupiter, see most recently Feeney, *The Gods in Epic* 221–22.

31. Cf. 13.858 where Polyphemus says to Galatea "your wrath is more savage than the thunderbolt" (*tua fulmine saevior ira est*).

32. With *legar* (52) cf. the same words at *M.* 15.878.

33. For recent readings of *C.* 3.30, see Putnam, "The Lyricist," and Woodman, "*Exegi*" passim.

34. In her final prayer to Ceyx, Alcyone consoles herself that both *littera* and *nomina* (11.706–7) will reunite the two lovers in their epitaph. Her final phrase—*si non / ossibus ossa meis, at nomen nomine tangam*—in conjoining death and life, loss of corporeality and still residual sexuality, owes much to Propertius 4.7.94. For Ovid sexuality lives on in naming, in the final act of procreation through *litterae*, in the different incarnations of Io, Byblis, Hyacinth, and Ajax.

35. On the interpretative difficulties of these lines see most recently Kovacs, "Ovid." In his précis of the poem at *Tr.* 2.560, Ovid carefully changes *mea* to *tua* as he addresses Augustus from the distance of Tomis.

36. There are close parallels (noted by Anderson, *Ovid's Metamorphoses*, on 10.483–87) between this brief description and the subsequent story of Myrrha. Cf. especially line 487 where metamorphosis is defined as the refusal by the gods to bestow either life or death by killing (*vitamque necemque*).

37. E.g., *Tr.* 2.179, 5.2.53; *e.p.* 1.2.126, 1.7.46.

38. Syme, *History in Ovid* 223.

39. *Clementia*: *Tr.* 4.4.53, 4.8.39, *e.p.* 1.2.59; *clementia* and *ira*: *Tr.* 5.4.17–19, *e.p.* 2.2.119–20.

40. The proximity of the word *casus* (the neighboring word in Ovid, in the next line in Virgil) strongly supports the plausibility of the allusion.

41. The parallels between exiled Ovid, linguistically bestialized by being forced to speak Getic, and the position of characters in the *Metamorphoses* such as Io and Callisto only confirms the horror. In the tale of Philomela, her loss of speech is the equivalent of exile while her tapestry emblematizes both the *Metamorphoses* and the books of exilic poetry. It and they, like the words, names, and myths they contain, are the only means both of survival for the inner self and of communication. (In the tale of the Sibyl these ingredients are reversed. She gradually becomes disembodied while her voice alone remains to tell *fata*: 14.153.)

42. Ovid himself makes somewhat the same point at *Tr.* 3.4.45–46.

43. On the deliberately paradoxical tone of this apostrophe, see most recently Ahl, "Lucan's *Pharsalia*" 139.

44. Deleted by Bentley.

45. The change from Ovid's *dicere* to Lucan's *expromere* is also telling. It puts particular stress on Lucan's own personal power, now that muses and gods no longer deeply influence human doings, to produce his poetry (cf. Cat. 65.3–4).

46. On Lucan's elimination of epic's traditional, wrathful gods see, most recently, Johnson, *Momentary Monsters* 6–7.

47. The phrase *sanguis meus*, which so caught Dante's fancy (*Par.* 15.28), possesses rich ambiguity when compared to *Geo.* 1.491 (quoted earlier) and Luc. 1.14. Anchises' offspring, from Aeneas to Caesar, will also be major shedders of blood as Roman history unfolds.

48. Lucan makes much of the word *manus* in battle scenes where they are images of doubling and twining. It is also worth remarking that the word *viscus* occurs a total of 15 times in Virgil's work, 43 in Lucan's poem. Of these appearances 9 are in book 7, twice the average for a single book.

49. The culmination of Lucan's poem might well have been the moment, adumbrated at 10.528, when the swords of his countrymen made their way *in viscera Caesaris*. The vengeance would have been Pompey's, but Caesar would still be center stage.

50. Cf. *Aen.* 12.453–54: *dabit . . . stragem . . . late*. The resonances of Virgil's simile are purposeful for at *Aen.* 6.590 *nimbi* are considered the particular attribute of Jupiter. Cf. as well *Geo.* 1.328–29, where *nimbi* and *fulmina* are complementary, and *Aen.* 8.354.

51. I must argue here against the standard interpretation of this phrase, represented by the comment of Getty, *Lucani* ad loc., who quotes approvingly the translation of Haskins: "rages against the quarter of the sky whence it came."

52. We may be meant to think of the grand temple of Jupiter Optimus Maximus, but a Roman of Lucan's time would also as likely see a reference to its neighbor, the smaller shrine of Jupiter Tonans which Augustus vowed in 26 B.C. and dedicated in 22. Suetonius (91) dwells on the emperor's fondness for the temple.

53. Once these associations have been made by Lucan, the reader finds it hard to dissociate Caesar with any mention of Jupiter, especially Jupiter the Thunderer, as the poem proceeds from 1.35 on.

54. Cf. also Caesar's words at 5.661.

55. After two intervening questions Scaeva also asks (155–56):

> "non ira saltem, iuvenes, pietate remota
> stabitis?"

"If loyalty is disregarded, will you not at least take your stand
in anger, youths?"

At least one major component of Caesarian militancy should
remain, even if his troops forget their *pietas*!

On the sheer power of Caesar in Lucan's portrait, see the
important discussion of Ahl, *Lucan: An Introduction* ch. 6 passim,
especially 201–9.

56. Cf. the narrator's more general definition at 10.407–8:

nulla fides pietasque viris qui castra secuntur,
venalesque manus . . .

Those who follow the camp have no trust, no loyalty: their
hands are for sale.

57. On the ambitions toward regal power of Caesar, his troops, and
his successors cf. 5.207, 7.240, 7.386, 9.90.

58. Cf. the narrator's comment (8.572–73) that *fides pura* and *vera
pietas* are missing on the part of the Egyptians toward Pompey
(again Ptolemy is a double for Caesar). There is another rich
authorial irony at 5.297–99 during the height of the mutiny
against Caesar. True *pietasque fidesque* have disappeared says the
editorial voice, because of Caesar. Would that *discordia*, the essence of civil war that Caesar has engendered, might destroy his
troops themselves!

59. The difficulties Lucan faced when dealing with Caesar's *clementia* are well treated by Ahl, *Lucan: An Introduction* 192–97.

60. 2.512–15, Caesar's words, followed by the narrator's comment
(516–21).

61. On this passage see most recently Masters, *Poetry and Civil War*
78–87, who feels that Caesar's response is genuine.

62. *Quantaene evertere . . . / me superis labor est* (654–55) where the
pun on *evertere* ("capsize," "overthrow") is to the point.

63. Quint, *Epic and Empire* 137–40, makes much of this episode in
developing his thesis that Lucan initiates a tradition of epic devoted to losers rather than winners, of poetry smacking as much
of romance withdrawal from action as of Iliadic heroic endeavor.
My own line of reasoning takes a different tack, arguing, in
general, that the *Aeneid* itself is richly and paradoxically an epic
of both losers and winners and, more particularly here, that
Lucan's poem, for all its Pompeian retrospection, has a central
figure who descends firmly from Virgil's Aeneas in his final,
most challenging incarnation.

64. *Ira* gathers force from its appearance at 146, the first specific
mention of Caesar's anger in the poem. The phrase *verbere caudae* is a reminiscence of Cat. 63.81 where the whole context has
strongly affected Lucan's imagination.

65. At 7.457 Lucan allows himself the apothegm that

bella pares superis facient civilia divos.

Civil war will make [Roman] deities equal to the gods above.

Lucan's poem has, of course, metaphorically done Caesar this
continuous honor during his lifetime!

66. Cf. 7.809.

67. See my chapter 7 and Barchiesi, *La Traccia* 111–19.

68. I agree here with Quint, *Epic and Empire* 78, that at least one type

of *pietas* is reconcilable with revenge. My disagreement lies with his contention (79) that *clementia* and *pietas* are separable entities, the one dominating the epic's first half, the other the second, a *pietas* of revenge superseding an allegiance to *clementia*. Anchises is very much present at the epic's end, in Turnus' words and in Aeneas' hesitation.

VIRGIL'S TRAGIC FUTURE:
SENECAN DRAMA
AND THE *AENEID*

Two salient facts emerge from a survey of the classical authors to whom
the younger Seneca refers in his prose works.[1] One is the paucity, in the
philosopher's citations, of direct allusion to writers of tragedy, whether
Greek or Roman.[2] The other, more positive, characteristic is the persistence of the bows that he makes to Virgil, *maximus vates* as he is styled
in *De Brevitate Vitae*.[3] For Seneca, the Mantuan is time upon time *Vergilius
noster*. On his verses the philosophical works regularly lay claim for analogies, with four times the frequency, for example, with which they draw
on Ovid, allusions to whom come second in number.

It would be a misjudgment rigidly to appropriate the same statistical
demarcations in a search for the imaginative sources of Seneca *tragicus*.
No critic would now question his thorough knowledge, and regular employment, of fifth-century tragedy for guidance in modeling the con-
struction of his plays, and there is little doubt that later developments in
Greek and Roman dramaturgy exerted influence as well.[4] Nevertheless,
as I argue in this essay, the impact of Virgil, and especially of the *Aeneid*'s
ethical framework, is salient in Senecan dramaturgy.[5] I am not thinking of
the bearing of specific passages in Virgil's chef d'oeuvre on individual
moments in Seneca's plays, though one Virgilian moment will be a primary focus of my argument.[6] Rather I refer to a larger pattern of influence, not widely studied by scholars, of what I would call tragic elements
in the *Aeneid* on both the processes and the conclusions of Senecan drama.

To illustrate this pattern I must first begin with a summary discussion
of the conclusion of Virgil's epic and especially of the relationship of the
finale to the poem as a whole. In bald précis, the ending centers around
two duels, of deeds and of words, between Aeneas and his antagonist
Turnus. The first is the physical contention between the two. After Jupiter sends down a Fury to frighten and enfeeble Turnus, Aeneas hurls
a spear, which wounds his enemy in the thigh and forces him to the
ground, his knee doubled under. The humbled warrior prays that he be
returned to his people, alive or, if Aeneas prefers, dead, then reminds him
of his father and asks for an end to hatred (12.931–38). Aeneas hesitates
but, seeing on Turnus the belt of young Pallas, who had become Aeneas'
protégé and was earlier killed in combat by Turnus, he becomes enraged
and, responding to Turnus as Pallas the avenger, he plunges his sword
into his adversary, whose soul flees under the shades as the epic ends.

The basic dissatisfactions of this ending are many (12.945–52).[7] If, as

Aeneas' tale reaches its culmination, we expect confirmation that we have been witnessing a thinly disguised paean of praise for Augustan Rome and, in particular, for its presumed ethics of restraint in the exercise of power, the concluding verses disappoint. Instead of some authorial reassurance that would lend justification to Aeneas' conduct and announce to the reader the dawn of a new era of peace after war, paradigm for the future post-Actian moment of Virgil's contemporary readers, we have only the indignant soul of Aeneas' enemy escaping to the Underworld. As at the end of Virgil's description of the shield of Aeneas, one of the great vehicles in the epic that sweeps us in its vision from Aeneas at Caere to the triple triumph of 29 and to the dedication of the temple to Apollo in 28, it is on the victim and his loss that the poet dwells, not on the implications which victory might carry for the political glory and moral excellence of time to come.[8]

To hold such expectations is to yearn for what Virgil does not say. His characterization of Aeneas' conduct raises doubts of another sort. Ever since the hero's meeting with Anchises in the world below, Aeneas has lived with his father's injunction, directed to him as *Romanus*, pattern for Roman behavior then and now, "to spare the humiliated and war down the proud" (*parcere subiectis et debellare superbos*).[9] It has not been fully appreciated exactly how closely this difficult maxim, with its play on *sub* and *super* and hence on the literal and figurative implications of positions expressively signified by what is superior and what inferior, applies to the postures in which Virgil places Aeneas and Turnus in the epic's final moments.

As most critics observe, the one trait that Virgil allots to Turnus alone among the epic's figures is *violentia*. He alludes to it four times, in conjunction not with physical action but with spoken response to a verbal challenge, whether it qualifies his energy in the act of persuasion or the impetuosity he manifests as he gives vent to a strong reply.[10] When it comes to deeds, Turnus' conduct seems to be motivated by traits that he shares with the poem's other main protagonists. But one characteristic sets him apart: Virgil allots the word *superbus* to him and to his exploits more than to any other figure in the *Aeneid*.[11] It is not hard to divine arrogance in many of his actions, but we should observe in particular here that pride is twice associated with his killing of Pallas. We hear before the clash begins of the *iussa superba* (10.445) by which Turnus clears the field of any competition and, after the duel has reached its deadly conclusion, the narrator addresses him as object of Aeneas' quest:

> proxima quaeque metit gladio latumque per agmen
> ardens limitem agit ferro, te, Turne, superbum
> caede nova quaerens.
>
> (10.513–15)

With the sword he mows down all the nearest ranks, and fiercely
drives with the steel a broad path through the host, seeking you,
Turnus, proud from your new-wrought slaughter.

In between, we are made to sense the moral connotations of his stance,
looming above the newly slain youth—*quem Turnus super assistens*
(10.490).[12] That he exemplifies *superbia* is reinforced, after he has taken
possession of Pallas' baldrick, by another narratorial intervention commenting on his lack of moderation.

This prideful pose is revenged at the end of the epic. We have been
readied for Turnus' punishment as early as the first moments of war's
outbreak when Latinus anticipates his *supplicium* (7.597). And, with specific reference to the death of Pallas, the youth's father, Evander, as he
prepares for his son's funeral, can demand vicariously the life of Turnus
from Aeneas (11.177–79). As the epic closes, the titular hero's hand has
done its pious duty of humbling the prideful by the wounding, not the
killing, of Turnus and, as we have seen, Aeneas hesitates. The terrifying
rage that overcomes him when he sights the sword belt of Pallas now
worn by Turnus directly contravenes Anchises' dictum urging *clementia*
once war has subjugated the haughty. Virgil is careful to make the reader
aware that Turnus' pride has been "warred down" even before he makes
his appeal for mercy. An injurious but not fatal wound is sufficient to
cause the *superbus* to become a suppliant whose eyes are *humilis*, earth-
bound and no longer dazzled by ambition for territory or a wife not due
him by fate. In Virgil's etymological wordplay, he has become graphically
sub-plex (930), in full view of the Trojan and Latin bystanders, because his
legs have been bent double underneath him (*duplicato poplite*, 927), forcing him to the ground. And Aeneas, we presume, towers above him,
ready to kill.

Virgil's working out of a son's duty to his father's pronouncement to
bring the prideful to their knees in battle—*pietas* at work—was of interest
to Seneca as he constructed his dramas. What happens next in the epic
exerted an even more profound influence. Virgil does not, perhaps cannot, have his hero offer mercy and spare the suppliant, nor is *clementia* a
viable option whenever it comes available in Senecan tragedy. But to have
the hero, in the poem's final moments, spurred to act by the memory of
ferocious resentment and "set aflame by furies and terrifying in his
wrath" is to transport him from the realm of rational thought into the
darker abysses of madness, and this inner, irrational realm of *saevitia*,
dolor, *furor*, and *ira* was one in which Seneca's characters, as well as
certainly their creator in working out their moments on life's stage, were
at home. If Virgil's reader is frustrated either that his hero cannot practice
restraint or that his enraged ferocity elicits no accolade from the poet, he

will be on the edge of appreciating what Seneca found so powerful in the *Aeneid*'s final words.

Before we move to the tragedies themselves we must look for a moment more closely at the *ira* and *furiae* to which Aeneas finally becomes prey.

First his furies. Those who defend his action often appeal to the dialogue between Jupiter and Juno that precedes the ending for arguments to bolster their contention that his conduct has support from, or can even claim analogy with, the (presumably) commendable behavior of the immortals. The general argument says that in declaring peace the two divinities, especially Juno, who forswears her enmity to the Trojans, somehow license a furious killing because the humbled hero, spared and, as a result, still apparently threatening, might stand in the way of this announced but as yet unreached miraculous era-to-come without war. The specific argument says that Aeneas' fury is defensible because it has the blessing of Jupiter.[13] But the king of the gods sends down his Dira not to lend justification to Aeneas' final deed but, first, to prevent Turnus' sister from offering him further aid and then, by declaring Jupiter's enmity so directly to Turnus, to weaken the hero to the point where the final clash loses all balance.

On the contrary, rather than being external forces that sanction his deed as though they conveyed divine approval, Aeneas' furies arise from violent, inner reactions. The narrative's dialogue between heaven and earth as the epic closes projects what might be against what actually is, an idealizing future against present emotionality. As such it could serve as metaphor for one aspect of Seneca's career which has often troubled his critics. How, it is often asked, could the philosopher, who spent so much of his career preaching an ethics of courageous restraint in which hatred, anger, and fury should have no part, in his dramas exploit these same abstractions as if they were the core motivating factors of human existence? Virgil compresses this contrast within the confines of his great poem. The prose works expound to a contemporary audience how it ought morally to live its life. The tragedies, through the condensed allegorizations of myth and the dynamism of metaphor, watch the more vital, more troubling evolution of authentic experience where the abstractions that the prose treatises are bent on exorcising now in large measure motivate the agenda of their protagonists.

As further preface I would like to dwell for a moment on what it means for Virgil to have Aeneas *furiis accensus et ira / terribilis*, especially when such *furiae* and *ira* have been motivated by *saevus dolor*. We should remember that within the space of the epic's first twenty-five lines we also hear three times of Juno's *ira*, twice of her *dolor*. In connection with the first mention of *ira* she is *saeva*, and at line 25 her resentments (*dolores*) are styled *saevi*. Twice also she is said to be set aflame. Virgil ends his catalog of her bitterness by styling her enkindled (*accensa*, 1.29), and as she approaches her minion, Aeolus, it is likewise with heart on fire (*flammato corde*, 1.50). In Juno's case there need be no intermediary to join cause and effect, the source of madness and its results.

Her anger and resentment take physical shape in Aeolus' horse-winds who, already used to rage and with their own angers, stand readily available as vehicles for, as well as incorporations of, her madness.[14] As the episode progresses her brother Neptune recognizes the results of Juno's anger in the furious sea,[15] and the poet reinforces the analogies of outer with inner nature through a simile where the whole imbroglio of explosive actors is compared to a mob which gives vent to its hysteria and to which *furor* lends arms.[16]

As at the end of the epic, memory plays a crucial role in the motivation for action. We first hear of Juno's "remembering wrath" (*memorem iram*, 1.4) and then that she dwells on recollection of the Trojan War where she took the Greek side (*veteris . . . memor . . . belli*, 1.23). Equally stored in her mind, as she prepares to initiate her revenge, and given most elaboration in Virgil's catalog are the residual grudges of jealousy for the judgment of Paris and the rape of Ganymede. And, as we recall, it is exactly *saevi monimenta doloris*, remembrance, not of piety owed Anchises or even Evander but of the intensity of personal suffering, that spurs Aeneas on to his final, ferocious act.

In book 1 Juno's fury takes tangible shape in the wildness of the winds. In book 7 her desire for vengeance is mediated by the fury Allecto whom she summons to incite Amata, Turnus, and the Latin farmers against the newly arrived Trojans. A Fury epitomizes her mentor's fury to drive others furious. The distinction with the emotional progress of the first book is subtle but important. In book 1 Juno preys directly on victims already lawless by instinct. In book 7 Allecto, though the external instrument of someone else's rage, also can take advantage of or, better, drive to the surface latent inner feelings of her subjects—Amata's incipient anger over the Trojans' advent, which portends the loss of Lavinia and (more suggestively) Turnus, then the latter's innate love of the madness of war (7.461),[17] and finally anger yet again, now of the Latins defending property that they see as their own (7.508).

The duality of fury here, as both externally instigated and internally triggered, is illustrated specifically in the case of Amata and her fellow mothers. On Amata Allecto's fury works like a snake and its venom "so that maddened by the pest she may embroil all the house" (*quo furibunda domum monstro permisceat omnem*, 7.348). And, as its poison finally strikes home:

    . . . penitusque in viscera lapsum
serpentis furiale malum totamque pererrat,
tum vero infelix ingentibus excita monstris
immensam siñe more furit lymphata per urbem.
    (7.374–77)
    . . . and when the serpent's maddening venom has glided deep into
her veins and courses through her whole frame, then indeed the
luckless queen, stung by monstrous horrors, in wild frenzy rages
from end to end of the city.

Virgil compares her to a top spun into a circle by boys at play, as if fury's
victims were ever, finally, mindless while her sport is both callous and
ignorant. She then abducts her daughter to a countryside fostering fan-
cied bacchic revelry. The mothers, by contrast, are aroused only indirectly by rumor and example:

    fama volat, furiisque accensas pectore matres
idem omnis simul ardor agit nova quaerere tecta.
    (7.392–93)
    Fame flies abroad, and the matrons, their breasts kindled with fury,
are driven on, all by the same passion, to seek new dwellings.

These *furiae* are not Allecto and her colleagues but emanate from within
as part of the women's response to Amata's suggestiveness.
    The distinction is significant because it anticipates the difference that I
illustrated earlier between the Dira of Jupiter and the fury of Aeneas at
the end of the epic. If anything, the discrepancy between the two types of
fury which the epic's final lines exemplify is even more substantial than in
book 7. In the latter instance there is at least an intimate, complementary
link between Fury and fury, between the provocative role of Allecto
toward Amata and the responsive reaction of the *matres*. In book 12 no
such link exists. As the epic concludes, outer and inner madness are
separate. The Dira dispatched by Jupiter is external envoy of his rage, one
of three sisters who sharpen the fear of sick mortals if on occasion, to
paraphrase Virgil's words, the king of the gods wields dreadful death, or
terrifies deserving cities with war (12.851–52). This creature is described
as highly visible, a perceived object of terror. Moreover upon noticing it
Juturna and her brother do not become furious but merely frightened. As
Turnus says in reply to Aeneas' final verbal challenge:

    . . . "non me tua fervida terrent
dicta, ferox; di me terrent et Iuppiter hostis."
    (12.894–95)

> "Your fiery words, fierce one, do not daunt me; the gods daunt me
> and the enmity of Jupiter."

Aeneas' fury, by contrast, is engendered within, a spiritual reaction triggered by remembrance of an equally grievous moment in the past. Like
the mothers *furiis . . . accensas*, he is *furiis accensus*, a target not of Jupiter's
emissary but of his Junonian *dolor*, a resentment and ferocity that allows
him an instant of supremacy never allotted even Juno at her counter-
balancing moments of savagery. He can now in anger take the life of his
enemy as the epic comes to its abrupt but powerful conclusion.

The ending of the *Aeneid* brings to final focus another moral issue that
deeply concerned Seneca as he wrote his tragedies, namely the confrontation between *odium* and *ira* on the one hand, *pietas* on the other.

Odium, we recall, is Turnus' word for the emotion prompting Aeneas'
preceding exploits (12.938), and *ira*, according to the narrator, inspires his
final deed. *Pietas*, though not directly mentioned by Virgil, is discovered
twice by Servius in Aeneas' comportment.[18] He is pious toward his father,
says the commentator, for hesitating, pious toward Evander for taking
vengeance for the death of Pallas (he does not add that the killing of
someone *subiectus* would be an act of impiety toward Anchises). The
tension will prove to be essential in several of Seneca's plays with *odium*
and *ira* pinpointed as the negative elements. For Seneca the philosopher,
the incompatibility of anger and piety is subject of some eloquent sen-
tences in *De Ira* but perhaps most succinctly phrased at 1.12.5: "Anger on
behalf of one's own is a token of a weak, not a pious spirit" (*Irasci pro suis
non est pii animi sed infirmi*).

It would have been apparent to Seneca that his thinking on this topic
was supported by Virgil's moralizing throughout the epic. As early as
lines 10 and 11 of the opening book, the narrator contrasts Aeneas' piety
with the *ira* of Juno, and this distinction reappears at the conclusion of the
initial episode, strengthened by allegory implicit in the simile already
touched on in which Neptune, calmer of the waves, is compared to a man
pietate gravem while Juno, Aeolus, and their lackeys are guilty of *saevitia*
and driven by *furor*.[19] The second book reverses the roles, with Aeneas, in
a series of episodes, taking the active part of the enraged warrior against
interlocutors who coax him toward what will prove the great emblematic
gesture of piety, when at last he leads his son and carries his father out of
Troy's smoldering ruins. In between we regularly find the hero adopting
the opposite role: with Hector, when he cautions Aeneas to depart with
Troy's sacred objects and the hero yields to *furor iraque* (2.316); with
Panthus, carrying both *sacra* and grandson while Aeneas again gives in to
fury; and especially with Venus who chides him:

"nate, quis indomitas tantus dolor excitat iras?
quid furis? aut quonam nostri tibi cura recessit?
non prius aspicies ubi fessum aetate parentem
liqueris Anchisen, superet coniunxne Creusa
Ascaniusque puer? . . ."
   (2.594–98)
"My son, what great resentment arouses your ungovernable anger?
Why are you raging? Or whither has your care for us gone? Will you
not first see where you left your father, Anchises spent with age,
whether your wife Creusa and the boy Ascanius survive?"

In spite of Servius' arguments to the contrary, Aeneas at the end is not
acting from *pietas* when he kills but from its opposites, *dolor*, *ira*, and
furor. We will see that Seneca would have agreed with this assessment.

One other aspect of the epic's finale deserves mention before we turn
to Seneca. The word Virgil has Aeneas use as he prepares to slay Turnus
is *immolo*. On the one hand the titular hero sees himself as surrogate for
Pallas, at last gaining the upper hand and with it the opportunity for
revenge. But the truth is that in fact Aeneas is offering Turnus as human
sacrifice to, and for, Pallas. We have been prepared for such a possibility
from the only two other occasions on which Virgil uses the verb. Each
instance is concerned with Aeneas and Pallas and each occurs shortly
after the latter has been killed by Turnus. When Aeneas learns of Pallas'
death, he goes on the rampage. He first takes eight captives to be used as
blood offering on Pallas' pyre (*immolet*, 519). The second victim he himself metaphorically offers:

nec procul Haemonides, Phoebi Triviaeque sacerdos,
infula cui sacra redimibat tempora vitta,
totus conlucens veste atque insignibus albis.
quem congressus agit campo, lapsumque superstans
immolat ingentique umbra tegit, arma Serestus
lecta refer umeris tibi, rex Gradive, tropaeum.
   (10.537–42)
Hard by was Haemon's son, priest of Phoebus and Trivia, his temples wreathed in the fillet's sacred band, all glittering in his robe and
in resplendent arms. Him he meets and drives over the plain; then,
bestriding the fallen, sacrifices him and wraps him in mighty darkness; his armor Serestus gathers and carries away on his shoulders, a
trophy, king Gradivus, for you!

The ironies here are multilayered. The headband and ribands that characterize Haemonides as priest also portend his incipient role as victim. The

sacrificer is sacrificed, the "priest" in this case being pious Aeneas, tendering as his living gift (to Pallas, we presume) a priest of Diana and Apollo, divinities especially dear to Augustus. Shortly later we meet again the earlier eight victims still alive, as Aeneas initiates definite preparations for the obsequies themselves. The final sacrificial offering is made by Aeneas as his last function in the poem.

In commenting on Aeneas' expropriation of live victims for sacrifice, Bailey succinctly remarks: "The idea here is wholly un-Roman."[20] There is, of course, a precedent in the *Iliad* in the twelve Trojan youths whom Achilles seizes (as blood price, he says) and then slaughters at the funeral of Patroclus (21.27–28). But even Homer's narrator censures the deed (23.175–76).[21] Why, then, does Virgil choose to end his poem with his precedent-setting hero offering human sacrifice, something no civilized Roman would have done, and following as example the conduct of Achilles at one of his most savage, barbaric moments? The answer must be that Virgil, too, would have us condemn his hero's final deed as the action of someone deranged, driven by fury to violate not only his father's injunction to behave with *clementia* but also a basic tenet of civilized behavior as already Homer would have known it.

Let us begin our survey of Seneca *tragicus* as a reader of Virgil with the play that comes first in the manuscript tradition, one that has fury at its center and in which human sacrifice, too, plays a conspicuous part, *Hercules Furens*.[22] The opening monologue of Juno, though it has parallels in Ovid's *Metamorphoses*, carefully echoes the initial lines of the *Aeneid* with phraseology not found in the later poem, to such a degree that it often resembles a powerful dramatization, in soliloquy, of what Virgil leaves implicit in his third-person narrative.[23] The goddess states her feelings most clearly at lines 27–29:

> non sic abibunt odia; vivaces aget
> violentus iras animus et saevus dolor
> aeterna bella pace sublata geret.

> Not in such fashion shall my hatred have its end; my angry soul shall keep up a long-living wrath, and my raging smart, banishing peace, shall wage unending wars.

Her words, which have resonances from moments we have analyzed at both the beginning and the end of the *Aeneid*, set the tone for what follows. At 34–35 we hear again of her *odia* and *ira*, which Hercules makes light of, and she styles herself *saeva*. Later, as her resolve strengthens, she apostrophizes her anger:

Perge, ira, perge et magna meditantem opprime,
congredere, manibus ipsa dilacera tuis:
quid tanta mandas odia?
   (75–77)
Then on, my wrath, and crush this plotter of big things; close with
him, yourself rend him in pieces with your own hands. Why to
another entrust such hate?

But the major ideological difference between this Juno and the angry
goddess of *Aeneid* I is that Seneca's character paves the way not for
someone else to incorporate and project her fury but for this fury to
originate spontaneously and destructively from within the hero so as to
appear self-engendered, not imposed from the outside. This is her prayer:
let him wage war with himself (*bella iam secum gerat*, 85), let him overcome himself (*se vincat*, 116), let the evil that finally grips him be Fury,
ever armed against itself (*in se semper armatus Furor*, 98)—

   hoc hoc ministro noster utatur dolor.
   (99)
This, this be the minister of my smarting wrath.[24]

And, in the course of his madness as he shifts the focus of his anger
from others to himself, Amphitryon describes the change as follows:

   Nondum tumultu pectus attonito carens
   mutavit iras, quodque habet proprium furor,
   in se ipse saevit.
   (1219–21)
His heart, not yet eased of frenzy's tumult, has shifted its wrath's aim
and now, sure sign of madness, he rages against himself.

Thus Seneca's Juno in her thinking, and his tragedy as its action unfolds, span the course of the *Aeneid*, from Juno's initial rage, exerted
against Aeneas by outside forces, to the hero's own fury, likewise incited
by *dolor* but this time welling up from inside and goading him directly
into action. The aftermath of this fury, even when Hercules returns to his
right mind, affects the play virtually to the end.[25] Both the way fury
pervades the play and the virtually unrelieved negativity of the ending
characterize in briefer compass the *Aeneid*'s conclusion as well. The final
impression of the play is that "evil, violence and death are stubbornly
rooted [in human nature and in the nature of the universe] and cannot be
eradicated."[26] The same can be said for the epic's finale.
   Two smaller, interrelated points. The madness of Hercules com-

mences at line 939, but it is preceded by two incidents that suggest its
incipience. First, he will not wash his bloodstained hands before offering
sacrifice and, more grievous, he is prepared to offer Lycus as human
victim to Jupiter.[27] Second, he claims that he will soon conceive prayers
worthy of Jupiter and himself. This combination of barbarity and hubris
gains full sway during the bout of madness itself, two main manifestations of which are his (imagined) attempt to defeat and supersede the
Olympians, and his murder of his family.

As Hercules kills his first child, Amphitryon sees him as prey of *caecus
Furor* (991), but the language of sacrifice is overwhelming in the words
given to Hercules and Amphitryon describing the massacre: *dicatum*
(1036; of his family, which he thinks is Lycus), *victimas alias* (1038; likewise
his own kin, though he expects them to be Eurystheus' household), and
finally Amphitryon himself:

> Nondum litasti, nate: consumma sacrum.
> stat ecce ad aras hostia, expectat manum
> cervice prona; praebeo, occurro, insequor;
> macta . . .
>   (1039–42)

You have not yet completed the sacrifice, son; bring the rite to
conclusion. See the victim stands before the altar; with bent neck he
awaits the stroke. I offer myself to death, I run to meet it, I follow
after it; smite.

The brutal propensity to replace animal with human sacrifice and a
tendency toward overweening pride are already operative earlier in Hercules' life.[28] His fury merely exaggerates their primacy.

In looking back to the *Aeneid* with *Hercules Furens* in mind we think, in
general, of the dissatisfactions of the ending, where not even Theseus'
offer of asylum in Athens seems to contravene the hero's mood of despair, and, in particular, of the hideous moments in both poems when
human blood sacrifice is threatening or perpetrated. But there is one
connection between the epic and this alone of Seneca's tragedies, the
figure of Hercules himself. He appears in *Aeneid* 8 during Evander's account of how, at the site of future Rome, he confronted the villain Cacus
and strangled him to death for stealing eight of his beautiful cattle.
Critical opinion generally sees Hercules as an allegorical prefiguration of
a sequence of Roman greats from Aeneas to Augustus, a sequence well
illustrated in book 8 itself as we progress in our mind's eye from Evander's primitive Palatine to the snowy threshold of the newly dedicated
Apollo temple, agleam in Luna marble.

But Virgil complicates too simple a reading of the human condition.

Cacus is haughty. He affixes the faces of his victims to "proud doorposts" (*foribus . . . superbis*, 8.196). But so is Hercules, proud from the killing of triple (-headed) Geryon and from the resulting spoils (*tergemini nece Geryonae spoliisque superbus*, 8.202). More important still, Cacus rages in wildness of mind (*furiis Caci mens effera*, 8.205)[29] as he contemplates the possibility of another crime. But so also does Hercules, twice over. In the first instance his rage is complementary to *dolor*:

> hic vero Alcidae furiis exarserat atro
> felle dolor . . .
>   (8.219–20)
> At this the resentment of Hercules had blazed forth, furiously, in black madness . . .

In the second instance we hear of him "furious in his spirit" (*furens animis*, 8.228) and shortly thereafter Virgil has Evander characterize him as "swollen in anger" (*fervidus ira*, 8.230), using the last adjective, in fact the last word, allotted Aeneas at the epic's end (12.951).[30] The twining of Cacus and Hercules by means of pride and anger questions not only the quality of Hercules' immediate mission but also any easy linkage between Hercules and future Roman political genius, especially if such a bond is meant to assert a sense of moral superiority. Rather, as we ponder the intricacies of Virgil's delineation of the Greek hero's progress through Pallanteum, we can with equal fairness claim him as spiritual ancestor of Seneca's Hercules, contemplating suicide and observing in the mirror of his psyche "a monstrous form, impious, savage, inexorable, wild" (*monstrum impium saevumque et immite ac ferum*, 1280).

Finally, there is another subtle link between *Aeneid* 8 and the Virgilian-Senecan Hercules who is at once tamer of monsters and monstrous, this time forged by the book's conclusion. In the final vignette of the shield that Vulcan crafts for Aeneas, many critics find the last exuberant parallel between Hercules' victory over Cacus' savagery and a crucial event in later Roman history when Octavian, soon to be Augustus, claims the support of Apollo and his fellow Olympians as he prepares to defeat Cleopatra and her bestial divinities. The description continues with Caesar's triple triumph and with the reception of gifts from conquered peoples. We must remember, however, that the ekphrasis concludes not with the emperor's glory but with the humiliation of nature:

> . . . Euphrates ibat iam mollior undis,
> extremique hominum Morini, Rhenusque bicornis,
> indomitique Dahae, et pontem indignatus Araxes.
>   (8.726–28)

And now went the Euphrates, calmer in its waves, and the Morini, remotest of mankind, the twin-horned Rhine, untamed Dahae, and the Araxes resenting its bridge.

The place of climax is given to the Araxes objecting to Caesar's bridge. Since the ancient reader would have recalled, with Servius, that Alexander the Great had also futilely bridged the same river,[31] we are therefore forced once again, through the figure of Hercules, to question the quality of the Augustan enterprise. If pride had previously linked Augustus with both Cacus and Hercules, here it is the hubris of one who thinks, now with Alexander as well as Hercules, that human physical prowess should be considered superior to nature's ongoing energies, and that, in Augustus' case, the art of politics, even in its most notable manifestations, could even be considered capable of dominating nature's more powerful continuities. As Seneca elsewhere demonstrates, this hubris is a vigorous incentive behind Hercules' frenzy. It is one in which Virgil carefully has Augustus also share.[32]

In *Hercules Furens* we watch the development and permutation of fury through the progress of a play whose demarcations in striking ways mimic the outline of the *Aeneid*. If we turn to *Troades*, we find that Seneca has expanded into the sweep of a complex drama ideas that Virgil concentrates at his epic's end: a debate between measured treatment of a conquered foe and unbridled vengeance, then moments of supplication followed by two violent deaths each caused by an enemy's anger and each interpreted by the playwright as human sacrifice performed before the faces of an enthralled audience.[33]

The moral nub that serves as ethical touchstone for the play's action is the early confrontation between Pyrrhus and Agamemnon—two set speeches (Pyrrhus, 203–49; Agamemnon, 250–91) followed by dialogue (292–352). Since neither character appears in Seneca's major model, Euripides' *Troiades*, it is a logical presumption that Seneca condensed into the dialectic arising from their mutual challenge his imagination's cleavage between a philosopher's adherence to reason, embodied in Agamemnon's call for restraint in the exercise of power, and a dramatist's acknowledgment of human nature's darker side, as illustrated in Pyrrhus' spirited defense of violence as well as in the evolving action of the play.

Seneca's meditation develops from Agamemnon's inquiry into "what the victor ought to do, the vanquished suffer" (257)—a question forthrightly answered by Pyrrhus at 335: "whatever he will, it is the victor's right to do."

For Pyrrhus might makes right. Agamemnon by contrast places on the victor the onus of moderation as requisite counterpose to his incipient *superbia*. His key statement comes at 279–85 and serves the same purpose of establishing a norm for future heroic conduct as does Anchises' appeal for clemency toward the defeated proud in *Aeneid* 6. His language, however, echoes that of Virgil's evaluations of Juno and Aeneas at the bounds of his epic. Agamemnon would have urged Trojan defeat, but razing Troy to the ground should not have been the Greek's intention:

> . . . sed regi frenis nequit
> et ira et ardens ensis et victoria
> commissa nocti. quidquid indignum aut ferum
> cuiquam videri potuit, hoc fecit dolor
> tenebraeque, per quas ipse se irritat furor,
> gladiusque felix, cuius infecti semel
> vecors libido est.
>
> (279–85)
>
> But wrath, the fiery sword, victory given to night's charge: these cannot be kept in hand. All that any might have deemed unworthy in me or brutal, this resentment wrought and darkness, whereby fury is spurred to greater fury, and the victorious sword, whose lust, when once stained with blood, is madness.

Ira, *dolor*, *furor*, and their instrument—here the burning, "happy" sword; for Virgil's Aeneas, the metonymical iron that complements his unbending stance—all come into play at the end of the epic.[34]

From this point on the play becomes a study in the victor's treatment of the conquered and, more particularly, of violence done in spite of, or in response to, a series of supplications for mercy. In other words Seneca elaborates in a drama's limited temporal compass what it means to go, in the epic's more expansive time-scheme, from Aeneas' hearing his father's prescription of moderation to the moment when he responds without *clementia* to Turnus' final plea.

The debate with Agamemnon prepares us for Pyrrhus' later behavior. At 313 Agamemnon reminds the younger man that Priam was his father's suppliant (*supplex paternus*), to which Pyrrhus replies that he knows his father's suppliants equally as enemies. At 333 Pyrrhus arrantly announces that "No law spares the captive or stays the penalty." Agamemnon caps the interchange by a contrastive appeal to equanimity:

> Compescere equidem verba et audacem malo
> poteram domare; sed meus captis quoque
> scit parcere ensis.
>
> (349–51)
>
> I could check your words and curb your recklessness by punishment; but my sword knows how to spare even captives.

The play's second great creator of violence foisted on the pitiable is Ulysses to whom we are introduced at 524 and among whose apothegms is the recognition that "resentment [*dolor*] is clearly no impartial judge" (545–46). There follow two acts of supplication, the first of Andromache, the second, in gesture only, of Astyanax, before Ulysses.[35] In the course of her appeal, Andromache twice reminds her foe of Hercules' gentleness toward the young Priam, alluding finally to his "merciful wrath" (*mites iras*, 730).[36] This in turn leads to the two acts of theater within theater. The messenger relates how Astyanax jumped to his death as Ulysses ushered him atop the city walls (1078–87) and how Pyrrhus slew Polyxena on Achilles' tomb while the throngs watched from a distance (1123–31).[37]

In both instances Seneca implies that what the spectators witnessed, and the drama's audience vicariously experiences, is a double human sacrifice. There is a precedent in Pyrrhus' earlier treatment of Priam. At the moment when he prepares to lead Polyxena off to death, Hecuba calls him "sacrificer of old men" (*mactator senum*, 1002), but she had already previously reminded us that he had performed the deed "at the very altars" (*ipsas . . . ad aras*, 45). The chorus shortly thereafter alludes still more explicitly to Priam as a victim offered to Jupiter:

> postrema pater funera cludis
> magnoque Iovi victima caesus
> Sigea premis litora truncus.
>   (139–41)

You, father, close the long funeral list and, slaughtered as a victim to mighty Jove, you lie headless on Sigeum's strand.[38]

Within the play his grandson and daughter share a similar fate. Ulysses sees the boy as a lustral sacrifice (*lustrale . . . sacrum*, 634–35) that should have been offered to the walls of Troy, and the messenger speaks of the *sacra* (1102) to which the Greek summons the gods as the boy prepares to leap. And already at 196 the ghost of Achilles claims Polyxena for sacrifice at the hands of Pyrrhus, and it is he who now prepares her as a *victima* (306) for his father whose monstrous anger lies behind the deed (190, 194). Hecuba later reinforces the notion of her daughter as blood offering to Achilles' ashes (943) and, as he reports the event, the messenger begins "the virgin has been sacrificed" (*mactata virgo est*, 1063) and concludes summarily, "such was the course of the rite" (*hic ordo sacri*, 1162).[39]

When we contemplate the future of its protagonists at the play's end, with Hecuba's final cry of despair and the messenger's command to the Troades to make for the ships, we listeners, viewers, readers are left with no satisfaction, only the memory of two merciless, highly theatric acts of ferocity stemming from anger vengeful enough to demand human sacrifice as its price.[40]

Phoenissae likewise is concerned with two spheres of savagery, this time potential rather than realized. In fact the drama's power revolves on the imminence rather than the actual use of force, and the argumentation of the plot centers on *pietas* as the great counterbalancing factor to the abstractions—anger, resentment, madness—that regularly induce the implementation of violence. Here, too, the *Aeneid* is in the intellectual background, explicitly in Anchises' appeal in *Aeneid* 6 to Caesar and Pompey not to maim their fatherland through civil strife (and, of course, to Aeneas-Romanus to spare the downtrodden), and implicitly, in Aeneas' hesitation before killing Turnus.

The first segment of this dual study in threatened action and in efforts at restraint concerns Oedipus. The potential violence stems from his self-anger and consequent will to suicide, which is averted (yet also transmuted) by the piety felt toward him by his daughter Antigone. Three times Oedipus speaks of the *dolor* that drives him to suicide (156, 189, 207) and twice of the concomitant *ira* (163, 186). Already previously the father had marveled that someone with his history could have begotten a pious child (*aliquis est ex me pius?* 82). But it is only after further persuasion that Oedipus gives her a proper accolade:

> . . . sola tu affectus potes
> mollire duros, sola pietatem in domo
> docere nostra.
> (309–11)
> You alone can soften my hard heart, you alone can teach piety in our house.

Shortly later, during the play's other great act of counsel, Jocasta can refer, in juxtaposition, to the *pietas* (536) of Antigone and to Oedipus' self-directed wrath (*irati sibi . . . parentis*, 537–38).

The old king fully comprehends his impiety—he speaks of the impious death he caused his father (*impia nece*, 260)—as well as his daughter's devotion. But he can also treat the virtue with irony. In fact, he straightaway speaks of how the *pietas* that his sons feel for each other, a piety soon to be reified in civil war as Eteocles and Polynices prepare to kill one another, will redeem his impious act (*hoc alia pietas redimet*, 261). He will become an important spiritual source for this brutal strife. Though Antigone's gentleness deflects his thoughts away from his self-mutilation and suicide, it merely displaces his negative energies elsewhere. A father's wish for self-slaughter is transformed by his desire into the "suicide" of civil strife as brother ponders killing brother. Though the messenger bids him forgo his *dolor* (348), his wish is triumphant:

> tumet animus ira, fervet immensum dolor,
> maiusque quam quod casus et iuvenum furor
> conatur aliquid cupio.
>   (352–54)

My heart swells with rage, my resentment burns measurelessly, and I long for some crime more dreadful than what the casual madness of young men attempts.

To his earlier *ira* and *dolor* he has now added *furor*, a fury greater than youth can imagine but left for youth to bring to fruition.

Both Antigone and Oedipus have already anticipated his words. Daughter has given father a reason for living, in his duty to avert the menace of impious war (*impii belli*) that his maddened (*furentes*) offspring are threatening (290). Oedipus responds by admitting the anger (*ira*, 299) that drives them headlong and noting how "their hearts are mad with lust of empire" (*regno pectus attonitum furit*, 302). But it remains for Jocasta to attempt to forestall incipient war between her sons. Though she can debate her piety were she to choose one brother over the other (380–81), it is really the piety of the brothers themselves that is at stake, their piety toward her (409–10). As the messenger puts her task:

> I, redde amorem fratribus, pacem omnibus,
> et impia arma matris oppositu impedi.
>   (401–2)

Go, restore love to brothers, peace to us all, and let a mother be the barrier to stay unholy arms.

Thereafter she can appeal forthrightly to her sons' *pietas* (451, 455) and, in particular, ask the returning Polynices to sheath his impious sword (467). It is to him that she directs her most pointed questions:

> . . . tam ferus durum geris
> saevumque in iras pectus? et nondum imperas.
> quid sceptra facient? pone vesanos, precor,
> animi tumores teque pietati refer.
>   (582–85)

Are you so wild, is your heart so hard, so full of savage rage? And you not yet a king. What will the scepter do? Oh, I beseech you, allay the mad ferment of your soul, and come back to duty's ways.

In sum, the play offers us two powerful figurations of *pietas* positioned against those who are about to have recourse to the madness of force.

Much of the play's vitality depends on this incipience, with words attempting to work their calming influence over potential deeds. Antigone's piety toward her father is saving, the persuasiveness of Jocasta over her sons apparently bootless. We will never know whether the dialogue between Eteocles and his mother, with which the manuscripts close, is meant to be the play's actual ending, and several factors (not least the drama's brevity vis-à-vis the other seven Senecan tragedies) tell against such a view. But perhaps this is the only way the play could end, before the *odium* and *ira*, which figure so prominently in Eteocles' final long speech (656–58), take effect in physical action. *Ulterius ne tende odiis* (12.938) are Turnus' last words of prayer to his enemy. Aeneas, of course, does kill, and by having him so do Virgil leaves his reader with a multitude of unanswered, perhaps unanswerable, questions.

Seneca naturally need not even imply to his listeners what lies in store for the play's protagonists. Those schooled in any version of the *Seven against Thebes* would have already known the general outcome. But their familiarity with Virgil, as well as with the other dramas of Seneca *tragicus*, would have forewarned them of the particularity that *pietas*, finally, holds no sway when *ira*, *odium*, and *furor* are its opponents.[41]

Readers of *Phoenissae* hold their breath in anticipation of how those subject to madness will, or will not, be animated by their inner feelings. *Medea*, by contrast, traces how the abstractions we have been watching directly operate on the play's murderous protagonist.

Unlike its Euripidean model, the drama begins with a monologue by Medea that both anticipates the play's ending and announces its main themes. Her appeal to the goddesses of vengeance (*ultrices deae*, 13) only comes to final fruition as she dismisses them in preparation for killing her first child (967).[42] But already at the start sexual jealousy is her motivating force along with hatred of her deserting husband, and she openly hints that her means of revenge against the latter is in the fact that she has borne children—*parta iam, parta ultio est* (25).[43] Only at the end of her monologue does she name the prompting impulses whose elaboration delimits the play's unfolding. They are by now a familiar trio: *dolor* (49), this time more grievous than any she had experienced even when she killed her brother; *ira*, with which she prays to be girded as if she were a snake-enswathed Fury; and *furor totus*, all-encompassing madness. Resentment becomes anger, which in turn will succumb to a frenzy of action.

Medea's next meditation is on her crimes (*scelera*) for Jason's sake, *impia* because in part directed against a brother, nevertheless spurred by *amor*, not *ira* (136), which is new. She addresses her *dolor furiose*, which, whatever its intensity or purpose, cannot contemplate the death of Jason. Her nurse's advice is to dissemble her emotions in order to increase her chances of requital.[44] Medea replies that only a "slight resentment" (*levis dolor*, 155), not one of her intensity, can react positively to counsel. There follows a scene of supplication whose irony lies in its role reversal: Creon grants Medea a day's grace to prepare for exile when in fact she will profit from the delay to make him one of her first victims. Once again the nurse warns of the impetuosity of her wrath (381, 394) and of the *furor* (386, 392), now become *Furor* (396), which drives her charge toward the bestial and impious. Medea replies that her *odium* is now the equal of her love (397–98) and that her fury is beginning to take its practical turn (*in poenas*, 406), as her wrath continues on.

Jason enters, notices her emotional state,[45] and receives her second act of supplication, it, too, ironic. He rebuffs, out of piety, her appeal to hand over their children to accompany her into exile, ignorant that his refusal will soon precipitate their deaths. She responds likewise ironically: might she see her children for one last time and could he bring himself to forgive what she has said out of *dolor* (554) and *ira* (556)—and to remain blind just a while longer to the plans she will soon execute under the influence of these very emotions, the gist of which the audience already knows (549–50).

We now turn from analogies to deeds, to the implementation of revenge, first through Medea's magic (740–848).[46] As her sons take the poisoned robes that will inflame father, daughter, and their setting, the chorus naively remarks on how she seems to interweave love and anger in her stance (866–69).[47] What they do not realize is that love for Jason has been changed into hatred and that the fervor of her former passion has suffered transmutation into the intensity of vengeance. As she turns to herself, *furiose*, in inner monologue, it is to a heightened degree of anger that she appeals (902). Her wrath up to now, which had encompassed the deaths of Creon and his child, would seem mere *pietas* (905), that is, the absence or opposite of anger, by comparison with what is to follow.[48] The resentment that had driven her to commit crime on behalf of Jason was a mere introduction (*prolusit dolor*, 907),[49] a young girl's rage (*puellaris furor*, 909), by comparison to Medea's true potential (*dolor*, 914; *ira*, 916).

The fluctuations in her final debate are predictable, first between *ira* and *amor* (938),[50] then, most trenchantly, between *ira* and *dolor* on the one hand, *pietas* on the other:

> . . . ira pietatem fugat
> iramque pietas—cede pietati, dolor.
> (943–44)
> Anger puts piety to flight, and piety, anger. O wrath, yield to piety.

She does not, of course, follow her own warning and, as her madness rises to its peak, to *dolor* (951) and *ira* (953) she adds first *odium* and then, in place of climax, the Furies themselves, individually and in banded force.[51]

Allusion to the *Furiae* is the major addition here to Seneca's ordinary vocabulary of emotion, and their presence links Medea's self-scrutiny and subsequent execution of vengeance closely to the end of the *Aeneid*. When she shouts to the approaching horde:

> . . . fige luminibus faces,
> lania, perure, pectus en Furiis patet . . .
>   (965–66)
> Plunge your brands into my eyes, tear, burn; see my breast is open
> to the Furies . . .

we are beholding someone caught up in a situation not unlike Aeneas, *furiis accensus* as well as consumed by *dolor* and *ira*. It is no coincidence that at the moment before the killing of her first son she twice addresses her brother (967, 969) and asks him to be the instrument for her vendetta just as Aeneas twice proclaims Pallas as the executor of Turnus.[52] Nor can it be accidental that the implications of Virgil's word choice as Aeneas-Pallas prepares to bury his sword in his enemy's chest, *immolat*, are made explicit by Medea at the moment of murder itself: "with this offering we appease your shade" (*victima manes tuos / placamus ista*, 970–71). Both protagonists see their victims as human sacrifice and both, I would argue, misappropriate the claims of lesser allegiances—Aeneas toward Pallas, Medea toward Apsyrtus—in disregard for the deeper loyalties and emotional bonds of son to father or of mother to son, as they yield to fury's frenzy. Seneca's play expands into dramatic form the climactic moment in the *Aeneid* when the epic's hero offers his final, equivocal display of severity.

Nearly fifty lines elapse before Medea kills her second son at the conclusion of the play.[53] These extended performances of slaying constitute another of Seneca's major divagations from his Euripidean prototype. Again *ira* and *dolor* pepper the speakers' language, of Jason as he appeals for forbearance, of Medea as she plunges ungovernably ahead.[54] And when we finally reach the ending, after Jason's anguished, ironic prayer that she refrain from sparing not their son but only further delay, we have perhaps Seneca's most uncompromising, unrelenting finale with Medea heading heavenward in her father's chariot toward a realm where, in Jason's boldly bitter declaration, there are no gods.

Though four murders highlight its plot, *Medea* unfolds essentially as a confrontation of multivalent loyalties, with demand of vengeful wrath taking precedence finally over any claims of piety. *Phaedra* deals in these same abstractions but now Seneca seems to pause more to analyze them as palpable entities. Not only are they given form in the human characters whose bodies they control, they are also reified externally, grand

266

shapes that demonstrate the horrors which ordinarily lurk within our consciences and behind our motivations.[55]

Where Euripides begins his *Hippolytus* with Aphrodite's long prayer for revenge, Seneca's play commences with an eighty line monologue by Hippolytus on the marvels, and violence, of the hunt. We may wonder about his addiction to the brutalities of the chase, but if we have a suspicion that Seneca deliberately forced our memories to overlay his description of the chaste hero's penchant for savagery against nature upon the extended demand for vengeance that Euripides puts in Aphrodite's mouth, it may be well grounded.

Our next figuration of emotion is Phaedra, victim of *dolor* (99) because of her love for Hippolytus, *furens* (112) because, in her obsession, she too has taken to hunting. Though her nurse urges restraint, Phaedra twice acknowledges that *furor* rules her life (by contrast to *sana consilia* [180] and *ratio* [184]).[56]

In the dialogue that follows, we hear in the words of the *nutrix* the play's first supplication: so strong is Hippolytus' *odium* (238, *bis*) for her and for all women that she had best forswear her madness (*furorem siste*, 248; *siste furibundum impetum*, 263). When Phaedra threatens to commit suicide, her confidante makes a rapid volte-face, pressing her to accept *furor* over *fama* and promising to approach the wild youth on her behalf (268–69). The chorus, though insisting on love's *furor* (279, 343–44), implements her new argument with the claim that *odium* and *irae* regularly surrender to *amor* (354–55). The nurse then remarks further on her charge's *furor* (363) and *dolor* (366), as does the chorus (404), but prays, with many levels of irony, to Diana to aid in ensnaring the youth's savage turn of mind.[57] The virgin goddess may not perform the work of Aphrodite, but it will not be long before the hunter becomes the hunted, enmeshed in the trappings of his art and feelings.

Meantime Hippolytus enters, inveighing self-assuredly against the "madness of a greedy mind" (*avarae mentis furor*, 486) which would never touch the hunter in his sylvan paradise. As for early man, his edenic existence was threatened only after unholy madness for gain (*impius lucri furor*), headlong anger (*ira praeceps*), and lust (*libido*) made inroads into its perfection, and *dolor* caused the manufacture of arms (540–42, 549). He would seem to see the destructive aspects of *ira*, *dolor*, and *furor* largely in socioeconomic terms. But matters here too take an ironic turn. For Hippolytus the chief menace to the idyllic stability of human life is woman:

> Detestor omnis, horreo fugio execror.
> sit ratio, sit natura, sit dirus furor:
> odisse placuit.
> (566–68)

I abominate them all, I dread, shun, curse them all. Be it reason, be it
instinct, be it wild rage: it is my joy to hate them.

Whatever Hippolytus may claim, the hatred he cherishes has nothing
to do with *ratio* and everything with rabid ferocity. The nurse expresses
the confidence that love might alter such *odia* (575), but Hippolytus reconfirms his addiction to a continued hatred (*odisse*, 579). He carries within him, and therefore into his imagined world of the chase, a type of
anger and rage that is as personally destructive as the other categories of
irrationality which he imagines capable of shattering early man's arcadia.
Its presence may in fact explain the violence that we have seen him bring
to his self-chosen life apart.

The dialogue that follows between Phaedra and Hippolytus has no
counterpart in Euripides. Its power rests in large measure on the relationship of word and gesture, in this case carefully tactile. Phaedra enters (the
nurse again remarks on her *furor*, 584), faints, and then is lifted up in
Hippolytus' arms. Reviving she remarks on the renewal of her *dolor* (589),
and the remainder of the scene brings the gradual revelation that this
suffering is elicited not by the absent Theseus but by Hippolytus himself.[58] Her supplication—"yet again, proud creature, I grovel before your
knees" (703)—calls forth from Hippolytus an astonishingly graphic response:

> . . . etiam in amplexus ruit?
> stringatur ensis, merita supplicia exigat.
> en impudicum crine contorto caput
> laeva reflexi: iustior numquam focis
> datus tuis est sanguis, arquitenens dea.
> (705–9)

Even rush into my arms? Let my sword be drawn and exact due
punishment. Watch, with my left hand in her twisted hair I have
bent back her shameless head. Never has blood been more justly
spilled upon your altar, goddess of the bow.

Hippolytus holds her head back with his left hand and presumably
with his right menaces her with the sword which she then grasps and he
immediately throws away. The last time that we heard of right and left
hands at work was in Hippolytus' opening paean to the weaponry of the
hunt, which soon turned to praise of Diana and her bow (49–50, 72).
Here, in one of the play's climactic scenes, Hippolytus threatens partially
to repeat the pattern of the *Aeneid*'s final scene as he prepares, out of an
innate *odium* now concentrated on a single figure, to kill a suppliant and
to offer her as human sacrifice to his liege, the goddess of the hunt. As he
rushes from the stage, it is the last that we see of him alive.

At this point in Euripides' play Phaedra commits suicide offstage. Seneca's version of the myth saves her for a confrontation with the newly returned Theseus. If in the previous scene her *dolor* had nearly driven Hippolytus to murder, now it gradually provokes two acts of violence.[59] The first stems from her lies to Theseus about his son's conduct. These cause him first to inveigh against the "fury" of Hippolytus' Amazonian inheritance and its "hatred" of the laws of Venus,[60] then to appeal to his father Neptune for vengeance. The results we only learn from the messenger's detailed account of how a monster, sent by the sea god, terrified the horses of Hippolytus, which, entangling their master in their reins, dismembered his body and scattered it over the landscape.

There are no doubt many levels of significance to Neptune's beast, but Seneca himself makes one meaning explicit.[61] Learning after the fact of Phaedra's mendacity and his son's innocence, Theseus can address his father as "complaisant approver of my wrath" (*irae facilis assensor meae*, 1207). We are prepared for its present manifestation because anger had figured prominently in Theseus' emotional past. Previously in the play the nurse had spoken of the "savage hand" that he had used in anger to kill his first wife,[62] Antiope, and in her last speech Phaedra finds in *odium* (1167) his motivating agent for the earlier murder. The messenger's depiction of the monster's preparation for action twice singles out anger as the spark for the horror that follows.[63] Moreover readers of *De Ira* will recall that Seneca has no difficulty conjuring up a vivid personification of Anger (2.35.5).[64] We have here in *Phaedra* its extraordinary dramatic counterpart where Theseus' anger, vented in haste and evoking from his father an equally hurried response, rends apart his son just as an earlier seizure of rage had helped encompass the death of the boy's mother.

The monster's terrible havoc brings the play in part full circle. The hunter-killer has become the murdered prey. The topography that, at the drama's opening, defines Hippolytus' freedom for the chase becomes the extent of landscape from which the servants must gather his broadcast corpse. The bloody procession of victory that opens the play becomes the ironic triumph of Theseus' criminal anger (*ovantem scelere tanto*, 1206). In more detail, the knotted cords with which the hunter controlled his hounds are repeated in the deadly tightened reins, his capturing noose becomes the reins' strangling halter,[65] while we are reminded of the left and right hands with which he wielded his weaponry when these same members are listed among the limbs that must be gathered to help recompose his body (49, 1258–59).[66] The "many a wound" (*vulnere multo*) that early on distinguished the stalked boar becomes the lacerations that have destroyed Hippolytus' beauty (30, 1101, 1266). Put abstractly, the hatred of women that drives Hippolytus to use his energies in slaughterous triumph over the natural world and nearly to kill Phaedra as

human sacrificial offering to Diana has given place to Theseus' butcher-
ing anger whose embodiment succeeds in implementing its vicious purpose.

The second act of violence that Phaedra precipitates is her suicide.
Theseus summarizes the emotions that have ruled her actions throughout the play as she makes her final entrance:

> quis te dolore percitam instigat furor?
> (1156)
> What fury pricks you on, wild with grief?

The grief and rage that had earlier signalized her passion for Hippolytus
and her consequent vindictiveness when scorned, which ultimately
caused his death, she now turns against herself (1200).[67]

The play thus ends with two deaths, two bodies, two imminent buri-
als. Again, in typical Senecan fashion, we find no gratification in present
action, no redeeming glimpses into a more promising future. In Euripides there is at least the final moment of reconciliation between dying
son and grieving father. From Seneca we take only the remembrance of
the constant immanence of *ira, odium, dolor*, and *furor* in our passional
lives and of the devastation which they are capable of wreaking.

From the beginning of *Agamemnon* we are swept into an intricate
emotional world interwoven of loyalty and infidelity, of love, hate, and
madness performed against the backdrop of history's repetitious demands for vengeance and atonement.

The ongoing impetus of cycles of revenge is felt at the start as the ghost
of Thyestes, replacing Aeschylus' discursive watchman, predicts a new
wave of *scelera, dolus, caedes, cruor*, of criminal deceit and bloodshed, in
conjunction with a banquet where Clytemnestra's murderous feast for
her returning husband will exact satisfaction for the cannibalistic repast
set out for Thyestes by his brother Atreus. The emotional action begins
with the appearance of the queen herself who visualizes the events before
her as the triumph of "blind love" (*amore caeco*, 118) over such virtues as
righteousness, grace, and piety (112). (She draws an explicit analogy
between herself and Medea, *ardens impia face*, ablaze with impious love,
119). The chorus had already commented on how royal palaces are regularly subject to crime and "impious arms" (78–79), while the nurse in
response pleads for delay and draws the customary distinction between
consilium and *ratio* on the one hand (126, 130), *dolor* on the other (128).
Clytemnestra replies that *dolor*, because of the death of Iphigenia, as well
as lust rule her actions.[68] As she succinctly puts her situation:

quocumque me ira, quo dolor, quo spes feret,
hoc ire pergam; fluctibus dedimus ratem.
   (142–43)
Where wrath, where anguish, where hope will carry me, there will I
make my way. To the waves I have given my bark.

Though an animal without reins has been transformed into a rudder-
less boat as analogy for emotion unconstrained, nevertheless anger and
resentfulness make their regular appearance as goads into action for
Seneca's characters. Both emotions gain confirmation in what follows.[69]
Though she might momentarily seem to falter in her murderous resolve,
as she debates with Aegistheus, nevertheless the outcome reaffirms
Clytemnestra's vocation as cruenta Tyndaris (306), sister of Helen who
had murdered her husband during Troy's destruction. The designation is
recalled by Cassandra at the moment she sees wife butcher husband
(Tyndaris furens, 897).

The theme of sacrifice, especially human sacrifice, linked closely with
the complementary recurrences of punishment and expiation, had already been broached at line 163 when Clytemnestra recalls the immolation of Iphigenia as lustral offering (lustrale caput) by her father, ad aras, so
that Aulis could send forth Greece's impious fleet (173) toward Troy.
Clytemnestra will retaliate in kind, as the nurse asks in horror:

   . . . hunc domi reducem paras
   mactare et aras caede maculare impia?
      (218–19)
   Are you preparing to kill him upon return home and to defile the
   altars with impious slaughter?

A third allusion to sacrifice is added in the play's long middle section
devoted to Eurybates' description of the storm that struck the Greek
ships on their journey back. The gods raised their furor (576) against the
fleet to claim victims in propitiation for the "killings" of Troy:

   postquam litatam est Ilio, Phoebus redit
   et damna noctis tristis ostendit dies.
      (577–78)
   Now that atonement has been made for Ilium, Phoebus returns and
   sad day reveals the havoc of the night.

Seneca pointedly frames this central discourse by allusion to altars, the
arae that Eurybates greets on his arrival (392) and the great altars on
which Clytemnestra asks for a white victim to fall in hopes of regaining

the gods' grace: "and let a white victim fall before the altars" (*et nivea magnas victima ante aras cadat*, 585).

Shortly later, in the course of a dialogue with Cassandra, Agamemnon again becomes the specific focus of the poet's analogies. At 448 Eurybates, alluding to Pyrrhus' murder of Priam, had spoken of "Hercean Jove sprinkled with royal blood" (*sparsam cruore regis Herceum Iovem*). The point is picked up first in Cassandra's reference to the *arae* on which both her brother Polites and her father had died (700), then again in the brilliant stichomythia at 791–93 when Agamemnon announces, "This is a festal day," to which Cassandra replies, "At Troy too there was festivity." "Let us venerate altars" (*Veneremur aras*), answers Agamemnon, to which Cassandra with terse specificity responds, "My father fell before the altar" (*Cecidit ante aras pater*). When Agamemnon continues vaguely, "Let us pray together to Jove," her keen riposte is, "Hercean Jove?"

We have been prepared for the analogy between Priam and Agamemnon and therefore for the latter's death as victim given for victim— whether of the gods for Troy or of a mother for her (equally victimized) daughter—or merely as prey of lovers' madness. Already in the play's opening lines the shade of Thyestes had predicted that Agamemnon would soon offer his throat to his wife (43), and the prognostication resonates in the Trojan women's vivid memory of Priam's death:

> vidi, vidi senis in iugulo
> telum Pyrrhi vix exiguo
>   sanguine tingui.
>   (656–58)
> I saw, I saw in the old man's throat the sword of Pyrrhus scarcely dampened by his scanty blood.

As the fatal moment approaches, Agamemnon, like his model in Virgil, the priest-victim Laocoon, promises to offer sacrifice to Juno (806–7), but shortly later himself becomes the object sacrificed.

We see the event through Cassandra's eyes (875–76, 885). A banquet has been prepared like the feast of Troy's final night. (This, too, Thyestes had also predicted along with allusions to the horrible meal to which he was subjected and to his grandfather Tantalus' serving of his father Pelops to the gods [11, 21, 48].) Appropriately Agamemnon dons as clothing the "proud spoils of Priam" (*Priami superbas corpore exuvias gerens*, 880), and, as history repeats and reverses itself, the old king and his Troy gain their revenge when the maddened daughter of Tyndareus takes on the unlikely role of "priestess":[70]

qualisque ad aras colla taurorum prius
designat oculis antequam ferro petat,
sic huc et illuc impiam librat manum.
habet, peractum est.
  (898–901)
And as at the altars [the priest] marks with his eye the oxen's neck
before he strikes with the knife, so now here, now there, she poises
her impious hand. He has it, the deed is done.

The play has another potential sacrificial victim, the "furious" seer
Cassandra who, with deadly clarity of mind, predicts the presence of the
Furies at Agamemnon's imminent murder.[71] The chorus comments on
the end of her "ravings":

Iam pervagatus ipse se fregit furor,
caditque flexo qualis ante aras genu
cervice taurus vulnus incertum gerens.
relevemus artus.
  (775–78)
Now has her rambling frenzy spent itself, and falls, as before the altar
with sinking knees falls the bull, receiving an ill-aimed stroke upon
his neck. Let us lift up her body.

In Aeschylus' *Agamemnon* Cassandra is killed offstage before the action
ceases. It is a masterstroke on Seneca's part to leave her death still in
abeyance at the play's last line:

CL. Furiosa, morere. CA. Veniet et vobis furor.
  (1012)
Clytemnestra: Madwoman, you will die. *Cassandra*: A madness will
also fall to your lot.

We end with a double vision of madness and death. Fury encloses the line
as much as it grips the lives, and forespeaks the violent ends, of the
protagonists. Raving Cassandra will soon be sacrificed to the vengeance
of Clytemnestra and Aegistheus. But her madness will then find suitable
replacement in the insanity of Orestes who in turn will revenge both her
death and Agamemnon's by slaying his mother and her paramour.

Thus this most Virgilian of Seneca's tragedies both proceeds and ends
in ways that again demonstrate the shaping influence of the *Aeneid*'s
conclusion. The challenge of delay to doing as the soul debates,[72] the
enclosing, persistent presence of *ira*, *odium*, *furor* in counterpoint to
pietas, the (here pervasive) constancy of human sacrifice as part of tragic
action[73]—all stem from Virgil's formative influence. And once more our

expectations of any spiritual compensation for horrors witnessed are disappointed. *Furor* rules our imaginations as *Agamemnon* concludes, allowing us to anticipate, in typical Senecan fashion, not the possibility of family reconciliation but only the further abidingness, both in imminent prospect and on a more distant horizon, of violence and retribution.

A heritage of macabre banquets and the ironic complementarity of happy offerings to the gods with human sacrifice are major themes in *Agamemnon*. They form the central thread of our last play, *Thyestes*, but again the types of emotionality we have been tracing in all the tragedies of Seneca are strands of cohesion woven through the whole.

We begin with a dialogue between the shade of Tantalus and Furia who commands:

> Perge, detestabilis
> umbra, et penates impios furiis age.
> certetur omni sceleri et alterna vice
> stringatur ensis; nec sit irarum modus
> pudorve, mentes caecus instiget furor . . .
> (23–27)
> Onward, damned shade, and goad your impious hearth with the furies' madness. Let it vie with every form of crime and let the sword be drawn on this side and on that; let there be no limit to anger, no shame, let blind fury incite their souls . . .[74]

The representation of *furor* is complemented by her personification of *ira*:

> . . . nihil sit ira quod vetitum putet . . .
> (39)
> Let there be nothing which anger considers unallowed . . .

Yet *ira* here, and the *odia* to which she soon refers (52), are essentially subservient to Fury's brooding presence, her grand comprehensive role as dramatized metaphor of human passion.[75] As such she is parallel, if we turn to the *Aeneid*'s conclusion, not to the Dira who embodies Jupiter's enmity and causes the isolation and, ultimately, humiliation of Turnus, but to those *furiae* that operate from within Aeneas' inflamed soul.

The plot begins in earnest with the appearance of Atreus who styles himself *iratus* (180). His attendant, paralleling the role of the nurse in *Agamemnon*, urges the restraint of *pietas* (216), whereupon the conversation evolves toward a distinction between *pietas* (248–49) and Furiae, Erinys and Megaera (250–52), and then, as Furia's opening address might lead us to expect, to the attribution of *furor* (253), *dolor* (255, 258, 274), and *ira* (259) to Atreus as his primary motivations for action.[76]

After a chorus commenting on the *furor* that inheres to the house of
Inachus, Thyestes enters with his three sons. His presence gives Atreus
the chance, in an aside, to recall his *odia* (494), *dolor* (496), now reinless
and compared to an Umbrian hound whose scent of prey overwhelms all
attempts at restraint, and *ira*. To his brother's face he voices an opposite
set of values:

> . . . quidquid irarum fuit
> transierit; ex hoc sanguis ac pietas die
> colantur, animis odia damnata excidant.
> (509–11)
> Let anger give place, a thing of the past; from this day let ties of
> blood and loyalty be cherished, let cursed hatred vanish from our
> hearts.

Thyestes, in trusting belief, prays that Atreus' obvious *pietas* (515) be a
sign that all anger (519) has left his thoughts, and as pledge offers his
children to Atreus' care, grasping his brother's knees in supplication. The
chorus, with corresponding naiveté, takes note in amazement of Atreus'
true piety (549) and remarks sententiously that, even when anger leads
men to the brink of war, *Pietas*, now grandly personified, will restore
them, however reluctant, to the hands of peace.[77] Whether such words be
spoken in truth or in deception, the opinion they voice is held consis-
tently throughout Seneca's works, either philosophical or dramatic.
Pietas and *ira* cannot operate in any one person contemporaneously.
They are opposites, and the one excludes the other.

The same antithesis pervades the messenger's recounting of Atreus'
ghastly vengeance. As he greedily eyes his young charges prior to putting
his plans into effect, we hear of his *impia ira* (712–13). The boy named
Tantalus in honor of his grandfather is the first to be murdered—lest you
think *pietas* be absent during the moment of slaying, says the reporter in
irony (717). As the spate of slaughter continues on, so do Atreus' anger,
ferocity, and fury.[78] But murder marks only half his vendetta, and here the
nuntius pauses to remark, as does Medea at a parallel moment in her
criminal progress, that Atreus' conduct up to now might be deemed
pious in comparison to what follows (745).[79] But even as he proffers his
brother a meal of the latter's children, his anger remains unsatiated because he had failed to pour the hot blood of the youths down Thyestes'
throat (1056), and his *dolor* (1066) is cheated because father and sons were
ignorant of what had happened to them.[80]

Save for the Oedipus plays, human sacrifice, as we have seen, is an
important literal and metaphoric theme in Senecan drama. Nowhere is it
more a focal element in the plot, more intimately conjoined to impiety or

more crucially implicated with *ira* and *dolor* that initiate tragic action and with *saevitia* and *furor* that expedite its resolution, than in *Thyestes*. We find here an element of the hideously grotesque missing even in *Agamemnon*. There the victim is metaphorically sacrificed while at a banquet, suitable enough setting for the heir of Tantalus and Atreus. In *Thyestes* the victims are not only seen as sacrificial offerings, they become in fact themselves the ghastly meal itself subsequently dispensed as ritual's festive accompaniment.

The tradition within which Atreus will operate stems, as the chorus presciently notes early on, from Tantalus' victimization of Pelops (144–48), and it is to his father and grandfather that he alludes as he asks his attendant for advice:[81]

> Profare, dirum qua caput mactem via.
> (244)
> Tell me in what manner I could bring ruin on Thyestes' wretched head.

Macto here means "afflict" or "vex." But since its most common meaning is "slay sacrificially," just beneath the surface, in Seneca's choice of words, is the suggestion: "How might I offer sacrifice in such a way as to torment Thyestes most."

The working out of the pattern begins at 544–45 as Atreus, with marked ambiguity in his phrasing, places the crown of rule on Thyestes' brow:

> Imposita capiti vincla venerendo gere;
> ego destinatas victimas superis dabo.
>
> Wear this bond, placed on your revered head; I will present the destined victims to the gods above.

The ritual of sacrifice itself begins at 682 where, in a dismal sequestered grove, according to the messenger's report, "altars were decked out" (*ornantur arae*, 684). Nothing is lacking. We have sacred wine and instrument to kill, visualized in a powerful series of metonymies:

> tangensque salsa victimam culter mola.
> servatur omnis ordo, ne tantum nefas
> non rite fiat.
> (688–90)
> ... and knife, touching the victim with salted meal. All (ritual) order is respected, lest so great a crime not be duly achieved.[82]

"He himself is the priest" (*Ipse est sacerdos*, 691), continues the messenger, he the one who makes certain that "no part of the sacred rite is left undone" (*nulla pars sacri perit*, 695). At the moment of slaughter

> . . . quem prius mactat sibi
> dubitat, secunda deinde quem caede immolet.
> (713–14)
> he hesitates within himself whom first to sacrifice, whom next to immolate in his second slaying.[83]

Tantalus is the first victim (*hostia*, 718), but all three children are given the same label at 759 and again at 915, though the word is ordinarily reserved for animal sacrifice. All in all, though frustrated in the last of his grisly maneuverings, nevertheless Atreus has accomplished much:

> . . . ferro vulnera impresso dedi,
> cecidi ad aras, caede votiva focos
> placavi, et artus, corpora exanima amputans,
> in parva carpsi frusta . . .
> (1057–60)
> With deep-driven sword I gave [them] their wounds, I slew them at the altars. I appeased the sacred fires with votive blood, and, hewing their lifeless bodies, I tore their limbs into small scraps.

And once more we have an ending that grants us no sense of spiritual relief in the foreclosing of horror, no feeling that abnormality is the exception rather than the rule, no easing of our pain, here in the presence of mutual affliction given and received.[84] We end with a dialogue between brothers:

> *TH.* Vindices aderunt dei;
> his puniendum vota te tradunt mea.
> *AT.* Te puniendum liberis trado tuis.
> (1110–12)
> *Thyestes*: The gods will be present to avenge; my prayers deliver you to them for punishment. *Atreus*: To your sons I deliver you for punishment.

Never were words more a mimicry of action nor dialogue more anticipatory of the physical horror it announces as ongoing or to come, to be perpetrated by and on its protagonists. Verbal sparring prepares for a continuance of suffering when the poet's lines have ended. Thyestes intones a future vendetta but Atreus has the last word, reminding us that

Thyestes must now endure constantly the vengeance Atreus has wreaked since he survives as living tomb for his dead children.

As for the *vindices dei*, the equally riveting ending of *Medea* had reminded us that there were no gods, at least gods as Seneca the philosopher might have us know them, with an interest in rewarding virtue and punishing vice. Rather here Seneca the dramatist, masterful student of our irrational side, may wish us to imagine not external, model divinities to whom we pray and offer sacrifice but the inner demons who drive us, in whatever manner, to indulge unethical rituals and to dispense ruthless hurt for the sake of retribution. These are the immortal creatures of our spirit's madness who we sense will flourish after the curtain has been raised on Seneca's troubling, truthful words.[85]

My goal in this essay has been to illustrate how the impact on Seneca of one particular moment in Virgil's epic, its conclusion, which must serve as summation of its hero's ethics of behavior, was particularly emphatic. Many of the major themes of the epic's last lines recur, in a variety of metamorphoses, throughout Senecan drama and propel its plot line—jealousy, often with sexual response at its base, as instigation for final vengeance; the regular adjacency of supplication with the wielder of power's hesitation between clemency and vengefulness before yielding to violence;[86] the debate between *pietas* and *ira*, restraint and emotional ferocity, in choosing a course of action, the constant presence of *dolor* and *furor* as that action evolves to its brutal conclusion, and the focus on human sacrifice as a fundamental element in the dynamics of reprisal.

My sense is that one of the more general aspects of the *Aeneid*'s finale that most impressed Seneca's imagination is its negative open-endedness, especially vis-à-vis the epics of Homer and Apollonius Rhodius. There is little if anything about Aeneas' furious slaughter of a suppliant hero become victim, whose soul departs indignant toward the shades, to recommend that we envisage a golden future soon to dawn after the poem's dark termination.

Rather, the manner in which Seneca understood the *Aeneid*'s denouement is, I have suggested, a way that should be equally persuasive to the modern reader of the epic. Whether we conclude with *Phaedra*'s two bodies, one mangled, the other execrated at burial, or with the *Dolor* of *Oedipus*[87] or *Agamemnon*'s double *furor*, whether it be murderess Medea's triumphant withdrawal into a heaven without gods or two brothers cursing each other with ever persisting reprisals, there is little or nothing to relieve suffering and everything to suggest its continuance. Likewise the poet spreads no halcyon future before us at the *Aeneid*'s end, and certainly no vision of a celestial rose or, for our repentant progenitors, of a "World before them . . . with Providence their guide." The gods of the

Aeneid may in their discourse speak of a future moment with man's *Furor* enchained or with their own *ira* forgone, but the poem's human present, especially the present figuring in, and anticipated by, the poem's last lines, tells an opposite tale. Its substance is one with which Seneca was in full sympathy.

But a final word of qualification is in order on the question of genre. What Seneca found enthralling in Virgil's poem was not the public authority, "something greater than the *Iliad*," in Propertius' contemporary appraisal, which it projects. During the unfolding of the immediate narrative and when future Roman action is adumbrated, Virgil provides, through the apparatus of divinity and through the *dicta* of paternal guidance, a framework that, ideally, should offer his hero a pattern for the control of violence in the present and set proper limitations to future uses of force. The moral excellence of history's protagonists, now and in an era of Augustan peace to come, is a goal that the poet elaborates for us on several crucial occasions. If human emotionality holds sway at the poem's conclusion, nevertheless throughout the poem it remains in counterpoint with gestures of temperateness and to stated expectations of restraint as Roman *imperium* evolves beyond the epic's time frame. Greek tragedy also regularly finds its heroes in search of ways to ameliorate their lot as they struggle against misfortune and evil, even inner evil. From this point of view Virgilian ideology continues and sustains the interpretative tradition of fifth-century drama stemming from Aristotle.

The contrast that in this regard the plays of Seneca offer both Greek tragedy and Virgilian epic is multivalent and ironic. The emotionality of the *Aeneid*'s ending is, for all its prominence, but a single moment, a sudden yielding by the hero to his passional side that previously, save in books 2 and 10, he had largely kept in check, and the protagonists of Greek tragedy habitually find the confidence to endure or master the evil which fortune brings. In the world of Senecan drama, self-enclosed as it is spiritually (and confined as it may well have been in public presentation), evil, usually self-generated, holds complete sway. The limitations to passion so strong in the Greek tragedians and so carefully suggested by Virgil's narrator to his heroes are constantly sprung by Seneca for whose dramatis personae evil regularly wells up without stint from within to help configure a series of monstrosities in human form.

The impetus toward violence that Virgil would have his characters moderate is, in Seneca, relentlessly pressed to an extreme. *Medea nunc sum.* For Seneca, as for Lucan, writing under Nero, passion's essential definition is its boundlessness.

Seneca the philosopher used his *maximus vates* largely for illustration, to augment, challenge, or merely adorn a text. Seneca the dramatist drew on something deeper in Virgil's art. However much, as philosopher,

Seneca owed to Stoic theorizing on the passions, as poet his greater debt is to the stylistic representation of emotionality that he discovered in Virgil.

Virgil not only offered Seneca the *exempla* of heroes yielding to un-bridled violence but the lexical means by which he could texture so intensely the unleashing of tragic destructiveness. Seneca's "reading" of the *Aeneid* follows in the line of superbly differentiated acceptances of the epic by Propertius, Horace, and Ovid. His is a more partial as well as, appropriately, a more passionate critique than those his predecessors advance. It construes as all-embracing for humanity what is only the *Aeneid*'s final truth: that political heroes in action base their lives on violence, not forgiveness, that history is germinated by individual emo-tionality, not collective restraint. There is no bow to a post-*Aeneid* renun-ciation of *furor* and *ira* which the late Horace finds operative, in his final collection of odes, nor do we encounter the panegyric of Augustus, which not long thereafter Ovid, in the *Metamorphoses*, both proclaims and brilliantly undermines. Instead we find Seneca reiterating in play after play evidence of man's destructiveness as if he felt that his role as inter-preter of Virgil's poem lay in insisting upon vital aspects of the epic which eulogists of empire and emperors would shunt aside or, at best, under-value.

Why, we may ask in conclusion, did he opt, of all genres, for drama to serve as counterpoint to his philosopher's prose? Why was it through the stage that he could best give shape to his own deepest thoughts on human nature and re-present Virgil's? Presumably any genre was avail-able to him, but lyric, for example, would have been too directly personal and therefore too perversely in opposition to the philosopher's solilo-quizing, authoritative "I." Were he to have chosen epic on whatever topic, he would have had to cope with Virgil's puissant legacy, which is to say with the *Aeneid*'s admixture of idealism and with the immediately contemporizing effect of its function as allegory. Rather it was drama, a genre dependent upon the universality of myth's paradigm with models drawn primarily from fifth-century Greece, that best served his purposes. Only through myth's combination of temporal remoteness with univer-sal applicability and through the drama's confrontational mien, where provocations, hesitations, and responses illustrate the ethical dilemmas of the private individual caught up in life's emotional thickets, could he compose an imaginative foil to philosophy's perfecting road of conver-sion and conviction. Philosophy's (finally) dogmatic, professorial speaker, though fully cognizant of the moral pitfalls ever dotting the path of humankind, preaches to his students the ideal, invariable schemata of what ought to be. Drama, especially Seneca's dramatizations of passions evolving within the intense framework of theatrical time, with their powerful probings into man's spirit as it analyzes and responds to its sufferings, exposes its reader-viewers to what we all experience together, to life's many voices, to what, in fact, truly is.

Donatus' vita of Virgil tells us that, had he lived on beyond September of 19 B.C., after completing the *Aeneid*'s polish, he would have wished to pass the remainder of his life in the study of philosophy.[88] But his epic is already, in the deepest sense, a philosophical poem. It soon helped furnish Seneca with the quintessence of his tragic poetry, the most authentically human and the most deeply visionary of the philosophical writings which he devised for our contemplation.

NOTES

I would like to thank Professor John Petruccione for his helpful critique of an earlier draft of this essay.

1. I list here standard essays on the criticism of Senecan drama-
    turgy which, though often cited in the notes, deserve to head
    any study of the tragedies: Eliot, "Seneca" and "Shakespeare";
    Regenbogen, "Schmerz und Tod"; Herington, "Senecan Trag-
    edy" and "Younger Seneca."
       In the interest of concision I have eliminated discussion of
    Oedipus and a survey of the beginnings of the six Senecan trag-
    edies, for which we have fifth-century prototypes, in relation to
    their Greek counterparts. This material can be found in the
    fuller version of the essay, cited on the page of acknowledg-
    ments.

2. For Seneca and earlier poetry, see Maguinness, "Seneca" 81–98;
    Mazzoli, *Seneca*; Dingel, *Seneca* and "Senecas Tragödien" 1052–
    99. Most of the commentators on individual plays cited in subse-
    quent notes have introductory sections devoted to Seneca's use
    of previous poets.

3. On Seneca's use of Virgil in his prose works see Wirth, *De Vergili*;
    Doppioni, *Virgilio*, with a valuable index of *loci citati* (201-S);
    Lurquin, *Citations*.

4. See especially Tarrant, "Senecan Drama" 213–63, for a survey of
    Seneca's inheritance from Hellenistic as well as fifth-century and
    earlier Roman drama, with a particular emphasis on matters of
    technique.

5. For Virgil's influence on Senecan tragedy, see ter Haar Romeny,
    De auctore; Runchina, "Tecnica" 163–324, especially 184–88, 206–
    7, 218–23; Fantham, "Virgil's Dido" 1–10.
       On the need for further study of the relationship between
    Virgil and Seneca's tragedies see, most recently, Seidensticker
    and Armstrong, "Seneca Tragicus" 916–88, in particular 923–24,
    where the authors lament the absence of investigations of the
    influence of Augustan poetry on Seneca "at a level more pro-
    found than merely philological or verbal"; Boyle, "Nature's
    Bonds" 1284–1347, especially 1338 and n. 105: "The relationship
    between Virgil and Seneca seems generally and profoundly mis-
    understood." For Boyle, "Seneca, not Lucan is [Virgil's] great
    Neronian successor."

6. It does not need recording again, to take *Agamemnon* as instance,
    how the description of the storm faced by the returning Greek

ships draws heavily on Virgil's lines early in the epic on the chaos which Juno elicits against Aeneas from Aeolus and his winds, or how much of the vitality of *Troades* stems from the reader's detailed knowledge of Virgil's brilliant staging of Troy's demise in *Aeneid* 2.

For the first cf., e.g., Tarrant, *Agamemnon* 248 and, on lines 466–69, 471; for the second, Fantham, *Troades* 214 on lines 41–45.

7. Others would argue that the ending is properly rounded off because both the hero's rage and the death of his opponent are justified. The most recent discussion favoring the righteousness of Aeneas' act is by Galinsky, "Anger of Aeneas" 321–48. That Turnus must die, largely because of flaws in his nature, and that therefore Aeneas' fury is warrantable, is the thesis of Stahl, "Death of Turnus." I have argued opposite points of view in chapter 9.

8. I give an emphasis antithetical to the largely eulogistic tone Virgil is perceived as adopting by Hardie, *Cosmos and Imperium* passim.

9. Williams, *Technique and Ideas*, by maintaining that Anchises here "addresses himself not to Aeneas but specifically to Romans" (208) and that therefore his words have no applicability to his son's future conduct, dispenses too readily with one of the most significant questions Virgil's readers must pose to themselves from that moment on: How are we expected to respond to Aeneas in his role as *tu . . . Romane* during the last six books and especially at its last moments? See further my "Review" 230.

10. 11.354, 11.376, 12.9, 12.45. For *violentia* as a speaker's trait cf., e.g., Quint. *IO* 2.12.11 and 11.1.3, and the example of Antiphanes in Quintus Curtius Rufus 7.1.16.

11. Virgil associates the adjective *superbus* directly with Turnus on three occasions (12.326, as well as the two instances mentioned later). Turnus' arrogance is well discussed by Williams, *Aeneid 7–12* on 10.439f.

12. The narrator's exclamation on Turnus' lack of *modus* is at 501–2.

13. Cf., e.g., Galinsky, "Anger of Aeneas" n. 9, 344.

14. *Furentibus austris* (51); *iras* (57).

15. *Furit aestus* (107); *irae* (130).

16. *Saevit* (149); *furor* (150).

17. "His love of the sword rages and the criminal madness of war" (*saevit amor ferri et scelerata insania belli*).

18. Servius on 12.940.

19. Cf. also 1.251–53 where Venus contrasts Juno's *ira* with Aeneas' *pietas*.

20. Bailey, *Religion* 285. He continues "for human sacrifice is unknown at any rate in the developed Roman religion."

21. Virgil, of course, does not show us Aeneas slaughtering his victims, as Homer does Achilles. Aeneas' direct killing of a human offering is saved for the epic's final climax.

22. The order in which I discuss the plays follows that of the Latin text also used in this essay, the Oxford Classical Text by Zwierlein, which in turn adheres to the arrangement of codex E (Etruscus).

The most recent attempt to list the plays in order of composition is that of Fitch, "Sense-Pauses" 289–307, who, basing his chronology on the relative occurrences of strong sense-pauses within the line and on a progression toward the freer shortening of final *o* in certain types of words, sees three groupings: 1, *Agamemnon, Phaedra, Oedipus*; 2, *Medea, Troades, Hercules Furens*; 3, *Thyestes, Phoenissa*. Cf. also ibid., *Hercules Furens* 53.

His arguments have been discussed and generally accepted by later editors. Cf. Fantham, *Troades* 14; Tarrant, *Thyestes* 10–13; Coffey and Mayer, *Phaedra* 4–5.

23. Fitch, *Hercules Furens* 117, sees the "primary model" of Juno's speech in Ovid *M.* 2.512–30, where the goddess dwells on her jealousy, Jupiter's misdemeanors, etc., but is fully aware of Virgil's strong presence as well (see, e.g., his comments on 28b–29, p. 131).

24. Cf. Herington, "Senecan Tragedy" 452, on Hercules as his own hellish fury.

25. As the drama's most recent commentator, John Fitch, writes (*Hercules Furens*, 36): "it is the continuing harshness of Hercules' character, and the conflict and pain which result from it, that remain dominant throughout the [final] act. Such an ending is absolutely typical of Seneca's practise as a tragedian."

26. Fitch, *Hercules Furens* 39.

27. 918–24: *victima* (922); *mactari* (923). Cf. *mactetur hostis* (*hostia*, Leo) (634).

28. Cf. further Fitch, *Hercules Furens* 386, on 1036–38.

29. For reason of manuscript authority alone, the reading *furiis* is to be preferred to *furis*.

30. The word is strongly placed, in enjambment at the start of the line but at the end of the sense unit. It is our last vision of Aeneas, "boiling hot" with emotion, before we look in conclusion to dying Turnus' limbs undone with cold (*solvuntur frigore*, later in the same line).

31. Servius on 8.728: "[Araxes] cui Alexander magnus pontem fecit, quem fluminis incrementa ruperunt. postea Augustus firmiore ponte eum ligavit, unde ad Augusti gloriam dixit 'pontem indignatus Araxes.'" Hardie, *Cosmos and Imperium* 208, argues that "the bridging of the Araxes provides the final answer to the threat of natural violence first represented in the storm of book 1." But, if we follow up Servius' observation, who is to say that Caesar will be, or even has the right to be, any more successful in taming a river's nature than his Hellenistic idol? And what of human nature?

32. Cf. Fitch, *Hercules Furens* 18–20, 23–24, 39, 41 n. 52, and 43, for further details on parallelisms Seneca elsewhere finds among Hercules, Alexander, Pompey, Julius Caesar, and Augustus.

33. This public display of brutality is an important parallel with the last scene of the *Aeneid*.

34. *Ferrum* (12.950).

35. Cf. especially lines 692–94, 709, and 733, to be compared with *Aen.* 12.930–34.

36. Cf. Pyrrhus' earlier allusion to Achilles' treatment of Telephus (217–18) with a hand that was at once strong and gentle (*fortem . . . et mitem*).

In various guises the collocation of might and mercy to describe Augustus and his Rome becomes nearly a commonplace in contemporary poetry (Prop. 2.16.41–42, 3.22.21–22; Ovid *Am.* 1.2.51–52). Cf. also *H.F.* 404–5 and *Octavia* 858.

37. *Theatri more*, 1125.
38. The last detail is from *Aen.* 2.557. For the sacrifice at the altars, cf. 2.513–14, 550.
39. Agamemnon's sacrifice of Iphigenia is always in the background here (248–49, 331, 555).
40. Cf. Fantham, *Troades* 18, on Seneca's "lack of a conciliatory ending."
41. There are far more uses (14) of words concerned with piety, relative to number of lines, in *Phoenissae* than in any other play of Seneca (the nearest is *Thy.* with 13). This is equally true for vocabulary of weaponry. (The relationship of Seneca's play to the *Phoenissae* of Euripides, especially given the former's very Roman emphasis on *pietas*, deserves separate study.)
42. Other examples of circular unity are the references to the chariot of Medea's father (32, 1025) as well as the branding of the murder of her brother as a mere girlish act (49, 909).
43. Cf. also 50.
44. *Dolor* (151), *ira* (153), *odia* (154), *furialem impetum* (157).
45. *Iratam* (444), *furit* (445), *odia* and *dolor* (446).
46. Before this the nurse once again remarks on her *dolor* (671) and on her furious appearance (*furentem*, 673).
47. They have already noted her uncontrolled *furor* (851–52) and *ira* (853).
48. Cf. *Thy.* 744–45.
49. Cf. *Phaedra* 1061.
50. Cf. also her previous reference to *ira* (927) and apostrophe to *demens furor* (930).
51. Erinys (953), Megaera (963), *turba Furiarum* (958), *Furiis* (966).
52. Cf. also 964.
53. The killing occurs between lines 1018 and 1019. The play ends at 1027.
54. 989, 1011, 1016, 1019.
55. The word *corpus*, e.g., occurs far more frequently in *Phaedra* than in any other Senecan drama; 17 uses versus 9 in *H.F.*, *Oed.*, *Aga.*, and *Thy.*
56. In what follows the nurse speaks of *furens libido* (195–96, if we accept the reading of E), and of *furor* as an unreal divinity. Cf. Segal, *Language and Desire* 45, on the apotheosis of *Furor* at 184.
57. *Ferum* (414); *innecte* (416).
58. *Furis* (645); *dolori* (670).
59. *Dolor*: in general (851), Phaedra's in particular (859).
60. *Furor* (909); *odisse* (910).
61. Segal, *Language and Desire* 75, sees the beast as a symbol of the distorted sexuality of Phaedra and Hippolytus.
62. *Saevam manum* (227); *coniugem iratum* (228).
63. *Iras parat* (1059); *prolusit irae* (1061).
64. Cf. Herington, "Senecan Tragedy" 442, and Coffey and Mayer, *Phaedra* 26, on Seneca and the physical symptoms of anger. The animality of anger and its constant need to be reined in are regular Senecan themes (e.g., *Aga.* 114, 203; *Thy.* 496; *Medea* 591–92, 866).
65. *Nodo . . . liga* (36–37); *nodos ligat* (1087); *laqueus*: 45, 76, 1086. Cf. the noose with which Phaedra threatens suicide (259).
66. The macabre details of the collection of Hippolytus' scattered limbs find no parallel in Euripides.

67. It is not fortuitous that, shortly before falling on her sword, Phaedra addresses Neptune as *profundi saeve dominator freti* (1159), as if to implicate Theseus' monstrous anger also in her death, which her last words see as a sacrifice to Hippolytus (1198).

68. *Dolor* (133); *cupido* (135).

69. *Dolet* (162); *ira* (261).

70. Zwierlein posits a lacuna between *oculis* and *antequam*.

71. Furies: 759–68; *furor*: 199, 720, 801, 869, 872, 1012.

72. Cf. 131, 192–95, 228.

73. It is noteworthy that the word *ira* occurs twelve times in *Agamemnon*, far more than in any other of Seneca's tragedies.

74. Cf. her allusion to the *furor* of Tantalus at 101. We recall the divination of *Furor* at *Phaedra* 184.

75. Cf. Tarrant, *Thyestes* 85 and n. 2. It would be wrong, I think, to press too far any resemblance between the *Furia* and Juno at the opening of *Hercules Furens*. Juno stands there as a character in her own right with her own parti pris. Her presence finally causes *furiae* to mushroom within Hercules with horrifying results. Here she is at once both the outside provocateur of action and its inner stimulus as well.

76. Cf. 259 (and 286) where his final weapon, or at least his final agent, according to Atreus, is Thyestes himself (*ipso Thyeste*). Seneca would perhaps have us think of Hercules as victim of his own madness (*H.F.* 85 et al.).

77. 552 (*ira*); 559 (*pietas*).

78. *Ira*: 735, 737; *saevitia*: 737, and cf. 743; *furor*: 739.

79. Cf. *Medea* 904–5. The difference lies in the fact that Medea's past impiety was exercised against her brother and against Pelias and his daughters, and therefore might be said to be of lesser criminality than her contemplated murder of her children. Atreus' impiety has only one goal but its achievement is divided into two parts, the second even more ghoulish than the first.

  Nevertheless in these two plays the confrontation of *ira* and *pietas* is more central an issue than in any other of the tragedies.

80. *Dolor* is a hideous part of Thyestes' own reaction as he eats (944, 968, 1003) and it continues on after the fact (1098, 1104).

81. Tantalus and Pelops are mentioned at 242.

82. The weapon stands in for its wielder who would ordinarily throw the sacred grain, touching momentarily softens stabbing, and the meal replaces the instrument's sharp edge.

83. The only other uses of *immolo* in Seneca *tragicus* are at *Tr.* 249 and 331.

84. Cf. the cogent summation of Tarrant, *Thyestes* 243, on line 1112.

85. See the eloquent comments of Segal, *Language and Desire* 105, on the question posed at *Phaedra* 184: "What power might reason have?" (*Quid possit ratio?*) and his summary judgment (8): "Senecan tragedy . . . goes beyond even the Greek and Elizabethan in projecting cosmic monstrosity as an image of immersion in self-destructive evil." Herington, "Younger Seneca" 522, offers a similar appraisal: "each of the Senecan tragedies, viewed as a whole, will make coherent sense as a concentrated study in one or more of the elemental terrors which ever threaten to disrupt human existence: omnipresent death, the passions, guilt voluntary and

involuntary, and political tyranny. Each is pervaded from end to end by an appalling aura of *evil*" (emphasis in original).

86. In the case of *Troades*, the acts of brutality are described as happening before an audience of bystanders and not simply as witnessed by the participating characters of the play.

87. For Regenbogen, "Schmerz und Tod" 193, the words of the nurse in [pseudo-Seneca] *Hercules Oetaeus* (252–53), describing the many shapes of anguish in Deianira's conduct—*formas dolor / errat per omnes* (anguish roams through every form [of life])—could stand for the complex configurations of passion throughout the authentic dramas of the playwright.

88. *Vita Donati* 35 in Hardie, *Vitae Vergilianae* 14.

VIRGIL'S

INFERNO

. . . Look, how the floor of heaven
Is thick inlaid with patines of bright gold.
There's not the smallest orb, which thou behold'st,
But in his motion like an angel sings,
Still quiring to the young-eyed cherubims;
Such harmony is in immortal souls:
But, whilst this muddy vesture of decay
Doth grossly close it in, we cannot hear it.
  SHAKESPEARE
  Merchant of Venice 5.1.58–65

  for within him hell
He brings, and round about him, nor from hell
One step no more than from himself can fly
By change of place . . .
  MILTON
  Paradise Lost 4.20–23

In the tenth canto of *Inferno*, where heretics are punished for their incontinence, Dante the pilgrim meets Cavalcante de' Cavalcanti who, weeping, asks concerning his poet son:

"... Se per questo cieco
carcere vai per altezza d'ingegno,
mio figlio ov'è? e perché non è teco?"
  (10.58–60)
"If you go through this blind prison by reason of high genius, where
is my son, and why is he not with you?"

The questions are fraught with richly Virgilian reminiscences, which make the moment metapoetic. Dante wants his reader to draw a parallel between Cavalcante and Andromache who, encountering Aeneas in Epirus, wonders in near delirium whether he is living or dead and, if dead, why has Hector himself not come in answer to her prayers (*Aen.* 3.310–12). But it is the phrase *cieco carcere* that most interests me.[1] For Dante, whether pilgrim or poet, the Underworld experience allegorizes our sinful life. The pilgrim's wandering through a *selva oscura*, his *cammino alto e silvestro*, is an analogy of our tainted journey through life, and the prison, both literally dark and morally blind, in which the eternally guilty are penned, signifies as well our confinement within the emotionality of ordinary existence.[2]

Dante adopts the phrase from the sixth book of the *Aeneid* at the poem's most metaphysical moment. Anchises is expounding the origin of life to his son who has ventured into the Underworld to find him and to learn of Rome's future. The spiritual side of man, the constructing seeds of his being, explains Aeneas' father, is fiery and would be instinctively heaven-bent were it not weighted down by bodies that do us harm, by the sluggishness of our moribund limbs. It is because we are physical entities that we are passion-ridden, that we fear, desire, grieve, or rejoice, closed, as we are, within our corporeal blackness as if in a sightless dungeon (*clausae tenebris et carcere caeco*, *Aen.* 6.734).[3]

This allegorical reading of the *Inferno* as emblematic of life's "dark prison" helps validate retrospectively an equally allegorical reading of the *Aeneid* and reconfirms its deep pessimism. Put briefly, the course of the *Commedia* takes us, in an extraordinary linear narrative complementing an equally powerful teleology, from a survey of our earthly misdeeds, with sinners frozen in Hell's circular eternity, to a purgation of them in the poem's second canticle, to the final reward—the subject of Dante's greatest metaphor, *Paradiso*—of reception into the timelessness of the celestial rose. The *Aeneid* has no *Paradiso*. Virgil's portrait of Elysium, in which few rest forever, or his idealizing glimpses of Augustan Rome, which remains ever in the future, far distant from the lived experience of the poem's immediate action, are scarcely parallel.[4] What Virgil offers us, symbolically, is a circle instead of Dante's line, with man's soul trapped in an inexorable cycle of births and deaths, undergoing an endless chain of one "inferno" and "purgatorio" after another.

This is not to say that Dante failed to make use of the circle as a model of perfection (or of circularity as a perfecting element in his own text). Nor am I maintaining that recourse to linearity, especially in the developmental progression from old Troy to new Rome, from Aeneas to Augustus, was not an essential Virgilian tactic. The tension between the two—the inexorability of Rome's manifest destiny in counterpoint with the inescapability of our immediate human plight and the emotions which reinforce it—is a basic, perhaps the basic, strategy of the epic. In my own reading, the "poetic" aspects of the poem, those which most magnetize our imagination, are constantly at odds with the programmatic, and the value of history, which the reader mainly sees as Aeneas' road to Rome, is proleptically, or tactically, questioned or undercut by both the evolution of the plot line itself and by Virgil's adherence to a poetics of repetitiveness. Hence my emphasis here is particularly on the final visions that remain in the foreground of the *Aeneid* and the *Divina Commedia*, particularly that of Virgil's epic.[5]

Virgil's souls, after their period of cleansing, are not assumed into a higher, holier sphere but accept again their tainting bodily carapaces, with only external circumstances changed. *Aeneid* 6 dramatizes the process of purification. *Quisque suos patimur manis*—"We all suffer our own shades"— explains Anchises (6.743). The rest of the epic discloses one man's experience of, or exposure to, hell, engendered by self and gods, who regularly either foster, mimic, or exemplify human madness.

The divergent modes in which Virgil and Dante treat their poetic inheritance generically complement these distinct eschatological views. The *Aeneid* is both spiritually fulfilled and generically incomplete. The spiritual wholeness is forged not around dreams of Rome's greatness at last implemented but around the emotion of anger. The epic begins with Juno's wrath unleashed against the Trojans and ends with Aeneas, in a rage, killing Turnus. The negative aspects of this cyclicity are reinforced by the imperfections of genre.

The funeral of Hector brings the *Iliad*'s exacting poetry to an end with communal ceremony. Forgiveness, reunion, a commitment to peace, and a statement by the narrator of an eternal pact to assure it are the gestures with which the *Odyssey* concludes. Reintegration of society betokens poetic wholeness. In Apollonius' *Argonautica* heroic journey and poetic voyage come to a parallel stop and the narrator proclaims final control over his material. Statius, Virgil's most obvious admirer among the silver Latin epicists, also ends his *Thebaid*, we should remember, not only with acts of reconciliation but with a poetic "seal" in which he places himself squarely in the tradition of his poetic mentor. The *Aeneid* lacks both the plot formulas that restore wholeness to society and the generic features by which the poet proclaims the completion of his accomplishment.

The *Aeneid*'s eccentric rounding off, therefore, offered Dante a double opportunity to bring his poem to a conclusion that spiritually reversed Virgil's tone and generically completed what the Augustan writer leaves unfinished. From both these aspects Dante is closer to Statius, and through him Homer, than he is to his beloved Virgil. In the pages that follow I will pursue this paradox from several angles. Dante, no doubt, understood Virgil, the creator of the *Aeneid*, as the great poet of empire, anticipating his own imaginings of a leader who would restore order to his troubled time. But Virgil, the figure in Dante's text, I would suggest, stands as emblem of the *Aeneid*'s own many-leveled incompletions, revealing Dante the poet fully cognizant of the poem's deep pessimism. Dante's Virgil is finally a figure of hopelessness, incapable of transcending the limitations of reason and therefore forced to return, in his own singular version of the *Aeneid*'s cycle, to Limbo whence his journey began.

I would like first to argue the case for the underlying circularity inherent in Virgil's text as it measures history's repetitiveness.[6] I will then turn to some of the passages in the *Aeneid* that most caught Dante's attention with two goals in mind: to demonstrate Virgil's own modulations on some of these very moments and to remind us as well of Dante's remarkable variations on Virgil's texts. I will look most closely at Dante's versions of Anchises, as they take shape in *Paradiso* 15 and especially in *Purgatorio* 30, in the characters of Cacciaguida and Virgil. Dante's Virgil, like Aeneas' father, can accompany his protégé only so far in his complex quest. I will examine in particular the parallels and differences in these limitations set to the father figure as guide. Finally, I will survey the ways in which Virgil and Dante treat Lethe and show how these variations serve to distinguish the poems in each of which the river stands as prominent symbol.

First a word on the "blind prison." The concept of the body as prison house for the soul, apparently Orphic in origin, enters literature through Plato's several uses of the analogy.[7] The soul is contaminated by the evils of the body from whose incarceration philosophy and the contemplation of higher forms can set it free.[8] Cicero adopts the symbolism in *De Re Publica* and *Tusculan Disputations*. In the first Scipio Africanus, after assuring his grandson that all those who have supported their fatherland enjoy eternal life in happiness, announces sententiously:

> Immo vero . . . hi vivunt, qui a corporum vinculis tamquam e carcere evolaverunt, vestra vero, quae dicitur, vita mors est.
> (*RP* 6.14)
> Surely indeed . . . these live on who have flown free of the bonds of their bodies as from a prison, but that so-called life of yours is death.[9]

And in the *Tusculans*, speaking of suicide, he remarks

> vir sapiens laetus ex his tenebris in lucem illam excesserit, nec tamen illa vincula carceris ruperit—leges enim vetant—, sed tamquam a magistratu aut ab aliqua potestate legitima, sic a deo evocatus atque emissus exierit.
> (*TD* 1.74)
> The wise man in his joy will pass from this darkness into the light beyond, yet nevertheless he will not break the bonds of the prison house—for the laws forbid it—but, as if at the bidding of a magistrate or some lawful authority, he will make his way out at the summons and release of god.[10]

The major point that distinguishes Virgil from Plato and Cicero in adducing the same analogy is the pessimism of his account. For the philosophers our souls are ultimately set free from corporeal bondage into eternal illumination. For Virgil, some few spirits, among them apparently Anchises, remain in the Happy Fields after death (*Aen.* 6.744). The majority, instead of returning after purification to their origin in the ether, as Orphic doctrine would have it, conceive a "wild" desire to embrace anew a bodily existence. This aim can only be achieved by drinking of Lethe

290

which, in Anchises' definition, offers in combination *securos latices et longa oblivia*, waters that bring with them "carelessness" and long-enduring oblivion of the past (*Aen.* 6.715). Thus, after purgation and a draft that washes away memory of life's troubles, the soul returns to the body and the cycle presses relentlessly on. It is no wonder that Aeneas, in the midst of this exposé of human destiny, asks his father the epic's most chilling questions:

> "o pater, anne aliquas ad caelum hinc ire putandum
> est sublimis animas iterumque ad tarda reverti
> corpora? quae lucis miseris tam dira cupido?"
> (*Aen.* 6.719–21)
> "O father, is it thinkable that some souls go aloft from here to the heavens above and return again to sluggish bodies? What dreadful yearning for the light holds these poor creatures?"

Aeneas, who is in the body and will remain so upon departure from the Underworld, knows that yearning for life is the equivalent of longing to re-create human bodily hell, that black prison from whose base motivations and actions man escapes only by death and its subsequent period of spiritual refinement.

Let us now examine other manifestations of "enclosure" with which Virgil complements his view of death and rebirth. First and most obvious is the apparent cyclicity of history. The idealizing thrust of the poem looks to the future moment of Augustus Caesar, whose wraith Anchises points out to his son,

> . . . aurea condet
> saecula qui rursus Latio regnata per arva
> Saturno quondam . . .
> (*Aen.* 6.792–94)
> who will establish again in Latium a golden age through countryside once ruled over by Saturn.[11]

Yet this dream is never of long duration. Evander, who also refers to Saturn's *aurea . . . saecula*, speaks of the peoples that he ruled in peace (*placida populos in pace*):

> deterior donec paulatim ac decolor aetas
> et belli rabies et amor successit habendi.
> (*Aen.* 8.326–27)
> until little by little an inferior, discolored age took its place, and a rage for war and love of possessions.[12]

Now *amor habendi* is a distinguishing characteristic of Virgil's very Roman bees, the Quirites of *Georgic* 4 (177), and passion for war erupts in Italy not before but after Aeneas' arrival, an event that occurs during the reign of Latinus:

> . . . Rex arva Latinus et urbes
> iam senior longa placidas in pace regebat.
>   (*Aen.* 7.45–46)
> King Latinus, now an old man, was ruling countryside and cities calm from length of peace.

The historical dialectic of Virgil's poem, as I said earlier, moves in two directions. On the visionary level it suggests an allegorical parallelism between Aeneas and Augustus. At the same time, on the experiential level, it warns against too trusting a belief in the capability of Aeneas-Augustus to renew a golden age, which means against the possibility of the renewal of any aspect of perfection or perfectibility.[13]

Virgil also makes regular use of poetic recollection to support his notion of history's repetitiousness. Through reliance on the reader's memory for verbal echoes that bring one context into another, he will often use the resultant juxtaposition as commentary on each separate passage. Let me offer an example where this friction undercuts idealism and simulates history's tendency to reecho itself, which in turn is but to reaffirm man's addiction to ineluctable, immutable patterns of action. Perhaps the most salient moments in the epic's eighth book are the adventure of Hercules and Cacus, as unfolded by Evander, and the narrator's description of the future events in Roman history crafted by Vulcan on Aeneas' shield. These Roman happenings are prospective for Aeneas, who in ignorance rejoices in what is to him only an *imago*, but retrospective for the all-knowing reader. On the most simplistic level Hercules is the savior who rids the site of Rome of an evil menace in the form of the beast Cacus, and Augustus is a modern revivification of this ancient prototype, heroically banishing Cleopatra and her monstrous gods from the Roman presence.

But on another deeper level history reiterates itself even here. Anger links Hercules and Cacus, and pride is in common between Cacus, who fixes the gory heads of his victims on his proud doors (*foribus superbis*, *Aen.* 8.196), and Augustus, who fits the gifts of the people he has conquered to proud doorjambs (*superbis postibus*, 8.721–22). Moreover there are further unexpected allusions through metaphor to the prehistorical context in the Augustan that urge us to reappraise the latter. Cacus is said to vomit forth smoke and flames as Hercules presses his attack, while, as we look ahead, Aeneas' Vulcan-made helmet vomits forth flames as do

the happy brows of Augustus, marshaling his forces at Actium.[14] When
the earlier duel is over the people are unable to satisfy their hearts (*ne-
queunt expleri*, 8.265) in gazing at the man-beast, and Virgil uses the same
phrase of happy Aeneas, unable to be satisfied as he gazes at the arms
brought by his mother (*expleri nequit*, 8.618). In sum, facile allegory promotes an equivalency of moral superiority among Hercules, Aeneas, and
Augustus. Verbal allusion suggests an opposite appraisal, that Cacus and
Augustus have their parallels and that there are monstral aspects to
Aeneas' arms, and to the history near and far that they reflect, which
equally link them with the apparent prototypical villain of Rome's locale.
Poetic language, then, by the very power of its repetitiousness, not only
subverts idealism but offers itself as exemplification of history's reiterative
tendencies.

Or, for a less morally charged but equally pessimistic example to which
I will return later, we might look at the funeral of young Marcellus, as
described by Anchises at the end of the sixth book, in relation to the
earlier depiction of the innumerable souls hovering around Lethe:

> hunc circum innumerae gentes populique volabant:
> ac veluti in pratis ubi apes aestate serena
> floribus insidunt variis et candida circum
> lilia funduntur, strepit omnis murmure campus.
>   (*Aen.* 6.706–9)

around this [stream] countless races and peoples were flying: and
just as in meadows in the calm of summer bees settle upon many-
colored flowers, and swarm around white lilies, the whole plain
resounds with the buzzing.

Lilies and flowers remain as, two hundred lines later, Anchises anticipates
his descendant's funeral:

> . . . manibus date lilia plenis,
> purpureos spargam flores animamque nepotis
> his saltem accumulem donis . . .
>   (*Aen.* 6.883–85)

Give lilies with full hands, I will scatter purple flowers and I will
heap up the soul of my offspring with at least these gifts . . .

But as Underworld changes to world above these blossoms are the fur-
nishings of death, not of life. The Lethe of forgetfulness becomes the
Tiber gliding by the burial tumulus, and the *campus* is no longer the
playground of bees in summer but the *Mavortis campus*, Mars' field where
funeral and burial took place (6.872–73). Buzzing is replaced by lamentation (though Virgil uses the same root word for each, *strepit* and *strepitus*,

6.709, 865), and what now swarms are not souls around Lethe but, in Aeneas' words, black night, with its dark shade, around the head of Marcellus (6.706, 866). As souls prepare to unite with bodies and return to earth, Virgil gives us, in the same language, one of his most poignant examples of what happens next—death again.

There are other, more direct ways in which history repeats itself in Virgil through the repeating of texts. Virgil's utilization of, and dependence on, Homer present the most obvious example. Homer's stylistic influence on the *Aeneid* is, of course, all-pervasive, but I am more interested here in the multivalent force of analogy as one poet adopts the other. Some comparisons are direct. When the Sibyl sees another Simois and another Achilles in Aeneas' future, she is simply telling Aeneas that the Tiber and Turnus will symbolically bring a renewal of his past (*Aen.* 6.87–89); and when Juno equates Aeneas with Paris, she, too, reminds the reader not of what is new in the Roman mission but of what remains irrepressibly Homeric (7.321).[15]

Then there is the subtler level of intent where the reader draws analogies from his memory of Homer as Virgil created them from his. To Juno, Aeneas may be Paris, but by the final moments of the epic, when the titular hero has Turnus at his mercy, to the reader watching his actions with the *Iliad* in mind he has become Achilles, and his victim shares in a double Homeric pedigree. He is Hector (in *Iliad* 22) about to be slain, and yet he becomes suddenly also the bereft but patriarchal Priam of book 24, reminding Achilles of his father as Turnus recalls Anchises to his son's memory.[16]

We might also dwell on the implications of the epic's first words, *Arma virumque*. The second entity in this doublet looks clearly to the opening word of the *Odyssey*, to the man of many turns whom the muse is asked to sing. But if "man" represents the *Odyssey*, "arms" in a profound sense symbolizes the *Iliad*. It is a striking metonymy for Homer's first word, Μῆνιν, weapons in place of the emotions that cause their use, and a reminder of the importance of resentment and wrath to the structure of the *Aeneid* as a whole. *Ira*, the anger of Juno, is mentioned prominently twice in the ten lines following on the opening. By the end of the epic, when Aeneas-Hector has metamorphosed for one last time into Aeneas-Achilles, her anger has become the hero's own as, *ira terribilis*, he prepares to slay his opponent. Her *saevi dolores*, her fierce resentments at past treatment by the Trojans, becomes Aeneas' memory of his own *saevus dolor* at Pallas' death.[17] This remembrance causes anger, fury, and the final deadly sword thrust. Wrath, arms, and the phantom presence of Achilles are amalgamated in the terrifying figure of Aeneas at the end of his epic. Its *incipit* had already duly forewarned us that this would be the case.

This interpretation casts in a highly ironic light Juno's pivotal concluding speech to Jupiter in which she seems to forgo her anger when her husband promises that the Trojans will be absorbed into the Latins and lose their identity.[18] The final suppression of Troy, its total absorption into fledgling Rome, means that the concluding events of the poem in one sense document the first moments of Roman history, the initial response to freedom from the Trojan past, which is to say, in particular, from *pietas* toward a father who had urged clemency toward suppliants.[19] These deeds are, in bald summary, Jupiter's ruthless unleashing of a Fury against Turnus, Juturna's succinct denunciation of the head of the gods, and Aeneas' own enraged response upon seeing the baldrick of Pallas.[20] Aeneas' motivation is, at the last, purely self-generated. No Venus appears to tell him to refrain from killing Helen, no Mercury orders him away from Carthage, nor does Tiber reveal the future in a dream. The irony is, of course, that Aeneas' action is one of the most Iliadic moments of the epic with Turnus wearing Pallas' sword belt standing in for Hector in Patroclus' armor. As so often in this poem, desire and wrath, eroticism and war, are entwined. They are as complementary as they are constant, Virgil would seem to say, in human affairs.

The ending of the *Aeneid* lacks the fulfillments that bring the *Iliad* to a conclusion, the ransoming of Hector's body and the lamentations and funeral that complete at once a life and a poem. Instead we are back to the beginning of the *Iliad* but without its satisfactions.[21] There are several moments in the *Aeneid*, among them the final pageant of book 6, that anticipate future Roman grandeur, an *imperium* founded on might but, at least in Anchises' final words, glorying in clemency. The "present" of the poem ultimately tells another tale. Virgil does not complete his text according to generic tradition, which is to say, with the emotional resolutions which Homer makes standard, but only with another release of aggressive, emotional energy which brings us back to the epic's start, to the start of the *Iliad*, and, presumably, to the resumption of a new cycle of human violence.

This multilevel enmeshment of Virgil's text with Homer's is a literary way of saying, again, that history is a constant reflection of itself.[22] To mimic and incorporate Homer is to reproject through further poetry the inner and outer history of his text, to retell it as history constantly retells itself. In other words poetry, like the histories it memorializes, is part of an unceasing continuum of cause and effect. The particular narratological figure that supports this evolution is ring composition, but I am not appealing to it as an aspect of style that directly or indirectly lends wholeness and balance to the text under discussion and proffers to the reader a concomitant sense of spiritual completion. Rather I see it as well, in Virgil's case, as a metaphor for enclosure, reinforcing a story line that speaks, finally, of a return whence we started and of human entrapment in certain modes of performance from which there is no escape. For Virgil, textual "space" resembles the spiritual enclosure of which it tells.

I have been looking at the poem in its entirety to exemplify my thesis, but I would like to offer one smaller illustrative instance. Aeneas leaves the Underworld by the gate of false dreams and we have already seen reasons why he could be said to embody exactly that, a *falsum insomnium*.[23] In no obvious sense has he been purged as the incorporeal souls of future Romans he has just witnessed presumably have been or will be.[24] Nevertheless the second half of the epic seems to offer a complex new beginning, for Aeneas himself (it is not accidental that the seventh book opens with an apostrophe to Caieta, Aeneas' recently deceased nurse), for Rome, and for Virgil's text:

> . . . maior rerum mihi nascitur ordo
> maius opus moveo.
>> (*Aen.* 7.44–45)
> A greater order of things is born for me. I set in motion a greater effort.

Yet Virgil does not speak here, as he had near the start of *Eclogue* 4, of a great order of the ages being born afresh—

> magnus ab integro saeclorum nascitur ordo
>> (*Ecl.* 4.5)

—but only of a greater stage in the events already begun which presents him with a greater task. Nothing is born anew as the result of Aeneas' Underworld journey. We are to be prepared for an enhanced version of what had occurred before. Aeneas' exit from Hell is soon followed by Juno's elicitation of the Fury Allecto from that same source, and it is she who sets in motion the "dreadful wars . . . the battle lines, and the kings driven by their emotions to deadly ruin" (*horrida bella . . . acies actosque animis in funera reges*, *Aen.* 7.41–42) that encapsulate the poet's heightened theme. Because of her, Amata and Turnus are roused to action, and battle begins after Iulus' hounds, stirred by her madness, wound the tamed stag of Silvia. But, at least as far as the first two are concerned, it is really in response to Aeneas that their emotions are aroused, and it is Aeneas' arrival in Latium that, in causing the death of a humanized animal, turns civilization back to nature. Unwittingly he brings his hell with him.[25]

The events that follow press inevitably toward the final confrontation, but the narrative of the intervening books, for all its richness of detail, goes both somewhere and nowhere, moving forward yet fraught with futility. A graphic example of this action that is equally nonaction is book 9, devoted primarily to Turnus, attacking and entering the Trojan camp, then forced to withdraw from it by plunging into the Tiber. It is a book of enclosures, of people inside and outside fortifications, of exclusions and hemmings in. If we look at the similes devoted to Turnus alone, he is first a wolf menacing a fold, then, as he attacks a Trojan attempting to scramble back inside the ramparts, he becomes an eagle or wolf, now snatching a lamb from the fold (*Aen.* 9.59–64, 563–66). Once inside the camp he is likened to a tiger in the midst of helpless flocks and finally, as he departs, to a lion pressed by men and weapons (9.731, 792–96). I detail all this because it not only confirms the animalizing of humans, the metamorphosis downward to bestiality particularly prominent in the book, but also strengthens a sense of spiritual imprisonment accompanying the events themselves.

This sense of psychic enclosure—and I come at last to my example—is nowhere in the epic more strongly projected than in the book's most famous episode, the adventures of Nisus and Euryalus who set out through the Rutulian camp to bring news to Aeneas and are themselves killed in the process. Nisus puts their inspiration as follows:

> . . . "dine hunc ardorem mentibus addunt,
> Euryale, an sua cuique deus fit dira cupido? . . ."
>   (*Aen.* 9.184–85)
> "Do the gods add this passion to our minds, Euryalus, or does his own dreadful yearning become for each person a god?"

Aside from the vital question of human motivation that Nisus' words raise, what most catches our attention here is the phrase *dira cupido*. It is used in the epic twice elsewhere, most pointedly by Aeneas when he questions the "dread yearning" of souls desirous again for the body's moral darkness.[26] If human life is a Hell of sorts, this is exactly what Nisus and Euryalus proceed to create in answer to their fateful desire, which, as so often in Virgil, motivates violence and anticipates death.

Even their initial intentions are morally blemished. Though involved with his friend *amore pio* (*Aen.* 5.296), Euryalus must suppress the tug of *pietas* by not telling their plans to his mother, who was the only woman to have stayed loyally with the Trojans. But matters grow worse. During their progress through the sleeping Rutulians, zeal for heroism becomes bloodlust. Nisus is equated with a starving lion setting sheepfolds in turmoil, who "roars with bloody mouth" (*fremit ore cruento* [9.341], a characteristic Virgil allots also to *impius Furor* in 1.296). Euryalus, equally on fire with rage (*incensus et ipse / perfurit*), continues his relentless slaughter until even Nisus recoils

> (sensit enim nimia caede atque cupidine ferri) . . .
>   (*Aen.* 9.354)
> (for he sensed that he was carried away with too much slaughter and lust) . . .

At this point greed for possessions replaces desire for murder, and Euryalus dons the helmet of Messapus. Reflections on this in the night's gloaming betray Euryalus, already impeded by darkness and his burden of booty. Nisus escapes from the troubled spot but, on looking back to find his friend absent, reenters the woods' perplexities:

> . . . rursus perplexum iter omne revolvens
> fallacis silvae simul et vestigia retro
> observata legit dumisque silentibus errat.
>   (*Aen.* 9.391–93)

Rescanning again the whole intertwined path of the deceiving woods, he forthwith tracks again his own traced steps and roams amid the silent thickets.

To save Euryalus is impossible, but Nisus kills his killer, Volscens, and in turn falls dead on the lifeless body of his friend.

I quoted at length the lines concerned with the topography of Nisus' return for Euryalus because they lend special support to a figurative reading of the whole episode. Nisus' reentering of the woods' deceitful labyrinth has its parallels with Aeneas' reprobing of Troy's embers in search of Creusa and with Orpheus' katabasis to find Eurydice in the Underworld, as told in *Georgic* 4.[27] The important difference is that here outer nature and the inner workings of the episode's protagonists conspire to fabricate a hell essentially of man's devising. The whole adventure desperately gets nowhere. It is Virgil's most vivid presentation of life as an enclosure, a hemming in of man by man himself, proof of the human inability to progress because of passions that become self-involved and self-defeating, not expansive and enhancing. Returning to our earlier metaphor, we could say that to follow the line is to idealize. It presumes our ability to surmount our emotionality, practice *pietas*, and find Aeneas. But Virgil regularly opts for the circle. No "Aeneas" is ever reached in Rome, however much we know he is there, in Virgil's *Aeneid*.

Here, too, verbal parallelism forms a counterpoint to linearity of narrative as once again the aesthetics of his presentation complements Virgil's moral design. We begin with Nisus' desire for mighty accomplishment:

> aut pugnam aut aliquid iamdudum invadere magnum
> mens agitat mihi, nec placida contenta quiete est.
>   (*Aen.* 9.186–87)

For a long time my mind spurs me on to do battle or attempt something great, nor is it satisfied with the quiet of peace.

But the quiet of peace is exactly what he, and we, return to at the end:

tum super exanimum sese proiecit amicum
confossus, placidaque ibi demum morte quievit.
  (*Aen.* 9.444–45)
Then, pierced through, he hurled himself on the lifeless body of his
friend and then at last grew quiet in the peace of death.

Quiet broken by human desires restored in the firmer quiet of death is
Virgil's cycle. It forms the narrative encasement for the labyrinthine
events in between in which *dira cupido* and its resultant fury conquer
piety—here toward both mother and Aeneas—for one of the most prominent, but far from the last, occasions in the epic. Passion quickly turns
heroic adventure into immoral adventuring and creates a hell wherein all
concerned, victors and victims alike, are finally trapped.[28]

In sum, then, the dread yearning for glory that lures Nisus and Euryalus into creating their own hell mimics *in parvo* the larger design into
which Virgil's philosophy sees man as bound—a dread yearning for life
which, in the larger cycle of the *Aeneid*, leads from anger to anger, the
termini of a larger inferno. The parallel between this cycle of desire and
anger and Homer's structuring of the *Iliad* confirms Virgil's own, fixed
multileveled allegiance to the Homeric texts above all others. Whatever it
may mean for Virgil to deal with projected schemata of history more all-
encompassing than Homer's and with the grander ethics of Roman *imperium*, the constants of human nature remain the same. At its base
Virgil's tale repeats Homer's. By ending his epic where Homer began,
with an act of anger, Virgil suggests that man is paralyzed by modes of
behavior that are eternally his.

I might seem to be arguing against one of Virgil's major symbolic
patterns—the containment of negative energies by barriers whose breaking down betokens the release of animality from confinement. In book 1,
impius Furor, as Jupiter imagines the future Augustan age, is at last
penned within the temple of War, its hands pinioned behind its back (*Aen.*
1.294–96). The epic begins when wild winds, curbed inside their mountain keep (Virgil uses the word *carcer*), are released with all their violence
against Aeneas' fleet (1.54). At the start of book 2 the breaching of the
wooden horse, pregnant with the armed might of the Greeks, augurs
Troy's doom. But it is my suggestion that the "prison" of our bodies can
be seen as complementary symbol to these more palpable models of
suppression and expression.

When he touches on the motivation for human action, Virgil often
considers it from two angles. We have seen Nisus pondering whether the
gods or one's own desire, the demon of one's inner self, urge a person to
act, and later in book 9 Remulus Numanus can shout to the Trojans,
"What god, what madness, drove you to Italy?"[29] There may be outside
forces, in appearance at least external to us, who loose the bonds of

irrationality. Juno, through her minion Aeolus, unpens the winds, and Sinon opens the horse. But there are also our overriding emotions, our psychic madnesses, those inner gods whose triggering from within their corporeal prison impel us toward action. The epic ends with Aeneas *furiis accensus*, set aflame by furies. Not long before, Jupiter had sent down a Fury to warn Turnus that his doom was imminent. The action proclaims a vendetta of the god against the Rutulian hero. By contrast the furies that impel Aeneas to his final deed are resentment, anger, and ferocity. They are the more powerful, and troubling, for being instinctive.[30]

It is one of Dante's primary accomplishments metaphorically to re-shape this circle into a line, to break the endless cycle of life, death, life—hell, purgatory, hell—which is to say emotion, purification, emotion, and to imagine his own brilliant Christian version of Orphic teleology where the soul, with body shed and the stains caused by its emotions washed away, enters not our wretched existence again but the luminosity of *Paradiso*, Dante's supreme evocation of an eternity of bliss in God's presence.

I would like to turn to Dante through one final Virgilian example of history's self-iteration, this time with the tale of Aeneas setting rather than following a precedent. As he nears the end of his "parade" of heroes in book 6, Anchises points out to Aeneas one of his most famous descendants, Julius Caesar, in company with Pompey, for five years in the 50s B.C. his son-in-law:

> illae autem paribus quas fulgere cernis in armis.
> concordes animae nunc et dum nocte prementur,
> heu quantum inter se bellum, si lumina vitae
> attigerint, quantas acies stragemque ciebunt,
> aggeribus socer Alpinis atque arce Monoeci
> descendens, gener adversis instructus Eois!
> ne, pueri, ne tanta animis adsuescite bella
> neu patriae validas in viscera vertite viris;
> tuque prior, tu parce, genus qui ducis Olympo.
> proice tela manu, sanguis meus!
>   (*Aen.* 6.826–35)

But those whom you perceive gleaming in like arms, souls in concord now and while they are pressed in night, alas how great a war will they set in motion between themselves, if they touch the lights of life, what great battle lines and slaughter, the father-in-law descending from Alpine heights and the citadel of Monaco, the son-in-law panoplied with eastern forces against his foe! Do not, my children, grow used to such wars in your thoughts, do not turn the powerful strength of your fatherland against its guts! Do you first, do you spare, who draw your descent from heaven, cast the weapons from your hand, o my blood!

The force of the last lines, as Anchises turns to Caesar, is particularly intense. It is the first instance in his survey where he directly addresses one of the ghosts, and line 835, with its play on *sanguis* and its incompletion, is especially powerful. Generation is replaced by death as inherited blood becomes, in the sublunar world, familial bloodshed, and incompletion brilliantly evidences not only Anchises' emotionality but the impossibility of finishing, which in lived experience would mean of obeying, his command.

Two items in this description look ahead into Virgil's text. The first is the categorization of the two souls as father-in-law and son-in-law. It will not be long before Juno will refer to the bloodbath in store from the potential marriage of Aeneas with Lavinia, that is, when Aeneas and Latinus are joined as *gener* and *socer*:

> hac gener atque socer coeant mercede suorum . . .
>   (*Aen.* 7.317)
> with this cost to their own people let son-in-law and father-in-law unite.

The goddess' words help anticipate later Roman civil war, finding in Aeneas' immediately subsequent action a model for future horrors, with familial alliances lending impetus to civil strife, not peace.

The second anticipatory item is the concomitant designation of Caesar and Pompey as *concordes animae*. *Concordia*, Anchises would seem to say, exists only in the Underworld when the passions that spur men to battle each other have been defused by purification.[31] Events would seem to prove his sentiments true. As Aeneas prepared to enter the "jaws" of the Underworld, he passed by, before its vestibule, a series of negative personifications ready to wreak havoc in the life of men. Among them were the Furies, *Somnia vana* (one of which Aeneas at the end of the book will arguably prove to be), death-bearing War (*mortiferum Bellum*), and maddened Discord (*Discordia demens*) (*Aen.* 6.280–81). These last suddenly become operative in Latium upon his arrival, to the point that Allecto, having carefully crafted for Juno the artifact of war, can boast:

> "en, perfecta tibi bello discordia tristi . . ."
>   (*Aen.* 7.545)
> "behold, complete for you—discord with the madness of war . . ."

The *Aeneid*, as we have grown to expect, suggests that *Concordia* can exist in its purgatory but that *Discordia* holds sway once men are released into the activity of living, of making history.

But it was the phrase *sanguis meus* that caught Dante's attention. In the fifteenth canto of *Paradiso*, in the sphere of Mars, Dante the pilgrim meets his twice-great-grandfather, the crusader Cacciaguida. Since the poet, in simile, first compares the ancestor's affection for his progeny to that with which Anchises greets his son in Elysium, the reader is prepared for the clear references to *Aeneid* 6 in Cacciaguida's first, imposing words:

> "O sanguis meus, o superinfusa
> gratia Dei, sicut tibi cui
> bis unquam coeli ianua reclusa?"
>   (*Par.* 15.28–30)
> "O my blood, o grace God poured down from above, for whom, as for you, has the gate of heaven ever been twice opened?"[32]

Cacciaguida's initial address is a reminder, as well, of the opening of *Aeneid* 6 where the Sibyl first assures Aeneas that the threshold of black Dis (*atri ianua Ditis*, 6.125–27) lies ever open and then outlines what tasks remain ahead if the enormous desire has seized him

> bis Stygios innare lacus, bis nigra videre
> Tartara . . .
>   (*Aen.* 6.134–35)
> twice to swim upon the Stygian meres, twice to see dark Tartarus . . .

For Aeneas, on the way to his father, the Sibyl can warn of the house of Dis being always receptive even for the heroic great who, after their exploits in Hell, return to their earthly life only to die again. For the pilgrim, Cacciaguida is directly prophesying that he must submit to a double exile on earth before final admission to Paradise. Analogically Dante the poet is drawing a careful distinction between the hero of the *Aeneid*, caught forever in the graceless pattern of Underworld, earth, Underworld (if it is to be his fate to be continually reborn) and his own protagonist. The pilgrim is both a St. Paul figure, for entering heaven twice, the first time whether in the body or not (*Inf.* 2.28–32),[33] and Christlike, for leaving heaven to endure the horrors of earth and Hell before reassuming forever his heavenly role.

There are two comparisons of Virgil's text with those of divine revelation during the Cacciaguida cantos, one directly pointing up its deficiencies for the Christian reader. The first is the sequence begun by the narrator's reference to Anchises and Aeneas meeting in the Underworld—

> se fede merta nostra maggior musa . . .
>   (*Par.* 15.26)
> if our greatest muse merits belief . . .

—followed by Cacciaguida's reference to "reading in the great volume where white or dark is never damaged" (*legendo del magno volume / du' non si muta mai bianco né bruno*, 15.50–51), namely the book of God's unalterable designs. More particular is the implicit distinction the poet makes in canto 17, when mentioning the *ambage*, the tortuous sayings

> . . . in che la gente folle
> gia s'inviscava pria che fosse anciso
> l'Agnel di Dio che le peccata tolle . . .
>   (*Par.* 17.31–33)
> in which the foolish folk of old once ensnared themselves, before the
> Lamb of God who takes away sins was slain . . .

The word *ambage* recalls the *ambages* of the Sibyl in *Aeneid* 6.99, in Dante standing for pagan writing in general. Mention of the *Agnel di Dio che le peccata tolle* is a bow to the Gospel of John, particularly and not coincidentally, to Christ's baptism, passion, and death (John 1.29).[34] We have here separated what the characters of Cacciaguida and the pilgrim within themselves configure. As we move from Aeneas' epic and Virgil's text to the *Divina Commedia*, we change from the tragedy of pagan darkness (and, I would add, from the dissonances implicit in Virgil's pessimistic cyclicity) to the "comedy" of Christian revelation (the *Commedia* as a type of *Novum Testamentum*) and the grace of its splendid acts of completion, in the concentrated focus on the Paradisal rose. We make the larger transitions metonymically in the smaller textual metamorphoses of Cacciaguida from Anchises (and, in part, the Sibyl) to God the Father, and of the pilgrim from Aeneas, entrapped finally in resentment, to a Christ figure who will suffer an immediate earthly "inferno" only to perform his own act of redemption for Florence by the endurance of his poetry.[35] By his act of figuration Dante the poet also symbolically redeems Aeneas, unchaining him from the passions of Virgil's text, and remaking him in the image of himself, capable, by divine grace and the imagination's fervor, of leaving earth's mutability for heaven's permanence.

But the most richly figurative appearances of Anchises in the poem are in canto 30 of *Purgatorio*, the canto in which Virgil the guide disappears while Virgil the poet remains intensely present. The first is the line

> "Manibus, oh, date lilia plenis"
>   (*Purg.* 30.21)
> "With full hands, oh, give lilies"

which angels chant from the chariot as they strew flowers before the arrival of Beatrice. The words, with the addition of the exclamation, begin the last sentence Anchises utters in the *Aeneid* and refer, as we saw, to flowers he imagines scattering at the funeral of Marcellus, perhaps on the bier itself. Dante's conversion of Virgil's line, as critics have noted, is astonishing, as lilies of the Roman, pagan dead become lilies of Christ's resurrection and Dante's imminent awareness of the loss of Virgil as guide is counterbalanced by the "restoration" of Beatrice, symbol of revelation, in the role of the resurrected Christ.[36]

The actual moment of loss and restoration is complemented, it has also been observed, by two other Virgilian echoes.[37] The first is the phrase *conosco i segni de l'antica fiamma* ("I recognize the traces of the ancient flame," *Purg.* 30.48), an Italian version of Dido's words to Anna near the opening of *Aeneid* 4, acknowledging that Aeneas stirs in her the same sensations as had her late husband Sychaeus (*agnosco veteris vestigia flamma*, 4.23). At this moment Dante notices Virgil's absence:

> Ma Virgilio n'avea lasciati scemi
> di sé, Virgilio dolcissimo patre,
> Virgilio a cui per mia salute die'mi . . .
> (*Purg.* 30.49–51)
> But Virgil had left us bereft of himself, Virgil sweetest father, Virgil to whom I gave myself for my salvation . . .[38]

Commentators rightly observe a parallel with the stunning lines in the fourth *Georgic* where Orpheus' voice, as his head floats down the Hebrus, calls on Eurydice in triple farewell. What we should also recognize is the particularly Virgilian power of the phrase *dolcissimo patre*. As Barolini points out, the adjective is the only use in the poem of the superlative of *dolce* to qualify a person—a climactic, emotional utterance coming at the moment when guide is utterly useless to pilgrim.[39] But the presence of Anchises is felt even here. The only time Virgil assigns a superlative to him is the apostrophe *pater optime*, addressed to Anchises by his son and contained among the last lines of Aeneas' narrative of his past exploits to Dido (*Aen.* 3.710). The Latinate ring of *dolcissimo patre* is intentional. It directly recalls the actual moment of Anchises' demise, that is, the point when he, too, is, at least in the body, totally lost to his son.[40]

This allusion serves two purposes. First, it confirms what the phrase *manibus, oh, date lilia plenis* had initially suggested, that Virgil the guide is to Dante the pilgrim a type of Anchises figure, leaving his son to fend for himself after his two major appearances as father-mentor. We are referred both to his death, at the conclusion of the exilic odyssey of book 3, and to his final words near the end of book 6, as he exposes Aeneas to future Rome and to his moral mission. Second, it helps underscore this crucial juncture in the pilgrim's journey by double reference to an equally im-portant transition in Virgil's text. As book 3 ends and the fourth book commences, Aeneas' first-person retelling of his past yields to third-person narrative. This change occurs at the instant when Anchises dies and Dido publicly admits her love. The advising old order passes, leaving Aeneas to face life and its responsibilities alone.

For Aeneas, therefore, the two withdrawals of Anchises occur at moments of crisis. The first is particular, the second more general. Book 4 dramatizes the more personal challenge. Aeneas, submitting to Dido, would have deviated from the road to Rome had not Mercury brought Jupiter's reminder of his duty, and caused his departure from Carthage. His yielding to passion leaves him unscathed but causes the suicide of his inamorata.

The second "disappearance" of Anchises, at the end of book 6, comes shortly after he has summarized for his son the essence of Roman imperialistic ethics in his famous apostrophe:

> ". . . tu regere imperio populos, Romane, memento
> (hae tibi erunt artes), pacique imponere morem,
> parcere subiectis et debellare superbos."
>   (*Aen.* 6.851–53)
> "Remember, O Roman, to rule peoples with might (these will be
> your arts), to spare the humbled and war down the proud."

This time the crisis of responsibility is a larger one. In the second half of the epic Aeneas is left on his own not only to avoid the private enticements of a Dido but actively to set a pattern for future Roman behavior, based on his father's novel, demanding code. In the epic's last moments Jupiter has agreed to Juno's demand that the Trojans be completely absorbed into the Latin race. This means that Aeneas' final deed of killing his archenemy Turnus is the first truly Roman action—Aeneas as *Romanus*, not *Troianus*. That he disobeys his father's exhortation to practice clemency and, in the heat of fury, kills a suppliant as the epic ends, therefore calls into question both the hero's much touted *pietas* and the possibility of any higher morality in the Roman design for rule. He is, finally, a spiritual failure in both the private and public spheres, but the consequences at the end of the epic are far larger than in the aftermath of the Dido interlude. Aeneas' final act demeans both father and son, and darkens the Roman future, at least as Virgil envisions it.

What wells up in Aeneas at the end of his epic is not *pietas*, an abstract sense of duty, of allegiance to father and the ideas he represents, but a remembrance of anguish (*dolor*) sparking violent anger (*ira*). Aeneas at last yields to a passionate action that betrays his inner self. In advertising his individuality, as well as abandoning recourse to *clementia*, he announces his independence from his father, which is to say, from the abstractions that ideally were to rule the Roman mission. Aeneas' final, public self-authentication, in the triumph of son over father, is also the freeing, at least momentarily, of the individual personality from collective destiny, of private, emotional response from subordination to the inherited authority of the patriarchal will and to an ideology where passion is deemed subject to reason.[41]

In the second half of the epic, after he has been shepherded to the gates of false dreams by his father, Aeneas cannot on his own restrain, much less rid himself of, the very emotionality that, as he well knows, is the source of human suffering. Dante's reminder of Aeneas' farewell to Anchises, therefore, resonates in several ways through his text. Just as Anchises comes to the limits of his mortality, so Virgil as guide must withdraw to Hell, a victim, in Dante's theology, of his ignorance of redemptive grace. He could be seen, as the Florentine poet portrays him, as a poignant symbol of the entrapment his own *Aeneid* imagines, with man, lacking a vision of paradise, caught in the cycle of hell, purgatory, hell where hell is earth and purgatory the final locale in the Underworld set aside for those preparing for renewed life as they become innocent of any taint. Virgil, returning to Hell, thus serves as analogy not only for Anchises and his single death but for his poetry's chief creation, Aeneas, launched on his own difficult journey. This voyage leads not to Roman idealizations and a transcendence of humanness but to life's horrors and their momentary obliteration in death.

Dante's major alteration to Virgil's text here, then, is the most obvious. The hero of the *Aeneid*, after his season in the Underworld, remains unguided except, finally, by the tugs of his emotions. What his father dictates in words—to establish a custom for peace—he does not implement by action that would also betoken a grand moral leap forward. In this sense the *Aeneid* is as incomplete spiritually as it is generically. There is to be no pagan parallel for *paradiso*. The pilgrim, by contrast, does not remain without direction, but gains for himself not a Dido, whose temptations of Aeneas follow on Anchises' demise, but Beatrice, Christlike symbol of revelation who will lead her charge into heaven.[42] She subjects the pilgrim to a withering interrogation bent on revealing, and hence purging, human inadequacy, not on arousing desires that serve to deflect a hero from his higher goals.

Finally, we should remember that Anchises does not disappear from Dante's text but is refigured in Cacciaguida, and therefore transumed into heaven just as is Aeneas himself in the guise of the pilgrim meeting his forebear. It is Cacciaguida, in *Paradiso* 17, who reveals to the pilgrim the trials in store for him when he returns for his period of earthly transience. He therefore parallels both the Sibyl and Anchises in book 6 who offer Aeneas the most direct prophecies of his and Rome's future. But here again we find an enormous difference between the two passages. Aeneas, as his saga progresses, seems not to remember, much less gain comfort from his father's revelations in the Underworld, as if history's future grandeur had small validity in the face of quotidian experience. The pilgrim, by contrast, responds to Cacciaguida's outline of exile's bitterness with understanding and an awareness of the power, and cost, of his poetry.

Let me return to Virgil with one last, familiar example of how Dante "straightens" Virgil's text, based on the figure of bees. We have seen the differing ways in which Virgil and Dante treat the lilies on which the bee-souls feed in Elysium. What happens, variously, to the bees themselves complements these metamorphoses. Bees appear twice in the last six books of the *Aeneid*. On the first occasion they serve as an omen for the newly arrived Trojans who will, the seer prophesies, lord it over the citadel of Latinus (7.64–67). The second finds the analogy applied to the besieged Latins themselves, stirred to anger by the "shepherd" Aeneas' attempt to smoke them out (12.587–92). Both instances speak of power, of domination, of martial energies—and epic heroes—spurred on by wrath, in other words of what happens to warriors before and after their season in the Underworld.

Dante does something tellingly different. Virgil's bee-souls become bee-angels who behave

> sì come schiera d'ape che s'infiora
> una fiata e una si ritorna
> la dove suo laboro s'insapora . . .
>   (*Par.* 31.7–9)
> like a swarm of bees which one moment enflower themselves, and
> the next return to where their work acquires savor . . .

These "bees," we learned from the previous canto, flit like sparks between the river of god's light and glory bringing, in an unexpected reversal, the grace of its nectar to the "flowers" of the blessed who line its banks. At Beatrice's urging the pilgrim drinks of the liquid.

This river of life, whether of water or fire, has numerous biblical precedents ranging from Ezekiel, Daniel, and Zechariah to the Book of Revelation where John speaks of the angel who "showed me the river of the water of life, clear as crystal, coming forth from the throne of God and of the Lamb" (*ostendit mihi fluvium aquae vitae, splendidum tamquam crystallum procedentem de sede Dei et Agni*, Apoc. 22.1).[43] But the reader of the *Divina Commedia* more immediately thinks back to the two streams emanating from a single source that flow through Eden and from which the pilgrim must drink before he can progress up into Paradise. The heavenly water of god's grace, which occasions the pilgrim's final, climactic draft, is biblical in origin. The purgatorial waters, named Lethe and Eunoe, are in the first instance Virgilian (and through Virgil, Platonic), in the second Dante's own invention:

"Da questa parte con virtù discende
che toglie altrui memoria del peccato;
de l'altra d'ogne ben fatto la rende."
    (*Purg.* 28.127–29)
"On this side it descends with virtue that takes from one the memory of sin; on the other side it restores the memory of every good deed."[44]

The expansion and mutation of his Virgilian heritage tells us something of Dante's, as well as of Virgil's, design. For Dante the two streams serve a theological purpose. They symbolize a final purgation of the pilgrim's guilty past and a preparation for the eternal rewards due his goodness. Drinking of their waters is an essential stage on the pilgrim's road to sanctity.

Virgil has no Eunoe, no revivification of any aspect of the past and, though his Lethe inspires forgetfulness, it is to force total eradication of all memory of a terrestrial existence. As we saw earlier, according to Anchises only by imbibing *securos latices et longa oblivia*, the liquid of lack-of-care and of lasting oblivions, so as to become *immemores*, totally forgetting, will souls be stricken with a desire to be reattached to bodies.[45] In other words, instead of Dante's symbolic purgation of the past's negativity and a readying for ultimate, irrevocable bliss, Virgil grants his souls complete oblivion of life's horrors only as preparation for becoming embroiled again in the body's passions and for a further internment in its blind prison. For Dante's souls, the memory of excellence endures as help in forming a continuum between our fugitive mundane existence and Paradise's eternity. Christ's Incarnation took place not only to redeem men from their evils but also to set a pattern for goodness that would persist even after the transition from earth to heaven. By contrast, Virgil's *animae*, required to forget what emotions have put them through while alive, are condemned to repeat the past. There is no linear ascent to God's presence, no climbing of the ladder of perfection, just a renewal of the cycle of earth, underworld, earth, or, with specific reference to *Aeneid* 6, care, forgetfulness, care.

It is no accident that two of the great symbols that bind book 6 of the *Aeneid* have their close counterparts in Dante's structuring of *Purgatorio*. We have examined how Dante's treatment of Lethe adapts his Virgilian inheritance, as he brings his second canticle to a close with a series of reminiscences of the finale of *Aeneid* 6. It is helpful to remember, in conclusion, how he begins. At the end of the first canto the guide Virgil girds his pilgrim with a *giunco schietto*, a straight reed that, after it has been tugged up from the ground, instantly renews itself (*Purg.* 1.95, 133–36). Dante clearly evokes the golden bough that, after Aeneas plucks it on the Sibyl's orders, will also immediately resprout (*Aen.* 6.143–44). This serves as a talisman that gains Aeneas entrance to the Underworld just as the pilgrim's encirclement with the symbol of humility is appropriate preparation for the ascent of purgation.[46] These comparable demarcations, plant and stream, suggest that Dante the poet saw in *Aeneid* 6 a document that constructs a type of purgatory to serve as model for his own *Purgatorio*.[47]

But the *aureus ramus* is no humble reed. At once wood and metal, it is, like Aeneas, alive and dead, symbol of a hero whose history is what Virgil sees as man's history, ever a mixture of life and death, passion and purgation.[48] Unlike the "sincere" reed that is attached to the pilgrim's body, the bough affirms Aeneas' heroism only for a transient moment. Symbolically its possession takes the hero nowhere beyond the continuous cycle of life's hellish experience and death's purgation of it. Whatever the inner yearnings of this *anima naturaliter Christiana*, Virgil seized no opportunity to imagine a metaphor for Paradise, and this is perhaps his greatest difference from his medieval successor's resplendent vision of eternity. Dante poetically and spiritually can fulfill what Virgil leaves incomplete.[49] He can release us, in his greatest comic gesture, from the dark enclosure of our humanity (and from Virgil's rich texturing of it) and place us, at least in our imagination, forever in God's graceful presence.

NOTES

I am most grateful to Polly Chatfield, Rachel Jacoff, Jeffrey Schnapp, and Eugene Vance for their helpful comments.

1. Compare Montefeltro's definition of Hell as *mondo cieco* (*Inf.* 27.25) with Marco the Lombard's view of earthly existence: "lo mondo è cieco" (*Purg.* 16.66).

2. *Inf.* 1.2, 2.142. For the allegory, Grandgent, *Companion* 64.

3. Anchises lists the four emotions at 733 (*metuunt cupiuntque, dolent gaudentque*). They are discussed by Cicero (*TD* 3.24 and 4.11; cf. *Fin.* 3.35) as disorders, arising in two cases from expected good, in the other two from expected bad. From expectations of good we experience *libido* and *laetitia* (Virgil's *cupiunt* and *gaudent*). From anticipations of evil, *metus* and *aegritudo* (Virgil's *metuunt* and *dolent*). The equation of *aegritudo* with *dolor* is confirmed from *TD* 3.25 where, after speaking of *aegritudo*, Cicero continues: *id autem est, ut is, qui doleat, oportere opinetur se dolere—* "now that is, that he who suffers believes that he ought to suffer." Virgil's four verbs are listed by Horace, in exactly reversed order, at *Epi.* 1.6.12.

4. It is noteworthy that the closest Dante comes to Virgil's Elysium is in his description of the Valley of the Princes in *Purg.* 7, a canto that abounds in Virgilian references, especially to the appropriate segments of *Aeneid* 6 (cf. Singleton, *Divine Comedy*, on lines 40 and 82). John Freccero, *Dante* 136–51, in his brilliant essay on Dante's Ulysses also uses the analogies of line and circle to distinguish Dante from the classical past, but both his purposes and results are different from mine.

5. Dante's use of the symbolism of circularity, especially as metaphor for conversion, has been discussed by Freccero in several of

his essays. See in particular, Freccero, *Dante* 70–92. My stress here on Dante's linearity is merely to emphasize that the spiritual force of the *Divina Commedia* leads the pilgrim triumphantly from beginning to final climax whereas the climax of the *Aeneid* projects us structurally and emotionally back whence we started. We end not with idealizing dreams fulfilled but only with further confirming evidence of the passionate individuality of gods and men.

6. My analysis of Virgil's view of history is strongly complemented by the discussion of Schnapp, *Transfiguration of History* especially ch. 2 passim. His reading of the nightmarish circular quality of *Aeneid* 6 is particularly important. Though book 6 is his chief concern, his insights are valid for the interpretation of the epic as a whole.

7. For details, and bibliography, see Austin, *Liber Sextus* on lines 724–51 and line 734. Solmsen, "Greek Ideas" and "World of the Dead," treats the religious and philosophical background of Virgil's Underworld in two important articles. His final conclusion about Virgil's tone, in the first article, is more sanguine than mine: "Man's worth and dignity lie in harboring in himself a spark of the divine, and there is a prospect of his being ultimately reabsorbed into the cosmic spirit" (14). The relationship of the blind prison to false *insomnia* and of both to Aeneas is discussed with insight by Tarrant, "Aeneas."

8. The major texts are *Phaedo* 66b and 82e; *Phaedrus* 250c; *Gorg.* 493a; *Crat.* 400c.

9. Cf. also 6.15: *corporis custodiis*.

10. Cf. also 1.75 and man's release *ex his vinculis*. At 1.72 Cicero speaks of those who are blinded (*caecati*) by sins and lusts. But the phrase *caeco carcere* with its implications of a double darkness seems Virgil's invention.

11. Cf. *Aen.* 1.286–88.

12. *Amor habendi* is a crucial psychological matrix for the final half of the poem. Greed for spoils causes the downfall of Nisus and Euryalus as well as Camilla, and the belt of Pallas carries its potent force from its initial possessor to Turnus and, finally, to Aeneas.

13. Virgil's allusions that suggest an equation of Aeneas with Augustus are set out in the greatest detail by Binder, *Aeneas und Augustus*.

14. *Aen.* 8.253, 259, 620, 681.

15. As another example we could note the virtual repetition of *Aen.* 1.100–101, as Aeneas, caught in a nearly disastrous storm, recalls the warring on the plains of Troy—

> . . . ubi tot Simois correpta sub undis
> scuta virum galeasque et fortia corpora volvit.

> where the Simois rolls so many shields of men snatched under its waves, and helmets and brave bodies.

—at 8.538–40 where Aeneas, once again speaking, anticipates the carnage of the future campaign:

> . . . quam multa sub undas
> scuta virum galeasque et fortia corpora volves,
> Thybri pater!

How many shields of men, father Tiber, and helmets and brave bodies will you roll under your waves!

The reiteration suggests that father Tiber will repeat the action of Trojan Simois, which is to say that in certain crucial respects the *Aeneid* repeats the *Iliad*, and in particular that the transfer of Troy to Rome represents at once topographical and temporal change and historical immutability. Johnson, "Figure of Laertes" 94, summarizes most sensitively the problematics of this verbal echo, which is also history's dismal reecho: "yet another bloody river, another image of murderous water—repetition, the determinism of historicist fate, its illusions and satanic mechanisms." (For a different interpretation of this repetition see Conte, *Rhetoric of Imitation* 65–66 and 66 n. 32.) The last appearance of the Tiber in the epic is at 12.35–36 where, in Latinus' words, it is "warm again with our blood" (*recalent nostro Thybrina fluenta / sanguine*). The Sibyl's prophecy at 6.87 of *Thybrim multo spumantem sanguine* has therefore been fulfilled by the end of the epic. In a less direct way her words may also anticipate the funeral of Marcellus past whose *tumulus* the Tiber will flow at a still later time (*Aen.* 6.873–74).

16. In perhaps the richest irony of all, Aeneas, killer of "Priam," adopts the role of Neoptolemus-Pyrrhus in book 2, the son of Achilles who does the actual deed itself. Knauer, *Aeneis und Homer*, has traced Virgil's reliance on Homer in greatest detail (cf. pages 316–27 for Homer and the end of the *Aeneid*).

17. The repetition has been evaluated by De Grummond, "*Saevus Dolor*," who feels, however, that Aeneas' anger is "born of love of others" (50) and that his acceptance of fate "brings harmony and prosperity to the land."

18. The qualified aspects of Juno's speech itself are well pointed out by Johnson, *Darkness Visible* 123–27, and Feeney, "Reconciliations of Juno." Cf. also Harrison, *Aeneid and Carthage* especially 111–12.

19. In spite of the epic's concluding lines and lengthy evidence of book 10, there are still those who believe that "Aeneas prefers to spare the conquered" (Griffin, "Augustus and the Poets" 214). I analyze the rationale behind Aeneas' final deed in greater detail in chapter 8.

20. The brief but telling Juturna scene has been searchingly discussed by Barchiesi, "Lamento," and Conte, *Rhetoric of Imitation* 157–58. Her disappearance is parallel to Apollo's abandonment of Hector in *Iliad* 22 save that the god departs in silence while she upbraids Jupiter. Her speech is rightly seen by Griffin, *Latin Poets* 129–30, as undercutting the idealism of Jupiter's preceding speech.

21. The ending of the *Aeneid* has as much in common with the conclusions of tragedy as with the finales of previous epics. Critics have noted parallels between the end of the *Oresteia* and that of the *Aeneid* (most recently Moskalew, *Formular Language* 158, n. 55) but these do not extend, in the text, beyond the similarities between Jupiter's final speech and Athena's address to the Eumenides. The conclusion of Aeschylus' trilogy offers nothing similar to Aeneas' final violence. Closer parallels, as we saw in the preceding chapter, can be found in the conclusions of Seneca's tragedies. In the *Medea*, for instance, the heroine yields to *dolor*, *odium*, and *ira* as she prepares to slay her first son (951–53), *dolor*, again, as she kills the second (1016; cf. 1019). And in the

Phaedra, as the queen enters with sword readied for suicide, Theseus exclaims (1156):

> Quis te dolore percitam instigat furor?

> What fury prods you on, provoked by pain?

But even here the ending, as the chorus helps reform the scattered corpse of Hippolytus and Theseus prepares for his funeral, has satisfactions, albeit macabre, which parallel more the *Iliad*'s conclusion than the *Aeneid*'s.

22. The very simultaneity of levels throughout the epic suggests the constant, continuous uniformity of history, not the developmental.

23. On the meaning of the word and its possible applications to Aeneas, see Michels, "Insomnium of Aeneas" passim. We never learn why Aeneas does not remember what his father has told him when he should have been guided and comforted by it. Is Aeneas, in his restoration to the world of the living, to be considered newborn and therefore as forgetful as those who have drunk of Lethe? Are the potentialities of the Roman future as "false" as the poetry that tells of them?

24. In meeting Palinurus, Dido and Deiphobus Aeneas reexperiences his recent life through a series of mortal moments in which the past is rehearsed and resuffered. His future he could surmise from his father's parade, but even this grand sequence has no effect on his post-Underworld existence. (The addition of Anchises' expansive vision of the future is Virgil's major alteration to his model, *Odyssey* 11, where Odysseus meets the ghosts of his past acquaintanceship. Homer's hero learns of his own personal future, near and far, from Tieresias, but there is nothing of the larger historical sweep that Anchises' words convey.) Michels, "Insomnium of Aeneas" 140 and 141 n. 5, probes the scholarship behind the misguided idea that, as a result of his visit to the underworld, Aeneas "abandons the past, and confidently faces the future, prepared to labour for the greatness of his race which lies centuries ahead." This reductive reading surfaces in even one of the most penetrating analyses of Virgil's art, that of Parry, "Two Voices" 121, "When he emerges, so strangely, from the ivory gate of false dreams, he is no longer a living man, but one who has at last understood his mission, and become identified with it." The text shows Aeneas with little or no understanding of or even interest in his mission and every evidence that he is an emotional human being. The prophetic vignettes depicted on the shield in book 8 appear only as an *imago* to him, even though certain characters on it overlap with those to whom he was introduced in book 6, and his father's ethical standards are by the end dispensable.

25. The association of Aeneas (and Iulus) with hunting, from his shooting of the stags in book 1 and his "hunting" of Dido in book 4 to his comparison to a hunter-hound in book 12, as he tracks the "deer" Turnus, deserves separate treatment.

26. The third instance is at *Aen.* 6.373 where the Sibyl rebukes the unburied Palinurus for his "dread yearning" to view the Styx before the allotted time, to transcend the immutable laws of fate. Dante was aware of the power of the passage (as Singleton, *Divine Comedy*, observes, commenting on *Purg.* 6.28–30). Another complementary use of the abstract *cupido* occurs later in

book 9 (760–61) when Turnus has forced his way into the Trojan camp. It would have been the final day for the war and for the Trojan race, says the narrator,

> sed furor ardentem caedisque insana cupido
> egit in adversos.

> But madness and a wild lust for slaughter drove him to violence against the enemy.

Once more, as throughout the episode of Nisus and Euryalus, human passions get the better of higher goals. The *irae* and *dolor* that Turnus experiences earlier in the book (66) on seeing the Trojan fortifications are not controlled once he has gained entrance. Neither are they mastered by Aeneas at the end of the epic (12.945–46).

27. I have discussed the connection in Putnam, *Poetry* 41–47.
28. The connection of Virgil with his model, the so-called Doloneia episode in *Iliad* 10, has been often noted (the most recent study is by Pavlock, "Epic and Tragedy"), but there are careful differences, some of which are important for my discussion. Diomede and Odysseus, the Greek protagonists of Homer's tale, have no purpose to their mission except to perform notable exploits. They kill the spy Dolon, enter the throng of the newly arrived Thracians, and slay Rhesus and twelve of his comrades, purloining his famous horses. On Athena's warning to leave off further bloodletting, they return to the Greek camp. Diomede first puts the horses to pasture with his own, then he and Odysseus wash off their sweat in the sea, bathe and anoint themselves, then eat. Nisus and Euryalus have a higher goal, to pass through the enemy camp and reach Aeneas. But passion, desire for slaughter and possessions, thwarts this noble purpose. They become Homeric, which is to say human. But there are basic differences from Homer. First, because the actors are young lovers who are setting forth to die, the progress of Virgil's narrative is endowed with a lyric sadness completely absent from Homer. Moreover, even discounting the element of mortality, there are final satisfactions to Homer's narrative that Virgil's lacks. No "civilizing" moment concludes the heroic adventuring of Nisus and Euryalus. Higher ideals, the *pietas* that motivates the search for Aeneas and restraint in seeing it through, are forgone. There is a "beyond" but no reaching it. Virgil does not allow his characters to surmount their inner-outer hell or to gain the (literal and figurative) fulfillment of taking us past Homer to "Rome."

Dante (*Inf.* 1.107–8) joins Nisus and Euryalus with Camilla and Turnus as heroes who, stricken with wounds, have died for the Italy to come, and Virgil, in an envoi, links their story to the puissance of his *carmina* and the endurance of Rome (*Aen.* 9.446–49). He would seem, in part, to share Dante's notion of a series of human sacrificial victims necessary for the establishment of Roman rule. (I need not recatalog the deaths that Aeneas leaves in his wake from Creusa to Turnus.) But the emotions imputed to Nisus and Euryalus, which cause their enterprise to founder, ironize against any idealizing vision of the future. It could be said that Virgil's text undercuts not only his own hopes for a perfected Roman future but also Dante's dream of *imperium* gloriously reestablished.

29. *Quis deus Italiam, quae vos dementia adegit?* (9.601).
30. The very last line of the epic (12.952), describing the death of Turnus—

> vitaque cum gemitu fugit indignata sub umbras

> and his life flees, resentful, with a groan under the shades

—is also important for my argument in several respects. Because it is exactly repeated from 11.831, where Camilla dies, the reader not only equates the two Italic warriors but ponders again the open-endedness of the epic. The denouement that follows on Aeneas' burst of anger appears abrupt because his violence is not dissipated by further narrative. But the epic's final line, because it repeats the poetic, which is to say also the epic's historical, past betokens not so much a full stop, demarcating a closed block of events, but a way station, a second occurrence in what the reader anticipates as a continuing series. Virgil elsewhere hints as much. The last image on the shield of Aeneas, which is also the last figure to appear in Virgil's delineation of Octavian's triple triumph of 29 B.C., is the Araxes, chafing at its bridge (*pontem indignatus Araxes, Aen.* 8.728). It is the finalizing resentfulness of those who suffer Rome's pride that not only marks a continuum of reiteration within the epic's temporal foreground but also forces our attention toward Rome's future Augustan age and its own fostering of the same motif. In the foreground of the poem's present and in its relation to the future, history repeats itself.
31. The abstraction *concordia* is never used in Virgil, and the adjective *concors* only again in the *Aeneid* at 3.542 where it is associated with hope for peace if the horses of war are tamed. By contrast *discordia*, personified or not, is mentioned at 6.280, 7.545, 8.702, 10.9, 10.106, 12.313, and 12.583. It appears in Virgil's poetry as early as *Ecl.* 1.71, and its uses at *Geo.* 2.496 and 4.68 help connect the martial bees with Roman civil strife.
32. It is worthy of note that Cacciaguida's sudden appearance before the pilgrim from out of the cross of the Church militant is compared to a shooting star (*Par.* 15.13–18). The only mention of such a sight (*stella facem ducens*) in the *Aeneid* is the omen in book 2 (692–98), which finally convinces Anchises, now divinely guided, of the appropriateness of departure from Troy. The first mention of Anchises in Dante's poem is at *Inf.* 1.73–74 where his son is *quel giusto / figliuol d'Anchise*. The last, a circumlocution for Sicily as the island *ove Anchise fini la lunga etate* (*Par.* 19.132), is a final reminder of his death at the end of *Aeneid* 3. The simile that precedes in *Paradiso* 15 (25–27) alludes to *Aeneid* 6.679–86 as Aeneas finally reaches his father in the Underworld. Anchises' subsequent words (687–88) are one of the most prominent allusions to Aeneas' *pietas* in the epic. The influence of Virgil's lines on *Inf.* 2.4–5 is pointed out by Ball, "Theological Semantics" especially 60–61, in the course of his larger survey of the relationship of Virgilian *pietas* and Dante's *pietà*.
33. Cf. *Par.* 31.138–39.
34. Cf. also 36.
35. Cf. *Par.* 17.98–99.
36. See especially the sensitive discussion by Freccero, *Poetics of Conversion* 80–82.

37. The most detailed analysis of the parallels is by Ryan, "Virgil's Wisdom" especially 11–14.

38. Singleton, *Divine Comedy* ad loc., noting the echo, refers to Moore, *Studies in Dante* 20–21.

39. Barolini, *Dante's Poets* 245. With this use of a superlative in connection with Virgil cf. the greeting that awaits him on his return to Limbo (*Inf.* 4.80: "*Onorate l'altissimo poeta . . .*"). The contrast highlights the emotionality of the pilgrim's farewell in *Purg.* 30.

40. The phrase *antica matre*, in the line immediately following (52), though it refers specifically to Eve, has also a careful Virgilian ring. Virgil's only use of the phrase *antiqua mater* is at *Aen.* 3.96 where Apollo's Delian oracle urges the Trojans to seek their ancient mother. Anchises immediately misinterprets the command as referring to Crete. Are we meant, as we remember this crucial mishearing, to have further corroboration from Virgil's text of the final uselessness of Virgil-Anchises as guide?

41. Of the many ironies operating at the end of the poem, none is more direct than the unexpected reversal of voice. By taking the active role (How far are we now from the hero to whom we were introduced in book 1, tossed about on the waves of someone else's passion!), Aeneas suddenly destroys the (presumably) masculine past of authoritative, paternal hierarchy in favor of solipsistic, passion-ridden "doing." His is a public statement, in theatrical view of all, of a noncivic, inner being. In slaying Turnus Aeneas kills his father thrice over. The first occurs when the reader recollects Priam ("Remember your father, Achilles like to the gods," are Priam's first words to the killer of his son [*Iliad* 24.486]), and the second from Turnus' direct reminder of Anchises (*Aen.* 12.933–34). In Turnus Virgil also has Aeneas kill an embodiment of Jupiter who a few lines earlier had preached restraint to Juno. *Ulterius temptare veto* ("I forbid you to attempt further"), Jupiter's final words in his first speech to his wife (12.806), are echoed and modified in Turnus' final words to Aeneas (12.938): *ulterius ne tende odiis* ("Do not press further in your hatred"). These are the only two uses of the comparative adverb in the Virgilian corpus. Through this triple patricide, Aeneas, instead of accepting and at last incorporating a father's abstractions that urge the implementation of peace through might, asserts the autonomy of private emotion.

42. However, during the pilgrim's encounter with Beatrice, Dante is careful to remind us of Dido and *Aeneid* 4 (the most obvious reference is at *Purg.* 31.72).

43. The symbolism of the river of life has been studied most recently by Quint, *Origin and Originality* 122.

44. The pilgrim drinks of Lethe at 31.101–2.

45. Virgil is drawing on Plato (*Rep.* 621a) with the significant difference that in the Myth of Er all souls must drink. Some do so only slightly, some, in their eagerness to forget past cares, imbibe too deeply. These latter are "defiled" (621c). The former share in ἀνάμνησις, collective memory of the past involving at least forms and their ultimate truths (cf. *Meno* 81–83, *Phaedo* 73–76, *Phaedrus* 250, 275). Virgil's more desperate vision includes total obliteration of what has gone before. Does it also mean that for him there are no ultimate truths? In his comment on *Aen.* 6.751, Austin, *Liber Sextus*, suggests that "their draught of Lethe has

made the souls forget their extra-bodily experience." It is far more likely that they are forgetting not their period of purgation but the horrors whence they came, as Austin, ibid., rightly notes on 715, "Lethe gives *securitas*, freedom from the cares of their finished life."

46. We expect the employment of some emblem parallel to the bough at *Inf.* 3.94 where guide and pilgrim approach Charon. Virgil's words alone take its place, leaving the reader still anticipating a later appearance.

47. There are other moments in *Purgatorio* where Dante is directly reflecting on *Aeneid* 6. I think especially of the Valley of the Princes in *Purgatorio* 7 and its close relation to Virgil's Elysium (see n. 4). There are parallels, too, between Daedalus' unfinished autobiography in sculpture, which Aeneas is made to turn away from by the Sibyl at the opening of book 6, and the three exemplifications of humility sculptured by god which the pilgrim views in *Purgatorio* 10.

48. The most suggestive modern study of the meaning of the golden bough remains that of Brooks, "Discolor Aura." Other important treatments are listed by Austin, *Liber Sextus* 83–84, in his note on lines 138f.

49. Within this larger frame he can also perform smaller acts of completion. For instance, with poetic magic playing the part of divine grace, he releases Rhipeus from the toils of Virgil's text, in which he dies at the fall of Troy, and places him to the right of the eye of Monarchy's eagle, symbol of justice (*Par.* 20.67–72, 118–26). In the double "hell" that Troy's dying represents, Rhipeus' superlative justice (*iustissimus unus / qui fuit in Teucris et servantissimus aequi* [*Aen.* 2.426–27]) matters no more than does the piety of the priest Panthus at a time when human violence and divine whimsy devalue the worth of such abstractions. In a recent essay Brodsky, "Reflections" 47, expresses the wish that Dante had included Virgil in his Paradise "for outstanding services to the linear principle." This is, in my view, to misinterpret both the tone and the structure of the *Aeneid*. Virgil does not pay poetic homage to linearity because of "a certain irresponsibility vis-à-vis the past" (ibid.). Rather, on the deepest levels of his text, his principle is desperate circularity based on the fact that man does not escape his past, especially the past of his own inherited feelings.

BIBLIOGRAPHY

AHL, F. M. *Lucan: An Introduction.* Cornell Studies in Classical Philology 39. Ithaca, 1976.

———. "Lucan's *Pharsalia.*" In *Roman Epic,* edited by A. J. Boyle, 125–42. London, 1993.

———. "Statius' *Thebaid*: A Reconsideration." *Aufstieg und Niedergang der römischen Welt* 2.32.5 (1986) 2803–2912.

ALEXIOU, M. *The Ritual Lament in Greek Tradition.* Cambridge, 1974.

ALLEN, A. W. "The Dullest Book of the *Aeneid.*" *Classical Journal* 47 (1951–52) 119–23.

ANDERSON, W. S. *The Art of the Aeneid.* Englewood Cliffs, N.J., 1969.

———, ed. *Ovid's Metamorphoses: Books 6–10.* Norman, Okla., 1972.

ANDERSSON, T. M. *Early Epic Scenery.* Ithaca, 1976.

AUSTIN, R. G., ed. *P. Vergili Maronis: Aeneidos Liber Secundus.* Oxford, 1964.

———, ed. *P. Vergili Maronis: Aeneidos Liber Sextus.* Oxford, 1977.

AVERY, W. T. "The Reluctant Golden Bough." *Classical Journal* 61 (1965–66) 269–72.

BAILEY, C. *Religion in Virgil.* Oxford, 1935.

BALL, R. "Theological Semantics: Virgil's *Pietas* and Dante's *Pietà.*" *Stanford Italian Review* 2 (1981) 59–79.

BARCHIESI, A. "Il lamento di Giuturna." *Materiali e Discussioni per l'Analisi dei Testi Classici* 1 (1978) 99–121.

———. *La Traccia del Modello: Effetti omerici nella narrazione virgiliana.* Biblioteca di *Materiali e Discussioni per l'Analisi dei Testi Classici* 1. Pisa, 1984.

BAROLINI, T. *Dante's Poets: Textuality and Truth in the Comedy.* Princeton, 1984.

BECKER, ERNEST. *Angel in Armor.* New York, 1969.

BENARIO, H. "The Tenth Book of the *Aeneid.*" *Transactions of the American Philological Association* 98 (1967) 23–36.

BINDER, G. *Aeneas und Augustus. Interpretationen zum 8. Buch der Aeneis.* Beiträge zur klassischen Philologie 38. Meisenheim, 1971.

BOYLE A. J. *The Chaonian Dove. Studies in the Eclogues, Georgics and Aeneid.* Mnemosyne suppl. 95. Leiden, 1986.

———. "In Nature's Bonds: A Study of Seneca's *Phaedra.*" *Aufstieg und Niedergang der römischen Welt* 2.32.2 (1985) 1284–1347.

———. "The Meaning of the *Aeneid.*" *Ramus* 1 (1972) 63–90.

BRISCOE, J. *A Commentary on Livy, Books XXXI–XXXIII.* Oxford, 1973.

BROCH, H. *The Death of Virgil.* Translated by Jean Starr Untermeyer. New York, 1945.

BRODSKY, J. "Reflections: Flight from Byzantium." *New Yorker* (October 28, 1985) 39–80.

BROOKS, R. A. "Discolor Aura: Reflections on the Golden
Bough." *American Journal of Philology* 74 (1953) 260–80.
Reprinted in *Virgil: A Collection of Critical Essays*, edited by S.
Commager, 143–63. Englewood Cliffs, N.J., 1966.

BURKE, P. "The Role of Mezentius in the *Aeneid*." *Classical
Journal* 69 (1974) 202–9.

CAIRNS, F. *Virgil's Augustan Epic*. Cambridge, 1989.

CLAUSEN, W. V. "An Interpretation of the *Aeneid*." *Harvard
Studies in Classical Philology* 68 (1964) 139–47.

———. *Virgil's Aeneid and the Tradition of Hellenistic Poetry*.
Berkeley, 1987.

CLAY, DISKIN. *Lucretius and Epicurus*. Ithaca, 1983.

COFFEY, M., and R. MAYER, eds. *Seneca: Phaedra*. Cambridge,
1990.

COLISH, MARCIA. *The Stoic Tradition from Antiquity to the Early
Middle Ages: I: Stoicism in Classical Latin Literature*. Studies in
the History of Christian Thought 34. Leiden, 1985.

CONTE, G. B. *The Rhetoric of Imitation: Genre and Poetic Memory in
Virgil and Other Latin Poets*. Cornell Studies in Classical
Philology 44. Ithaca, 1986.

D'ARMS, J. H. "Virgil's *cunctantem* (*ramum*): *Aeneid* VI 211."
Classical Journal 59 (1963–64) 265–68.

DE GRUMMOND, W. "*Saevus Dolor*: The Opening and Closing of
the *Aeneid*." *Vergilius* 27 (1981) 48–52.

DI CESARE, M. *The Altar and the City: A Reading of Vergil's Aeneid*.
New York, 1974.

DINGEL, J. *Seneca und die Dichtung*. Bibliothek der klassischen
Altertumswissenschaft, n.f. 51. Heidelberg, 1974.

———. "Senecas Tragödien: Vorbilder und poëtische Aspekte."
Aufstieg und Niedergang der römischen Welt 2.32.2 (1985) 1052–99.

DODDS, E. R., ed. *Euripides Bacchae*. Oxford, 1960.

DOPPIONI, L. *Virgilio nell'arte e nel pensiero di Seneca*. Florence,
1939.

DUBOIS, P. *History, Rhetorical Description and the Epic*.
Cambridge, 1982.

DUCKWORTH, G. "The *Aeneid* as a Trilogy." *Transactions of the
American Philological Association* 88 (1957) 1–10.

———. *Structural Patterns and Proportions in Vergil's Aeneid*. Ann
Arbor, Mich., 1962.

DUDLEY, D. R. "A Plea for Aeneas." *Greece and Rome* 8 (1961) 52–
60.

EARL, D. C. *The Political Thought of Sallust*. Amsterdam, 1966.

EDGEWORTH, R. J. "The Ivory Gate and the Threshold of
Apollo." *Classica et Mediaevalia* 37 (1986) 145–60.

EGGERDING, F. "Parcere subiectis. Ein Beitrag zur
Vergilinterpretation." *Gymnasium* 59 (1952) 31–52.

ELIADE, M. *The Sacred and the Profane*. New York, 1959.

ELIOT, T. S. "Seneca in Elizabethan Translation." In *Selected
Essays*, 65–105. 3rd ed. London, 1951.

———. "Shakespeare and the Stoicism of Seneca." In *Selected Essays*, 126–40. 3rd ed. London, 1951.

ENK, P. J. "De Labyrinthi Imagine in Foribus Templi Cumani Insculpta." *Mnemosyne*, ser. 4, 11 (1958) 322–30.

FANTHAM, E. *Seneca's Troades: A Literary Introduction with Text, Translation, and Commentary.* Princeton, 1982.

———. "Virgil's Dido and Seneca's Tragic Heroines." *Greece and Rome* 22 (1975) 1–10.

FARRON, S. "The *Furor* and *Violentia* of Aeneas." *Acta Classica* 20 (1977) 204–8.

FEENEY, D. C. *The Gods in Epic: Poets and Critics of the Classical Tradition.* Oxford, 1991.

———. "The Reconciliations of Juno." *Classical Quarterly* 34 (1984) 179–94.

FITCH, J. G. "Sense-Pauses and Relative Dating in Seneca, Sophocles and Shakespeare." *American Journal of Philology* 102 (1981) 289–307.

———, ed. *Seneca's Hercules Furens: A Critical Text with Introduction and Commentary.* Ithaca, 1987.

FITZGERALD, W. "Aeneas, Daedalus and the Labyrinth." *Arethusa* 17 (1984) 51–65.

FOWLER, W. W. *Virgil's "Gathering of the Clans."* Oxford, 1918.

FRAENKEL, E. "Some Aspects of the Structure of *Aeneid* VII." *Journal of Roman Studies* 35 (1945) 1–14.

FRAZER, J. G., ed. *The Fasti of Ovid.* London, 1929.

FRECCERO, J. *Dante: The Poetics of Conversion.* Edited by R. Jacoff. Cambridge, Mass., 1986.

FRISK, H. *Griechisches Etymologisches Wörterbuch.* Heidelberg, 1970.

FRONTISI-DUCROUX, F. *Dédale: Mythologie de l'artisan en Grèce ancienne.* Paris, 1975.

FRYE, NORTHROP. *The Return of Eden.* Toronto, 1965.

GALINSKY, G. K. *Aeneas, Sicily and Rome.* Princeton, 1969.

———. "The Anger of Aeneas." *American Journal of Philology* 109 (1988) 321–48.

GERNENTZ, W. *Laudes Romae.* Dissertation. Rostock, 1918.

GETTY, R. J., ed. *M. Annaei Lucani: De Bello Civili: Liber 1.* Cambridge, 1955.

GILLIS, DANIEL. *Eros and Death in the Aeneid.* Rome, 1983.

GLENN, J. "Mezentius and Polyphemus." *American Journal of Philology* 92 (1971) 129–55.

———. "Virgil's Polyphemus." *Greece and Rome* 19 (1972) 47–59.

GOOLD, G. P. "Servius and the Helen Episode." *Harvard Studies in Classical Philology* 74 (1970) 101–68.

GOTOFF, HAROLD C. "The Difficulty of the Ascent from Avernus." *Classical Philology* 80 (1985) 35–40.

GOW, A. S. F., ed. *Theocritus.* Cambridge, 1952.

GRANDGENT, C. *Companion to the Divine Comedy.* Edited by C. S. Singleton. Cambridge, Mass., 1975.

GRANSDEN, K. W. *Virgil's Iliad*. Cambridge, 1984.
——, ed. *Aeneid: Book 8*. Cambridge, 1976.
GRIFFIN, J. "Augustus and the Poets: Caesar qui cogere posset."
   In *Caesar Augustus: Seven Aspects*, edited by F. Millar and E.
   Segal, 189–218. Oxford, 1984.
——. *Latin Poets and Roman Life*. Chapel Hill, N.C., 1986.
GRIMM, R. E. "Aeneas and Andromache in *Aeneid* III." *American
   Journal of Philology* 88 (1967) 151–62.
HALTER, T. *Vergil und Horaz*. Bern, 1970.
HARDIE, C., ed. *Vitae Vergilianae Antiquae*. Oxford, 1966.
HARDIE, P. *Virgil's Aeneid: Cosmos and Imperium*. Oxford, 1986.
HARRISON, E. *The Aeneid and Carthage*. In *Poetry and Politics in the
   Age of Augustus*, 95–115. Cambridge, 1984.
HEINZE, R. *Virgils epische Technik*. Stuttgart, 1957.
HENRY, J. *Aeneidea*. Dublin and London, 1873–92. Reprinted,
   New York, 1972.
HERINGTON, C. J. "Senecan Tragedy." *Arion* 5 (1966) 422–71.
——. "The Younger Seneca." In *The Cambridge History of Classical
   Literature: II, Latin Literature*, edited by E. J. Kenney, 511–32.
   Cambridge, 1982.
HIGHET, G. *The Speeches in Vergil's Aeneid*. Princeton, 1972.
HÜGI, M. *Vergils Aeneis und die Hellenistische Dichtung*. Bern and
   Stuttgart, 1952.
JACKSON KNIGHT, W. F. "Pairs of Passages in Virgil." *Greece and
   Rome* 13 (1944) 10–14.
JACOFF, RACHEL. "Intertextualities in Arcadia: *Purgatorio* 30.49–
   51." In *The Poetry of Allusion: Virgil and Ovid in Dante's
   Commedia*, edited by R. Jacoff and J. Schnapp, 131–44. Stanford,
   1991.
JENS, W. "Der Eingang des dritten Buches der *Aeneis*." *Philologus*
   97 (1948) 194–97.
JOHNSON, W. R. *Darkness Visible: A Study of Vergil's Aeneid*.
   Berkeley, 1976.
——. "The Figure of Laertes: Reflections on the Character of
   Aeneas." In *Vergil at 2000*, edited by J. D. Bernard, 85–105. New
   York, 1986.
——. *Momentary Monsters: Lucan and His Heroes*. Cornell Studies
   in Classical Philology 47. Ithaca, 1987.
JONES, J. W., JR. "Mezentius the Isolated Hero." *Vergilius* 23
   (1977) 50–54.
KERMODE, F. *The Sense of an Ending: Studies in the Theory of
   Fiction*. Oxford, 1967.
KNAUER, G. *Die Aeneis und Homer. Hypomnemata* 7. Göttingen,
   1979.
KOERNER, J. K. *Die Suche nach dem Labyrinth*. Frankfurt, 1983.
KOVACS, D. "Ovid, *Metamorphoses* 1.2." *Classical Quarterly* 37
   (1987) 458–65.
KRAGGERUD, E. *Aeneisstudien. SO* suppl. 22. Oslo, 1968.
KRIS, E., and O. KURZ. *Legend, Myth, and Magic in the Image of the
   Artist*. New Haven, Conn., 1979.

LEACH, E. W. "The Blindness of Mezentius." *Arethusa* 4 (1971) 83–89.

LESKY, A. "Zu den Katalogen der *Aeneis*." In *Forschungen zur Römischen Literatur: Festschrift K. Büchner*, 189–96. Wiesbaden, 1970.

LLOYD, R. B. "*Aeneid* III: A New Approach." *American Journal of Philology* 78 (1957) 133–51.

——. "*Aeneid* III and the Aeneas Legend." *American Journal of Philology* 78 (1957) 382–400.

LURQUIN, G. *Les citations virgiliennes dans les ouvrages en prose de Sénèque le philosophe*. Louvain, 1941.

LYNE, R. O. A. M. *Further Voices in Vergil's Aeneid*. Oxford, 1987.

MACDONALD, RONALD R. *The Burial-Places of Memory*. Amherst, Mass., 1987.

MACKAIL, J. W. *The Aeneid of Virgil*. Oxford, 1930.

MACKAY, L. A. "Hero and Theme in the *Aeneid*." *Transactions of the American Philological Association* 94 (1963) 157–66.

MAGUINNESS, W. S. "Seneca and the Poets." *Hermathena* 88 (1956) 81–98.

MASTERS, J. *Poetry and Civil War in Lucan's Bellum Civile*. Cambridge, 1992.

MAZZOLI, G. *Seneca e la Poesia*. Pubblicazioni della Facoltà di lettere e filosofia dell' università di Pavia. Milan, 1970.

MCKAY, A. G. "The Achaemenides Episode: Vergil, *Aeneid* III, 588–691." *Vergilius* 12 (1966) 31–38.

——. "Recent Work on Virgil: A Bibliographical Survey, 1964–73." *Classical World* 68 (1974–75) 1–92.

MICHELS, A. "The Insomnium of Aeneas." *Classical Quarterly* 31 (1981) 140–46.

MOMMSEN, T. "Die Remuslegende." *Hermes* 16 (1881) 1–23. Reprinted in *Gesammelte Schriften IV*, 1–21. Berlin, 1906.

MOORE, E. *Studies in Dante. First Series: Scripture and Classical Authors in Dante*. Oxford, 1896.

MOSKALEW, W. *Formular Language and Poetic Design in the Aeneid*. Leiden, 1982.

MOULTON, C. "The End of the *Odyssey*." *Greek, Roman and Byzantine Studies* 15 (1974) 153–69.

NETHERCUT, W. R. "Invasion in the *Aeneid*." *Greece and Rome* 15 (1968) 82–95.

NEWTON, F. L. "Recurrent Imagery in *Aeneid* IV." *Transactions of the American Philological Association* 88 (1957) 31–43.

NORDEN, E. *P. Vergilius Maro Aeneis Buch VI*. 4th ed. Stuttgart, 1957.

NORTH, H. *Sophrosyne*. Ithaca, 1966.

OGILVIE, R. M. *A Commentary on Livy, Books 1–5*. Oxford, 1965.

O'HARA, J. *Death and the Optimistic Prophecy in Vergil's Aeneid*. Princeton, 1990.

OTIS, B. "The Originality of the Aeneid." In *Studies in Latin Literature and Its Influence: Virgil*, edited by D. R. Dudley, 27–66. London, 1969.

——. *Virgil: A Study in Civilized Poetry*. Oxford, 1963.

PARRY, A. "The Two Voices of Virgil's *Aeneid*." *Arion* 2 (1963) 66–80. Reprinted in *Virgil: A Collection of Critical Essays*, edited by S. Commager, 107–23. Englewood Cliffs, N.J., 1966.

PAVLOCK, B. "Epic and Tragedy in Vergil's Nisus and Euryalus Episode." *Transactions of the American Philological Association* 115 (1985) 207–24.

PEASE, ARTHUR STANLEY, ed. *Publi Vergili Maronis: Aeneidos: Liber Quartus*. Cambridge, Mass., 1935.

PÖSCHL, V. *Die Dichtkunst Virgils*. Innsbruck, 1950. Translated by G. Seligson as *The Art of Vergil*. Ann Arbor, Mich., 1962.

——. "Die Tempeltüren des Dädalus in der Aeneis [6.14–33]." *Würzburger Jahrbücher für die Altertumswissenschaft*, n.f. 1 (1975) 119–23.

PUCCI, P. *The Violence of Pity*. Ithaca, 1980.

PUTNAM, M. C. J. "Introduction." *Arethusa* 14 (1981) 7–15.

——. "The Lyricist as Hero." *Ramus* 2 (1973) 1–19. Reprinted in *Essays on Latin Lyric, Elegy and Epic*, 133–51. Princeton, 1982.

——. *The Poetry of the Aeneid*. Cambridge, 1965. Reprinted, Ithaca, 1988.

——. Review of *Technique and Ideas in the Aeneid*, by G. Williams. *American Journal of Philology* 105 (1984) 228–31.

QUINN, K. *Virgil's Aeneid: A Critical Description*. London, 1968.

QUINT, D. *Epic and Empire: Politics and Generic Form from Virgil to Milton*. Princeton, 1993.

——. *Origin and Originality in Renaissance Literature*. New Haven, Conn., 1983.

RECKFORD, K. J. "Helen in *Aeneid* 2 and 6." *Arethusa* 14 (1981) 85–99.

——. "Latent Tragedy in *Aeneid* VII, 1–285." *American Journal of Philology* 82 (1961) 252–69.

——. "Some Trees in Virgil and Tolkien." In *Perspectives of Roman Poetry*, edited by G. K. Galinsky, 57–91. Austin, 1974.

REEKER, H. D. *Die Landschaft in der Aeneis*. *Spudasmata* 27. Hildesheim, 1971.

REGENBOGEN, O. "Schmerz und Tod in den Tragödien Senecas." *Vorträge der Bibliothek Warburg* 1927/8, 167–218. Berlin, 1930. Reprinted in *Kleine Schriften*, ed. F. Dirlmeier, 409–62. Munich, 1961.

RÖMISCH, E. "Die Achaemenides-Episode in Vergils Aeneis." In *Studien zum antiken Epos*, 208–27. Meisenheim, 1976.

RUNCHINA, G. "Tecnica drammatica e retorica nelle tragedie di Seneca." *Annali della Facoltà di lettere dell' università di Cagliari* 28 (1960) 163–324.

RUTLEDGE, H. "Vergil's Daedalus." *Classical Journal* 62 (1967) 309–11.

RYAN, C. J. "Virgil's Wisdom in the *Divine Comedy*." *Medievalia et Humanistica* 11 (1982) 1–38.

SACHS, JOE. "The Fury of Aeneas." *St. John's Review* 14 (Winter 1982) 75–82.

SANDERLIN, G. "Aeneas as Apprentice—Point of View in the
Third *Aeneid*." *Classical Journal* 71 (1975–76) 53–56.

SAYLOR, C. "Toy Troy: The New Perspective of the Backward
Glance." *Vergilius* 16 (1970) 26–28.

SCHNAPP, J. *The Transfiguration of History at the Center of Dante's
Paradise*. Princeton, 1986.

SEGAL, C. P. "*Aeternum per saecula nomen*, the Golden Bough and
the Tragedy of History: Part I." *Arion* 4 (1965) 617–57.

———. "*Aeternum per saecula nomen*, the Golden Bough and the
Tragedy of History: Part II." *Arion* 5 (1966) 34–72.

———. "Art and the Hero: Participation, Detachment and Narrative Point of View in *Aeneid* 1." *Arethusa* 14 (1981) 67–83.

———. "Circean Temptations." *Transactions of the American Philological Association* 99 (1968) 419–42.

———. "The Hesitation of the Golden Bough: A Reexamination."
Hermes 96 (1968) 74–79.

———. *Language and Desire in Seneca's Phaedra*. Princeton, 1986.

SEIDENSTICKER, B., and D. ARMSTRONG. "Seneca Tragicus 1878–
1978 (with addenda 1979ff.)." *Aufstieg und Niedergang der
römischen Welt* 2.32.2 (1985) 916–68.

SEMPLE, W. H. "A Short Study of *Aeneid*, Book III." *Bulletin of the
Rylands Library* 38 (1955) 225–40.

SINGLETON, C. S., ed. and trans. *The Divine Comedy*. 3 vols.
Princeton, 1970–75.

SKUTSCH, OTTO, ed. *The Annals of Quintus Ennius*. Oxford, 1985.

SMALL, S. G. P. "The Arms of Turnus: *Aeneid* 7.783–92." *Transactions of the American Philological Association* 90 (1959) 243–52.

———. "Vergil, Dante and Camilla." *Classical Journal* 54 (1958–59)
295–301.

SOLMSEN, F. "Greek Ideas of the Hereafter in Virgil's Roman
Epic." *Proceedings of the American Philosophical Society* 112
(1968) 8–14.

———. "The World of the Dead in Book 6 of the *Aeneid*." *Classical
Philology* 67 (1972) 31–41.

SPERONI, C. "The Motif of the Bleeding and Speaking Trees of
Dante's Suicides." *Italian Quarterly* 9 (1965) 44–55.

STAHL, H.-P. "Aeneas—An Unheroic Hero?" *Arethusa* 14 (1981)
157–77.

———. "The Death of Turnus: Augustan Vergil and the Political
Rival." In *Between Republic and Empire*, edited by K. Raaflaub
and M. Toher, 174–211. Berkeley, 1990.

SULLIVAN, F. A. "Mezentius: A Virgilian Creation." *Classical
Philology* 64 (1969) 219–25.

SYME, R. *History in Ovid*. Oxford, 1978.

TARRANT, R. J. "Aeneas and the Gates of Sleep." *Classical Philology* 77 (1982) 51–55.

———. "Senecan Drama and Its Antecedents." *Harvard Studies in
Classical Philology* 82 (1978) 213–63.

———, ed. *Seneca: Agamemnon*. Cambridge, 1976.

———. *Seneca's Thyestes*. Atlanta, 1985.

TER HAAR ROMENY, B. *De auctore tragoediarum quae sub Senecae nomine feruntur Vergilii imitatore.* Dissertation. Leiden, 1877.

THANIEL, G. "A Note on *Aeneid* 3.623–626." *Classical Bulletin* 50 (1973) 10–12.

THORNTON, AGATHE. *The Living Universe: Gods and Men in Virgil's Aeneid. Mnemosyne* suppl. 46. Leiden, 1976.

TODD, F. "Virgil's Invocation of Erato." *Classical Review* 45 (1931) 216–18.

TREU, M. "Zur clementia Caesars." *Museum Helveticum* 5 (1948) 197–217.

VAN NORTWICK, T. "Aeneas, Turnus and Achilles." *Transactions of the American Philological Association* 110 (1980) 303–14.

VAN SICKLE, J. B. "Studies of Dialectical Methodology in the Virgilian Tradition." *Modern Language Notes* 85 (1970) 884–928.

WAGENVOORT, H. "The Crime of Fratricide." In *Studies in Roman Literature, Culture and Religion,* 169–83. Leiden, 1956.

WEBER, C. "Gallus' Grynium and Vergil's Cumae." *Annual Report of the Collegium Mediterranistorum* 1 (1978) 45–76.

WEINSTOCK, S. *Divus Iulius.* Oxford, 1971.

WEST, D. *The Bough and the Gate.* Exeter, 1987.

———. "The Deaths of Hector and Turnus." *Greece and Rome* 21 (1974) 21–31.

WICKERT, L. "Neue Forschungen zum römischen Principat." *Aufstieg und Niedergang der römischen Welt* 2.1 (1974) 3–76.

WIESEN, D. S. "The Pessimism of the Eighth *Aeneid.*" *Latomus* 32 (1973) 737–65.

WILLIAMS, G. *Technique and Ideas in the Aeneid.* New Haven, Conn., 1983.

———. *Tradition and Originality in Roman Poetry.* Oxford, 1968.

WILLIAMS, R. D. "The Function and Structure of Virgil's Catalogue in *Aeneid* 7." *Classical Quarterly* 55 (1961) 146–53.

———. "The Purpose of the *Aeneid.*" *Anticthon* 1 (1967) 29–41.

———, ed. *The Aeneid of Virgil: Books 7–12.* London, 1973.

———. *P. Vergili Maronis: Aeneidos Liber Tertius.* Oxford, 1962.

WIRTH, H. *De Vergili apud Senecam philosophum usu.* Dissertation. Freiburg, 1900.

WOODMAN, A. J. "*Exegi Monumentum*: Horace, Odes 3.30." In *Quality and Pleasure in Latin Poetry,* 115–28. Cambridge, 1974.

ZANKER, G. "The Love Theme in Apollonius Rhodius' *Argonautica.*" *Wiener Studien* 92 (1979) 52–75.

ZWIERLEIN, O., ed. *L. Annaei Senecae Tragoediae.* Oxford, 1986. Reprinted with corrections. Oxford, 1987.